STATISTICAL CONCEPTS

A SECOND COURSE FOR EDUCATION AND THE BEHAVIORAL SCIENCES

SECOND EDITION

STATISTICAL CONCEPTS

A SECOND COURSE FOR EDUCATION AND THE BEHAVIORAL SCIENCES

SECOND EDITION

RICHARD G. LOMAX
THE UNIVERSITY OF ALABAMA

LEA LAWRENCE ERLBAUM ASSOCIATES, PUBLISHERS

2001 MAHWAH, NEW JERSEY   LONDON

Credits
Tables found in the Appendix have been reprinted from the following sources: Tables 1, 2, 3, 4, 5, 6 from Pearson, E. S. & Hartley, H. O. (1966), *Biometrika Tables for Statisticians*, respectively Tables 1, 12, 8, 18, 14, 47, by permission of Oxford University Press; Table 7 from Dunnett, C. W. (1955), A multiple comparison procedure for comparing several treatments with a control, *Journal of the American Statistical Association*, *50*, 1096–1121, by permission of the American Statistical Association, and from Dunnett, C. W. (1964), New tables for multiple comparisons with a control, *Biometrics*, *20*, 482–491, by permission of the Biometric Society; Table 8 from Games, P. A. (1977), An improved *t* table for simultaneous control of *g* contrasts, *Journal of the American Statistical Association*, *72*, 531–534, by permission of the American Statistical Association; Table 9 from Harter, H. L. (1960), Tables of range and studentized range, *Annals of Mathematical Statistics*, *31*, 1122–1147, by permission of the Institute of Mathematical Statistics; Table 10 from Duncan, D. B. (1955), Multiple range and multiple *F* tests, *Biometrics*, *11*, 1–42, by permission of the Biometric Society; Table 11 from Bryant, J. L., & Paulson, A. S. (1976), An extension of Tukey's method of multiple comparisions to experimental designs with random concomitant variables, *Biometrika*, *63*, 631–638, by permission of Oxford University Press.

Lawrence Erlbaum Associates, Inc., Publishers
10 Industrial Avenue
Mahwah, NJ 07430

Cover design by Kathryn Houghtaling Lacey

Library of Congress Cataloging-in-Publication Data

Lomax, Richard G.
  Statistical concepts : a second course for education and the behavioral sciences /
Richard G. Lomax.— 2nd ed.
    p. cm.
    Includes bibliographical references and index.
  ISBN 0-8058-3783-3 (pbk. : alk. paper)
  Statistics. I. Title.
    QA276. 12L66 2000
  519.5—dc21   00-059299
                                                        CIP

Books published by Lawrence Erlbaum Associates are printed on
acid-free paper, and their bindings are chosen for strength and durability.

Printed in the United States of America
10 9 8 7 6 5

This book is dedicated to
Lea and Kristen
and to students who have seen the light

CONTENTS

PREFACE

APPROACH

I know, I know! I've heard it a million times before. When you hear someone at a party mention the word *statistics* or *statistician*, you probably say "I hate statistics" and turn the other cheek. In the more than 20 years I have been in the field of statistics, I can only recall four or five times when someone did not have that reaction. Enough is enough. With the help of this text, the "I hate statistics" slogan will become a distant figment of your imagination.

As the title suggests, this text is designed for a second or intermediate course in statistics for students in education and the behavioral sciences. The content coverage includes a number of regression and analysis of variance models, all subsumed under the general linear model (GLM). The text is designed for you to become a better-prepared researcher and a more intelligent consumer of research. It is assumed that you have already completed an introductory course in statistics (covering descriptive statistics up through *t*-tests). However, I do not assume that you have an extensive and/or recent training in mathematics. Many of you have only had algebra, some more than 20 years ago. Rest assured, you will do fine.

I believe that a text should serve as an effective instructional tool. You should find this text to be more than a reference book; you might actually use it to learn statistics (what an oxymoron, that a statistics book can actually teach something). This text is not a theoretical statistics book, nor is it a cookbook on computing statistics. Recipes have to be memorized, consequently you tend not to understand how or why you obtain the desired product. Besides, what happens if you run out of salt or forget to add butter?

GOALS AND CONTENT COVERAGE

My goals for this text are lofty, but the effort and its effects will be worthwhile. First, the text provides a comprehensive coverage of topics that could be included in an undergraduate or graduate intermediate course in statistics. The text is flexible enough so that instructors can select those topics that they desire to cover as they deem relevant in their particular discipline. In other words, chapters and sections of chapters from this text can be included in a statistics course as the instructor sees fit. Most of the popular as well as many of the lesser-known procedures and models are described in the text. A particular feature is a thorough and up-to-date discussion of assumptions, the effects of their violation, and how to deal with their violation.

The first two chapters of the text cover simple regression and multiple regression analyses, both for linear and nonlinear models. The remaining six chapters of the text cover different analysis of variance (ANOVA) models. Specifically, we describe the following procedures: the one-factor model; factorial models; multiple comparison procedures; analysis of covariance (ANCOVA); random- and mixed-effects models, including repeated measures and split-plot designs; and hierarchical and randomized blocks models.

Second, the text communicates a conceptual, intuitive understanding of statistics, which requires only a rudimentary knowledge of basic algebra, and emphasizes the important concepts in statistics. The most effective way to learn statistics is through the conceptual approach. Statistical concepts tend to be easy to learn because (a) concepts can be simply stated, (b) concepts can be made relevant thorough the use of real-life examples, (c) the same concepts are shared by many procedures, and (d) concepts can be related to one another.

This text will allow you to reach these goals. The following indicators will provide some feedback as to how you are doing. First, there will be a noticeable change in your attitude toward statistics. Thus one outcome is for you to feel that "statistics isn't half bad", or "this stuff is OK." Second, you will feel comfortable using statistics in your own work. Finally, you will begin to "see the light." You will know when you have reached this highest stage of statistics development when suddenly, in the middle of the night, you wake up from a dream and say "now I get it." In other words, you will begin to think statistics rather than think of ways to get out of doing statistics.

NEW TO THE SECOND EDITION

A number of changes have been made in the second edition based on the suggestions of reviewers, instructors, and students. These improvements have been made in order to better achieve the goals of the text. The changes include the following: (a) additional chapter problems have been added at the end of each chapter, including more concrete examples; (b) an instructor's guide has been written to assist the teaching of statistics (further described in the next section); (c) the sequence of some of the chapters has been altered to provide a better conceptual flow for the ANOVA models (i.e., the ANCOVA chapter was moved up to follow the factorial ANOVA chapter so that more direct comparisons could be made of design vs. statistical control); (d) more examples have been included in the text and those examples have been made more concrete; (e) additional tables have been added to enhance student understanding; (f) objectives have been written for each chapter; (g) the multivariate chapter was omitted because a single chapter on this topic simply could not stand on its own—instead a multivariate text is recommended for a complete discussion of these methods; and (h) updated content has been provided where applicable.

PEDAGOGICAL TOOLS

The text contains several important pedagogical features to allow you to attain these goals. First, each chapter begins with an outline (so you can anticipate what will be covered), and a list of key concepts (which you will need to really understand what you are doing). Second, realistic examples from education and the behavioral sciences are used to illustrate the concepts and procedures covered in each chapter. Each of these examples includes a complete set of computations, an examination of assumptions where necessary, as well as tables and figures to assist you. Third, the text is based on the conceptual approach. That is, material is covered so that you obtain a good understanding of statistical concepts. If you know the concepts, then you know statistics. Finally, each chapter ends with two sets of problems, computational and conceptual. Pay particular attention to the conceptual problems as they provide the best assessment of your understanding of the concepts in the chapter. I strongly suggest using the example data sets and the computational problems for additional practice through hand computations and available statistics software. This will serve to reinforce the concepts covered. Answers to the odd-numbered problems are given at the end of the text.

For the instructor, an instructor's guide can be obtained free of charge from the publisher. The guide provides a more complete look at the problems, including their solution and an explanation of the solution where necessary. Also included in the instructor's guide is an example syllabus as well as some statistical humor to use in your teaching of statistics.

ACKNOWLEDGMENTS

There are many individuals whose assistance enabled the completion of this book. First, I would like to thank the following individuals whom I studied with at the University of Pittsburgh: Jamie Algina (now at the University of Florida), Lloyd Bond (University of North Carolina - Greensboro), Jim Carlson (CTB / McGraw-Hill), Bill Cooley, Harry Hsu, Charles Stegman (University of Arkansas), and Neil Timm. Next, numerous colleagues have played an important role in my personal and professional life as a statistician. Rather than include an admittedly incomplete listing, I just say "thank you" to all of you. You know who you are.

Thanks also to all of the wonderful people at Lawrence Erlbaum Associates, in particular, to Ray O'Connell for inspiring this project back in 1986 when I began writing the first edition of this text, and to Debra Riegert for supporting the development of the second edition you now see. Thanks also to Larry Erlbaum and Joe Petrowski for behind the scenes work on all of my textbooks. I am most appreciative of the insightful suggestions provided by the reviewers of this text, Dr. Matt L. Riggs of Loma Linda University, Dr. Leo Edwards of Fayetteville State University and Dr. Harry O'Neil of the University of Southern California. A special thank you to all of the terrific students that I have had the pleasure of teaching at the University of Pittsburgh, the University of Illinois - Chicago, Louisiana State University, Boston College, Northern Illinois University, and the University of Alabama. For all of your efforts, and the many lights that you have seen and shared with me, this book is for you. I am most grateful to my family, in particular, to Lea and Kristen. It is because of your love and understanding that I was able to cope with such a major project. Thank you one and all.

—RGL
Tuscaloosa, AL

1

SIMPLE LINEAR REGRESSION

Chapter Outline

1. Introduction to the concepts of simple linear regression
2. The population simple linear regression equation
3. The sample simple linear regression equation
   Unstandardized regression equation
   Standardized regression equation
   Prediction errors
   Least squares criterion
   Proportion of predictable variation (coefficient of determination)
   Significance tests and confidence intervals
   Assumptions
   Graphical techniques: Detection of assumption violations

Key Concepts

1. Slope and intercept of a straight line
2. Regression equation
3. Prediction errors/residuals
4. Standardized and unstandardized regression coefficients
5. Proportion of variation accounted for; coefficient of determination

Your first course in statistical principles exposed you to descriptive statistics (measures of central tendency, measures of dispersion or variability, various theoretical distributions, types of scores, and measures of relationship or association) and an introduction to inferential statistics (probability, hypothesis testing, types of decision errors, test statistics, critical values, all leading up to inferences about means and other statistics). We pick up the trail of statistics where the first course left off.

When considering the relationship between two variables (say X and Y), the researcher will typically calculate some measure of the relationship between those variables, such as a correlation coefficient (e.g., r_{XY}, the Pearson product–moment correlation coefficient). Another way of looking at how two variables may be related is through regression analysis, in terms of prediction. That is, the ability of one variable to predict a second is evaluated. Here we adopt the usual notation where X is defined as the *independent* or *predictor variable*, and Y as the *dependent* or *criterion variable*.

For example, an admissions officer might want to use Graduate Record Exam (GRE) scores to predict graduate-level grade point averages (GPA) to make admissions decisions for a sample of applicants to a university or college. For those unfamiliar with the GRE, the test assesses general aptitude for graduate school. The research question of interest would be, how well does the GRE (the independent or predictor variable) predict performance in graduate school (the dependent or criterion variable)? This is an example of simple linear regression where only a single predictor variable is included in the analysis. Thus we have a bivariate situation where only two variables are being considered, one predictor variable and one criterion variable. Chapter 2 considers the case of multiple predictor variables in multiple linear regression. As is shown later in this chapter, the use of the GRE in predicting GPA requires the condition that these variables have a correlation different from zero. If the GRE and GPA are uncorrelated (i.e., the correlation is essentially zero), then the GRE will have no utility in predicting GPA.

In this chapter we consider the concepts of slope, intercept, regression equation, unstandardized and standardized regression coefficients, residuals, proportion of variation accounted for, as well as considering tests of significance and statistical assumptions. Our objectives are that by the end of this chapter, you will be able to (a) understand the concepts underlying simple linear regression, (b) compute and interpret the results of simple linear regression, and (c) understand and evaluate the assumptions of simple linear regression.

INTRODUCTION TO THE CONCEPTS OF SIMPLE LINEAR REGRESSION

Let us consider the basic concepts involved in simple linear regression. Many years ago when you had algebra, you were taught about an equation that was used to describe a straight line,

$$Y = bX + a$$

Here X (the predictor variable) is being used to predict Y (the criterion variable). The *slope* of the line is denoted by b and indicates the number of Y units the line changes for a one-unit change in X. The Y-intercept is denoted by a and is the point at which the line intersects or crosses the Y axis. To be more specific, a is the value of Y when X is equal to zero. Hereafter we use the term *intercept* rather than Y-intercept to keep it simple.

Consider the plot of the straight line $Y = 0.5X + 1.0$ as shown in Fig. 1.1. Here we see that the line clearly intersects the Y axis at $Y = 1.0$; thus the intercept is equal to 1. The slope of a line is defined, more specifically, as the change in Y divided by the change in X.

$$b = \frac{\Delta Y}{\Delta X} \quad or \quad \frac{Y_2 - Y_1}{X_2 - X_1}$$

For instance, take two points shown in Fig. 1.1, (X_1, Y_1) and (X_2, Y_2), that fall on the straight line with coordinates $(0,1)$ and $(4,3)$, respectively. We compute the slope for those two points to be $(3 - 1)/(4 - 0) = 0.5$. If we were to select any other two points that fall on the straight line, then the slope for those two points would also be equal to 0.5. That is, regardless of the two points on the line that we select, the slope will always be the same, constant value of 0.5. This is true because we only need two points to define a particular straight line. That is, with the points $(0,1)$ and $(4,3)$ we can draw only one straight line that passes through both of those points, and that line has a slope of 0.5 and an intercept of 1.0.

Let us take the concepts of slope, intercept, and straight line and apply them in the context of correlation so that we can study the relationship between the variables X and Y. Consider the examples of straight lines plotted in Fig. 1.2. In Fig. 1.2(a) the diagonal line indicates a slope of +1.00, which is used as a reference line. Any line drawn from the lower left portion of the plot to the upper right portion of the plot indicates a slope

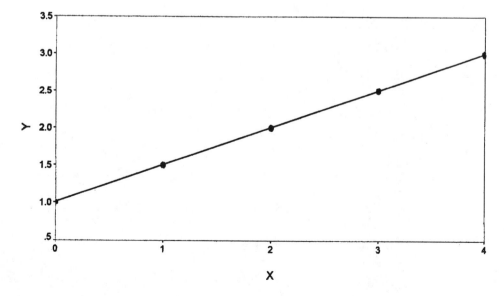

FIG. 1.1 Plot of line: $Y = 0.5X + 1.0$.

with a positive value (i.e., greater than 0). In other words, as X increases, Y also increases. This describes a positive relationship or correlation between variables X and Y. In Fig. 1.2(b) the slope is equal to 0 as the line is horizontal to the X axis. As X increases, Y remains constant; the correlation is also equal to 0. In Fig. 1.2(c) the diagonal line indicates a slope of -1.00, which is used as a reference line. Any line drawn from the upper left portion of plot to the lower right portion of the plot indicates a slope with a negative value (i.e., less than 0). In other words, as X increases, Y decreases. This describes a negative relationship or correlation between variables X and Y. Notice

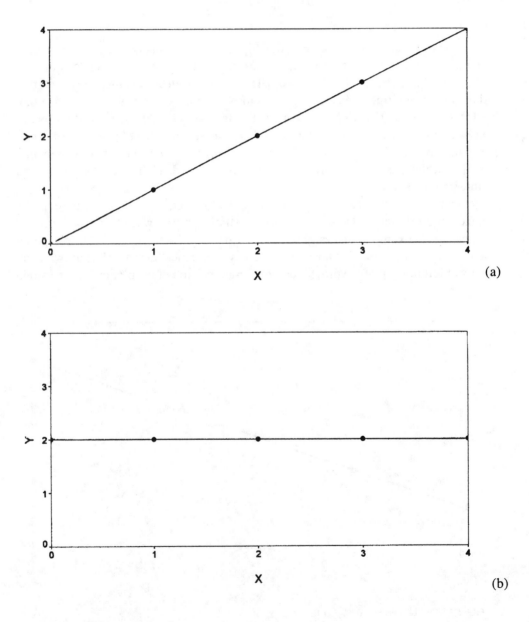

(a)

(b)

FIG. 1.2   Possible Slopes: (a), (b),   *(continued on next page)*

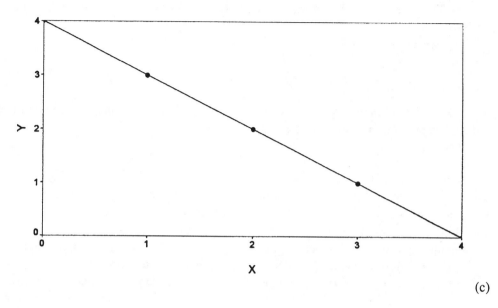

(c)

FIG. 1.2 (*con't.*) **(c).**

that the sign of the slope (i.e., positive or negative) will be the same as the sign of the correlation coefficient. That is, if both X and Y are increasing, the slope and the correlation coefficient will both be positive; if X is increasing while Y is decreasing, the slope and the correlation coefficient will both be negative.

THE POPULATION SIMPLE LINEAR REGRESSION EQUATION

Let us take these concepts and place them into the formal context of simple linear regression. First consider the situation where we have the entire population of individuals' scores on both variables X (GRE) and Y (GPA). Typically, X is used to predict Y; thus X is defined as the predictor variable and Y as the criterion variable. Next we define the linear regression equation as the equation for a straight line. This yields the equation for the regression of Y the criterion, given X the predictor or, as we like to say in statistics, the regression of Y on X.

The *population regression equation* for the regression of Y on X is

$$Y_i = \beta_{YX} X_i + \alpha_{YX} + \varepsilon_i$$

where Y is the criterion variable, X is the predictor variable, β_{YX} is the population slope of the regression line for Y predicted by X, α_{YX} is the population intercept of the regression line for Y predicted by X, ε_i are the population residuals or errors of prediction (the part of Y_i not predicted from X_i), and i represents an index for a particular individual (or object). The index i can take on values from 1 to N, where N is the size of the population, written as $i = 1, \ldots , N$.

The *population prediction equation* is

$$Y'_i = \beta_{YX}X_i + \alpha_{YX}$$

where Y'_i is the predicted value of Y given a specific value of X. Thus, we see that the population prediction error is defined as

$$\varepsilon_i = Y_i - Y'_i$$

There is only one difference between the regression and prediction equations. The regression equation explicitly includes prediction error as ε_i, whereas the prediction equation includes prediction error implicitly as part of Y'_i.

Consider for a moment a practical application of the difference between the regression and prediction equations. Frequently a researcher will develop a regression equation for a population with known values of X and Y, and then will use the prediction equation for an equivalent population to actually predict Y from known values of X (i.e., Y will not be known until later). Using the GRE example, the admissions officer first develops a regression equation for a population of students currently attending the university so as to have a current measure of GPA. This yields the slope and intercept. Finally, the prediction equation is used to predict future GPA and make admission decisions for next year's population of applicants based on their GRE scores.

The population slope and intercept in simple linear regression can be computed as

$$\beta_{YX} = \frac{N\sum_{i=1}^{N} XY - (\sum_{i=1}^{N} X)(\sum_{i=1}^{N} Y)}{N\sum_{i=1}^{N} X^2 - (\sum_{i=1}^{N} X)^2}$$

and

$$\alpha_{YX} = \mu_Y - \beta_{YX}\mu_X$$

where μ_Y is the population mean for Y, and μ_X is the population mean for X. Note that the previously used method for calculating the slope and intercept of a straight line is not used in regression analysis. The numerator of the slope comes from the covariance formula and the denominator of the slope comes from the variance formula.

THE SAMPLE SIMPLE LINEAR REGRESSION EQUATION

Unstandardized Regression Equation

If we return to the real world of sample statistics, let us consider the sample simple linear regression equation. As usual, Greek letters refer to population parameters and

English letters refer to sample statistics. The sample regression equation for the regression of Y on X is

$$Y_i = b_{YX} X_i + a_{YX} + e_i$$

where Y and X are as before, b_{yx} is the sample slope of the regression line for Y as predicted by X, a_{yx} is the sample intercept of the regression line for Y as predicted by X, e_i are sample residuals or errors of prediction (that part of Y_i that is not predictable from X_i), and i represents an index for an individual (or object). The index i can take on values from 1 to n, where n is the size of the sample, and is written as $i = 1, \dots , n$.

The sample prediction equation is

$$Y'_i = b_{YX} X_i + a_{YX}$$

where Y'_i is the predicted value of Y given a specific value of X. Thus, we see that the sample prediction error is defined as

$$e_i = Y_i - Y'_i$$

The difference between the regression and prediction equations is the same as previously discussed except that we are now dealing with a sample rather than a population.

The sample slope and intercept can be computed as

$$b_{YX} = \frac{n \sum_{i=1}^{n} XY - (\sum_{i=1}^{n} X)(\sum_{i=1}^{n} Y)}{n \sum_{i=1}^{n} X^2 - (\sum_{i=1}^{n} X)^2}$$

and

$$a_{YX} = \overline{Y} - b_{YX} \overline{X}$$

where $\overline{Y}$ is the sample mean for Y, and $\overline{X}$ is the sample mean for X. The sample slope is referred to alternately as (a) the expected or predicted change in Y for a one unit change in X, (b) the influence of X on Y, and (c) the unstandardized or raw regression coefficient. The sample intercept is referred to alternately as (a) the point at which the regression line intersects (or crosses) the Y axis and (b) the value of Y when X is zero.

Consider now the analysis of a realistic example to be followed throughout this chapter. Let us use the GRE–Quantitative (GRE–Q) subtest to predict midterm scores of an introductory statistics course. The GRE–Q has a possible range of 20 to 80 points (if we remove the last digit of zero for computational ease), and the statistics midterm has a possible range of 0 to 50 points. Given the sample of 10 statistics students, shown in Table 1.1, let us work through a simple linear regression analysis. The observation numbers ($i = 1, \dots , 10$), and values for the GRE–Q and midterm variables are given in the first three columns of the table, respectively. The other columns are discussed as we go along.

As sample means, we compute for the GRE–Q that $\overline{X} = 55.5$ and for the statistics midterm $\overline{Y} = 38$. The sample slope and intercept are computed as follows:

$$b_{YX} = \frac{n\sum_{i=1}^{n} XY - (\sum_{i=1}^{n} X)(\sum_{i=1}^{n} Y)}{n\sum_{i=1}^{n} X^2 - (\sum_{i=1}^{n} X)^2}$$

$$= [10(21,905) - (555)(380)]/[10(32,355) - (555)^2] = 8,150/15,525 = 0.5250$$

and

$$a_{YX} = \overline{Y} - b_{YX}\overline{X}$$

$$= 38 - 0.5250\ (55.5) = 8.8625$$

Let us interpret the slope and intercept values. A slope of 0.5250 would mean that if your score on the GRE–Q was increased by one point, then your predicted score on the statistics midterm would be increased by 0.5250 points. An intercept of 8.8625 would mean that if your score on the GRE–Q was zero (although not possible), then your score on the statistics midterm would be 8.8625. The sample simple linear regression equation then is

$$Y_i = b_{YX}X_i + a_{YX} + e_i$$

$$= 0.5250X_i + 8.8625 + e_i$$

TABLE 1.1
Statistics Midterm Example Data

Student	GRE–Q	Midterm	Residual	Predicted Midterm
1	37	32	3.7125	28.2875
2	45	36	3.5125	32.4875
3	43	27	–4.4375	31.4375
4	50	34	–1.1125	35.1125
5	65	45	2.0125	42.9875
6	72	49	2.3375	46.6625
7	61	42	1.1125	40.8875
8	57	38	–0.7875	38.7875
9	48	30	–4.0625	34.0625
10	77	47	–2.2875	49.2875

Sums: $\Sigma X = 555$; $\Sigma Y = 380$; $\Sigma X^2 = 32,355$; $\Sigma Y^2 = 14,948$; $\Sigma XY = 21,905$

If your score on the GRE–Q is 63, then your predicted score on the statistics midterm is

$$Y'_i = .5250\ (63) + 8.8625 = 41.9375$$

Thus based on the prediction equation developed, one would predict that your score on the midterm to be approximately 42; however, as becomes evident, predictions are usually somewhat less than perfect.

Standardized Regression Equation

Until this point in the chapter, all of the computations in simple linear regression have involved the use of raw scores. For this reason we referred to the equation as the unstandardized regression equation. The slope estimate is an unstandardized or raw regression slope because it is the predicted change in Y raw score units for a one raw score unit change in X. We can also express the regression of Y on X in standard z-score units rather than in raw score units, where

$$z(X_i) = \frac{X_i - \overline{X}}{s_X} \quad \text{and} \quad z(Y_i) = \frac{Y_i - \overline{Y}}{s_Y}$$

and s_x and s_y are the sample standard deviations for X and Y, respectively. The computations are immediately simplified. The means and variances of both standardized variables (i.e., z_x and z_y) are 0 and 1, respectively. The sample standardized linear prediction equation becomes

$$z(Y'_i) = b^*_{YX}\ z(X_i) = r_{XY}\ z(X_i)$$

The standardized regression slope, b^*_{yx}, is equal to r_{xy}, the sample Pearson correlation between X and Y where $z(Y'_i)$ and $z(X_i)$ are individual z scores for the predicted criterion and predictor variables, respectively. No intercept term is necessary in the prediction equation as the mean of the z scores for both X and Y is zero (i.e., $a^*_{yx} = \overline{z}_y - b^*_{yx}\overline{z}_x = 0$ in standard score form). In summary, the standardized slope is equal to the correlation coefficient and the standardized intercept is equal to zero.

For our statistics midterm example, the sample Pearson correlation is computed as

$$r_{XY} = \frac{n\sum_{i=1}^{n} XY - (\sum_{i=1}^{n} X)(\sum_{i=1}^{n} Y)}{\sqrt{\left[n\sum_{i=1}^{n} X^2 - (\sum_{i=1}^{n} X)^2 \right]\left[n\sum_{i=1}^{n} Y^2 - (\sum_{i=1}^{n} Y)^2 \right]}}$$

$$= [10(21,905) - (555)(380)]/\sqrt{[10(32,355) - (555)^2][10(14,948) - (380)^2]} = 0.9177$$

Thus, the sample standardized linear prediction equation is

$$z(Y'_i) = .9177z(X_i)$$

The slope of .9177 would be interpreted as the expected increase in the statistics mid-term in z-score units for a 1 z-score unit increase in the GRE–Q. A 1 z-score unit increase is also the same as a one standard deviation increase because the standard deviation of a distribution of z-scores is equal to 1.

In what situations would you want to use the standardized or unstandardized regression analyses? According to Pedhazur (1997), b^* is not very stable from sample to sample. For example, at Ivy-Covered University, b^* would vary across different graduating classes (or samples), whereas b would be much more consistent across classes. Thus, most researchers prefer the use of b to compare the influences of a particular predictor variable across different samples and/or populations.

Prediction Errors

Previously, we mentioned that perfect prediction of Y from X is extremely unlikely. Perfect prediction can only occur with a perfect correlation between the predictor and criterion variables (i.e., $r_{xy} = \pm 1.0$). When we are developing the regression equation, the values of Y are known. Once the slope and intercept have been estimated, we would like to use the prediction equation to predict Y from X when the values of Y are unknown. We have already defined the predicted values of Y as Y'. In other words, a predicted value Y' can be computed by plugging the obtained value for X into the prediction equation. It can be shown that $Y'_i = Y_i$ for all i only when there is perfect prediction. However, this is extremely unlikely in reality where many variables are interrelated, and particularly in simple linear regression using only a single predictor variable.

We can compute a value of Y' for each of the i individuals or objects from the prediction equation. In comparing the actual Y values with the predicted Y values, we obtain the residuals as

$$e_i = Y_i - Y'_i$$

for all $i = 1 , \ldots , n$ individuals or objects in the sample. The e_i are also known as *errors of estimate*, or *prediction errors*, and are that portion of Y_i that is not predictable from X_i. The residual terms are random values that are unique to each individual or object.

The residuals and predicted values as computed for the statistics midterm example are shown in the last two columns of Table 1.1, respectively. Consider observation 2, where the observed GRE–Q score is 45 and the observed midterm score is 36. The predicted midterm score is 32.4875 and the residual is +3.5125. This indicates that person 2 had a higher observed midterm score than was predicted using the GRE–Q as a predictor. We see that a positive residual indicates the observed criterion score is larger than the predicted criterion score, whereas a negative residual (such as in observation 3) indicates the observed criterion score is smaller than the predicted criterion score. For observation 3, the observed GRE–Q score is 43, the observed midterm score is 27, the predicted midterm score is 31.4375, and thus the residual is –4.4375. Person 2 scored higher on the midterm than we predicted, and person 3 scored lower on the midterm than we predicted.

The regression of midterm on GRE–Q is shown graphically in the scatterplot of Fig. 1.3. The straight diagonal line represents the regression line, and the curved diagonal lines are not considered until later in the chapter. Observation 2 is depicted by scores of GRE–Q = 45 and midterm = 36. The vertical distance along the Y axis between the point and the regression line denotes the size and sign of the residual. Observation 2 is above the regression line, as the observed midterm score is larger than the predicted midterm score; thus the residual is positive. Person 2 exceeded our prediction by 3.5125 points shown by a vertical line between the observed and predicted midterm scores. Observation 3 is shown by scores of GRE–Q = 43 and midterm = 27. Observation 3 is below the regression line, as the observed midterm score is smaller than the predicted midterm score; thus the residual is negative. Person 3 fell below our prediction by 4.4375 points shown by a vertical line. In other words, points falling above the regression line have positive residuals and points falling below the regression line have negative residuals.

If we look at the residual column in Table 1.1, we see that half of the residuals are positive and half negative, and in Fig. 1.3 that half of the points fall above the regression line and half below the regression line. It can be shown that the mean of the residuals is always zero (i.e., $\bar{e} = 0$) because the sum of the residuals is always zero. This results from the fact that the mean of the observed criterion scores is equal to the mean of the predicted criterion scores (i.e., $\overline{Y} = \overline{Y'}$; 38 for the example).

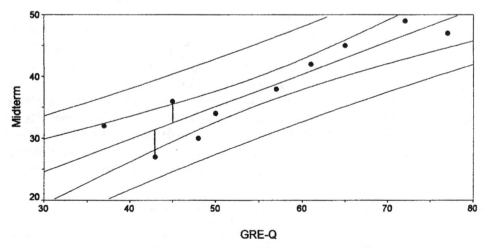

*The curved lines closest to the regression line are for the 95% CI and
the curved lines furthest from the regression line are for the 95% PI

FIG. 1.3 Regression of midterm on GRE–Q. The curved lines closest to the regression line are for the 95% CI and the curved lines furthest from the regression line are for the 95% PI.

Least Squares Criterion

How was one particular method selected for determining the slope and intercept of a straight line? Could everyone just use his or her own favorite method? The answer to these questions is simple. On a practical level, it just would not do for everyone to use his or her own favorite method for estimating the slope and intercept. Obviously, some standard procedure has to be used. On a statistical level, there are statistical criteria that help us decide which method to use in calculating the slope and intercept. The criterion usually used in linear regression analysis (and in all linear models for that matter) is the *least squares criterion*. According to the least squares criterion, the sum of the squared prediction errors or residuals is smallest. That is, we want to find that regression line, defined by a particular slope and intercept, that minimizes the sum of the squared residuals. Given the value that we place on the accuracy of prediction, this would also seem to be the most logical choice of a method for estimating the slope and intercept of a line. One might also consider other criteria, such as the most illogical choice of the "most squares criterion," where the sum of the squared residuals would be the largest.

In summary then, the least squares criterion gives us a particular slope and intercept, and thus a particular regression line, such that the sum of the squared residuals is smallest. We often refer to this particular method for calculating the slope and intercept as *least squares estimation*, because b and a represent sample estimates of the population parameters β and α obtained using the least squares criterion. In addition, the mean is defined as the value where the sum of the squared deviations of the raw scores from the mean is less than the sum of the squared deviations of the raw scores from any other value. Thus the particular method of estimating the mean as a measure of central tendency was also selected on the basis of the least squares criterion.

Let us examine several criteria with the example data set. Figure 1.4 consists of four scatterplots of the GRE–Q versus statistics midterm data, each drawn with a different regression line (i.e., different slopes and/or intercepts). Figure 1.4(a) is a plot of the points with the least squares regression line drawn. The remaining plots include regression lines drawn using other criteria. Figure 1.4(d) is drawn with the most squares regression line included. From the figure it is obvious that the least squares regression line is the best description of the plotted points. The other plots have many more large residuals than the least squares line. In computing the sum of the squared residuals for each regression line drawn, Table 1.2 shows that the least squares regression line has the smallest value. For these data, and in general, the least squares criterion is statistically better than any of the other criteria, and is the criterion that we typically use.

Proportion of Predictable Variation (Coefficient of Determination)

How well is the criterion variable Y predicted by the predictor variable X? For our example, you might be interested in how well the statistics midterm scores are predicted by the GRE–Q. Let us consider two possible situations with respect to this example. First, if the GRE–Q was found to be a really good predictor of statistics midterm scores, then instructors could use the GRE–Q information to individualize their instruction to the skill level of each student or class. They could, for example, provide special instruction to those students with low GRE–Q scores, or in general, adjust the level of instruction to fit the quantitative skills of their students. Second, if the GRE–Q was not found to be a very good predictor of statistics midterm scores, then instructors would not find very much use for the GRE–Q in terms of their preparation for the statistics course. Perhaps they would search for some other more useful predictor, such as prior grades in quantitatively oriented courses or the number of years since the student had algebra. In other words, if a predictor is not found to be particularly useful in pre-

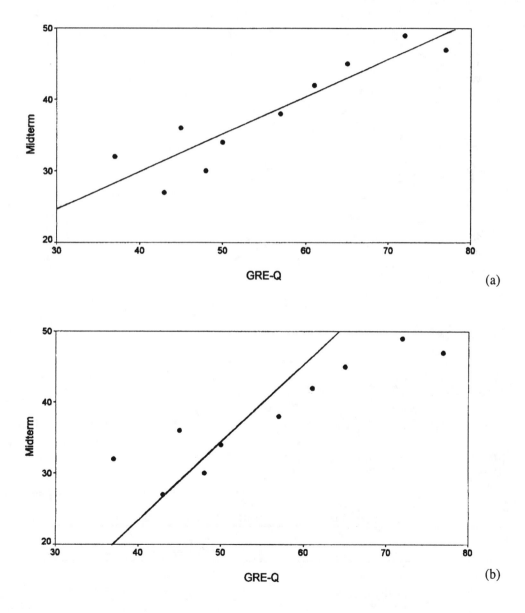

(a)

(b)

FIG. 1.4 Example regression lines: (a), (b),   (continued on next page)

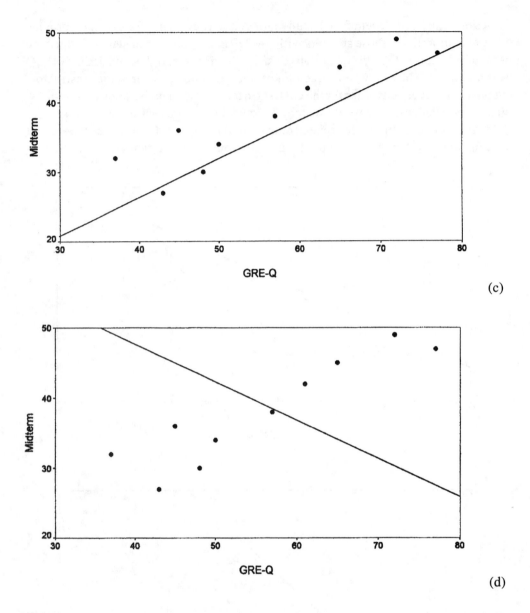

(c)

(d)

FIG. 1.4 (con't.) Example regression lines: (c), (d).

TABLE 1.2
Sum of Squared Residuals for Different Regression Lines

Line	Sum of Squared residuals
a	80.1578
b	833.0000
c	281.7500
d	1,481.7500

dicting the criterion variable, then the researcher (or teacher) might want to consider other relevant predictors.

How do we determine the utility of a predictor variable? The simplest method involves partitioning the sum of squares in Y, which we denote as SS_Y. As is shown in chapter 3, this is very much like partitioning the sum of squares used in the analysis of variance.

In simple linear regression, we can partition SS_Y into

$$SS_Y = SS_{reg} + SS_{res}$$

$$\sum_{i=1}^{n}(Y - \overline{Y})^2 = \sum_{i=1}^{n}(Y' - \overline{Y})^2 + \sum_{i=1}^{n}(Y - Y')^2$$

where SS_Y is the sum of squares in Y, SS_{reg} is the sum of squares of the regression of Y on X (often written as $SS_{Y'}$), SS_{res} is the sum of squares of the residuals, and the sums are taken over all observations from $i = 1, \ldots, n$. The term SS_Y represents the total variation in the observed Y scores, SS_{reg} the variation in Y predicted by X, and SS_{res} the variation in Y not predicted by X (i.e., residual variation). For computational purposes, let us write SS_Y, SS_{reg}, and SS_{res} as follows:

$$SS_Y = \frac{n\sum_{i=1}^{n}Y^2 - (\sum_{i=1}^{n}Y)^2}{n}$$

$$SS_{reg} = \frac{\left(\left[n\sum_{i=1}^{n}XY - (\sum_{i=1}^{n}X)(\sum_{i=1}^{n}Y)\right]/n\right)^2}{\left[n\sum_{i=1}^{n}X^2 - (\sum_{i=1}^{n}X)^2\right]/n}$$

and

$$SS_{res} = SS_Y - SS_{reg}$$

where the denominator of SS_{reg} is actually SS_X {i.e., $[n\Sigma X^2 - (\Sigma X)^2]/n$}, the sum of squares in X. The last step is to take the ratio of predicted variation to total variation as

$$\frac{SS_{reg}}{SS_Y} = r_{XY}^2$$

This ratio tells us the proportion of total variation (or sum of squares) in Y predictable using the regression equation (where X is the predictor variable). It turns out this ratio is equal to r_{XY}^2, the square of the Pearson correlation, commonly referred to as the *coefficient of determination*.

In general, there is no magical rule of thumb as to how large the coefficient of determination needs to be in order to say a meaningful proportion of variation has been predicted. The coefficient is determined not just by the quality of the predictor variable included in the model, but also by the quality of relevant predictor variables not included in the model and the amount of total variation in Y. This becomes clearer as we move through this chapter and the next.

With the sample data of predicting midterm statistics scores from the GRE–Q, let me illustrate the computation of the sums of squares. We can write SS_Y as follows:

$$SS_Y = \frac{n \sum_{i=1}^{n} Y^2 - (\sum_{i=1}^{n} Y)^2}{n}$$

$$= [10(14,948) - (380)^2]/10 = 508.0000$$

Next we can compute SS_{reg} and SS_{res}, where

$$SS_{reg} = \frac{\left(\left[n \sum_{i=1}^{n} XY - (\sum_{i=1}^{n} X)(\sum_{i=1}^{n} Y) \right] / n \right)^2}{\left[n \sum_{i=1}^{n} X^2 - (\sum_{i=1}^{n} X)^2 \right] / n}$$

$$= \frac{([10(21,905) - (555)(380)]/10)^2}{[10(32,355) - (555)^2]/10} = \frac{664,225}{1,552.5} = 427.8422$$

and

$$SS_{res} = SS_Y - SS_{reg}$$

$$= 508.0000 - 427.8422 = 80.1578$$

Let us note for later use that the computed denominator of SS_{reg}, which is SS_X, is equal to 1,552.5000. The last step is to take the ratio of SS_{reg} to SS_Y, or more formally,

$$\frac{SS_{reg}}{SS_Y} = r_{XY}^2$$

$$427.8422/508.0000 = 0.8422$$

Finally, let us check our results for the example data. Using the partitioning of sum of squares method, we found that the coefficient of determination was equal to .8422. If we take the sample Pearson correlation value of .9177 and square it, then we once again obtain the value of .8422. Thus the GRE–Q predicts approximately 84% of the variation in the midterm statistics exam. Several tests of significance are discussed in the next section.

Significance Tests and Confidence Intervals

This section describes five procedures used in the simple linear regression context. The first three are tests of statistical significance that generally involve testing whether or not X is a significant predictor of Y. Then we consider two confidence interval techniques.

Test of Significance of r_{XY}^2.   The first test is the test of the significance of r_{XY}^2 (alternatively known as the test of the proportion of variation in Y predicted by X). The null and alternative hypotheses, respectively, are as follows:

$$H_0: \rho_{XY}^2 = 0$$

$$H_1: \rho_{XY}^2 > 0$$

This test is based on the following test statistic:

$$F = \frac{r^2 / m}{(1 - r^2) / (n - m - 1)}$$

where F indicates that this is an F statistic, r^2 is the coefficient of determination (i.e., r_{XY}^2, the proportion of variation in Y predicted by X), $1 - r^2$ is the proportion of variation in Y that is not predicted by X, m is the number of predictors (which in the case of simple linear regression is always 1), and n is the sample size. The F test statistic is compared to the F critical value, always a one-tailed test and at the designated level of significance, with degrees of freedom m and $(n - m - 1)$, as taken from the F table in Appendix Table 4. That is, the tabled critical value is $_{(1-\alpha)}F_{m,(n-m-1)}$.

For the statistics midterm example, we compute the test statistic as

$$F = \frac{r^2 / m}{(1 - r^2) / (n - m - 1)}$$

$$= \frac{.8422 / 1}{(1 - .8422) / (10 - 1 - 1)} = 42.6971$$

From Appendix Table 4, the critical value, at the .05 level of significance, is $_{.95}F_{1,8} = 5.32$. The test statistic exceeds the critical value; thus we reject H_0 and conclude that ρ_{XY}^2 is not equal to zero at the .05 level of significance (i.e., GRE–Q does predict a significant proportion of the variation on the midterm exam).

Test of Significance of Sum of Squares.   The second test is the test of proportion of sum of squares in Y predicted by X. The null and alternative hypotheses, respectively, are as follows:

$$H_0: SS_{reg} = 0$$

$$H_1: SS_{reg} > 0$$

This test is based on the following test statistic:

$$F = \frac{SS_{reg} / m}{SS_{res} / (n - m - 1)}$$

where each of these terms is the same as previously discussed. A conceptually simpler way of thinking about this test statistic is as the standard F ratio,

$$F = \frac{SS_1 / df_1}{SS_2 / df_2} = \frac{MS_1}{MS_2}$$

Applying the standard F ratio to this particular situation we have

$$F = \frac{SS_{reg} / df_{reg}}{SS_{res} / df_{res}} = \frac{MS_{reg}}{MS_{res}}$$

where $df_{reg} = m$ and $df_{res} = (n - m - 1)$. As before, the F test statistic is compared to the F critical value, which is always a one-tailed test, and at the designated level of significance, with degrees of freedom m and $(n - m - 1)$, as taken from the F table in Appendix Table 4. The tabled critical value is $_{(1 - \alpha)}F_{m, (n - m - 1)}$. Algebraically, the first two tests are identical.

For the statistics midterm example, the test statistic is computed as

$$F = \frac{SS_{reg} / df_{reg}}{SS_{res} / df_{res}} = \frac{MS_{reg}}{MS_{res}}$$

$$= \frac{427.8422 / 1}{80.1578 / 8} = \frac{427.8422}{10.0197} = 42.7001$$

The critical value, at the .05 level of significance, is again $_{.95}F_{1,8} = 5.32$. The F test statistic exceeds the F critical value, so we reject H_0 and conclude that SS_{reg} is not equal to zero at the .05 level of significance (i.e., X does predict a significant proportion of the sum of squares in Y). We also see that the test statistics for the first two tests are equal to 42.70, within rounding error.

Test of Significance of b_{YX}.   The third test is the test of the significance of the slope or regression coefficient, b_{YX}. In other words, is the unstandardized regression coefficient statistically significantly different from zero? This is actually the same as the test of b^*, so we need not develop a separate test for b^*. The null and alternative hypotheses, respectively, are as follows:

$$H_0: \beta_{YX} = 0$$

$$H_1: \beta_{YX} \neq 0$$

To test whether the regression coefficient is equal to zero, we need to develop a standard error for b. However, before we get into the particulars of the standard error of b, we need to develop some additional new concepts. The first new concept is the *variance error of estimate*. Although this is the correct statistical term, it is easier to think of this concept as the *variance of the residuals*. The variance error of estimate, or variance of the residuals, is defined as

$$s_{res}^{2} = \Sigma\ e_i^2/df_{res} = SS_{res}/df_{res} = MS_{res}$$

where the summation is taken from $i = 1, \ldots, n$ and $df_{res} = (n - m - 1)$ (or $n - 2$ with a single predictor). Two degrees of freedom are lost because we have to estimate the population slope and intercept, β and α, from the sample data. The variance error of estimate indicates the amount of variation among the residuals. If there are some extremely large residuals, this will result in a relatively large value of s_{res}^{2}, indicating poor prediction overall. If the residuals are generally small, this will result in a comparatively small value of s_{res}^{2}, indicating good prediction overall.

The next new concept is the *standard error of estimate*, alternatively known as the *root mean square error*. The standard error of estimate is simply the positive square root of the variance error of estimate, and can be thought of as the standard deviation of the residuals or errors of estimate. To keep it simple, call it the standard error of estimate, and denote it as s_{res}. Recall from introductory statistics that the concept of the standard error of the mean was related to the standard (or unit) normal distribution. The range of one standard error about the mean (i.e., the mean ± one standard error) covers approximately 68% of the distribution. The range of two standard errors about the mean covers approximately 95% of the distribution. The range of three standard errors about the mean covers approximately 99% of the distribution.

The final new concept is the *standard error of b*. We denote the standard error of b as s_b and define it as

$$s_b = \frac{s_{res}}{\sqrt{[n\Sigma X^2 - (\Sigma X)^2]/n}} = \frac{s_{res}}{\sqrt{SS_X}}$$

where the summation is taken over $i = 1, \ldots, n$. We want s_b to be small in order to reject H_0, so we need s_{res} to be small and SS_X to be large. In other words, we want there to be a large spread of scores in X. If the variability in X is small, it is not likely that X will be a significant predictor of Y.

Now we are ready to put these concepts together into a test statistic to test the significance of b. As in many significance tests, the test statistic is formed by the ratio of a parameter estimate divided by its respective standard error. A ratio of the parameter estimate of the slope b to its standard error s_b is formed as

$$t = \frac{b}{s_b}$$

The test-statistic t is compared to the critical values of t, a two-tailed test for a nondirectional H_1, at the designated level of significance, and with degrees of freedom $(n - m - 1)$, as taken from the t table in Appendix Table 2. That is, the tabled critical values are $\pm_{(\alpha/2)} t_{(n - m - 1)}$ for a two-tailed test.

It should be noted for the test statistics F and t just discussed (i.e., for the first two and third test statistics, respectively) that $t^2 = F$. This will always occur when a single predictor is used, as is the case in simple linear regression, and when it is hypothesized that the values of ρ^2 and β are equal to zero. This occurs because the two theoretical distributions are related in this particular situation. The square of the value for a t distribution with ν degrees of freedom at a particular percentile (P_i) will always be equal to the value of an F distribution with 1 and ν degrees of freedom, numerator and denominator, respectively, at the same percentile (P_i). That is, the degrees of freedom for the t and for the denominator of the F distributions must be the same, and the degrees of freedom for the numerator of the F distribution must be equal to 1. Try comparing Appendix Tables 2 and 4.

In addition, all other things being equal (i.e., same data, same degrees of freedom, same level of significance), each of the three tests will yield the same result. That is, if X is a significant predictor of Y, then H_0 will be rejected for all three tests in favor of the alternative H_1. If X is not a significant predictor of Y, then H_0 will not be rejected for any of these tests. In the case of simple linear regression, each of these tests is a method for testing the same general hypothesis and logically ought to lead the researcher to the same conclusion. Thus, there is no real need to implement each of the three tests in simple linear regression.

We can also form a confidence interval around b. As in most confidence interval procedures, it follows the form of the sample estimate plus or minus the tabled critical value multiplied by the standard error. The confidence interval (CI) around b is formed as follows:

$$\mathbf{CI}(b) = b \pm _{(\alpha/2)} t _{(n - m - 1)} s_b$$

Recall that the null hypothesis was written as H_0: $\beta = 0$. Therefore, if the confidence interval contains zero, then β is not significantly different from zero at the specified α level. This is interpreted to mean that in $(1 - \alpha)\%$ of the sample confidence intervals that would be formed from multiple samples, β will be included.

Next we work out the third test statistic for the midterm statistics example. We specify H_0: $\beta = 0$ and conduct a two-tailed test. First we calculate the variance error of estimate as

$$s^2_{res} = \Sigma\, e_i^2/df_{res} = SS_{res}/df_{res} = MS_{res}$$

$$= 80.1578/8 = 10.0197$$

The standard error of estimate, s_{res}, is computed to be $+\sqrt{10.0197} = 3.1654$. Next the standard error of b is found to be

$$s_b = \frac{s_{res}}{\sqrt{SS_X}} = \frac{3.1654}{\sqrt{1,552.5000}} = .0803$$

where SS_X is taken from a previous computation. Finally, we calculate the test statistic to be

$$t = \frac{b}{s_b} = \frac{.5250}{.0803} = 6.5380$$

To evaluate the null hypothesis, we compare this test statistic to its respective critical value $\pm_{.025} t_8 = \pm 2.306$. The test statistic exceeds the critical value, so H_0 is rejected in favor of H_1. We conclude that the slope is indeed significantly different from zero, at the .05 level of significance. Compare the two F-test statistics previously computed with the t-test statistic just computed. The F-test statistics were calculated to be around 42.70, whereas the t-test statistic was 6.5380. We see then that t^2 is indeed equal to F, within rounding error.

Finally let us compute the confidence interval for b as follows:

$$\textbf{CI } (b) = b \pm {}_{(\alpha/2)} t_{(n - m - 1)} \, s_b = b \pm {}_{.025} t_8 (s_b)$$

$$= 0.5250 \pm 2.306(0.0803) = 0.5250 \pm 0.1852$$

$$= (0.3398, 0.7102)$$

The interval does not contain zero, the value specified in H_0; thus we conclude that β is significantly different from zero, at the .05 level of significance.

Confidence Interval for the Predicted Mean Value of Y. The fourth procedure is the development of a confidence interval for the predicted mean value of Y, denoted by $\overline{Y}'_0$, at a specific value of X_0. Alternatively, $\overline{Y}'_0$ is referred to as the fitted or expected value of Y, or as the conditional mean of Y given X (there is more about conditional means in the next section). In other words, given a particular predictor score X_0, we would like to know how confident we can be in the predicted mean for Y.

The standard error of $\overline{Y}'_0$ is

$$s(\overline{Y}'_0) = s_{res} \sqrt{(1 / n) + [(X_0 - \overline{X})^2 / SS_X]}$$

As we can see from the standard error $s(\overline{Y}'_0)$, the further X_0 is from $\overline{X}$, the larger the standard error. Thus, the standard error is dependent on the particular value of X_0 selected. In other words, we expect to make our best predictions at the center of the distribution of X scores, and to make our poorest predictions for extreme values of X. Thus, the closer the values of the predictor are to the center of the distribution of the X scores, the better the prediction.

A confidence interval around $\overline{Y}'_0$ is formed as follows:

$$\mathbf{CI}(\overline{Y}'_0) = \overline{Y}'_0 \pm {}_{(\alpha/2)} t_{(n-2)} s(\overline{Y}'_0)$$

We would interpret the confidence interval to mean that in $(1 - \alpha)\%$ of the sample confidence intervals that would be formed from multiple samples, the population mean value of Y for a given value of X will be included.

Let us consider an example of this confidence interval procedure with the midterm statistics data. If we take a GRE–Q score of 50, the predicted score on the statistics midterm would be 35.1125. A confidence interval for the predicted mean value of 35.1125 would be developed as follows:

$$s(\overline{Y}'_0) = s_{\text{res}} \sqrt{(1 / n) + [(X_0 - \overline{X})^2 / SS_X]}$$

$$= 3.1654 \sqrt{(1 / 10) + [(50 - 55)^2 / 1{,}552.5000]} = 1.0786$$

and

$$\mathbf{CI}(\overline{Y}'_0) = \overline{Y}'_0 \pm {}_{(\alpha/2)} t_{(n-2)} s(\overline{Y}'_0) = \overline{Y}'_0 \pm {}_{(.025)} t_{(8)} s(\overline{Y}'_0)$$

$$= 35.1125 \pm (2.306)(1.0786) = 35.1125 \pm 2.4873$$

$$= (32.6252, 37.5998)$$

Returning to Fig. 1.3, the confidence interval around $\overline{Y}'_0$ given X_0 is plotted as the pair of curved lines closest to the regression line. Here we see graphically that the width of the confidence interval increases the further we move from $\overline{X}$ (where $\overline{X} = 55.5000$).

Prediction Interval for Individual Values of Y. The fifth and final procedure is the development of a prediction interval for an individual predicted value of Y'_0 at a specific value of X_0. That is, the predictor score for a particular individual is known, but the criterion score for that individual has not yet been observed. This is in contrast to the confidence interval just discussed where the individual Y scores have already been observed. Thus the confidence interval deals with the mean of the predicted values, whereas the prediction interval deals with an individual predicted value not yet observed.

The standard error of Y'_0 is

$$s(Y'_0) = s_{\text{res}} \sqrt{1 + (1 / n) + [(X_0 - \overline{X})^2 / SS_X]}$$

The standard error of Y'_0 is similar to that of the standard error of $\overline{Y}'_0$ with the addition of 1 to the equation. Thus the standard error of Y'_0 will always be greater than the standard error of $\overline{Y}'_0$ in that there is more uncertainty about individual values than about the mean. Once again we can see from the standard error, $s(Y'_0)$, that the further X_0 is from $\overline{X}$, the larger the standard error. The standard error is again dependent on the particular value of X selected, where we will have more confidence in our predictions for values of X close to $\overline{X}$.

The prediction interval (PI) around Y'_0 is formed as follows

$$PI(Y'_0) = Y'_0 \pm_{(\alpha/2)} t_{(n-2)} s(Y'_0)$$

Thus, the prediction interval will always be wider than its corresponding confidence interval. We would interpret the prediction interval to mean that in $(1 - \alpha)\%$ of the sample prediction intervals that would be formed from multiple samples, the new observation Y_0 for a given value of X will be included.

Consider an example of this prediction interval procedure with the midterm statistics data. If we take a GRE–Q score of 50, the predicted score on the statistics midterm would be 35.1125. A prediction interval for the predicted individual value of 35.1125 would be developed as follows:

$$s(Y'_0) = s_{res} \sqrt{1 + (1/n) + [(X_0 - \overline{X})^2 / SS_X]}$$

$$= 3.1654 \sqrt{1 + (1/10) + [(50 - 55)^2 / 1,552.5000]} = 3.3441$$

$$PI(Y'_0) = Y'_0 \pm_{(\alpha/2)} t_{(n-2)} s(Y'_0) = Y'_0 \pm_{.025} t_8 s(Y'_0)$$

$$= 35.1125 \pm (2.306)(3.3441) = 35.1125 \pm 7.7115 = (27.4010, 42.8240)$$

In Fig. 1.3, the prediction interval around Y'_0 given X_0 is plotted as the pair of curved lines furthest from the regression line. Here we see graphically that the prediction interval is always wider than its corresponding confidence interval.

Assumptions

Until this point in the chapter, we have not mentioned the assumptions underlying the regression analysis. In this section we present the three general assumptions involved in simple linear regression: (a) linearity, (b) the distribution of the errors in prediction, and (c) X being a fixed variable. In the next section, we consider more specifically how assumption violations can be detected graphically and handled.

The Regression of Y on X is Linear. First assume the regression of Y on X is linear; this was also assumed for correlations in chapter 10. Consider the scatterplot and fitted regression line in Fig. 1.5 where X and Y are not linearly related. In fact, X and Y form a perfect curvilinear relationship because all of the points fall precisely on a curve. However, fitting a straight line to these points would result in a slope of zero as indicated by the solid horizontal line, not useful at all for predicting Y from X. For example, age and performance are not linearly related.

Let us take a look at a second example of a perfect curvilinear relationship. In this example, I intentionally choose a regression equation such that

$$1/Y_i = b_{YX} X_i + a_{YX} + e_i$$

Thus, an inverse or reciprocal relationship exists between X and Y. Let us predetermine b_{yx} to be equal to 5 and a_{yx} to be equal to 0. Then select as X_i values from 1 to 20, and proceed to calculate the Y values directly from the regression equation with residuals of zero.

In the analysis of this data I consider two forms of simple regression: simple linear regression, and simple reciprocal regression. The simple linear regression analysis, although obviously an inappropriate model for these data, yields as the regression equation

$$Y_i = -.0053X_i + .0921 + e_i$$

where the Pearson correlation between X and Y is computed to be $-.7076$ for an r^2 value of .5007. A plot of the regression line is shown by the solid diagonal line in Fig. 1.6. Obviously, fitting the points with a straight line does not yield the best fit possible for these data.

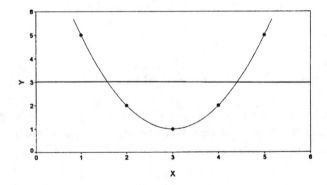

FIG. 1.5   Nonlinear regression example 1.

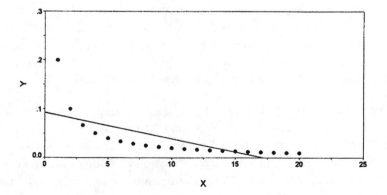

FIG. 1.6   Nonlinear regression example 2, wrong.

The simple reciprocal regression analysis, which we know to be an appropriate model for these data, yields as the regression equation

$$1/Y_i = 5X_i + 0 + e_i$$

where the nonlinear correlation between X and Y is computed to be $+1.0$ for an r^2 value of 1.0. A plot of the regression line is shown by the solid curve in Fig. 1.7. Here we see that the points are exactly fitted with the curved line; this should not be surprising, as we manufactured the data set to have this characteristic. Thus, the choice of a regression model to use for these data has an effect on the magnitude of the relationship between X and Y, in terms of both the Pearson correlation coefficient, and the regression slope and intercept.

If the relationship between X and Y is linear, then the sample slope and intercept will be unbiased estimators of the population slope and intercept, respectively. The linearity assumption is important because, regardless of the value of X_i, we always expect Y_i to increase by b_{yx} units for a 1-unit increase in X_i. If a nonlinear relationship exists, this means that the expected increase in Y_i depends on the value of X_i. Strictly speaking, linearity in a model refers to there being linearity in the parameters of the model (i.e., in simple linear regression, β and α).

The Distribution of the Errors in Prediction.   The second assumption is actually a set of four statements about the form of the errors in prediction or residuals, the e_i. First, the errors in prediction are assumed to be random and independent errors. That is, there is no systematic pattern about the errors, and each error is independent of the other errors. An example of a systematic pattern would be where for small values of X the residuals tended to be small, whereas for large values of X the residuals tended to be large. Thus there would be a relationship between X and e. Dependent errors would oc-

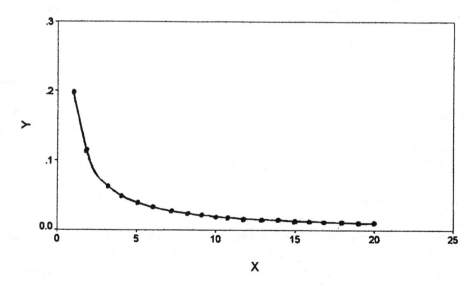

FIG. 1.7   Nonlinear regression example 2, right.

cur when the error for one individual depends on or is related to the error for another individual as a result of some predictor not being included in the model. For our midterm statistics example, students similar in age might have similar residuals because age was not included as a predictor in the model. Independence is conceptually the same as assuming that the errors are uncorrelated. In fact, with normally distributed variables, a zero correlation does imply independence.

Prior to discussing the remaining portions of the second assumption, we need to examine the concept of a *conditional distribution*. In regression analysis, a conditional distribution is defined as the distribution of Y for a particular value of X. For instance, in the midterm statistics example, we could consider the conditional distribution of midterm scores for GRE–Q = 50: in other words, what the distribution of Y would look like for $X = 50$. We call this a conditional distribution because it represents the distribution of Y conditional on a particular value of X (sometimes denoted as $Y|X$, read as Y given X). However, here we are interested in examining the conditional distribution of the prediction errors, that is, the distribution of the prediction errors conditional on a particular value of X (i.e., $e|X$, read as e given X).

According to the second part of the assumption, the conditional distributions of the prediction errors for all values of X have a mean of zero. That is, for say $X = 50$, there are some positive and some negative errors in prediction, but on the average the errors in prediction are zero. This is assumed for all values of X. If the first two parts of the assumption are satisfied, then Y' is an unbiased estimator of the mean of each conditional distribution.

The third part of the assumption is the conditional distributions of the prediction errors have a constant variance, s_{res}^2, for all values of X. Often this is referred to as the assumption of *homogeneity of variance* or *homoscedasticity*, where homoscedasticity means "same scatter" (previously assumed for t tests). That is, for all values of X, the conditional distributions of the prediction errors will have the same variance. If the first three parts of the assumption are satisfied, then s_{res}^2 is an unbiased estimator of the variance of each conditional distribution.

The fourth and final part of the assumption is the conditional distributions of the prediction errors are normal in shape. That is, for all values of X, the prediction errors are normally distributed. Now we have a complete assumption about the conditional distributions of the prediction errors. Each conditional distribution of e_i consists of random and independent (I) values that are normally (N) distributed, with a mean of zero, and a variance of s_{res}^2. In statistical notation, the assumption is that $e_i \sim NI(0, s_{res}^2)$. If all four parts of the second assumption and the first assumption are satisfied, then we can validly test hypotheses and form confidence intervals.

The Fixed X Model.   According to the third and final assumption, the values of X are *fixed*. That is, X is a fixed variable rather than a random variable. This results in the regression model being valid only for those particular values of X that were actually observed and used in the analysis. We see a similar concept in the fixed-effects analysis of variance model in chapter 3. Thus the same values of X would be used in replications or repeated samples.

Strictly speaking, the regression model and its parameter estimates are only valid for those values of X actually sampled. The use of a prediction equation, based on one sample of individuals, to predict Y for another sample of individuals may be suspect. Depending on the circumstances, the new sample of individuals may actually call for a different set of parameter estimates. Two obvious situations that come to mind are the *extrapolation* and *interpolation* of values of X. In general we may not want to make predictions about individuals having X scores outside of the range of values used in developing the prediction equation; this is defined as extrapolating beyond the sample predictor data. We cannot assume that the function defined by the prediction equation is the same outside of the values of X that were initially sampled. The prediction errors for the nonsampled X values would be expected to be larger than those for the sampled X values because there is no supportive prediction data for the former.

On the other hand, we may not be quite as concerned in making predictions about individuals having X scores within the range of values used in developing the prediction equation; this is defined as interpolating within the range of the sample predictor data. We would feel somewhat more comfortable in assuming that the function defined by the prediction equation is the same for other new values of X within the range of those initially sampled. For the most part, the fixed X assumption would be satisfied if the new observations behaved like those in the prediction sample. In the interpolation situation, we expect the prediction errors to be somewhat smaller as compared to the extrapolation situation because there is at least some similar supportive prediction data for the former.

In our midterm statistics example, we will have a bit more confidence in our prediction for a GRE–Q value of 52 (which did not occur in the sample, but falls within the range of sampled values) than in a value of 20 (which also did not occur, but is much smaller than the smallest value sampled, 37). In fact, this is precisely the rationale underlying the prediction interval developed in the preceding section, where the width of the interval increased as an individual's score on the predictor (X_i) moved away from the predictor mean $(\overline{X})$. If all of the other assumptions are upheld, and if e is statistically independent of X (i.e., the residuals are independent of the predictor scores), then X can be a random variable without affecting the estimators a and b. Thus if X is a random variable and is independent of e, then a and b are unaffected, allowing for the proper use of tests of significance and confidence intervals. It should also be noted that Y is considered to be a random variable, and thus no assumption is made about fixed values of Y.

A summary of the assumptions and the effects of their violation for simple linear regression is presented in Table 1.3.

Graphical Techniques: Detection of Assumption Violations

So as to better evaluate the data and the assumptions stated in the previous section, the use of various graphical techniques is absolutely essential. In simple linear regression, two general types of plots are typically constructed. The first is the scatterplot of Y versus X (where Y is plotted on the vertical axis and X on the horizontal axis). The second plot involves plotting some type of residual versus X (or alternatively versus Y').

TABLE 1.3
Assumptions and Violation of Assumptions—Simple Linear Regression

Assumption	Effect of Assumption Violation
1. Regression of Y on X is linear	Bias in slope and intercept; expected change in Y is not a constant and depends on value of X; reduced magnitude of coefficient of determination
2. Independence of residuals	Influences standard errors of the model
3. Residual means equal 0	Bias in Y'
4. Homogeneity of variance of residuals	Bias in s^2_{res}; may inflate standard errors and thus increase likelihood of a Type II error; may result in nonnormal conditional distributions
5. Normality of residuals	Less precise slope, intercept, and coefficient of determination
6. Values of X are fixed	(a) Extrapolating beyond the range of X: prediction errors larger, may also bias slope and intercept (b) Interpolating within the range of X: smaller effects than in (a); if other assumptions met, negligible effect

Prior to considering these graphical techniques, we need to look at different types of residuals. So far we have only discussed the raw residuals, e_i. These are appropriately termed *raw residuals* for the same reason that X_i and Y_i are termed *raw scores*. They have not been altered in any way and remain in their original metric or scale. Thus the raw residuals are on the same raw score scale as Y with a mean of zero and a variance of $s_{res}^{\ 2}$. Some researchers dislike raw residuals in that their scale is dependent on the scale of Y, and therefore they must temper their interpretation of the residual values. Thus standardized residuals have also been developed.

There are several types of standardized residuals. The original form of standardized residual is the result of e_i/s_{res}. These values are measured along the z-score scale with a mean of 0, a variance of 1, and approximately 95% of the values are within ±2 units of zero. Some researchers prefer these over raw residuals because they find it easier to detect large residuals. However, if you really think about it, one can easily look at the middle 95% of the raw residuals by just considering the range of ±2 standard errors (i.e., ±2 s_{res}) around zero. Other types of standardized residuals will not be considered here (cf. Atkinson, 1985; Cook & Weisberg, 1982; Dunn & Clark, 1987; Weisberg, 1985).

The Linearity Assumption.   Let us first consider detecting violation of the linearity assumption. Initially look at the scatterplot of Y versus X. Here an obvious violation is easily viewed. If the linearity assumption is met, we would expect to see no systematic pattern of points deviating from the regression line and accompanying elliptical scatter of points. Recall from the previous section the blatant violations of the linearity assumption as shown in Fig. 1.5 and 1.6. While examination of this plot is often satisfactory in simple linear regression, less obvious violations will be more easily detected in a residual plot. Therefore I recommend that you examine at a minimum both the scatterplot and the residual plot.

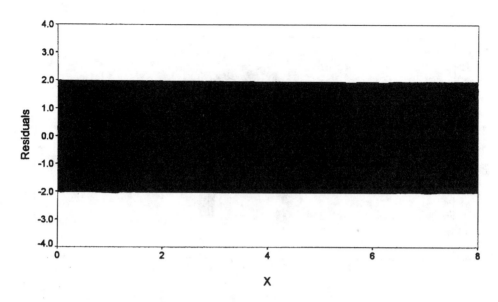

FIG. 1.8 Residual plot showing linearity.

The type of residual plot most often used to detect nonlinearity is the plot of e versus either X or Y'. With just a single predictor the plot of e versus X will look exactly the same as the plot of e versus Y', except that the scale on the horizontal axis is obviously different. If the linearity assumption is met, then we would expect to see a horizontal band of residuals mainly contained within $\pm 2\, s_{res}$ (or standard errors) across the values of X (or Y'), as shown in Fig. 1.8.

An example of an obvious nonlinear relationship is shown in the residual plot of Fig. 1.9. Here we see negative residuals for small and large values of X, and positive residuals for moderate values of X. In general, a nonlinear relationship yields alternating series of positive and negative residuals across the values of X. That is, we see a systematic pattern between e and X such as that shown in Fig. 1.9, rather than the random pattern that was observed in the linear relationship depicted by Fig. 1.8. A residual plot for the midterm statistics example is shown in Fig. 1.10. Even with a very small sample, we see a fairly random pattern of residuals, and therefore feel fairly confident that the linearity assumption has been satisfied.

There is also a statistical method for determining nonlinearity known as the *correlation ratio*. The correlation ratio is a measure of linear as well as nonlinear relationship and is denoted by η^2. The formula for computing the correlation ratio in the simple linear regression context is

$$\eta_{YX}^2 = 1 - \frac{SS_{with}}{SS_Y}$$

where SS_{with} is known as sum of squares within groups and computed as follows. If we let all individuals with the same value of X constitute a group, then we can compute a mean for that group on Y. These group means are denoted by $\overline{Y}_{.j}$, where the dot signifies

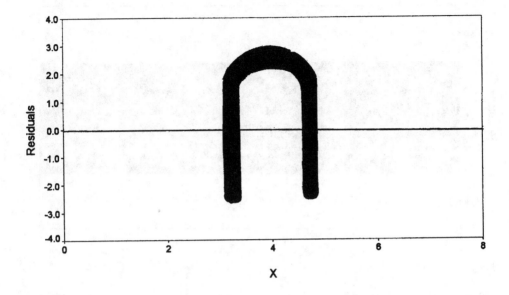

FIG. 1.9   Residual plot showing nonlinearity.

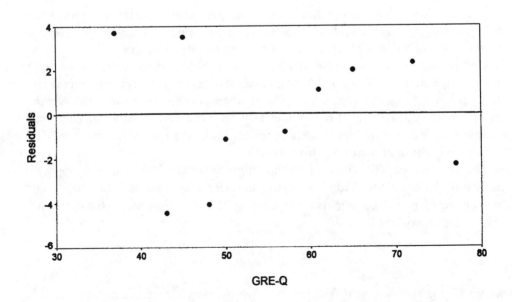

FIG. 1.10   Residual plot for midterm example.

we have averaged across the i scores in a group, and the j designates the particular group. SS_{with} is computed as

$$SS_{with} = \sum_{i=1}^{n} \sum_{j=1}^{J} (Y_{ij} - \overline{Y}_{\cdot j})^2$$

where the summation is taken over all individuals in each group (all i) and then over all groups (all j). The correlation ratio η_{YX}^2 is then compared with the coefficient of determination r_{XY}^2. If the coefficients are approximately equal, then the regression is linear. If the correlation ratio is meaningfully greater than the coefficient of determination, then the regression is not linear. The correlation ratio cannot be less than the coefficient of determination.

A more formal statistical test is

$$F = \frac{(\eta_{YX}^2 - r_{XY}^2) / (J - 2)}{(1 - \eta_{YX}^2) / (N - J)}$$

where J is the total number of groups and N is the total number of observations. This test statistic is then compared to the critical value $_{(1-\alpha)}F_{(J-2),(N-J)}$. Here the null and alternative hypotheses, respectively, are as follows:

$$H_0: H_{YX}^2 - \rho_{XY}^2 = 0$$

$$H_1: H_{YX}^2 - \rho_{XY}^2 > 0$$

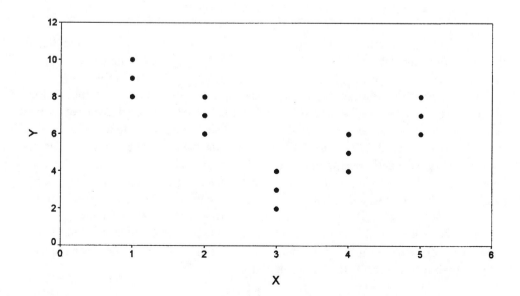

FIG. 1.11 Plot for test of linearity.

TABLE 1.4
Results for Test of Linearity

Summary statistics:

r_{XY} = .1492

SS_Y = 72.4000

SS_{with} = 10.0000

Computation of η_{YX}^2:

$\eta_{YX}^2 = 1 - (SS_{with}/SS_Y)$

$= 1 - (10.0000/72.4000)$

$= .8619$

Hypotheses:

H_0: $H_{YX}^2 - \rho_{XY}^2 = 0$

H_1: $H_{YX}^2 - \rho_{XY}^2 > 0$

Test statistic:

$$F = \frac{(\eta_{YX}^2 - r_{XY}^2)/(J-2)}{(1-\eta_{YX}^2)/(N-J)}$$

$$= \frac{(.8619 - .1492)/3}{(1 - .8619)/10}$$

$$= 17.2025$$

Critical value: $_{.95}F_{3,10} = 3.71$

Conclusion: Reject H_0 and conclude that the relationship is nonlinear

where ρ_{XY}^2 is the population coefficient of determination as estimated by r_{XY}^2, and H_{YX}^2 is the population correlation ratio as estimated by η_{YX}^2. A complete example of this procedure for an obvious nonlinear relationship is shown in Fig. 1.1 and Table 1.4.

Once a serious violation of the linearity assumption has been detected, the obvious question is how to deal with it. There are two alternative procedures that the researcher can utilize, *transformations* or *nonlinear models*. The first option is to transform either one or both of the variables to achieve linearity. That is, the researcher selects a transformation that subsequently results in a linear relationship between the transformed variables. Then the method of least squares can be used to perform a linear regression analysis on the transformed variables. However, because you are dealing with transformed variables measured along a scale different from your original variables, your results need to be described in terms of the transformed rather than the original variables. A better option is to use a nonlinear model to examine the relationship between the variables in their original form (further discussed in chap. 12).

The Normality Assumption. Next let us examine violation of the normality assumption. Often nonnormal distributions are largely a function of one or a few extreme observations, known as *outliers*. Extreme values may cause nonnormality and seriously affect the regression results. The regression estimates are quite sensitive to outlying observations such that the precision of the estimates is affected, particularly the slope. Also the coefficient of determination can be affected. In general, the regression line will be pulled toward the outlier, because the least squares principle always attempts to find the line that best fits all of the points.

Various rules of thumb are used to crudely detect outliers from a residual plot or scatterplot. A commonly used rule is to define an outlier as an observation more than two or three standard errors from the mean (i.e., a large distance from the mean), when all of the data points are included. There are several reasons why an observation may be an outlier. The observation may be a result of (a) a simple recording or data entry error, (b) an error in observation, (c) an improperly functioning instrument, (d) inappropriate use of administration instructions, or (e) a true outlier. If the outlier is the result of an error, correct the error if possible and redo the regression analysis. If the error cannot be corrected, then the observation could be deleted. If the outlier represents an accurate observation, then this observation may contain important theoretical information, and one would be more hesitant to delete it.

A simple procedure to use for single case outliers (i.e., just one outlier) is to perform two regression analyses, both with and without the outlier being included. A comparison of the regression results will provide some indication of the effects of the outlier. Other methods for dealing with outliers are available, but are not described here (e.g., robust regression, nonparametric regression).

Let us examine with the midterm statistics example the effect of one outlier. Here we add an additional 11th observation, an individual with a GRE–Q score of 38 (a low score) and a midterm statistics score of 50 (a very high score). It should be obvious that this observation is quite different from the others. A summary of the regression results, with and without the outlier, is shown in Table 1.5. The outlier dramatically changes the prediction equation from $Y' = 0.5250X + 8.8625$ without the outlier to $Y' = 0.3409X + 20.7152$ with the outlier. In addition, the standard error of the slope is doubled, so that the test of the significance of the slope goes from being significant at the .05 level to nonsignificant. The value of r_{XY}^2 drops from .8422 to .3330 and the standard error of estimate doubles. Although this is a rather extreme example, it nevertheless serves to illustrate the effect that a single outlier can have on the results of a regression analysis. Some references for outlier detection are Cook (1977), Andrews and Pregibon (1978), Barnett and Lewis (1978), Hawkins (1980), Beckman and Cook (1983), and Rousseeuw and Leroy (1987).

How does one go about detecting violation of the normality assumption? There are two commonly used procedures. The simplest procedure involves checking for symmetry in a histogram, frequency distribution, boxplot, or through calculation of skewness and kurtosis. Although *nonzero kurtosis* (i.e., a distribution that is either flat or has a sharp peak) will have minimal effect on the regression estimates, *nonzero skewness* (i.e., a distribution that is not symmetric) will have much more impact on these estimates. Thus, looking for asymmetrical distributions is a must. For the midterm statistics example, the skewness value for the raw residuals is –0.2692. One rule of thumb is to be concerned if the skewness value is extreme—say, larger than 1.5 or 2.0 in magnitude.

Another useful graphical technique is the normal probability plot. With normally distributed data or residuals, the points on the normal probability plot will fall along a straight diagonal line, whereas nonnormal data will not. There is a difficulty with this plot because there is no criterion with which to judge deviation from linearity. A normal probability plot of the raw residuals for the midterm statistics example is shown in Fig. 1.12. Taken together, the skewness and normal probability plot results indicate that the normality assumption is satisfied. It is recommended that a look at symmetry and/or the normal probability plot be considered at a minimum (available in many statistical packages).

There are also several statistical procedures available for the detection of nonnormality. Tests of nonnormality of the residuals have been proposed (e.g., An-

TABLE 1.5
Regression Results With and Without an Outlier

Result	Without Outlier	With Outlier
a_{YX}	8.8625	20.7152
b_{YX}	0.5250	0.3409
s_b	0.0803	0.1608
p level of b	0.0002	0.0631
r_{XY}^2	0.8422	0.3330

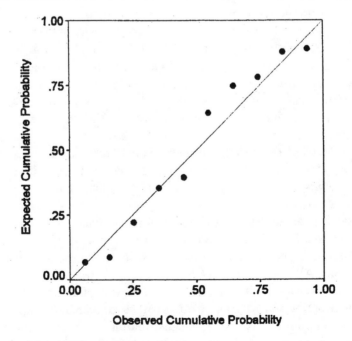

FIG. 1.12 Normal probability plot for example data.

drews, 1971; Belsley, Kuh, & Welsch, 1980; Ruppert & Carroll, 1980; Wu, 1985). In addition, various transformations are available to transform a nonnormal distribution into a normal distribution. Some of the more commonly used transformations in regression analysis are the log and the square root. However, again there is a problem because you will be dealing with transformed variables that are measured along some other scale than that of your original variables. A nice review of these procedures is described by Cook and Weisberg (1982).

The Homogeneity Assumption. The third assumption we need to consider is the homogeneity or homoscedasticity of variance assumption. In a plot of the residuals versus X (or alternatively Y'), the consistency of the variance of the conditional residual distributions can be examined. A common violation of this assumption occurs when the conditional residual variance increases as X (or Y') increases. Here the plot is cone- or fan-shaped where the cone opens toward the right. An example of this violation would be where weight is predicted by age. A scatterplot of residuals versus age would take on a cone shape, in that weight is more predictable for young children than it is for adults. Thus, residuals would tend to be larger for adults than for children.

Another method for detecting violation of the homogeneity assumption is the use of formal statistical tests. Tests have been proposed that are specifically designed for regression models (e.g., Miller, 1997). Other tests more general in scope can also be used. Usually, however, the residual plot indicates obvious violations of the assumption.

As a result of violation of the homogeneity assumption, the estimates of the standard errors are larger, and although the regression coefficients remain unbiased, as a net result the validity of the significance tests is affected. In fact, with larger standard errors, it will be more difficult to reject H_0, and therefore the result is a larger number of Type II errors. Minor violations of this assumption will have a small net effect; more serious violations occur when the variances are greatly different. In addition, nonconstant variances may also result in the conditional distributions being nonnormal in shape.

What should you do if the homogeneity assumption is violated? The simplest solution is to use some sort of transformation, here known as *variance-stabilizing transformations* (e.g., Weisberg, 1985). Some commonly used transformations are the log and square root of Y. These transformations often improve on the nonnormality of the conditional distributions. However, as before, you will be dealing with transformed variables rather than your original variables. A better solution is to use generalized or weighted least squares rather than ordinary least squares as the method of estimation (e.g., Weisberg, 1985). A third solution is to use a form of robust estimation (e.g., Carroll & Ruppert, 1982).

The Independence Assumption. The final assumption to be examined is *independence of the residuals*. Once again, the simplest procedure for assessing this assumption is to examine a residual plot (e.g., e vs. X). If the independence assumption is satisfied, then the residuals should fall into a random display of points. If the assumption is violated, then the residuals will fall into some type of cyclical pattern, such that negative residuals will tend to cluster together and positive residuals will tend to cluster together.

Violation of the independence assumption generally occurs in three situations. The first and most common situation is when the observations are collected over time (e.g., time-series data [Box & Jenkins, 1976] or longitudinal data). Here the independent variable is some measure of time. In this context a violation is referred to as autocorrelated errors or serial correlation because errors are correlated for adjacent time points. For example, say we measure the weight of a sample of individuals at two different points in time. The correlation between these two measures is likely to be much higher when weight is measured 1 week apart as compared to 1 year apart. Thus, for example, those individuals with large positive residuals in week 1 are quite likely to also have large positive residuals in week 2, but not as likely 1 year later.

Nonindependence will affect the estimated standard errors, being under or overestimated depending on the type of autocorrelation (i.e., for positive or negative autocorrelation, respectively). A statistical test for autocorrelation is the Durbin–Watson test (1950, 1951, 1971). The Durbin-Watson test statistic is not appropriate for the midterm statistics example because the independent variable is not a measure of time.

Violations can also occur (a) when observations are made within blocks, such that the observations within a particular block are more similar than observations in different blocks; or (b) when observation involves replication. As with the homogeneity assumption, for serious violations of the independence assumption a standard procedure is to use generalized or weighted least squares as the method of estimation.

Summary.   The simplest procedure for assessing assumptions is to plot the residuals and see what the plot tells you. Take the midterm statistics problem as an example. Although sample size is quite small in terms of looking at conditional distributions, it would appear that all of our assumptions have been satisfied. All of the residuals are within two standard errors of zero, and there does not seem to be any systematic pattern in the residuals. The distribution of the residuals is nearly symmetric and the normal probability plot looks good. The scatterplot also strongly suggests a linear relationship. The more sophisticated statistical programs have implemented various regression diagnostics to assist the researcher in the evaluation of assumptions. In addition, several textbooks have been written that include a discussion of the use of regression analysis with statistical software (e.g., Barcikowski, 1983; Cody & Smith, 1997).

SUMMARY

In this chapter the method of simple linear regression was described. First we discussed the basic concepts of regression such as the slope, intercept, and regression and prediction equations. Next, a formal introduction to the population simple linear regression model was given. These concepts were then extended to the sample situation where a more detailed discussion was given. In the sample context we considered unstandardized and standardized regression coefficients, errors in prediction, the least squares criterion, the coefficient of determination, various tests of significance, the underlying statistical assumptions of the model and of the significance tests, and finally the use of graphical techniques to detect assumption violations. At this point you should have met the following objectives: (a) be able to understand the concepts underlying simple linear regression, (b) be able to compute and interpret the results of simple linear regression, and (c) be able to understand and evaluate the assumptions of simple linear regression. Chapter 2 follows up with a description of multiple regression, where regression models are developed based on two or more predictors.

PROBLEMS

Conceptual Problems

1. The regression lines' intercept represents
   a. the slope of the line.
   b. the amount of change in Y given a one unit change in X.
   c. the value of Y when X is equal to zero.
   d. the strength of the relationship between X and Y.

2. The regression line for predicting final exam grades in history from midterm scores in the same course is found to be $Y' = .61X + 3.12$. If the value of X increases from 74 to 75, the value of Y will
   a. increase .61 points.
   b. increase 1.00 points.
   c. increase 3.12 points.
   d. decrease .61 points.

3. Given that $\mu_x = 14$, $\sigma^2_x = 36$, $\mu_y = 14$, $\sigma^2_y = 49$, and $Y' = 14$ is the prediction equation for predicting Y from X, the variance of the predicted values of Y' is
   a. 0
   b. 14
   c. 36
   d. 49

4. In regression analysis, the prediction of Y is *most* accurate for which of the following correlations between X and Y?
   a. −.90
   b. −.30
   c. +.20
   d. +.80

5. If the relationship between two variables is linear,
   a. all the points fall on a curved line.
   b. the relationship is best represented by a curved line.
   c. all the points must fall on a straight line.
   d. the relationship is best represented by a straight line.

6. If both X and Y are measured on a standard z-score scale, the regression line will have a slope of
    a. 0.00
    b. +1 or −1
    c. r_{XY}
    d. s_y/s_x

7. If the simple linear regression equation for predicting Y from X is $Y' = 25$, then the correlation between X and Y is
    a. 0.00
    b. 0.25
    c. 0.50
    d. 1.00

8. The slope of the regression equation
    a. may never be negative.
    b. may never be greater than +1.00.
    c. may never be greater than the correlation coefficient r_{xy}.
    d. none of the above.

9. If two individuals have the same score on the predictor, their residual scores will
    a. be necessarily equal.
    b. depend *only* on their observed scores on Y.
    c. depend *only* on their predicted scores on Y.
    d. depend *only* on the number of individuals that have the same predicted score.

10. If $r_{xy} = .6$, the proportion of variation in Y that is *not* predictable from X is
    a. .36
    b. .40
    c. .60
    d. .64

11. Homoscedasticity assumes that
    a. the range of Y is the same as the range of X.
    b. the X and Y distributions have the same mean values.
    c. the variability of the X and the Y distributions is the same.
    d. the variability of Y is the same for all values of X.

12. The linear regression slope b_{yx} represents the
    a. amount of change in X expected from a one unit change in Y.
    b. amount of change in Y expected from a one unit change in X.
    c. correlation between X and Y.
    d. error of estimate of Y from X.

13. If the correlation between X and Y is zero, then the best prediction of Y that can be made is the mean of Y. True or false?

14. If the slope of the regression line for predicting Y from X is greater than 1, then the mean of the predicted scores of Y is larger than the mean of the observed scores of Y. True or false?

15. If X and Y are highly nonlinear, linear regression is more useful than the situation where X and Y are highly linear. True or false?

16. If the pretest (X) and the posttest (Y) are positively correlated, and your friend receives a pretest score below the mean, then the regression equation would predict that your friend would have a posttest score that is above the mean. True or false?

17. Two variables are linearly related so that given X, Y can be predicted without error. I assert that r_{xy} must be equal to either $+1.0$ or -1.0. Am I correct?

18. I assert that the simple regression equation is structured so that at least two of the actual data points will fall on the regression line. Am I correct?

Computational Problems

1. You are given the following pairs of scores on X and Y.

X	Y
4	5
4	6
3	4
7	8
2	4

   a. Find the linear regression equation for the prediction of Y from X.
   b. Use the prediction equation obtained to predict the value of Y for a person who has an X value of 6.

2. The regression equation for predicting Y from X is $Y' = 2.5X + 18$. What is the observed mean for Y if $\mu_x = 40$ and $\sigma^2_x = 81$?

3. An educational consultant collected data from 10 school districts. Measures were taken of the number of hours per week of instructional time that were allocated to reading instruction at the district level (X) and the district mean achievement in reading (Y). Summary values from the raw data are given as follows: $\Sigma X = 58$, $\Sigma Y = 60$, $\Sigma X^2 = 410$, $\Sigma Y^2 = 398$, $\Sigma XY = 299$.
   a. Find the linear regression equation for the prediction of Y from X.

   b. If the district's instructional time was 9 hours, what would be the predicted
       reading achievement level?

4. You are given the following pairs of scores on X and Y:

X	Y
2	2
2	1
1	1
1	1
3	5
4	4
5	7
5	6
7	7
6	8
4	3
3	3
6	6
6	6
8	10
9	9
10	6
9	6
4	9
4	10

   Perform the following computations using $\alpha = .05$.
   a. the regression equation of Y on X
   b. test of the significance of X as a predictor
   c. plot Y versus X
   d. compute the residuals
   e. plot residuals versus X

2

MULTIPLE REGRESSION

Chapter Outline

1. Partial and semipartial correlations
   Partial correlation
   Semipartial (part) correlation
2. Multiple linear regression
   Unstandardized regression equation
   Standardized regression equation
   Coefficient of multiple determination and multiple correlation
   Significance tests
   Assumptions
3. Variable selection procedures
4. Nonlinear regression

Key Concepts

1. Partial and semipartial (part) correlations
2. Standardized and unstandardized regression coefficients
3. Coefficient of multiple determination and multiple correlation
4. Increments in proportion of variation explained
5. Variable selection procedures
6. Nonlinear relationships

In chapter 1 our concern was with the prediction of a dependent or criterion variable (Y) by a single independent or predictor variable (X). However, given the types of phenomena we typically deal with in the social and behavioral sciences, the use of a single predictor variable is quite restrictive. In other words, given the complexity of most human and animal behaviors, one predictor is often insufficient in terms of understanding the criterion. In order to account for a sufficient proportion of variability in the criterion, more than one predictor is necessary. This leads us to analyze the data via multiple regression where two or more predictors are used to predict the criterion variable. Here we adopt the usual notation where the Xs are defined as the independent or predictor variables, and Y as the dependent or criterion variable.

For example, our admissions officer might want to use more than just Graduate Record Exam (GRE) scores to predict graduate-level grade point averages (GPA) to make admissions decisions for a sample of applicants to your favorite local university or college. Other potentially useful predictors might be undergraduate grade point average, recommendation letters, writing samples, or an evaluation from a personal interview. The research question of interest would now be, how well do the GRE, undergraduate GPA, recommendations, writing samples, and interview scores (the independent or predictor variables) predict performance in graduate school (the dependent or criterion variable)? This is an example of a situation where multiple regression using multiple predictor variables might be the method of choice.

Most of the concepts used in simple linear regression from chapter 1 carry over to multiple regression. However, due to the fact that multiple predictor variables are used, the computations become necessarily more complex. For simplicity, we only examine the computations for the two-predictor case. The computations for more than two predictors require the use of matrix algebra and/or calculus, which neither of us really wants. However, these computations can easily be carried out through the use of a statistical computer software package.

This chapter considers the concepts of partial, semipartial, and multiple correlations, standardized and unstandardized regression coefficients, the coefficient of multiple determination, increments in the proportion of variation accounted for by an additional predictor, several variable selection procedures, and nonlinear regression, and examines various tests of significance and statistical assumptions. Our objectives are that by the end of this chapter, you will be able to (a) compute and interpret the results of part and semipartial correlations, (b) understand the concepts underlying multiple linear regression, (c) compute and interpret the results of multiple linear regression, (d) understand and evaluate the assumptions of multiple linear regression, (e) compute and interpret the results of the variable selection procedures, and (f) understand the concepts underlying nonlinear regression.

PARTIAL AND SEMIPARTIAL CORRELATIONS

Prior to a discussion of regression analysis, we need to consider two related concepts in correlational analysis. Specifically, we address partial and semipartial correlations. Multiple regression involves the use of two or more predictor variables and one criterion variable; thus, there are at a minimum three variables involved in the analysis. If we think about these variables in the context of the Pearson correlation, we have a problem because this correlation can only be used to relate two variables at a time. How do we incorporate additional variables into a correlational analysis? The answer is, through partial and semipartial correlations, and, later in this chapter, multiple correlations.

Partial Correlation

First we discuss the concept of *partial correlation*. The simplest situation consists of three variables, which we label X_1, X_2, and X_3. Here an example of a partial correlation would be the correlation between X_1 and X_2 where X_3 is held constant (i.e., controlled or partialed out). That is, the influence of X_3 is removed from both X_1 and X_2 (both have been adjusted for X_3). Thus the partial correlation here represents the linear relationship between X_1 and X_2 independent of the linear influence of X_3. This particular partial correlation is denoted by $r_{12.3}$, where the Xs are not shown for simplicity and the dot indicates that the variables preceding it are to be correlated and the variable(s) following it are to be partialed out. A method for computing $r_{12.3}$ is as follows:

$$r_{12.3} = \frac{r_{12} - r_{13}r_{23}}{\sqrt{(1 - r_{13}^2)(1 - r_{23}^2)}}$$

It should be obvious that this method takes a fairly complicated combination of bivariate (two-variable) correlations.

Let us take an example of a situation where a partial correlation might be computed. Say a researcher is interested in the relationship between height (X_1) and weight (X_2). The sample consists of individuals ranging in age (X_3) from 6 months to 65 years. The sample correlations are $r_{12} = .7$, $r_{13} = .1$, and $r_{23} = .6$. We compute $r_{12.3}$ as

$$r_{12.3} = \frac{r_{12} - r_{13}r_{23}}{\sqrt{(1 - r_{13}^2)(1 - r_{23}^2)}} = \frac{.7 - (.1).6}{\sqrt{(1-.01)(1-.36)}} = .8040$$

We see here that the bivariate correlation between height and weight, ignoring age ($r_{12} = .7$), is smaller than the partial correlation between height and weight controlling for age ($r_{12.3} = .8040$). That is, the relationship between height and weight is stronger when age is held constant (i.e., for a particular age) than it is across all ages. Although we often talk about holding a particular variable constant, in reality variables such as age cannot be held constant artificially.

Some rather interesting partial correlation results can occur in particular situations. At one extreme, if both r_{13} and r_{23} equal zero, then $r_{12} = r_{12.3}$. That is, if the variable being partialed out is uncorrelated with each of the other two variables, then the partialing process will not have any effect. This seems logical, as an unrelated variable should have no influence. At the other extreme, if either r_{13} or r_{23} equals 1, then $r_{12.3}$ cannot be calculated as the denominator is equal to zero (you cannot divide by zero). Thus $r_{12.3}$ is undefined. Later in this chapter we see an example of perfect multicollinearity, a serious problem. In between these extremes, it is possible for the partial correlation to be greater than or less than its corresponding bivariate correlation (including a change in sign), and even for the partial correlation to be equal to zero when its bivariate correlation is not. Although space prohibits showing an example of each of these situations, it is fairly easy to construct such examples by playing with the bivariate correlations.

Thus far we have considered what is referred to as the *first-order partial correlation*. In other words, only one variable has been partialed out. This can be extended to second-order (e.g., $r_{12.34}$) and higher order partial correlations (e.g., $r_{12.345}$). In general, we may represent any partial correlation by $r_{12.w}$, where W represents all of the variables to be controlled. These partial correlations are computationally more complex than first-order partials in that the former are a function of other types of correlations (e.g., partial or multiple correlations). The topic of multiple correlation is taken up later in this chapter. It is unlikely that you will see applications of partial correlations beyond the first order (Cohen & Cohen, 1983).

To perform a test of significance on a partial correlation, the procedure is very similar to a test of significance on a bivariate correlation. One can conduct a test of a simple bivariate correlation (i.e., $H_0: \rho = \rho_0$), where ρ_0 is the hypothesized value (often zero), as follows:

$$z = (Z_r - Z_0)(\sqrt{n-3})$$

where Z_r and Z_0 are the Fisher's transformed values of the obtained and hypothesized correlations, respectively (see Appendix Table 5), and the z table is used to obtain critical values (see Appendix Table 1). For a two-tailed test the critical values are $_{\alpha/2}z$ and $_{1-\alpha/2}z$. For a one-tailed test the critical value is either $_\alpha z$ or $_{1-\alpha}z$, depending on the alternative hypothesis specified.

The test of a partial correlation (i.e., $H_0: \rho_{12.w} = \rho_0$) then is as follows:

$$z = [Z(r_{12.w}) - Z_0]\sqrt{n - 3 - n_w}$$

where n_w represents the number of variables to be controlled. The z table is again used for obtaining critical values.

Semipartial (Part) Correlation

Next the concept of *semipartial correlation* (or part correlation) is discussed. The simplest situation consists again of three variables, which we label $X_1, X_2,$ and X_3. Here an example of a semipartial correlation would be the correlation between X_1 and X_2 where X_3 is removed from X_2 only. That is, the influence of X_3 is removed from X_2 only. Thus the semipartial correlation here represents the linear relationship between X_1 and X_2 after that portion of X_2 that can be linearly predicted from X_3 has been removed from X_2. This particular semipartial correlation is denoted by $r_{1(2.3)}$, where the Xs are not shown for simplicity and within the parentheses the dot indicates that the variable(s) following it are to be removed from the variable preceding it. A method for computing $r_{1(2.3)}$ is as follows:

$$r_{1(2.3)} = \frac{r_{12} - r_{13}r_{23}}{\sqrt{1 - r_{23}^2}}$$

Again, this method obviously takes a fairly complicated combination of bivariate correlations.

Let us take an example of a situation where a semipartial correlation might be computed. Say a researcher is interested in the relationship between GPA (X_1) and GRE scores (X_2). The researcher would like to remove the influence of intelligence (IQ: X_3) from GRE scores, but not from GPA. The sample correlations are $r_{12} = .5$, $r_{13} = .3$, and $r_{23} = .7$. We compute $r_{1(2.3)}$ as

$$r_{1(2.3)} = \frac{r_{12} - r_{13} r_{23}}{\sqrt{1 - r_{23}^2}} = \frac{.5 - (.3).7}{\sqrt{1 - .49}} = .4061$$

It becomes evident that the bivariate correlation between GPA and GRE ignoring IQ ($r_{12} = .50$) is larger than the semipartial correlation between GPA and GRE controlling for IQ in GRE ($r_{1(2.3)} = .4061$). As was the case with a partial correlation, various values of a semipartial correlation can be obtained depending on the particular combination of the bivariate correlations.

Thus far we have considered what is referred to as the *first-order semipartial correlation*. In other words, only one variable has been removed from X_2. This notion can be extended to second-order (e.g., $r_{1(2.34)}$) and higher order semipartial correlations (e.g., $r_{1(2.345)}$). In general, we may represent any semipartial correlation by $r_{1(2.w)}$, where W represents all of the variables to be controlled in X_2. These semipartial correlations are computationally more complex than first-order semipartials in that the former are a function of other types of correlations (e.g., multiple correlations). It is unlikely that you will see applications of semipartial correlations beyond the first order (Cohen & Cohen, 1983). Finally, the procedure for testing the significance of a semipartial correlation is the same as that of a partial correlation described earlier in this chapter.

Now that we have considered the correlational relationships among two or more variables (i.e., partial and semipartial correlations), let us move on to an examination of the multiple regression model where there are two or more predictor variables.

MULTIPLE LINEAR REGRESSION

Let us take the concepts we have learned in this and the previous chapter and place them into the context of multiple linear regression. For purposes of brevity, we do not consider the population situation because the sample situation is invoked 99.44% of the time. In this section we discuss the unstandardized and standardized multiple regression equations, the coefficient of multiple determination, multiple correlation, various tests of significance, and statistical assumptions.

Unstandardized Regression Equation

Consider the sample multiple linear regression equation for the regression of Y on $X_{1,2, ..., m}$ as

$$Y_i = b_1 X_{1i} + b_2 X_{2i} + ... + b_m X_{mi} + a + e_i$$

where Y is the criterion variable, the X_ks are the predictor variables where $k = 1, \ldots, m$, b_k is the sample partial slope of the regression line for Y as predicted by X_k, a is the sample intercept of the regression line for Y as predicted by the set of X_ks, e_i are the residuals or errors of prediction (the part of Y not predictable from the X_ks), and i represents an index for an individual (or object). The index i can take on values from 1 to n where n is the size of the sample (usually written as $i = 1, \ldots, n$). The term *partial slope* is used because it represents the slope of Y on a particular X_k in which we have partialed out the influence of the other X_ks, much as we did with the partial correlation.

The sample prediction equation is

$$Y'_i = b_1 X_{1i} + b_2 X_{2i} + \ldots + b_m X_{mi} + a$$

where Y'_i is the predicted value of Y given specific values of the X_ks, and the other terms are as before. The difference between the regression and prediction equations is the same as discussed in chapter 1. We can also compute residuals, the e_i, for each of the i individuals or objects from the prediction equation. By comparing the actual Y values with the predicted Y values, we obtain the residuals as

$$e_i = Y_i - Y'_i$$

for all $i = 1, \ldots, n$ individuals or objects in the sample.

Calculation of the sample partial slopes and the intercept in the multiple predictor case is not as straightforward as in the case of a single predictor. To keep the computations simple, we use a two-predictor model for illustrative purposes. Usually the computer will be used to perform the computations involved in multiple regression; thus we need not concern ourselves with the computations for models involving more than two predictors.

For the two-predictor case the sample partial slopes and the intercept can be computed as

$$b_1 = \frac{(r_{Y1} - r_{Y2} r_{12}) s_Y}{(1 - r_{12}^2) s_1}$$

$$b_2 = \frac{(r_{Y2} - r_{Y1} r_{12}) s_Y}{(1 - r_{12}^2) s_2}$$

$$a = \overline{Y} - b_1 \overline{X}_1 - b_2 \overline{X}_2$$

The sample partial slope b_1 is referred to alternately as (a) the expected or predicted change in Y for a one unit change in X_1 with X_2 held constant (or for individuals with the same score on X_2), (b) the influence of X_1 on Y with X_2 held constant, and (c) the unstandardized or raw regression coefficient. Similar statements may be made for b_2. The sample intercept is referred to as the value of Y when X_1 and X_2 are both zero.

An alternative method for computing the sample partial slopes that involves the use of a partial correlation is as follows:

$$b_1 = r_{Y1.2} \frac{s_Y \sqrt{1 - r_{Y2}^2}}{s_1 \sqrt{1 - r_{12}^2}}$$

and

$$b_2 = r_{Y2.1} \frac{s_Y \sqrt{1 - r_{Y1}^2}}{s_2 \sqrt{1 - r_{12}^2}}$$

What statistical criterion was used to arrive at the particular values for the partial slopes and intercept of a linear regression equation? The criterion usually used in multiple linear regression analysis (and in all general linear models [GLM] for that matter, including simple linear regression as described in chap. 1) is the least squares criterion. The least squares criterion arrives at those values for the partial slopes and intercept such that the sum of the squared prediction errors or residuals is smallest. That is, we want to find that regression equation, defined by a particular set of partial slopes and an intercept, that minimizes the sum of the squared residuals. We often refer to this particular method for calculating the slope and intercept as least squares estimation, because a and the b_ks represent sample estimates of the population parameters α and the β_ks obtained using the least squares criterion.

Consider now the analysis of a realistic example we will follow in this chapter. We use the GRE–Quantitative + Verbal Total (GRETOT) and undergraduate grade point average (UGPA) to predict graduate grade point average (GGPA). GRETOT has a possible range of 40 to 160 points (if we remove the last digit of zero for computational ease), and GPA is defined as having a possible range of 0.00 to 4.00 points. Given the sample of 11 statistics students as shown in Table 2.1, let us work through a multiple linear regression analysis.

TABLE 2.1
GRE–GPA Example Data

Student	GRETOT	UGPA	GGPA
1	145	3.2	4.0
2	120	3.7	3.9
3	125	3.6	3.8
4	130	2.9	3.7
5	110	3.5	3.6
6	100	3.3	3.5
7	95	3.0	3.4
8	115	2.7	3.3
9	105	3.1	3.2
10	90	2.8	3.1
11	105	2.4	3.0

48 CHAPTER 2

As sample statistics, we compute for GRETOT (X_1 or subscript 1) that $\overline{X}_1 = 112.7273$ and $s_1^2 = 266.8182$, for UGPA (X_2 or subscript 2) that $\overline{X}_2 = 3.1091$ and $s_2^2 = 0.1609$, whereas for GGPA (Y) that $\overline{Y} = 3.5000$ and $s_Y^2 = 0.1100$. In addition, we compute $r_{Y1} = .7845$, $r_{Y2} = .7516$, and $r_{12} = .3011$. The sample partial slopes and intercept are computed as follows:

$$b_1 = \frac{(r_{Y1} - r_{Y2}r_{12})s_Y}{(1 - r_{12}^2)s_1}$$

$$= \frac{[.7845 - .7516(.3011)].3317}{(1 - .3011^2)16.3346} = .0125$$

$$b_2 = \frac{(r_{Y2} - r_{Y1}r_{12})s_Y}{(1 - r_{12}^2)s_2}$$

$$= \frac{[.7516 - .7845(.3011)].3317}{(1 - .3011^2).4011} = .4687$$

and

$$a = \overline{Y} - b_1\overline{X}_1 - b_2\overline{X}_2$$

$$= 3.5000 - (.0125)(112.7273) - (.4687)(3.1091) = .6337 .$$

Let us interpret the partial slope and intercept values. A partial slope of .0125 for GRETOT would mean that if your score on the GRETOT was increased by 1 point, then your graduate grade point average would be increased by .0125 points, controlling for undergraduate grade point average. Likewise, a partial slope of .4687 for UGPA would mean that if your undergraduate grade point average was increased by 1 point, then your graduate grade point average would be increased by .4687 points, controlling for GRE total. An intercept of .6337 would mean that if your scores on the GRETOT and UGPA were 0, then your graduate grade point average would be .6337. However, it is impossible to obtain a GRETOT score of 0 because you receive 40 points for putting your name on the answer sheet. In a similar way, an undergraduate student could not obtain a UGPA of 0 and be admitted to graduate school. To put all of this together then, the sample multiple linear regression equation is

$$Y_i = b_1X_{1i} + b_2X_{2i} + a + e_i$$

$$= .0125X_{1i} + .4687X_{2i} + .6337 + e_i$$

If your score on the GRETOT was 130 and your UGPA was 3.5, then your predicted score on the GGPA would be

$$Y'_i = .0125(130) + .4687(3.5000) + .6337 = 3.8992$$

Based on the prediction equation, we predict your GGPA would be around 3.9; however, as we have already seen from chapter 1, predictions are usually somewhat less than perfect.

Standardized Regression Equation

Until this point in the chapter, all of the computations in multiple linear regression have involved the use of raw scores. For this reason we referred to the equation as the unstandardized regression equation. A partial slope estimate is an unstandardized or raw partial regression slope because it is the predicted change in Y raw score units for a one raw score unit change in X_k, controlling for the remaining X_ks. Often we may want to express the regression in terms of standard z-score units rather than in raw score units (as in chap. 11). The means and variances of the standardized variables (i.e., z_1, z_2, and z_y) are 0 and 1, respectively. The sample standardized linear prediction equation becomes

$$z(Y'_i) = b_1{}^*z_{1i} + b_2{}^*z_{2i} + \dots + b_m{}^*z_{mi}$$

where $b_k{}^*$ represents a sample standardized partial slope and the other terms are as before. As was the case in simple linear regression, no intercept term is necessary in the standardized prediction equation, as the mean of the z scores for all variables is zero. The sample standardized partial slopes are, in general, computed by

$$b_k{}^* = b_k(s_k/s_Y)$$

For the two predictor case, the standardized partial slopes can be calculated by

$$b_1{}^* = b_1(s_1/s_Y) \quad \text{or} \quad (r_{Y1} - r_{Y2}r_{12})/(1 - r^2{}_{12})$$

and

$$b_2{}^* = b_2(s_2/s_Y) \quad \text{or} \quad (r_{Y2} - r_{Y1}r_{12})/(1 - r^2{}_{12})$$

As you can see, if $r_{12} = 0$, where the two predictors are uncorrelated, then $b_1{}^* = r_{Y1}$ and $b_2{}^* = r_{Y2}$.

For our graduate grade point average example, the standardized partial slopes are equal to

$$b_1{}^* = b_1(s_1/s_Y)$$

$$= .0125 \ (16.3346/.3317) = .6156$$

and

$$b_2{}^* = b_2 \ (s_2/s_Y)$$

$$= .4687 \ (.4011/.3317) = .5668$$

The prediction equation is then

$$z(Y'_i) = .6156z_{1i} + .5668z_{2i}$$

The standardized partial slope of .6156 for GRETOT would be interpreted as the expected increase in GGPA in z-score units for a one z-score unit increase in the GRETOT, controlling for UGPA. A similar statement may be made for the standardized partial slope of UGPA. The b_k^* can also be interpreted as the expected standard deviation change in Y associated with a one standard deviation change in X_k when the other X_ks are held constant.

When would you want to use the standardized versus unstandardized regression analyses? According to Pedhazur (1997), b_k^* is sample specific and is not very stable across different samples due to the variance of X_k changing (as the variance of X_k increases, the value of b_k^* also increases, all else being equal). For example, at Ivy-Covered University, b_k^* would vary across different graduating classes (or samples) whereas b_k would be much more consistent across classes. Thus most researchers prefer the use of b_k to compare the influence of a particular predictor variable across different samples and/or populations. However, the b_k^* are useful for assessing the relative importance of the predictor variables (relative to one another) for a particular sample, but not their absolute contributions. This is important because the raw score predictor variables are typically measured on different scales. Thus for our GGPA example, the relative contribution of GRETOT is slightly greater than that of UGPA, as shown by the values of the standardized partial slopes. This is verified later, when we test for the significance of the two predictors.

Coefficient of Multiple Determination and Multiple Correlation

An obvious question now is, How well is the criterion variable predicted by the predictor variables? For our example, we are interested in how well the graduate grade point averages are predicted by the GRE total scores and the undergraduate grade point averages. In other words, what is the utility of the set of predictor variables?

The simplest method involves the partitioning of the sum of squares in Y, which we denote as SS_Y. In multiple linear regression, we can write SS_Y as follows:

$$SS_Y = [n \; \Sigma \; Y_i^2 - (\Sigma \; Y_i)^2]/n \;\; \text{or} \;\; (n-1)s_Y^2$$

where we sum over Y for $i = 1, \dots, n$. Next we can conceptually partition SS_Y as

$$SS_Y = SS_{\text{reg}} + SS_{\text{res}}$$

or

$$\Sigma(Y_i - \overline{Y})^2 = \Sigma(Y_i' - \overline{Y})^2 + \Sigma(Y_i - Y_i')^2$$

where SS_{reg} is the sum of squares due to the regression of Y on the X_ks (often written as $SS_{Y'}$), and SS_{res} is the sum of squares due to the residuals. The SS_Y term represents the total variation in Y. The SS_{reg} term represents the variation in Y that is predicted by the X_ks. The SS_{res} term represents the variation in Y that is not predicted by the X_ks (i.e., residual variation).

Before we consider computation of SS_{reg} and SS_{res}, let us look at the coefficient of multiple determination. Recall from chapter 1 the coefficient of determination, r_{XY}^2. Now consider the multiple version of r_{XY}^2, here denoted as $R_{Y.1,...,m}^2$. The subscript tells us that Y is the criterion variable and that $X_{1,...,m}$ are the predictor variables. The simplest procedure for computing R^2 is as follows:

$$R_{Y.1,...,m}^2 = b_1*r_{Y1} + b_2*r_{Y2} + ... + b_m*r_{Ym}$$

The coefficient of multiple determination tells us the proportion of total variation in Y that is predictable using the set of predictor variables in a linear regression equation. Often we see the coefficient in terms of SS as

$$R_{Y.1,...,m}^2 = SS_{reg} / SS_Y$$

Thus, one method for computing the SS_{reg} and SS_{res} is from R^2 as follows:

$$SS_{reg} = R^2 SS_Y$$

and

$$SS_{res} = (1 - R^2)SS_Y$$

$$= SS_Y - SS_{reg}$$

In general, as was the case in simple linear regression, in multiple linear regression there is no magical rule of thumb as to how large the coefficient of multiple determination needs to be in order to say that a meaningful proportion of variation has been predicted. The coefficient is determined not just by the quality of the predictor variables included in the model, but also by the quality of relevant predictor variables not included in the model, as well as by the amount of total variation in Y. Several tests of significance are discussed in the next section. Note also that $R_{Y.1,...,m}$ is referred to as the multiple correlation coefficient.

With the sample data of predicting GGPA from GRETOT and UGPA, let us examine the partitioning of the SS_Y. We can write SS_Y as follows:

$$SS_Y = (n - 1) s_Y^2$$

$$= (10)(.1100) = 1.1000$$

Next we can compute R^2 as

$$R_{Y.12}^2 = b_1*r_{Y1} + b_2*r_{Y2}$$

$$= .6156(.7845) + .5668(.7516) = .9089$$

We can also partition SS_Y into SS_{reg} and SS_{res}, where

$$SS_{reg} = R^2 SS_Y$$

$$= .9089(1.1000) = 0.9998$$

and

$$SS_{res} = (1 - R^2)SS_Y$$

$$= (1 - .9089)1.1000 = .1002$$

Finally, let us summarize these results for the example data. We found that the coefficient of multiple determination was equal to .9089. Thus the GRE total score and the undergraduate grade point average predict around 91% of the variation in the graduate grade point average. This would be quite satisfactory for the college admissions officer in that there is little variation left to be explained.

It should be noted that R^2 is sensitive to sample size and to the number of predictor variables. R is a biased estimate of the population multiple correlation due to sampling error in the bivariate correlations and in the standard deviations of X and Y. Because R systematically overestimates the population multiple correlation, an adjusted coefficient of multiple determination has been devised. The adjusted R^2 is calculated as follows:

$$\text{adjusted } R^2 = 1 - (1 - R^2)\left(\frac{n-1}{n-m-1}\right)$$

Thus, the adjusted R^2 adjusts for sample size and the number of predictors in the equation, and allows us to compare equations fitted to the same set of data with differing numbers of predictors or with multiple samples of data. The difference between R^2 and adjusted R^2 is called *shrinkage*.

When n is small relative to m, the amount of bias can be large as R^2 can be expected to be large by chance alone. In this case the adjustment will be quite large; this is why we need to make the adjustment. In addition, with small samples, the regression coefficients (i.e., the b_ks) may not be very good estimates of the population values anyway. When n is large relative to m, bias will be minimized and your generalizations are likely to be better about the population values.

When a large number of predictors is used in multiple regression, power (the likelihood of rejecting H_0 when H_0 is false) is reduced, and there is an increased likelihood of a Type I error (rejecting H_0 when H_0 is true) over the total number of significance tests (i.e., one for each predictor and overall, as we show in the next section). In the case of multiple regression, power is a function of sample size, the number of predictors, the level of significance, and the size of the population effect (i.e., for a given predictor, or overall). There are no hard and fast rules about how large a sample you need relative to the number of predictors. Although many rules of thumb exist, none can really be substantiated. The best advice is to design your research such that the ratio of n to m is large. We return to the adjusted R^2 in the next section.

For the example data, we compute the adjusted R^2 to be

$$\text{adjusted } R^2 = 1 - (1 - R^2)\left(\frac{n-1}{n-m-1}\right) = 1 - (1 - .9089)\left(\frac{11-1}{11-2-1}\right) = .8861$$

which in this case indicates a very small adjustment in comparison to R^2.

Significance Tests

In this subsection, I describe three procedures used in multiple linear regression. These involve testing the significance of the overall regression equation, each individual partial slope (or regression coefficient), and the increments in the proportion of variation accounted for by each predictor.

Test of Significance of the Overall Regression Equation. The first test is the test of significance of the overall regression equation, or alternatively the test of significance of the coefficient of multiple determination. The test is essentially a test of all of the b_ks simultaneously. The null and alternative hypotheses, respectively, are as follows

$$H_0: \rho_{Y.1,\dots,m}^{2} = 0$$

$$H_1: \rho_{Y.1,\dots,m}^{2} > 0$$

If H_0 is rejected, then one or more of the individual regression coefficients (i.e., the b_k) *may* be statistically significantly different from zero. However, it is possible to have a significant overall R^2 when none of the individual predictors are significant. This would indicate that none of the individual predictors are strong given the other predictors, not that each one is a weak predictor by itself. Do not forget that the predictors may be correlated, making the notion "controlling for the other predictors" an important one. If H_0 is not rejected, then none of the individual regression coefficients will be significantly different from zero.

The test is based on the following test statistic,

$$F = \frac{R^2 / m}{(1 - R^2) / (n - m - 1)}$$

where F indicates that this is an F statistic, R^2 is the coefficient of multiple determination (the proportion of variation in Y predicted by the X_ks), $1 - R^2$ is the coefficient of multiple nondetermination (the proportion of variation in Y that is not predicted by the X_ks), m is the number of predictors, and n is the sample size. The F-test statistic is compared with the F critical value, always a one-tailed test and at the designated level of significance, with degrees of freedom being m and $(n - m - 1)$, as taken from the F table in Appendix Table 4. That is, the tabled critical value is $_{(1-\alpha)}F_{m,(n-m-1)}$. The test statistic can also be written in equivalent form as

$$F = \frac{SS_{\text{reg}} / df_{\text{reg}}}{SS_{\text{res}} / df_{\text{res}}} = \frac{MS_{\text{reg}}}{MS_{\text{res}}}$$

where $df_{\text{reg}} = m$ and $df_{\text{res}} = (n - m - 1)$.

For the GGPA example, we compute the test statistic as

$$F = \frac{R^2 / m}{(1 - R^2) / (n - m - 1)} = \frac{.9089 / 2}{(1 - .9089) / (11 - 2 - 1)} = 39.9078$$

or as

$$F = \frac{SS_{\text{reg}} / df_{\text{reg}}}{SS_{\text{res}} / df_{\text{res}}} = \frac{0.9998 / 2}{.1002 / 8} = 39.9122$$

The critical value, at the .05 level of significance, is $_{.95}F_{2,8} = 4.46$. The test statistic exceeds the critical value, so we reject H_0 and conclude that ρ^2 is not equal to zero at the .05 level of significance (i.e., GRETOT and UGPA together do predict a significant proportion of the variation in GGPA) (the two F-test statistics differ slightly due to rounding error).

Test of Significance of b_k.   The second test is the test of the statistical significance of each partial slope or regression coefficient, b_k. That is, are the unstandardized regression coefficients statistically significantly different from zero? This is actually the same as the test of b_k^*, so we need not develop a separate test for b_k^*. The null and alternative hypotheses, respectively, are as follows:

$$H_0: \beta_k = 0$$

$$H_1: \beta_k \neq 0$$

where β_k is the population partial slope for X_k.

In multiple regression it is necessary to compute a standard error for each b_k. Recall from chapter 1 the variance error of estimate concept. The variance error of estimate is similarly defined for multiple linear regression as

$$s_{\text{res}}^2 = SS_{\text{res}} / df_{\text{res}} = MS_{\text{res}}$$

where $df_{\text{res}} = (n - m - 1)$. The degrees of freedom are lost because we have to estimate the population partial slopes and intercept, that is, the β_ks and α, respectively, from the sample data. The variance error of estimate indicates the amount of variation among the residuals. The standard error of estimate is simply the positive square root of the variance error of estimate, and can be thought of as the standard deviation of the residuals or errors of estimate. We call it the *standard error of estimate* and denote it as s_{res}.

Finally, we need to compute a standard error for each b_k. Denote the standard error of b_k as $s(b_k)$ and define it as

$$s(b_k) = \frac{s_{\text{res}}}{\sqrt{(n-1)s_k^2 (1 - R_k^2)}}$$

where s_k^2 is the sample variance for predictor X_k, and R_k^2 is the squared multiple correlation between X_k and the remaining X_ks. The R_k^2 terms represent essentially the overlap between that predictor (X_k) and the remaining predictors. In the case of two predictors, R_k^2 is equal to r_{12}^2.

We are now ready to examine the test statistic for testing the significance of the b_ks. As in many tests of significance, the test statistic is formed by the ratio of a parameter estimate divided by its respective estimated standard error. The ratio is formed as

$$t = \frac{b}{s(b_k)}$$

The test statistic t is compared to the critical values of t, a two-tailed test for a nondirectional H_1, at the designated level of significance, and with degrees of freedom $(n - m - 1)$, as taken from the t table in Appendix Table 2. That is, the tabled critical values are $\pm_{(\alpha/2)} t_{(n - m - 1)}$ for a two-tailed test.

If desired, we can also form a confidence interval around b_k. As in many confidence interval procedures encountered, it follows the form of the sample estimate plus or minus the tabled critical value multiplied by the relevant estimated standard error. The confidence interval around b_k is formed as follows:

$$\mathbf{CI}(b_k) = b_k \pm {}_{(\alpha/2)}t_{(n - m - 1)}s(b_k)$$

Recall that the null hypothesis specified that β_k is equal to zero (i.e., H_0: $\beta_k = 0$). Therefore, if the confidence interval contains zero, then b_k is not significantly different from zero at the specified α level. This is interpreted to mean that in $(1 - \alpha)$ % of the sample confidence intervals that would be formed from multiple samples, β_k will be included.

Let us compute the second test statistic for the GGPA example. We specify the null hypothesis to be $\beta_k = 0$ and conduct two-tailed tests. First we calculate the variance error of estimate as

$$s_{res}^2 = SS_{res}/df_{res} = MS_{res}$$

$$= .1002/8 = .0125$$

The standard error of estimate, s_{res}, is computed to be .1118. Next the standard errors of the b_k are found to be

$$s(b_1) = \frac{s_{res}}{\sqrt{(n-1)s_1^2(1-r_{12}^2)}} = \frac{.1118}{\sqrt{(10)266.8182(1-.3011^2)}} = .0023$$

and

$$s(b_2) = \frac{s_{res}}{\sqrt{(n-1)s_2^2(1-r_{12}^2)}} = \frac{.1118}{\sqrt{(10)0.1609(1-.3011^2)}} = .0924$$

Finally we calculate the t test statistics to be

$$t_1 = b_1/s(b_1) = .0125/.0023 = 5.4348$$

and

$$t_2 = b_2/s(b_2) = .4687/.0924 = 5.0725$$

To evaluate the null hypotheses, we compare these test statistics to the respective critical values of $\pm_{.025}t_8 = \pm2.306$. Both test statistics exceed the critical value; consequently, H_0 is rejected in favor of H_1 for both predictors. We conclude that the partial slopes are indeed significantly different from zero, at the .05 level of significance.

Finally, let us compute the confidence intervals for the b_ks as follows:

$$\text{CI}(b_1) = b_1 \pm {}_{(\alpha/2)}t_{(n-m-1)}s(b_1) = b_1 \pm {}_{.025}t_8s(b_1)$$

$$= .0125 \pm 2.306(.0023) = (.0072, .0178)$$

and

$$\text{CI}(b_2) = b_2 \pm {}_{(\alpha/2)}t_{(n-m-1)}s(b_2) = b_2 \pm {}_{.025}t_8s(b_2)$$

$$= .4687 \pm 2.306(.0924) = (.2556, .6818)$$

The intervals do not contain zero, the value specified in H_0; then we again conclude that both b_ks are significantly different from zero, at the .05 level of significance.

Test of the Increment in the Proportion of Variation Accounted For. A third and final test is that of the increment in the proportion of variation accounted for by each predictor. As an example, take a two-predictor model. You may want to test for the increment or increase in the proportion of variation accounted for by two predictors as compared to one. This would essentially be a test of a two-predictor model versus a one-predictor model. To test for the increment in X_1, the test statistic would be

$$F = \frac{(R_{Y.12}^2 - R_{Y.2}^2) / (m_2 - m_1)}{(1 - R_{Y.12}^2) / (n - m_2 - 1)}$$

where $R_{Y.2}{}^2 = r_{Y2}{}^2$, m_2 is the number of predictors in the two-predictor model (i.e., 2) and m_1 is the number of predictors in the one-predictor model (i.e., 1). The F-test statistic is compared to the F critical value, always a one-tailed test at the designated level of significance, and denoted as ${}_{(1-\alpha)}F_{(m2-m1, n-m2-1)}$. To test for the increment in X_2, the test statistic would be

$$F = \frac{(R_{Y.12}^2 - R_{Y.1}^2) / (m_2 - m_1)}{(1 - R_{Y.12}^2) / (n - m_2 - 1)}$$

where $R_{Y.1}^2 = r_{y1}^2$, m_2 is the number of predictors in the two-predictor model (i.e., 2) and m_1 is the number of predictors in the one-predictor model (i.e., 1). Again, the F-test statistic is compared to the F critical value, always a one-tailed test at the designated level of significance, and denoted as $_{(1 - \alpha)}F_{(m2 - m1, \, n - m2 - 1)}$.

In general, we can compare two regression models for the same sample data, where the full model is defined as one having all predictor variables of interest included and the reduced model is defined as one having a subset of those predictor variables included. That is, for the reduced model one or more of the predictors included in the full model have been dropped. A general test statistic can be written as

$$F = \frac{(R_{full}^2 - R_{reduced}^2) \, / \, (m_{full} - m_{reduced})}{(1 - R_{full}^2) \, / \, (n - m_{full} - 1)}$$

where m_{full} is the number of predictors in the full model, and $m_{reduced}$ is the number of predictors in the reduced model. The F-test statistic is compared to the F critical value, always a one-tailed test at the designated level of significance, and denoted as $_{(1 - \alpha)}F_{(mfull - mreduced, \, n - mfull - 1)}$.

Let us examine these tests for the GGPA example. To test for the increment in X_1 (e.g., GRETOT), the test statistic would be

$$F = \frac{(R_{Y.12}^2 - R_{Y.2}^2) \, / \, (m_2 - m_1)}{(1 - R_{Y.12}^2) \, / \, (n - m_2 - 1)} = \frac{(.9089 - .7516^2) \, / \, (2 - 1)}{(1 - .9089) \, / \, (11 - 2 - 1)} = 30.2083$$

The F-test statistic is compared to the F critical value $_{(1 - \alpha)}F_{(mfull - mreduced, \, n - mfull - 1)}$, which is $_{.95}F_{1,8} = 5.32$. To test for the increment in X_2 (e.g., UGPA), the test statistic would be

$$F = \frac{(R_{Y.12}^2 - R_{Y.1}^2) \, / \, (m_2 - m_1)}{(1 - R_{Y.12}^2) \, / \, (n - m_2 - 1)} = \frac{(.9089 - .7845^2) \, / \, (2 - 1)}{(1 - .9089) \, / \, (11 - 2 - 1)} = 25.7703$$

The second test has the identical critical value. Thus, we would conclude that the inclusion of a second predictor (either GRETOT or UGPA) adds a significant amount of variation to predicting GGPA beyond a single predictor. Incidentally, because $t^2 = F$ when there is one degree of freedom in the numerator of F, we can compare these tests to the tests of the regression coefficients (i.e., b_k). You can verify these results for yourself. Note that the incremental tests are not always provided in statistical packages.

Other Tests.   One can also form confidence intervals for the predicted mean of Y and for the prediction intervals for individual values of Y, along the same lines as we developed in chapter 1. However, with multiple predictors the computations become unnecessarily complex and are not included in this text (cf. Myers, 1986). Many of the comprehensive statistical packages allow you to compute these intervals.

Assumptions

A considerable amount of space in chapter 1 was dedicated to the assumptions of simple linear regression. For the most part, the assumptions of multiple linear regression are the same, and thus we need not devote as much space here. The assumptions are concerned with linearity of the regression, the distribution of the errors in prediction, the fixed X model, and multicollinearity. This subsection also mentions those graphical techniques appropriate for evaluating each assumption.

The Regression of Y on the X_ks is Linear.   The first assumption is that the regression of Y on the X_ks is linear. If the relationships between the individual X_ks and Y are linear, then the sample partial slopes and intercept will be unbiased estimators of the population partial slopes and intercept, respectively. The linearity assumption is important because regardless of the value of X_k, we always expect Y to increase by b_k units for a 1-unit increase in X_k, controlling for the other X_ks. If a nonlinear relationship exists, this means that the expected increase in Y depends on the value of X_k; that is, the expected increase is not a constant value. Strictly speaking, linearity in a model refers to there being linearity in the parameters of the model (i.e., α and the β_ks).

Violation of the linearity assumption can be detected through residual plots of e versus each X_k and of e versus Y' (alternatively, one can look at plots of Y vs. each X_k and of Y vs. Y'). The residuals should be located within a band of $\pm 2\ s_{res}$ (or standard errors) across the values of X_k (or Y'), as previously shown in chapter 1 by Fig. 1.8. Residual plots for the GGPA example are shown in Fig. 2.1, where Fig. 2.1(a) represents e versus Y', Fig. 2.1(b) represents e versus GRETOT, and Fig. 2.1(c) represents e versus UGPA. Even with a very small sample, we see a fairly random pattern of residuals (although there is a slight pattern in each plot), and therefore feel fairly confident that the linearity assumption has been satisfied. Note also that there are other types of residual plots developed especially for multiple regression, such as the added variable and partial residual plots (Larsen & McCleary, 1972; Mansfield & Conerly, 1987; Weisberg, 1985).

There are two procedures that can be used to deal with nonlinearity, transformations (of one or more of the X_ks and/or Y as described in chapt. 1) and nonlinear models. Nonlinear models are discussed further in a later section of this chapter.

The Distribution of the Errors in Prediction.   The second assumption is actually a set of four statements about the form of the errors in prediction or residuals, the e_i terms. First, the errors in prediction are assumed to be random and independent errors. That is, there is no systematic pattern about the errors and each error is independent of the other errors. An example of a systematic pattern is one where for small values of X_k the residuals tend to be small, whereas for large values of X_k the residuals tend to be large. Thus, there is a relationship between X_k and e.

The simplest procedure for assessing independence is to examine residual plots. If the independence assumption is satisfied, then the residuals should fall into a random display of points. If the assumption is violated, then the residuals will fall into some type of cyclical pattern. As discussed in chapter 1, the Durbin–Watson statistic (1950, 1951, 1971) can be used to test for autocorrelation. As mentioned in chapter 1, violations of the independence assumption generally occur in three situations: time-series data, observations within blocks, or replication. Nonindependence will affect the standard errors of the regression model. For serious violations of the independence as-

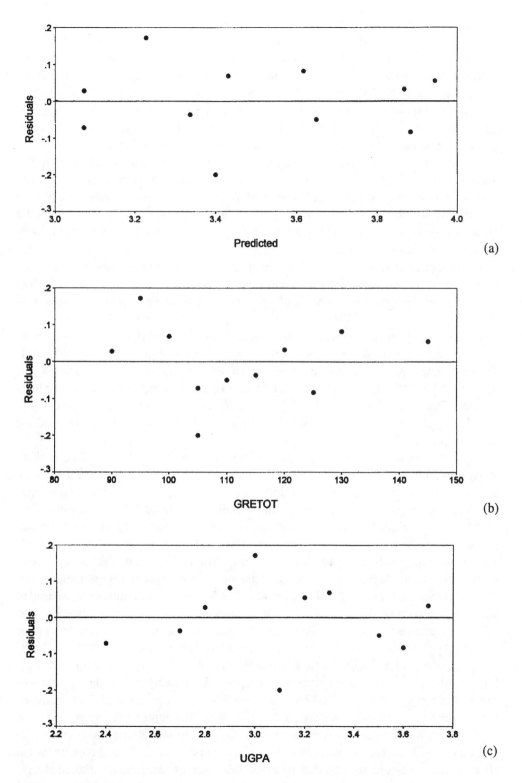

FIG. 2.1   Residual plots for GRE–GPA example: (a), (b), (c).

sumption, one can use generalized or weighted least squares as the method of estimation (Myers, 1986), or use some type of transformation. The residual plots shown in Fig. 2.1 do not suggest any independence problems.

The second part of the assumption purports that the conditional distributions of the prediction errors for all values of X_k have a mean of zero. This is assumed for all values of X_k. If the first two parts of the assumption are satisfied, then Y' is an unbiased estimator of the mean of each conditional distribution. Due to the small sample size, consistency of the conditional means cannot really be assessed for the sample data.

The third part of the assumption is that the conditional distributions of the prediction errors have a constant variance, s_{res}^2, for all values of X_k. This again is the assumption of homogeneity or homoscedasticity of variance. Thus for all values of X_k, the conditional distributions of the prediction errors have the same variance. If the first three parts of the assumption are satisfied, then s_{res}^2 is an unbiased estimator of the variance for each conditional distribution.

In a plot of residuals versus the X_ks as well as Y', the consistency of the variance of the conditional residual distributions may be examined. As discussed in chapter 1, another method for detecting violation of the homogeneity assumption is the use of formal statistical tests (see Miller, 1997). Violation of the homogeneity assumption may lead to inflated standard errors or nonnormal conditional distributions. Several solutions are available for dealing with violations, as previously described in chapter 1. These include the use of variance stabilizing transformations (such as the square root of Y or the log of Y), generalized or weighted least squares rather than ordinary least squares as the method of estimation (Myers, 1986), or robust regression (Myers, 1986; Wu, 1985). Due to the small sample size, homogeneity cannot really be assessed for the example data.

The fourth and final part of the assumption holds that the conditional distributions of the prediction errors are normal in shape. That is, for all values of X_k, the prediction errors are normally distributed. Violation of the normality assumption may be a result of outliers, as discussed in chapter 1. The simplest outlier detection procedure is to look for observations that are more than two or three standard errors from the mean. Other procedures were described in chapter 1. Several methods for dealing with outliers are available, such as conducting regressions with and without suspected outliers, robust regression (Myers, 1986; Wu, 1985), and nonparametric regression (Miller, 1997; Rousseeuw & Leroy, 1987; Wu, 1985). The following procedures can be used to detect normality violations: viewing the frequency distributions and/or normal probability plot, and calculation of a skewness statistic. For the example data, the normal probability plot is shown in Fig. 2.2, and even with a small sample looks good. Violations can lead to imprecision particularly in the partial slopes and the coefficient of determination. There are also several statistical procedures available for the detection of nonnormality (e.g., the Shapiro–Wilk test, 1965; D'Agostino's test, 1971); transformations can also be used to normalize the data. Review chapter 1 for more details.

Now we have a complete assumption about the conditional distributions of the prediction errors. Each conditional distribution of e_i consists of random and independent (I) values that are normally (N) distributed with a mean of zero, and a variance of s_{res}^2.

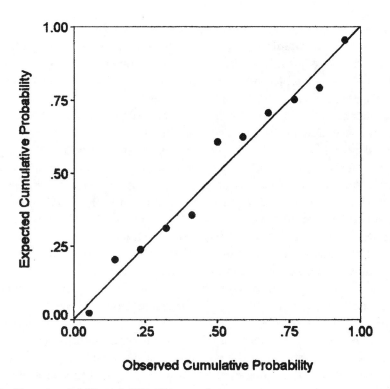

FIG. 2.2   Normal probability plot: GRE–GPA example.

In statistical notation, this is written as $e_i \sim NI(0, s^2_{res})$. If all four parts of the second assumption and the first assumption are satisfied, then we can test hypotheses and form confidence intervals about the β_ks. By meeting these assumptions then, inferential statistics based on b_k become valid such that the estimates of b_k are normally distributed with population mean β_k and population variance $\sigma(\beta_k)^2$.

The Fixed X Model.   The third assumption puts forth that the values of X_k are fixed. That is, the X_ks are fixed variables rather than random variables. This results in the regression model being valid only for those particular values of X_k that were actually observed and used in the analysis. Thus, the same values of X_k would be used in replications or repeated samples. A similar concept is presented in the fixed and random-effects analysis of variance models in subsequent chapters.

Strictly speaking, the regression model and its resultant parameter estimates are only valid for those values of X_k actually sampled. The use of a prediction equation developed to predict Y, based on one sample of individuals, may be suspect for another sample of individuals. Depending on the circumstances, the new sample of individuals may actually call for a different set of parameter estimates. Two obvious situations that come to mind are the extrapolation and interpolation of values of X_k. In general, we may not want to make predictions about individuals having combinations of X_k scores outside of the range of values used in developing the prediction equation; this is defined as extrapolating beyond the sample predictor data. We cannot assume that the function defined by the prediction equation is the same outside of the combinations of values of X_k that were initially sampled. The prediction errors for the nonsampled X_k values would be expected to be larger than those for the sampled X_k values because there is no supportive prediction data for the former.

On the other hand, we may not be quite as concerned in making predictions about individuals having combinations of X_k scores within the range of values used in developing the prediction equation; this is defined as interpolating within the range of the sample predictor data. We would feel somewhat more comfortable in assuming that the function defined by the prediction equation is the same for other new values of combinations of X_k scores within the range of those initially sampled. For the most part, the fixed X assumption would be satisfied if the new observations behave like those in the prediction sample. In the interpolation situation, we expect the prediction errors to be somewhat smaller as compared to the extrapolation situation because there is at least some similar supportive prediction data for the former.

If all of the other assumptions are upheld, and if e is statistically independent of the X_ks, then X_k can be either a fixed or a random variable without affecting the estimators, a and the b_ks (Wonnacott & Wonnacott, 1981). Thus if X_k is a random variable and is independent of e, then a and the b_ks are unaffected, allowing for the proper use of tests of significance and confidence intervals. It should also be noted that Y is considered to be a random variable, and thus no assumption is made about fixed values of Y.

Multicollinearity. The final assumption is unique to multiple linear regression, being unnecessary in simple linear regression. We define multicollinearity as a strong linear relationship between two or more of the predictors. The presence of severe multicollinearity is problematic in several respects. First, it will lead to instability of the regression coefficients across samples, where the estimates will bounce around quite a bit in terms of magnitude and even occasionally result in changes in sign (perhaps opposite of expectation). This occurs because the standard errors of the regression coefficients become larger, thus making it more difficult to achieve statistical significance. Another result that may occur involves an overall R^2 that is significant, but none of the individual predictors are significantly different from zero. This is interpreted to mean that none of the individual predictors are significant given the other predictors being included, and does not mean that each one is a weak predictor by itself. Also the variances of the regression coefficients tend to be large in the presence of severe multicollinearity. Multicollinearity will also serve to restrict the utility and generalizability of the estimated regression model.

Recall from earlier in the chapter when we discussed the notion of partial regression coefficients, where the other predictors were held constant. In the presence of severe multicollinearity the other predictors cannot really be held constant because they are so highly intercorrelated. Multicollinearity may be indicated when there are large changes in estimated coefficients due to (a) a variable being added or deleted and/or (b) an observation being added or deleted (Chatterjee & Price, 1977). Multicollinearity is also likely when a composite variable as well as its component variables are used as predictors (e.g., GRETOT as well as GRE–Quantitative [GRE–Q] and GRE–Verbal [GRE–V]).

How do we detect violations of this assumption? The simplest procedure is to conduct a series of special regression analyses. For example, say there are three predictors. The procedure is to conduct the following three regression analyses: (a) to regress the first predictor X_1 on the other two predictors (i.e., X_2 and X_3); (b) to regress the second predictor X_2 on X_1 and X_3; and (c) to regress the third predictor X_3 on X_1 and X_2. Thus these regressions only involve the predictor variables, not the criterion variable. If any of the resultant R_k^2 values are close to 1 (greater than .9 might be a good rule of thumb), then there may be a problem. However, the large R^2 value may also be due to small sample size, and thus collecting more data would be useful. For the example data, $R_{12}^2 =$ .0907 and therefore multicollinearity is not a concern.

Also, if the number of predictors is greater than or equal to n, then perfect multicollinearity is a possibility. Another statistical method for detecting multicollinearity is to compute a variance inflation factor (VIF) for each predictor, which is equal to $1/(1 - R_k^2)$. The VIF is defined as the inflation that occurs for each regression coefficient above the ideal situation of uncorrelated predictors. Wetherill (1986) suggested that the largest VIF should be less than 10 in order to satisfy this assumption.

There are several possible methods for dealing with a multicollinearity problem. First, one can remove one or more of the correlated predictors. Second, ridge regression techniques can be used (see Hoerl & Kennard, 1970a, 1970b; Marquardt & Snee, 1975; Myers, 1986; Wetherill, 1986). Third, principal component scores resulting from principal component analysis can be utilized rather than raw scores on each variable (see Kleinbaum, Kupper, Muller, & Nizam, 1998; Myers, 1986; Weisberg, 1985; Wetherill, 1986). Fourth, transformations of the variables can be used to remove or reduce the extent of the problem. The final solution, and probably my last choice, is to use simple linear regression, where multicollinearity cannot exist.

Summary. For the GGPA example, although sample size is quite small in terms of looking at conditional distributions, it would appear that all of our assumptions have been satisfied. All of the residuals are within two standard errors of zero, and there does not seem to be any systematic pattern in the residuals. The distribution of the residuals is nearly symmetric and the normal probability plot looks good. The scatterplot also strongly suggests a linear relationship. The more sophisticated statistical software packages have implemented various regression diagnostics to assist the researcher in the evaluation of assumptions.

A summary of the assumptions and the effects of their violation for multiple linear regression is presented in Table 2.2.

VARIABLE SELECTION PROCEDURES

The multiple predictor models that we have considered thus far can be viewed as simultaneous. That is, all of the predictors to be used are entered (or selected) simultaneously, such that all of the regression parameters are estimated simultaneously; here the set of predictors has been selected *a priori*. There is also another class of models where the predictor variables are entered (or selected) systematically; here the set of predictors has not been selected *a priori*. This class of models is referred to as *variable*

TABLE 2.2

Assumptions and Violation of Assumptions—Multiple Linear Regression

Assumption	Effect of assumption violation
1. Regression of Y on the X_ks is linear	Bias in partial slopes and intercept; expected change in Y is not a constant and depends on value of X_k
2. Independence of residuals	Influences standard errors of the model
3. Residual means equal zero	Bias in Y'
4. Homogeneity of variance of residuals	Bias in s_{res}^2; may inflate standard errors or result in nonnormal conditional distributions
5. Normality of residuals	Less precise partial slopes and coefficient of determination
6. Values of X_k are fixed	(a) Extrapolating beyond the range of X_k combinations: prediction errors larger, may also bias partial slopes and intercept (b) Interpolating within the range of X_k combinations: smaller effects than in (a); if other assumptions met, negligible effect
7. Nonmulticollinearity of the X_ks	Regression coefficients can be quite unstable across samples (as standard errors are larger); R^2 may be significant, yet none of the predictors are significant; restricted generalizability of the model

selection procedures. There are several types of variable selection procedures. This section introduces the following procedures: backward elimination, forward selection, stepwise selection, and all possible subsets regression. None of these procedures are recommended with multicollinear data.

First let us discuss the *backward elimination* procedure. Here variables are eliminated from the model based on their minimal contribution to the prediction of the criterion variable. In the first stage of the analysis, all potential predictors are included in the model. In the second stage, that predictor is deleted from the model that makes the smallest contribution to the explanation of the dependent variable. This can be done by eliminating that variable having the smallest t or F statistic such that it is making the smallest contribution to SS_{reg} or R^2. In subsequent stages, that predictor is deleted that makes the next smallest contribution to the prediction of Y. The analysis continues until each of the remaining predictors in the model is a significant predictor of Y. This could be determined by comparing the t or F statistics for each predictor to the critical value, at a preselected level of significance. Some computer programs use as a stopping rule the maximum F-to-remove criterion, where the procedure would be stopped when all of the selected predictors' F values were greater than the specified F criterion. Another stopping rule is where the researcher stops at a predetermined number of predictors (see Hocking, 1976; Thompson, 1978).

Next consider the *forward selection* procedure. Here variables are added or selected to the model based on their maximal contribution to the prediction of the criterion variable. Initially, none of the potential predictors are included in the model. In the first stage, the predictor is added to the model that makes the largest contribution to the explanation of the dependent variable. This can be done by selecting that variable having the largest t or F statistic such that it is making the largest contribution to SS_{reg} or R^2. In subsequent stages, the predictor is selected that makes the next largest contribution to the prediction of Y. The analysis continues until each of the selected predictors in the model is a significant predictor of Y, whereas none of the unselected predictors is a significant predictor. This could be determined by comparing the t or F statistics for each predictor to the critical value, at a preselected level of significance. Some computer programs use as a stopping rule the minimum F-to-enter criterion, where the procedure would be stopped when all of the unselected predictors' F values were less than the specified F criterion.

For the same set of data and at the same level of significance, the backward elimination and forward selection procedures may not necessarily result in the exact same model, due to the differences in how variables are selected. It is often recommended (e.g., Wetherill, 1986) that the backward elimination procedure be used over the forward selection procedure. It is easier to keep a watch on the effects that each stage has on the regression estimates and standard errors with the backward elimination procedure.

The *stepwise selection* procedure is a modification of the forward selection procedure with one important difference. Predictors that have been selected into the model can at a later step be deleted from the model; thus the modification conceptually involves a backward elimination mechanism. This situation can occur for a predictor when a significant contribution at an earlier step later becomes a nonsignificant contribution given the set of other predictors in the model. That is, the predictor loses its significance due to new predictors being added to the model.

The stepwise selection procedure is as follows. Initially, none of the potential predictors are included in the model. In the first step, that predictor is added to the model that makes the largest contribution to the explanation of the dependent variable. This can be done by selecting that variable having the largest t or F statistic such that it is making the largest contribution to SS_{reg} or R^2. In subsequent stages, the predictor is selected that makes the next largest contribution to the prediction of Y. Those predictors that have entered at earlier stages are also checked to see if their contribution remains significant. If not, then that predictor is eliminated from the model. The analysis continues until each of the predictors remaining in the model is a significant predictor of Y, while none of the other predictors is a significant predictor. This could be determined by comparing the t or F statistics for each predictor to the critical value, at a preselected level of significance. Some computer programs use as stopping rules the minimum F-to-enter and maximum F-to-remove criteria, where the F-to-enter value selected is usually equal to or slightly greater than the F-to-remove value selected (to prevent a predictor from continuously being entered and removed). For the same set of data and at the same level of significance, the backward elimination, forward selection, and stepwise selection procedures may not necessarily result in the exact same model, due to the differences in how variables are selected.

One final variable selection procedure is known as *all possible subsets regression*. Let us say, for example, that there are five potential predictors. In this procedure, all possible one-, two-, three-, and four-variable models are analyzed (with five predictors there is only a single five-predictor model). Thus there will be 5 one-predictor models, 10 two-predictor models, 10 three-predictor models, and 5 four-predictor models. The best k predictor model can be selected as the model that yields the largest R^2. For example, the best three-predictor model would be that model of the 10 estimated that yields the largest R^2. The best overall model could also be selected as that model with the largest adjusted R^2; that is, the model with the largest R^2 for the smallest number of predictors. With today's powerful computers, this procedure is easier and more cost efficient than in the past. However, the researcher is not advised to consider this procedure, or for that matter any of the other variable selection procedures, when the number of potential predictors is quite large. Here the researcher is likely to invoke the garbage in, garbage out principle, where number crunching takes precedence over thoughtful analysis. Also, the number of models will be equal to 2^m, so that for 10 predictors there are 1,024 possible subsets. It seems clear that examination of that number of models is not a thoughtful analysis.

In closing our discussion of variable selection procedures, there are two other procedures I would like to briefly mention. In *hierarchical regression*, the researcher specifies a priori a sequence for the variables. Thus, the analysis proceeds in a forward selection (or backward elimination) mode according to a specified theoretically based sequence rather than an unspecified statistically based sequence. In *setwise regression* (also known as *blockwise*, *chunkwise*, or *forced stepwise regression*), the researcher specifies a priori a sequence for sets of variables. The sets of variables are determined by the researcher such that variables within a set share some common theoretical ground (e.g., home background variables in one set and aptitude variables in another set). Variables within a set are selected according to one of the variable selection procedures (e.g., backward elimination, forward selection, stepwise selection). Those variables selected for a particular set are then entered in the specified sequence. Thus, these procedures are a bit more theoretically based than the four previously discussed. For further information on the variable selection procedures, see Cohen and Cohen (1983), Kleinbaum et al. (1998), Miller (1990), Pedhazur (1997), and Weisberg (1985).

Consider a new example set of data to illustrate some of the variable selection procedures. The data to be analyzed consist of four potential predictor variables and 20 observations, as shown in Table 2.3. The criterion variable is reading comprehension, whereas the predictor variables are letter identification (X_1), word knowledge (X_2), decoding skill (X_3), and reading rate (X_4). First look at the results from the forward selection procedure shown in Table 2.4. In stage 0, we see that no predictors have yet to enter the model, but decoding will be the first to be selected into the model. Decoding has indeed been added to the model in stage 1, the adjusted R^2 value is .4730, and letter identification will be the next variable to enter the model. In stage 2, letter identification is added to the model, the adjusted R^2 increases to .5672, and word knowledge will next be selected into the model. At the .05 level of significance, no other predictors would be added to the model, and we would normally stop adding new variables. However, let us continue until all variables have been selected just as an exercise. In stage 3, word knowledge is added to the model, the adjusted R^2 only increases to .6139, and rate will next be selected into the model. Finally, in stage 4, rate is selected into the model, the adjusted R^2 actually decreases to .6019, and all of the potential predictors have been included in the model.

TABLE 2.3
Reading Example Data

Student	Reading Comprehension	Letter Identification	Word Knowledge	Decoding Skill	Reading Rate
1	54	2	26	16	3
2	53	10	29	15	4
3	40	4	6	5	3
4	53	5	20	16	5
5	49	9	10	8	4
6	53	10	25	11	6
7	53	7	21	11	5
8	54	9	25	13	4
9	50	8	6	13	4
10	40	4	11	6	5
11	51	5	19	7	3
12	47	5	9	10	3
13	46	9	6	5	2
14	53	9	26	16	3
15	53	7	34	16	6
16	53	10	20	16	5
17	52	10	14	5	4
18	52	9	23	15	6
19	48	6	28	10	4
20	52	7	10	16	5

For this particular data set, the results for the backward elimination and stepwise selection procedures are essentially the same as for the forward selection procedure; that is, letter identification and decoding are selected for the model at the .05 level of significance. As previously mentioned, this will not always be the case, particularly with a larger number of predictor variables. The results of the backward elimination and stepwise selection procedures are not presented here, but feel free to analyze the data on your own.

Finally, consider analyzing the same data with the all possible subsets regression procedure. A summary of these results is contained in Table 2.5. Here we see that the best one-predictor model is with decoding (adjusted $R^2 = .4730$), the best two-predictor model is with letter identification and decoding (adjusted $R^2 = .5672$), the best three-predictor model is with letter identification, word knowledge, and decoding (adjusted $R^2 = .6139$) and, of course, the best and only four-predictor model is with all four predictors included (adjusted $R^2 = .6019$). Based on statistical significance at the .05 level, the two-predictor model (with letter identification and decoding) is the best overall model,

TABLE 2.4
Forward Selection Regression Results

	Variables in Model	Coefficient	F	Variables Not in Model	F
Stage 0:	None			X_1	3.6405
				X_2	12.2938
				X_3	18.0538
				X_4	1.9535
$R^2 = .0000$	Adjusted $R^2 = .0000$				
Stage 1:	X_3	.6986	18.0538	X_1	4.9173
				X_2	3.0729
				X_4	0.0118
$R^2 = .5008$	Adjusted $R^2 = .4730$				
Stage 2:	X_1	.5840	4.9173	X_2	3.0561
	X_3	.6622	19.5150	X_4	0.1335
$R^2 = .6128$	Adjusted $R^2 = .5672$				
Stage 3:	X_1	.5473	4.8070	X_4	0.5184
	X_2	.1483	3.0561		
	X_3	.4874	7.9093		
$R^2 = .6749$	Adjusted $R^2 = .6139$				
Stage 4:	X_1	.5863	5.1166	None	
	X_2	.1599	3.3295		
	X_3	.5205	8.1896		
	X_4	−.4371	0.5184		
$R^2 = .6857$	Adjusted $R^2 = .6019$				

as the remaining predictors do not make a significant additional contribution to the prediction of comprehension. Based on parsimony (i.e., simplicity), one may select either the one-predictor model (with decoding) or the two-predictor model (with letter identification and decoding), depending on the relative costs of these models.

Let me make a few comments about the variable selection procedures. There is a bit of controversy as to when these procedures are most applicable. We can define exploratory research as inquiry that is not guided by theory or previous research, and confirmatory research as inquiry that is guided by theory or research. Although some researchers suggest that variable selection procedures are always useful (i.e., the num-

TABLE 2.5
All Possible Subsets Regression Results

Variables in Model	R^2	Adjusted R^2
One-variable models:		
X_1	.1682	.1220
X_2	.4058	.3728
X_3	.5007	.4730
X_4	.0979	.0478
Two-variable models:		
X_1, X_2	.5141	.4570
X_1, X_3	.6128	.5672
X_1, X_4	.2162	.1240
X_2, X_3	.5772	.5274
X_2, X_4	.4108	.3415
X_3, X_4	.5011	.4424
Three-variable models:		
X_1, X_2, X_3	.6749	.6139
X_1, X_2, X_4	.5141	.4230
X_1, X_3, X_4	.6160	.5440
X_2, X_3, X_4	.5785	.4995
Four-variable model:		
X_1, X_2, X_3, X_4	.6857	.6019

ber crunchers) or they are never useful (e.g., the statistical purists), my personal philosophy lies somewhere in between. I believe that the best situation to use these procedures is in exploratory research where prior research and theory are weak or lacking. Thus in some sense, the data are used to guide the analysis. I also feel that these procedures are not the best to use in confirmatory research. If the interest is in confirming a theory, then test it with one or perhaps a few theoretically based regression models. It also seems useful to try to strike a balance between a fairly simple model, in terms of just a few important predictors, and the model that yields the best prediction, in terms of maximizing R^2. Also, do not forget to evaluate the assumptions once you have selected a model. Regression diagnostics (e.g., residual plots) are just as necessary with the variable selection procedures as they are with multiple linear regression.

As an example, consider being given 100 observations. A two-predictor model with an R^2 of .05 is about as useless as a 90-predictor model with an R^2 of .90. If you compute the adjusted R^2 values for this example, you would find that for the two-predictor model with an R^2 of .05, the adjusted R^2 is about .03. Compare this to the 90-predictor model with an R^2 of .90, where the adjusted R^2 is about $-.10$. Remember, both the number of predictors and the value of R^2 are important for assessing the utility of a regression model. In addition, other criteria may be used, such as minimizing MS_{res}, having small standard errors for the b_ks, or Mallows C_p (1973).

NONLINEAR REGRESSION

The last section of this chapter continues our discussion on how to deal with nonlinearity in multiple regression analysis. Previously in chapter 1 we considered the correlation ratio, which serves as a measure of linear and nonlinear relationship, as well as when nonlinear regression analysis might be necessary. Here I would like to formally introduce some nonlinear multiple regression models. In other words, what options are available if the criterion variable is not linearly related to the predictor variables?

First we examine polynomial regression models. Polynomial models consist of a very broad class of models, of which linear models are a special case. In polynomial models, powers of the predictor variables are used. In general, a sample polynomial regression model would look like the following:

$$Y = b_1X + b_2X^2 + ... + b_mX^m + a + e$$

where the independent variable X is taken from the first power through the mth power, and the i subscript for observations has been deleted to simplify the notation. If the model consists of only X taken to the first power, then this represents a *simple linear regression model* (also known as a *first-degree polynomial*). A *second-degree polynomial* includes X taken to the second power, which is also known as a *quadratic model* (rather than a linear one). The quadratic model is

$$Y = b_1X + b_2X^2 + a + e$$

A *third-degree polynomial* includes X taken to the third power, also known as a *cubic model*. Examples of these polynomial models are shown in Fig. 2.3.

Thus far, these polynomial models contain only one predictor variable, where we have used a single predictor and taken powers of it. A multiple predictor polynomial model can also be utilized. An example of a second-degree polynomial model with two predictors would be

$$Y = b_1X_1 + b_2X_1^2 + b_3X_2 + b_4X_2^2 + a + e$$

This model may also include an interaction term, such as $b_5X_1X_2$, described later in this section.

In terms of obtaining estimates of the parameters for the polynomial regression model, we can, for example, identify X^2 as X_2. We can then proceed to use the ordinary least squares method of estimation. The same can be done for other terms in the polynomial model. The assumptions of such models are the same as with linear regression models. Once each of the parameters is estimated, the statistical significance of each of the b_ks can be determined. For instance, in a second-degree model, if the quadratic term is not significant this tells us that a linear model is better suited for the data. One could also compare the R^2 values from a linear and a quadratic model, using the F statistic, to determine the most statistically plausible model.

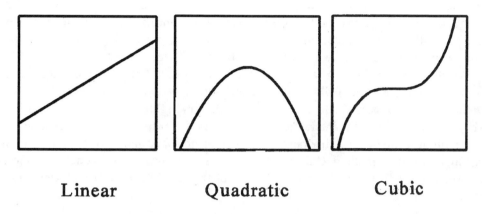

Linear   Quadratic   Cubic

FIG. 2.3   Three polynomial regression models

One does have to be careful when implementing polynomial models. First of all, we can fit a set of data with n observations perfectly with an $(n-1)$th degree polynomial. This obviously places too much value on each observation. The same may be said of letting one or two outliers determine the degree of the polynomial. Going from, say, a linear model to a quadratic model because of one obvious outlier is placing too much importance and validity on that outlier. As pointed out before, one observation should not be the major determinant of the regression equation. We recommend that a simple model that explains Y fairly well is to be preferred over a complex, higher order polynomial that does not explain Y much better. Moreover, higher order polynomial models may result in multicollinearity problems as some of the variables tend to be highly correlated (e.g., X_1 and X_1^2). For more information on polynomial regression models, see Bates and Watts (1988), Kleinbaum et al. (1998), Pedhazur (1997), Seber and Wild (1989), and Weisberg (1985).

Under other circumstances, one might prefer to transform the criterion variable and/or the predictor variables to obtain a more linear form. Some commonly used transformations are log, reciprocal, exponential, and square root. See Berry and Feldman (1985) for more information.

A final type of nonlinear model involves the use of interaction terms. *Interaction* is a term commonly used in the analysis of variance when there are two or more independent variables (to be discussed in chap. 5). Interaction terms may also be used in regression analysis. Let us write a simple two-predictor interaction-type model as

$$Y = b_1X_1 + b_2X_2 + b_3X_1X_2 + a + e$$

where X_1X_2 represents the interaction of predictor variables 1 and 2. An interaction can be defined as occurring when the relationship between Y and X_1 depends on the level of X_2. For example, suppose one were to use quantitative ability and motivation to predict statistics performance. One might expect that high levels of statistics performance would not only be related to quantitative ability and motivation individually, but to an interaction of those predictors together as well. That is, a high level of statistics performance may be a function of some minimal level of both ability and motivation taken together. Without motivation, students would probably not apply their quantitative ability, and thus would have a low level of statistics performance.

An interaction between X_1 and X_2 indicates that those variables are not additive. In other words, there is a contribution of the $X_1 X_2$ interaction above and beyond the individual contributions of X_1 and X_2. If X_1 and X_2 are very highly correlated, multicollinearity of X_1 and X_2 with the interaction term is likely. In terms of parameter estimation, one could just call the $X_1 X_2$ interaction X_3 and then go ahead and use the ordinary least squares estimation method. One may also use nonlinear interactive models. For more information see Berry and Feldman (1985), Cohen and Cohen (1983), and Kleinbaum et al. (1998).

SUMMARY

In this chapter, methods involving multiple predictors in the regression context were considered. The chapter began with a look at partial and semipartial correlations. Next, a lengthy discussion of multiple linear regression was conducted. Here we extended many of the basic concepts of simple linear regression to the multiple predictor situation. In addition, several new concepts were introduced, including the coefficient of multiple determination, multiple correlation, tests of the individual regression coefficients, and testing increments in the proportion of variation accounted for by a predictor. Next we examined variable selection procedures, such as the forward selection, backward elimination, stepwise selection, and all possible subsets procedures. Finally, nonlinear regression was described for the single and multiple predictor cases. At this point you should have met the following objectives: (a) be able to compute and interpret the results of part and semipartial correlations, (b) be able to understand the concepts underlying multiple linear regression, (c) be able to compute and interpret the results of multiple linear regression, (d) be able to understand and evaluate the assumptions of multiple linear regression, (e) be able to compute and interpret the results of the variable selection procedures, and (f) be able to understand the concepts underlying nonlinear regression. In chapter 3 we begin our discussion of the analysis of variance with the one-factor model and relate it to simple linear regression analysis as well.

PROBLEMS

Conceptual Problems

1.   Variable 1 is to be predicted from a combination of variable 2 and one of variables 3, 4, 5, or 6. The correlations of importance are as follows:

$r_{13} = .8$ $r_{23} = .2$
$r_{14} = .6$ $r_{24} = .5$
$r_{15} = .6$ $r_{25} = .2$
$r_{16} = .8$ $r_{26} = .5$

1. Which of the following multiple correlation coefficient will have the largest value?
   a. $r_{1.23}$
   b. $r_{1.24}$
   c. $r_{1.25}$
   d. $r_{1.26}$

2. The most accurate predictions are made when the standard error of estimate equals
   a. $\bar{Y}$
   b. s_Y
   c. 0
   d. 1

3. The intercept can take on a positive value only. True or false?

4. Adding an additional predictor to a regression equation will necessarily result in an increase in R^2. True or false?

5. The best prediction in multiple regression will result when each predictor has a high correlation with the other predictor variables and a high correlation with the dependent variable. True or false?

6. Consider the following two situations:
   Situation 1 $r_{y1} = .6$ $r_{y2} = .5$ $r_{12} = .0$
   Situation 2 $r_{y1} = .6$ $r_{y2} = .5$ $r_{12} = .2$
   I assert that the value of R^2 will be greater in Situation 2. Am I correct?

7. Values of variables X_1, X_2, X_3 are available for a sample of 50 students. The value of $r_{12} = .6$. I assert that if the partial correlation $r_{12.3}$ were calculated it would be larger than .6. Am I correct?

Computational Problems

1. You are given the following data, where X_1 and X_2 are used to predict Y:

Y	X_1	X_2
40	100	10
50	200	20
50	300	10
70	400	30
65	500	20
65	600	20
80	700	30

   Compute the following values: intercept; b_1; b_2; SS_{res}; SS_{reg}; F; s_{res}^2; $s(b_1)$; $s(b_2)$; t_1; t_2; F increment in X_1; F increment in X_2.

2. Complete the missing information for this regression equation (df = 23).

$$Y' = 25.1 + 1.2\,X_1 + 1.0\,X_2 - .50\,X_3$$

(2.1)	(1.5)	(1.3)	(.06)	standard errors
(11.9)	( )	( )	( )	t ratios
	( )	( )	( )	significant at .05?

3. Consider a sample of elementary school children. Given that r (strength, weight) = .6, r (strength, age) = .7, and r (weight, age) = .8, what is the first-order partial correlation coefficient between strength and weight holding age constant?

4. For a sample of 100 adults, you are given that $r_{12} = .55$, $r_{13} = .80$, $r_{23} = .70$. What is the value of $r_{1(2.3)}$?

5. A researcher would like to predict salary from a set of four predictor variables for a sample of 45 subjects. Multiple linear regression was used to analyze these data. Complete the following summary table ($\alpha = .05$) for the test of significance of the overall regression equation.

Source	SS	df	MS	F	Critical Value and Decision
Regression	—	—	20	—	—
Residual	400	—	—		
Total	—	—			

6. Calculate the partial correlation $r_{12.3}$ and the part correlation $r_{1(2.3)}$ from the following bivariate correlations: $r_{12} = .5$, $r_{13} = .8$, $r_{23} = .9$.

7. Calculate the partial correlation $r_{13.2}$ and the part correlation $r_{1(3.2)}$ from the following bivariate correlations: $r_{12} = .21$, $r_{13} = .40$, $r_{23} = -.38$.

8. You are given the following data, where X_1 (verbal aptitude) and X_2 (prior reading achievement) are to be used to predict Y (reading achievement):

Y	X_1	X_2
2	2	5
1	2	4
1	1	5
1	1	3
5	3	6
4	4	4
7	5	6
6	5	4
7	7	3

8	6	3
3	4	3
3	3	6
6	6	9
6	6	8
10	8	9
9	9	6
6	10	4
6	9	5
9	4	8

Compute the following values: intercept; b_1; b_2; SS_{res}; SS_{reg}; F; s_{res}^2; $s(b_1)$; $s(b_2)$; t_1; t_2; F increment in X_1; F increment in X_2.

3

One-Factor Analysis of Variance—Fixed-Effects Model

Chapter Outline

Key Concepts

1. Between- and within-groups variability
2. Sources of variation
3. Partitioning the sums of squares
4. The ANOVA model
5. Expected mean squares
6. Kruskal–Wallis one-factor ANOVA

In the last two chapters our discussion dealt with the simple and multiple regression models. The next six chapters are concerned with various analysis of variance models. All of these regression and analysis of variance models are forms of the general linear model (GLM). In this chapter we consider the simplest form of the analysis of variance (ANOVA), known as the one-factor analysis of variance model. Recall the independent *t* test where the means from two independent samples were compared. What if you wish to compare more than two means? The answer is to use the *analysis of variance*. At this point you may be wondering why the procedure is called the analysis of variance rather than the analysis of means, because the intent is to study possible mean differences. One way of comparing a set of means is to think in terms of the variability among those means. If the sample means are all the same, then the variability of those means would be zero. If the sample means are not all the same, then the variability of those means would be somewhat greater than zero. In general, the greater the mean differences, the greater is the variability of the means. Thus mean differences are studied by looking at the variability of the means; hence, the term analysis of variance is appropriate rather than the analysis of means (see third section, this chapter).

As in the previous two chapters, *X* is used to denote our single independent variable, which we also refer to as a *factor*, and *Y* to denote our *dependent* (or *criterion*) *variable*. Thus the one-factor ANOVA is a bivariate procedure, as was the case in simple regression. Our interest here is in determining whether mean differences exist on the dependent variable. Stated another way, the researcher is interested in the influence of the independent variable on the dependent variable. For example, a researcher may want to determine the influence that method of instruction has on statistics achievement. The independent variable or factor would be method of instruction and the dependent variable would be statistics achievement. Three different methods of instruction that might be compared are large lecture hall instruction, small-group instruction, and computer-assisted instruction. Students would be randomly assigned to one of the three methods of instruction and at the end of the semester evaluated as to their level of achievement in statistics. These results would be of interest to a statistics instructor in determining the most effective method of instruction. Thus, the instructor may opt for the method of instruction that yields the highest mean achievement.

A few of the concepts we developed in the last two chapters on regression are utilized in the analysis of variance. These concepts include the independent and dependent variables, the linear model, partitioning of the sums of squares, degrees of freedom, mean square terms, and F ratios, as well as the assumptions of normality, homoscedasticity, and independence. However, there are also several new concepts to consider, such as between- and within-groups variability, fixed and random effects, the ANOVA summary table, the expected mean squares, balanced and unbalanced models, and the Kruskal–Wallis one-factor ANOVA. Our objectives are that by the end of this chapter, you will be able to (a) understand the characteristics and concepts underlying the one-factor ANOVA (balanced, unbalanced, nonparametric), (b) compute and interpret the results of a one-factor ANOVA (balanced, unbalanced, nonparametric), and (c) understand and evaluate the assumptions of the one-factor ANOVA (balanced, unbalanced, nonparametric).

CHARACTERISTICS OF THE ONE-FACTOR ANOVA MODEL

This section describes the distinguishing characteristics of the one-factor ANOVA model. Suppose you are interested in comparing the means of two independent samples. Here the independent t test would be the method of choice (or perhaps Welch's t' or the Mann–Whitney–Wilcoxon test). What if your interest is in comparing the means of more than two independent samples? One possibility is to conduct multiple independent t tests on each pair of means. For example, if you wished to determine whether the means from five independent samples are the same, you could do all possible pairwise t tests. In this case the following null hypotheses could be evaluated: $\mu_1 = \mu_2$, $\mu_1 = \mu_3$, $\mu_1 = \mu_4$, $\mu_1 = \mu_5$, $\mu_2 = \mu_3$, $\mu_2 = \mu_4$, $\mu_2 = \mu_5$, $\mu_3 = \mu_4$, $\mu_3 = \mu_5$, and $\mu_4 = \mu_5$. Thus we would have to carry out 10 different independent t tests. An easy way to determine the number of possible pairwise t tests that could be done for J means is to compute the value of $\frac{1}{2}[J(J-1)]$.

What is the problem with conducting so many t tests? The problem has to do with the probability of making a Type I error (i.e., α), where the researcher incorrectly rejects a true null hypothesis. Although the α level for each t test can be controlled at a specified nominal level, say .05, what happens to the overall α level for the entire set of tests? The overall α level for the entire set of tests (i.e., α_{total}), often called the *experiment-wise Type I error rate*, is larger than the α level for each of the individual t tests.

In our example we are interested in comparing the means for 10 pairs of groups. A t test is conducted for each of the 10 pairs of groups at $\alpha = .05$. Although each test controls the α level at .05, the overall α level will be larger because the risk of a Type I error accumulates across the tests. For each test we are taking a risk; the more tests we do, the more risks we are taking. This can be explained by considering the risk you take each day you drive your car to school or work. The risk of an accident is small for any one day; however, over the period of a year the risk of an accident is much larger.

For C independent (or orthogonal) tests we compute the experiment-wise error as follows:

$$\alpha_{total} = 1 - (1 - \alpha)^C$$

Assume for the moment that our 10 tests are independent (although they are not). If we go ahead with our 10 t-tests at $\alpha = .05$, then the experiment-wise error rate is

$$\alpha_{total} = 1 - (1 - .05)^{10}$$

$$= 1 - .60 = .40$$

Although we are seemingly controlling our α level at the .05 level, the probability of making a Type I error across all 10 tests is .40. In other words, in the long run, 4 times out of 10 we will make a Type I error. Thus we do not want to do all possible t tests. Before we move on, the experiment-wise error rate for C dependent tests (which would be the case when doing all possible pairwise t tests, as in our example) is more difficult to determine, so let us just say that

$$\alpha \leq \alpha_{total} \leq C\alpha$$

Are there other options available to us where we can maintain better control over our experiment-wise error rate? The optimal solution, in terms of maintaining control over our overall α level as well as maximizing power, is to conduct one overall test, often called an *omnibus test*. Recall that power has to do with the probability of correctly rejecting a false null hypothesis. The omnibus test could assess the equality of all of the means simultaneously. This test is the one used in the analysis of variance. The one-factor analysis of variance, then, represents an extension of the independent t test for two or more independent sample means, where the experiment-wise error rate is controlled.

In addition, the one-factor ANOVA has only one independent variable or factor with two or more levels. The levels represent the different samples or groups or treatments whose means are to be compared. In our example, method of instruction is the independent variable with three levels: large lecture hall, small group, and computer assisted. There are two ways of conceptually thinking about the selection of levels. In the fixed-effects model, all levels that the researcher is interested in are included in the design and analysis for the study. As a result, generalizations can only be made about those particular levels of the independent variable that are actually selected. For instance, if a researcher is only interested in three methods of instruction—large lecture hall, small group, and computer assisted—then only those levels are incorporated into the study. Generalizations about other methods of instruction cannot be made because no other methods were considered for selection. Other examples of fixed-effects independent variables might be gender, type of drug treatment, or marital status.

In the random-effects model, the researcher randomly samples some levels of the independent variable from the population of levels. As a result, generalizations can be made about all of the levels in the population, even those not actually sampled. For instance, a researcher interested in teacher effectiveness may have randomly sampled history teachers (i.e., the independent variable) from the population of history teachers in a particular school district. Generalizations can then be made about other history teachers in that school district not actually sampled. The random selection of levels is much the same as the random selection of individuals or objects in the random sampling process. This is the nature of inferential statistics, where inferences are made about a population (of individuals, objects, or levels) from a sample. Other examples of random-effects independent variables might be classrooms, animals, or time (e.g., hours, days). The remainder of this chapter is concerned with the fixed-effects model. Chapter 7 discusses the random-effects model in more detail.

In the fixed-effects model, once the levels of the independent variable are selected, subjects (i.e., persons or objects) are randomly assigned to the levels of the independent variable. In certain situations, the researcher does not have control over which level a subject is assigned to. The groups already may be in place when the researcher arrives on the scene. For instance, students may be assigned to their classes at the beginning of the year by the school administration. Researchers typically have little input regarding class assignments. In another situation, it may be theoretically impossible to assign subjects to groups. For example, until genetics research is more advanced than at present, researchers will not be able to assign individuals to a level of gender. Thus, a distinction needs to be made about whether or not the researcher can control the assignment of subjects to groups. Although the analysis will not be altered, the interpretation of the results will. When researchers have control over group assignments, the extent to which they can generalize their findings is greater than for those researchers who do not have such control. For further information on the differences between true experimental designs (i.e., with random assignment) and quasi-experimental designs (i.e., without random assignment), see Campbell and Stanley (1966) and Cook and Campbell (1979).

Moreover, in the model being considered here, each subject is exposed to only one level of the independent variable. Chapter 7 deals with models where a subject is exposed to multiple levels of an independent variable; these are known as *repeated-measures models*. For example, a researcher may be interested in observing a group of young children repeatedly over a period of several years. Thus, each child might be observed every 6 months from birth to age 5 years. This would require a repeated-measures design because the observations of a particular child over time are obviously not independent observations.

One final characteristic is the measurement scale of the independent and dependent variables. In the analysis of variance, it is assumed that the scale of measurement on the dependent variable is at the interval or ratio level. If the dependent variable is measured at the ordinal level, then the nonparametric equivalent, the Kruskal–Wallis test, should be used (discussed later in this chapter). If the dependent variable shares properties of both the ordinal and interval levels (e.g., grade point average), then both the ANOVA and Kruskal–Wallis procedures should be used to cross-reference any potential effects of the measurement scale. The independent variable is a grouping or categorical variable, so it can be measured on any scale.

In summary, the characteristics of the one-factor analysis of variance fixed-effects model are as follows: (a) control of the experiment-wise error rate through an omnibus test; (b) one independent variable with two or more levels; (c) the levels of the independent variable are fixed by the researcher; (d) subjects are randomly assigned to these levels; (e) subjects are exposed to only one level of the independent variable; and (f) the dependent variable is measured at least at the interval level, although the Kruskal–Wallis one-factor ANOVA can be used for an ordinal-level dependent variable. In the context of experimental design, the one-factor analysis of variance is referred to as the *completely randomized design*.

THE LAYOUT OF THE DATA

Before we get into the theory and subsequent analysis of the data, let us examine the form in which the data is typically placed, known as the layout of the data. We designate each observation as Y_{ij}, where the j subscript tells us what group or level the observation belongs to and the i subscript tells us the observation or identification number within that group. For instance, Y_{34} would mean this is the third observation in the fourth group or level of the independent variable. The first subscript ranges over $i = 1$, ... , n and the second subscript ranges over $j = 1$, ... , J. Thus there are J levels of the independent variable and n subjects in each group, for a total of $Jn = N$ observations. For now, assume there are n subjects in each group in order to simplify matters; this is referred to as the *equal* ns *or balanced case*. Later on in this chapter, we consider the *unequal* ns *or unbalanced case*.

The layout of the data is shown in Table 3.1. Here we see that each column represents the observations for a particular group or level of the independent variable. At the bottom of each column are the group sample means ($\overline{Y}_{.j}$), the sums of the observations for group j ($\Sigma Y_{.j}$), and the sums of the squared observations for group j ($\Sigma Y_{.j}^{2}$). Also included is the overall sample mean ($\overline{Y}_{..}$). In conclusion, the layout of the data is one form in which the researcher can place the data to set up the analysis.

ANOVA THEORY

This section examines the underlying theory and logic of the analysis of variance, the sums of squares, and the ANOVA summary table. As noted previously, in the analysis of variance mean differences are tested by looking at the variability of the means. This section shows precisely how this is done.

General Theory and Logic

We begin with the hypotheses to be tested in the analysis of variance. In the two-group situation of the independent t test, the null and alternative hypotheses for a two-tailed test are as follows:

$$H_0: \mu_1 = \mu_2$$

$$H_1: \mu_1 \neq \mu_2$$

TABLE 3.1
Layout for the One-Factor ANOVA

Level of the Independent Variable					
1	2	3	...	J	
Y_{11}	Y_{12}	Y_{13}	...	Y_{1J}	
Y_{21}	Y_{22}	Y_{23}	...	Y_{2J}	
Y_{31}	Y_{32}	Y_{33}	...	Y_{3J}	
Y_{41}	Y_{42}	Y_{43}	...	Y_{4J}	
.	.	.	.	.	
.	.	.	.	.	
.	.	.	.	.	
Y_{n1}	Y_{n2}	Y_{n3}	...	Y_{nJ}	
—	—	—		—	
$\bar{Y}_{.1}$	$\bar{Y}_{.2}$	$\bar{Y}_{.3}$	...	$\bar{Y}_{.J}$	$\bar{Y}_{..}$
$\Sigma Y_{.1}$	$\Sigma Y_{.2}$	$\Sigma Y_{.3}$	...	$\Sigma Y_{.J}$	
$\Sigma Y_{.1}^2$	$\Sigma Y_{.2}^2$	$\Sigma Y_{.3}^2$	...	$\Sigma Y_{.J}^2$	

In the multiple-group situation, we have already seen the problem that occurs when multiple independent t tests are conducted for each pair of population means (i.e., increased likelihood of a Type I error). We concluded that the solution was to use an omnibus test where the equality of all of the means could be assessed simultaneously. The hypotheses for the omnibus analysis of variance test are as follows:

$$H_0: \mu_1 = \mu_2 = \mu_3 = ... = \mu_J$$

$$H_1: \text{not all the } \mu_j \text{ are equal.}$$

Here H_1 is purposely written in a general form to cover the multitude of possible mean differences that could arise. These range from only two of the means being different to all of the means being different from one another. Thus, because of the way H_1 has been written, only a nondirectional alternative is appropriate. If H_0 were to be rejected, then the researcher might want to consider a multiple comparison procedure so as to determine which means or combination of means are significantly different (see chap. 4).

As was mentioned in the introduction to this chapter, the analysis of mean differences is actually carried out by looking at variability of the means. At first this seems strange. If one wants to test for mean differences, then do a test of means. If one wants to test for variance differences, then do a test of variances. These statements should make sense because logic pervades the field of statistics. And they do for the two-group situation. For the multiple-group situation, we already know things get a bit more complicated.

Say a researcher is interested in the influence of amount of daily study time on statistics achievement. Three groups were formed based on the amount of daily study time in statistics: ½ hour, 1 hour, and 2 hours. Is there a differential influence of amount of time studied on subsequent mean statistics achievement (e.g., statistics final exam)? We would expect that the more one studied statistics, the higher the statistics mean achievement would be. One possible outcome in the population is where the amount of study time does not influence statistics achievement; here the population means will be equal. That is, the null hypothesis of equal group means is true. Thus the three groups will actually be three samples from the same population of students, with mean μ. The means are equal; thus there is no variability among the three group means. A second possible outcome in the population is where the amount of study time does influence statistics achievement; here the population means will not be equal. That is, the null hypothesis is false. Thus the three groups will not be three samples from the same population of students, but rather, each group will represent a sample from a distinct population of students receiving that particular amount of study time, with mean μ_j. The means are not equal, so there is variability among the three group means. In summary, the statistical question becomes whether the difference between the sample means is due to the usual sampling variability expected from a single population, or the result of a true difference between the sample means from different populations.

We conceptually define *within-groups variability* as the variability of the observations within a group combined across groups, and *between-groups variability* as the variability of the group means. In Fig. 3.1, the horizontal axis represents low and high variability within the groups. The vertical axis represents low and high variability between the groups. In the upper left-hand plot, there is low variability both within and between the groups. That is, performance is very consistent, both within each group as well as across groups. Here, within- and between-group variability are both low, and it is quite unlikely that one would reject H_0. In the upper right-hand plot, there is high variability within the groups and low variability between the groups. That is, performance is very consistent across groups, but quite variable within each group. Here, within-group variability exceeds between group variability, and again it is quite unlikely that one would reject H_0. In the lower left-hand plot, there is low variability within the groups and high variability between groups. That is, performance is very consistent within each group, but quite variable across groups. Here, between-group variability exceeds within-group variability, and it is quite likely that one would reject H_0. In the lower right-hand plot, there is high variability both within and between the groups. That is, performance is quite variable within each group, as well as across the groups. Here, within- and between-group variability are both high, and depending on the relative amounts of between and within group variability, one may or may not reject H_0. In summary, the optimal situation in terms of seeking to reject H_0 would be the one represented by high variability between the groups and low variability within the groups.

Partitioning the Sums of Squares

The partitioning of the sums of squares was an important concept in regression analysis (chaps. 1 and 2) and is also important in the analysis of variance. In part this is be-

Variability Within Groups

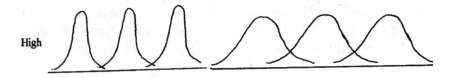

Variability
between
Groups

FIG. 3.1 Conceptual look at between- and within-groups variability.

cause both are forms of the general linear model (GLM). Let us begin with the sum of squares in Y, which we previously denoted as SS_Y, but instead denote here as SS_{total}. The term SS_{total} represents the amount of total variation in Y. The next step is to partition the total variation into variation between the groups, denoted by SS_{betw}, and variation within the groups, denoted by SS_{with}. In the one-factor analysis of variance we partition SS_{total} as follows:

$$SS_{total} = SS_{betw} + SS_{with}$$

or

$$\sum_{i=1}^{n} \sum_{j=1}^{J} (Y_{ij} - \overline{Y}_{..})^2 = \sum_{i=1}^{n} \sum_{j=1}^{J} (\overline{Y}_{.j} - \overline{Y}_{..})^2 + \sum_{i=1}^{n} \sum_{j=1}^{J} (Y_{ij} - \overline{Y}_{.j})^2$$

where SS_{total} is the total sum of squares due to variation among all of the observations without regard to group membership, SS_{betw} is the between-groups sum of squares due to the variation between the group means, and SS_{with} is the within-groups sum of squares due to the variation within the groups combined across groups.

We refer to this particular formulation of the partitioned sums of squares as the *definitional formula*, because each term literally defines a form of variation. In regression terminology, with these sums-of-squares terms the total variation in Y is partitioned into variation explained or predicted by the mean differences in the levels of X (i.e., like SS_{reg}) and variation due to within-group or residual error (i.e., individual differences or other factors, like SS_{res}). We return to the similarities of the ANOVA and regression general linear models later in this chapter.

Due to computational complexity and computational error, the definitional formula is rarely used with real data. Instead, a computational formula for the partitioned sums of squares is used for hand computations. The computational formula for the partitioning of the sums of squares is as follows.

$$SS_{total} = SS_{betw} + SS_{with}$$

$$\left[\sum_{i=1}^{n}\sum_{j=1}^{J}Y_{ij}^{2} - \frac{\left(\sum_{i=1}^{n}\sum_{j=1}^{J}Y_{ij}\right)^{2}}{N}\right] = \left[\frac{\sum_{j=1}^{J}\left(\sum_{i=1}^{n}Y_{ij}\right)^{2}}{n} - \frac{\left(\sum_{i=1}^{n}\sum_{j=1}^{J}Y_{ij}\right)^{2}}{N}\right] + \left[\sum_{i=1}^{n}\sum_{j=1}^{J}Y_{ij}^{2} - \frac{\sum_{j=1}^{J}\left(\sum_{i=1}^{n}Y_{ij}\right)^{2}}{n}\right]$$

Although this formula initially looks a bit overwhelming, it is not all that difficult. A careful look at the computations shows that there are only three different terms in the entire equation, each of which occurs twice. In the first term of SS_{total} and SS_{with}, each score is squared and then summed across all observations (both within and across groups). In the second term of SS_{total} and SS_{betw}, all of the observations are summed (both within and across groups); the total quantity is squared and is then divided by the total number of observations ($nJ = N$). For the first term in SS_{betw} and the second term in SS_{with}, the observations are summed within each group, squared, and summed across groups, and finally divided by n. Do you actually need to compute the total sum of squares? No, because the sum of squares between and within will add up to the sum of squares total. The only reason to compute the total sum of squares is as a check on hand computations. A complete example of the analysis of variance is considered later.

The ANOVA Summary Table

Now that we have partitioned the sums of squares, the next step is to assemble the *ANOVA summary table*. The purpose of the summary table is to simply summarize the analysis of variance. A general form of the summary table is shown in Table 3.2. The first column lists the sources of variation in the model. As we already know, in the one-factor model the total variation is partitioned into between-groups variation and within-groups variation. The second column notes the sums of squares terms for each source (i.e., SS_{betw}, SS_{with}, and SS_{total}).

The third column gives the degrees of freedom for each source. Recall that, in general, degrees of freedom has to do with the number of observations that are free to vary. For example, if a sample mean and all of the sample observations except for one are known, then the final observation is not free to vary. That is, the final observation is predeter-

TABLE 3.2
Analysis of Variance Summary Table

Source	SS	df	MS	F
Between groups	SS_{betw}	$J-1$	MS_{betw}	MS_{betw}/MS_{with}
Within groups	SS_{with}	$N-J$	MS_{with}	
Total	SS_{total}	$N-1$		

mined to be a particular value. Let us take an example where the mean is 10 and there are three observations, 7, 11, and an unknown observation. First we know that the sum of the three observations must be 30 for the mean to be 10. Second, we know that the sum of the known observations is 18. Finally, we determine that the unknown observation must be 12. Otherwise the sample mean would not be exactly equal to 10.

For the between-groups source, in the definitional formula we deal with the deviation of each group mean from the overall mean. There are J group means, so the df_{betw} must be $J-1$. Why? If there are J group means and we know the overall mean, then only $J-1$ of the group means are free to vary. In other words, if we know the overall mean and all but one of the group means, then the final unknown mean is predetermined. For the within-groups source, in the definitional formula we deal with the deviation of each observation from its respective group mean. There are n observations in each group; consequently, there are $n-1$ degrees of freedom in each group and J groups. Why are there $n-1$ degrees of freedom in each group? If there are n observations in each group, then only $n-1$ of the observations are free to vary. In other words, if we know the group mean and all but one of the observations for that group, then the final unknown observation for that group is predetermined. There are J groups, so the df_{with} is $J(n-1)$ or $N-J$. For the total source, in the definitional formula we deal with the deviation of each observation from the overall mean. There are N total observations; thus the df_{total} must be $N-1$. Why? If there are N total observations and we know the overall mean, then only $N-1$ of the observations are free to vary. In other words, if we know the overall mean and all but one of the N observations, then the final unknown observation is predetermined.

Why should we be concerned about the number of degrees of freedom in the analysis of variance? Suppose two researchers have conducted similar studies, with Researcher A using 20 observations per group and Researcher B only using 10 observations per group. Each researcher obtains a SS_{with} of 15. Would it be fair to say that the result for the two studies was the same? Such a comparison would be unfair because the SS_{with} is influenced by the number of observations per group. A fair comparison would be to weight the SS_{with} terms by their respective number of degrees of freedom. Similarly, it would not be fair to compare the SS_{betw} terms from two similar studies based on different numbers of groups. A fair comparison here would be to weight the SS_{betw} terms by their respective number of degrees of freedom. The method of weighting a sum-of-squares term by the number of degrees of freedom on which it is based yields what is called a *mean squares* term. Thus $MS_{betw} = SS_{betw}/df_{betw}$ and $MS_{with} = SS_{with}/df_{with}$, as shown in the fourth column of Table 3.2. They are referred to as *mean squares*, like the mean, because they represent a summed quantity that is weighted by the number of observations used in the sum itself. The mean squares terms are also variance estimates, like the sample variance s^2, because they represent the sum of the squared deviations divided by their degrees of freedom. We return to the notion of mean squares terms as variance estimates later.

The last column in the ANOVA summary table, the F value, is the summary test statistic of the summary table. The F value is computed by taking the ratio of the two mean squares or variance terms. Thus for the one-factor ANOVA fixed-effects model, the F value is computed as $F = MS_{betw}/MS_{with}$. As originally developed by Sir Ronald A. Fisher in the 1920s, this test statistic was originally known as the variance ratio because it represents the ratio of two variance estimates. Later the variance ratio was renamed the F ratio by George W. Snedecor (who worked out the table of F values, discussed momentarily) in honor of Fisher (F for Fisher).

The F ratio tells us whether there is more variation between groups than there is within groups, which must be the case if we are to reject H_0. Thus if there is more variation between groups than there is within groups, then MS_{betw} will be larger than MS_{with}. As a result of this, the F ratio of MS_{betw}/MS_{with} will be greater than 1. If, on the other hand, the amount of variation between groups is about the same as there is within groups, then MS_{betw} and MS_{with} will be about the same, and the F ratio will be approximately 1. Thus we want to find large F values in order to reject the null hypothesis. The F-test statistic is then compared with the F critical value so as to make a decision about the null hypothesis. The critical value is found in the F table of Appendix Table 4 as $_{(1-\alpha)}F_{(J-1, N-J)}$. Thus the degrees of freedom are df_{betw} for the numerator of the F ratio and df_{with} for the denominator of the F ratio. The significance test is a one-tailed test so as to be consistent with the alternative hypothesis. The null hypothesis is rejected if the F-test statistic exceeds the F critical value.

If the F-test statistic does exceed the F critical value, and there are more than two groups, then it is not clear where the differences among the means lie. In this case, some multiple comparison procedure may be used to determine where the mean differences are in the groups; this is the topic of chapter 4. When there are only two groups, it is obvious where the mean difference lies, between groups 1 and 2. For the two-group situation, it is also interesting to note that the F and t-test statistics follow the rule of $F = t^2$, for a nondirectional alternative hypothesis in the independent t test. This result also occurred in simple regression analysis and is another example of the case where $F = t^2$ when the numerator degrees of freedom for the F ratio is 1. In an actual ANOVA summary table (shown in the next section), except for the source of variation column, each of the other entries is entered in quantitative form. That is, for example, instead of entering SS_{betw}, we would enter the computed value of the SS_{betw}.

THE ANOVA MODEL

In this section we introduce the analysis of variance linear model, the estimation of parameters of the model, various measures of association between X and Y, and finish up with an example.

The Model

The analysis of variance model is a general linear model much like the simple and multiple regression models of chapters 1 and 2. The one-factor ANOVA fixed-effects model can be written in terms of population parameters as

$$Y_{ij} = \mu + \alpha_j + \varepsilon_{ij}$$

where Y is the observed score on the criterion variable for individual i in group j, μ is the overall or grand population mean (i.e., regardless of group designation), α_j is the group effect for group j, and ε_{ij} is the random residual error for individual i in group j. The residual error can be due to individual differences, measurement error, and/or other factors not under investigation (i.e., other than X). The population group effect and residual error are computed as

$$\alpha_j = \mu_{.j} - \mu$$

and

$$\varepsilon_{ij} = Y_{ij} - \mu_{.j}$$

respectively, and $\mu_{.j}$ is the population mean for group j, where the initial dot subscript indicates we have averaged across all i individuals in group j. That is, the group effect is equal to the difference between the population mean of group j and the overall population mean, whereas the residual error is equal to the difference between an individual's observed score and the population mean of group j. The group effect can also be thought of as the average effect of being a member of a particular group. The residual error in the analysis of variance is similar to the residual error in regression analysis, which in both cases represents that portion of Y not accounted for by X.

There is a special condition of the model, known as a *side condition*, that should be pointed out. For the equal ns or balanced model under consideration here, the side condition is

$$\sum_{j=1}^{J} \alpha_j = 0$$

where the summation is taken over $j = 1, \dots, J$. Thus the sum of the group effects is equal to 0. This implies that if there are any nonzero group effects, the group effects will balance out around zero with some positive and some negative effects. A positive group effect implies a group mean greater than the overall mean, whereas a negative group effect implies a group mean less than the overall mean.

Estimation of the Parameters of the Model

To estimate the parameters of the model μ, α_j, and ε_{ij}, the least squares method of estimation is used, as the least squares method is generally most appropriate for general linear models (i.e., regression, ANOVA). These sample estimates are represented as $\overline{Y}_{..}$, a_j, and e_{ij}, respectively, where the latter two are computed as

[handwritten: sample estimate of group effect (α_j)]

$$a_j = \overline{Y}_{.j} - \overline{Y}_{..}$$

and

$$e_{ij} = Y_{ij} - \overline{Y}_{.j}$$

[handwritten: sample estimate of random/residual error for indiv i in group j (ε_{ij})]

respectively. Note that $\overline{Y}_{..}$ represents the overall sample mean, where the double dot subscript indicates we have averaged across both the i and j subscripts, and that $\overline{Y}_{.j}$ represents the sample mean for group j, where the initial dot subscript indicates we have averaged across all i individuals in group j.

Consider again a question from chapters 1 and 2. Why was least squares selected as the statistical criterion used to arrive at the particular parameter estimates for the ANOVA model? The criterion used in parametric analysis of variance (and in all general linear models) is the least squares criterion. The least squares criterion arrives at those estimates for the parameters of the model (i.e., μ, α_j, and ε_{ij}) such that the sum of the squared residuals is smallest. That is, we want to find the set of estimates that minimizes the sum of the squared residuals. We often refer to this particular method of estimation as *least squares estimation*, because $\overline{Y}_{..}$, a_j, and e_{ij} represent sample estimates of the population parameters μ, α_j, and ε_{ij}, respectively, obtained using the least squares criterion.

Measures of Association

Various measures of the strength of association between X and Y, or of the relative strength of the group effect have been proposed. These include η^2, adjusted η^2 or ε^2, and ω^2. Although tests of significance exist for each of these measures, they are not really necessary because in effect their significance is assessed by the F test in the analysis of variance.

Let us examine briefly each of these measures, all of which assume equal variances across the groups. First η^2 (eta), known as the correlation ratio, represents the proportion of variation in Y explained by the group differences (i.e., by X). We can compute η^2 as

$$\eta^2 = SS_{\text{betw}}/SS_{\text{total}}$$

This statistic is conceptually similar to the R^2 statistic used in regression analysis.

Like R^2, η^2 is a positively biased statistic (i.e., overestimates the association). The bias is most evident for ns less than 30. There is an adjusted version of η^2, known as adjusted η^2 or ε^2, computed by

$$\varepsilon^2 = 1 - (MS_{\text{with}}/MS_{\text{total}})$$

where $MS_{\text{total}} = (SS_{\text{total}}/df_{\text{total}})$. This measure ($\varepsilon^2$) is not affected by sample size and is unrelated to residual error, unfortunately also denoted by ε.

Another measure of the strength of the association between X and Y is the statistic ω^2 (omega), which is also not affected by sample size. We can compute ω^2 as

$$\omega^2 = \frac{SS_{betw} - (J-1)MS_{with}}{SS_{total} + MS_{with}}$$

Thus, a safe recommendation would be to use either ε^2 or ω^2 so that bias resulting from sample size will not be a concern. As far as deciding between ε^2 and ω^2, because ω^2 is more popular and has been extended to more ANOVA models and designs, ω^2 can serve as a nice across-the-board measure of association. For further discussion, see Keppel (1982), O'Grady (1982), and Wilcox (1987). In addition, there is no magical rule of thumb for interpreting the size of these statistics, only that they are scaled theoretically from zero (no association) to one (perfect association). It is up to researchers in the particular substantive area of research to interpret the magnitude of these measures by comparing their results to the results of other similar studies.

An Example

Consider now an example problem used throughout this chapter. Our dependent variable is the number of times a student attends statistics lab during one semester (or quarter), whereas the independent variable is the attractiveness of the lab instructor (assuming each instructor is of the same gender and is equally competent). Thus the researcher is interested in whether the attractiveness of the instructor influences student attendance at the statistics lab. The attractiveness groups are defined as follows: Group 1, unattractive; Group 2, slightly attractive; Group 3, moderately attractive; and Group 4, very attractive. Students were randomly assigned to a group at the beginning of the semester, and attendance was taken by the instructor. There were 8 students in each group for a total of 32. Students could attend a maximum of 30 lab sessions. In Table 3.3 we see the data, sample statistics (means and variances) for each group and overall, and the necessary summation terms for computing the sums of squares.

First we compute the sums of squares as follows

$$SS_{total} = \sum_{i=1}^{n}\sum_{j=1}^{J}Y_{ij}^2 - \frac{\left(\sum_{i=1}^{n}\sum_{j=1}^{J}Y_{ij}\right)^2}{N}$$

$$= 12{,}591 - (346{,}921/32) = 1{,}749.7188$$

$$SS_{betw} = \frac{\sum_{j=1}^{J}\left(\sum_{i=1}^{n}Y_{ij}\right)^2}{n} - \frac{\left(\sum_{i=1}^{n}\sum_{j=1}^{J}Y_{ij}\right)^2}{N}$$

$$= (92{,}639/8) - (346{,}921/32) = 738.5938$$

$$SS_{\text{with}} = \sum_{i=1}^{n} \sum_{j=1}^{J} Y_{ij}^2 - \frac{\sum_{j=1}^{J} \left(\sum_{i=1}^{n} Y_{ij} \right)^2}{n}$$

$$= 12,591 - (92,639/8) = 1,011.1250$$

Next we compute the mean squares as follows:

$$MS_{\text{betw}} = SS_{\text{betw}}/df_{\text{betw}} = 738.5938/3 = 246.1979$$

$$MS_{\text{with}} = SS_{\text{with}}/df_{\text{with}} = 1,011.1250/28 = 36.1116$$

Finally, we compute the F-test statistic as follows:

$$F = MS_{\text{betw}}/MS_{\text{with}} = 246.1979/36.1116 = 6.8177$$

The test statistic is compared to the critical value $_{.95}F_{3,28} = 2.95$ obtained from Appendix Table 4, using the .05 level of significance. The test statistic exceeds the critical value, so we reject H_0 and conclude that the levels of attractiveness are related to mean differ-

TABLE 13.3
Data and Summary Statistics for the Statistics Lab Example

	Number of Statistics Labs Attended by Group			
	Group 1	*Group 2*	*Group 3*	*Group 4*
	15	20	10	30
	10	13	24	22
	12	9	29	26
	8	22	12	20
	21	24	27	29
	7	25	21	28
	13	18	25	25
	3	12	14	15
ΣY_{ij}	89	143	162	195
$\overline{Y}_j$	11.1250	17.8750	20.2500	24.3750
s_j^2	30.1250	35.2679	53.0714	25.9821

$\overline{Y}_{..} = 18.4063 \qquad s_{..}^2 = 56.4425$

$\Sigma_j \, (\Sigma_i \, Y_{ij})^2 = (89)^2 + (143)^2 + (162)^2 + (195)^2 = 92,639$

$\Sigma_i \, \Sigma_j \, Y_{ij}^2 = 12,591$

$(\Sigma_i \, \Sigma_j \, Y_{ij})^2 = (589)^2 = 346,921$

$df_{\text{with}} = 4(8-1) = (n-1)$

28

ences in statistics lab attendance. These results are summarized in the ANOVA summary table as shown in Table 3.4.

Next we estimate the group effects and residual errors. The group effects are estimated as

$$a_1 = \overline{Y}_{.1} - \overline{Y}_{..} = 11.125 - 18.4063 = -7.2813$$

$$a_2 = \overline{Y}_{.2} - \overline{Y}_{..} = 17.875 - 18.4063 = -0.5313$$

$$a_3 = \overline{Y}_{.3} - \overline{Y}_{..} = 20.250 - 18.4063 = +1.8437$$

$$a_4 = \overline{Y}_{.4} - \overline{Y}_{..} = 24.375 - 18.4063 = +5.9687$$

You can then show that the sum of the group effects is equal to zero (i.e., the side condition of $\Sigma \alpha_j = 0$). In chapter 4 we use the same data to determine statistically through the use of multiple comparison procedures which group means, or combination of group means, are different. The residual errors for each individual by group are shown in Table 3.5, and as we can see, the sum of the residual errors is zero (i.e., $\Sigma e_{ij} = 0$), and thus the mean residual error is also zero (i.e., $\overline{e} = 0$).

TABLE 3.4
Analysis of Variance Summary Table—Statistics Lab Example

Source	SS	df	MS	F
Between groups	738.5938	3	246.1979	6.8177[*]
Within groups	1,011.1250	28	36.1116	
Total	1,749.7188	31		

[*]$_{.95}F_{3,28} = 2.95.$

TABLE 3.5
Residuals for the Statistics Lab Example by Group

Group 1	Group 2	Group 3	Group 4
3.875	2.125	−10.250	5.625
−1.125	−4.875	3.750	−2.375
0.875	−8.875	8.750	1.625
−3.125	4.125	−8.250	−4.375
9.875	6.125	6.750	4.625
−4.125	7.125	0.750	3.625
1.875	0.125	4.750	0.625
−8.125	−5.875	−6.250	−9.375

$\Sigma_i \Sigma_j e_{ij} = 0.0000$

Finally we estimate the measures of association. First we calculate the correlation ratio η^2 to be

$$\eta^2 = SS_{betw}/SS_{total} = 738.5938/1{,}749.7188 = .4221$$

Next we calculate ε^2 to be

$$\varepsilon^2 = 1 - (MS_{with}/MS_{total}) = 1 - (36.1116/56.4425) = .3602$$

where $MS_{total} = SS_{total}/df_{total}$.

Lastly we calculate ω^2 to be

$$\omega^2 = \frac{SS_{betw} - (J-1)MS_{with}}{SS_{total} + MS_{with}} = \frac{738.5938 - (3)36.1116}{1749.7188 + 36.1116} = .3529$$

Based on the measures of association, and without knowledge of other research on instructor attractiveness, one would conclude that there is some evidence of a relationship between instructor attractiveness and lab attendance. We can order the instructor group means from unattractive (lowest mean) to very attractive (highest mean); this relationship implies that the more attractive the instructor, the more inclined the student is to attend lab.

Several textbooks have been written about using statistical packages in the ANOVA context. These include Barcikowski (1983; SAS, SPSS), Cody and Smith (1997; SAS), and Levine (1991; SPSS). These references describe how to use the computer to conduct the analysis of variance for many of the designs discussed in this text.

EXPECTED MEAN SQUARES

There is one more theoretical concept, called *expected mean squares*, to introduce in this chapter. The notion of expected mean squares provides the basis for determining what the appropriate error term is when forming an F ratio. In other words, when forming an F ratio to test a certain hypothesis, how do we know which source of variation to use as the error term in the denominator? For instance, in the one-factor fixed-effects ANOVA model, how did we know to use MS_{with} as the error term in testing for differences between the groups?

Before we get into expected mean squares, though, consider the definition of an expected value. An expected value is defined as the average value of a statistic that would be obtained with repeated sampling. Using the sample mean as an example statistic, the expected value of the mean would be the average value of the sample means obtained from an infinite number of samples. The expected value is also known as the mean of the sampling distribution of the statistic under consideration. In this example, the expected value of the mean is the mean of the sampling distribution of the mean.

An expected mean square for a particular source of variation represents the average mean square value for that source obtained if the same study were to be repeated an infinite number of times. For instance, the expected value of mean square between, represented by $E(MS_{betw})$, is the average value of MS_{betw} over repeated samplings. Thus a mean square estimate represents a sample from a population of mean square terms. Sampling distributions and sampling variability are as much a concern in the analysis of variance as they are in other situations.

Let us examine the expected mean squares in more detail. Consider the alternative situations of H_0 actually being true and H_0 actually being false. If H_0 is actually true, such that there are no differences between the population group means, then the expected mean squares are

$$E(MS_{betw}) = \sigma_\varepsilon^2$$

$$E(MS_{with}) = \sigma_\varepsilon^2$$

and thus

$$E(MS_{betw})/E(MS_{with}) = 1$$

where σ_ε^2 is the population variance of the residual errors, and $E(F) = df_{with}/(df_{with} - 2)$. If H_0 is actually true, then each of the J samples actually comes from the same population with mean μ.

If H_0 is actually false, such that there are differences between the population group means, then the expected mean squares are

$$E(MS_{betw}) = \sigma_\varepsilon^2 + \frac{n \sum_{j=1}^{J} \alpha_j^2}{J-1}$$

$$E(MS_{with}) = \sigma_\varepsilon^2$$

and thus

$$E(MS_{betw})/E(MS_{with}) > 1$$

where $E(F) > df_{with}/(df_{with} - 2)$. If H_0 is actually false, then the J samples do actually come from different populations with different means μ_j. There is a difference in $E(MS_{betw})$ between when H_0 is actually true as compared to when H_0 is actually false because in the latter situation there is a second term. The important part of this term is $\Sigma \ \alpha_j^2$, which represents the sum of the squared group effects or mean differences. The larger this term becomes, the larger the F ratio becomes. We also see that $E(MS_{with})$ is the same whether H_0 is actually true or false, and represents a reliable estimate of σ_ε^2. This term is mean free because it does not depend on group mean differences. To cover all possibilities, F can be less than 1 [or actually $df_{with}/(df_{with} - 2)$] due to sampling error, nonrandom samples, and/or assumption violations. For a mathematical proof of the $E(MS)$ terms, see Kirk (1982, pp. 66–71).

In general, the F ratio represents

$$F = \frac{\text{systematic variability} + \text{error variability}}{\text{error variability}}$$

where for the one-factor fixed-effects model, systematic variability is variability between the groups and error variability is variability within the groups. The F ratio is formed in a particular way because we want to isolate the systematic variability in the numerator. For this model, the only appropriate F ratio is $MS_{\text{betw}}/MS_{\text{with}}$, because it does serve to isolate the systematic variability represented by the variability between the groups. Therefore the appropriate error term for testing a particular effect is the mean square that is identical to the mean square of that effect, except that it lacks a term due to the effect of interest. For this model, the appropriate error term to use for testing differences between groups is the mean square that is identical to MS_{betw}, except that it lacks a term due to the between groups effect [i.e., $(n \sum \alpha_j^2)/(J-1)$], which of course is MS_{with}. It should also be noted that the F ratio is a ratio of two independent variance estimates, here being MS_{betw} and MS_{with}.

ASSUMPTIONS AND VIOLATION OF ASSUMPTIONS

In the last two chapters we devoted considerable attention to the assumptions of regression analysis. For the most part, the assumptions of the one-factor analysis of variance are the same; thus we need not devote as much space to the assumptions here. The assumptions are again concerned with the distribution of the residual errors. We also mention those techniques that are appropriate to use in evaluating each assumption.

Random and Independent Errors

The assumption of the distribution of the residual errors is actually a set of three statements about the form of the residual errors, the ε_{ij}. First, the residual errors are assumed to be random and independent errors. That is, there is no systematic pattern about the errors and the errors are independent across individuals. An example of a systematic pattern would be where for one group (e.g., X_1) the residuals tended to be small, whereas for another group (e.g., X_2) the residuals tended to be large. Thus there would be a relationship between X and ε.

The use of independent random samples is crucial in the analysis of variance. The F ratio is very sensitive to violation of the independence assumption in terms of increased likelihood of a Type I and/or Type II error. A violation of the independence assumption may affect the standard errors of the sample means and thus influence any inferences made about those means. One purpose of random assignment of individuals to groups is to achieve independence of the ε_{ij} terms. If each individual is only observed once and individuals are randomly assigned to groups, then the independence assumption is usually met.

The simplest procedure for assessing independence is to examine residual plots by group. If the independence assumption is satisfied, then the residuals should fall into a random display of points for each group. If the assumption is violated, then the residuals will fall into some type of cyclical pattern. As discussed in chapter 1, the Durbin–Watson statistic (1950, 1951, 1971) can be used to test for autocorrelation. Violations of the independence assumption generally occur in the three situations mentioned in chapter 1: time-series data, observations within blocks, or replication. For severe violations of the independence assumption, there is no simple "fix," such as the use of transformations or nonparametric tests (e.g., Scariano and Davenport, 1987). For the example data, a plot of the residuals by group is shown in Fig. 3.2, and there does appear to be a random display of points for each group.

Homogeneity of Variance

According to the second part of the assumption, the distributions of the residual errors for each group have a constant variance, σ_{res}^2. This is again the assumption of *homogeneity of variance* or *homoscedasticity*. In other words, for all values of X (i.e., for each group), the conditional distributions of the residual errors have the same variance. If the first two parts of the assumption are satisfied, then s_{res}^2 is an unbiased estimator of the error variance σ_{res}^2 for each group.

A violation of the homogeneity assumption may lead to bias in the SS_{with} term, as well as an increase in the Type I error rate and possibly an increase in the Type II error rate. The effect of the violation seems to be small with equal or nearly equal ns across the groups (nearly equal ns might be defined as a maximum ratio of largest n_j to smallest n_j of 1.5). There is a more serious problem if the larger ns are associated with the smaller variances (actual $\alpha >$ nominal α, which is a liberal result), or if the larger ns are associated with the larger variances (actual $\alpha <$ nominal α, which is a conservative result).

In a plot of residuals versus each value of X, the consistency of the variance of the conditional residual distributions may be examined. Another method for detecting

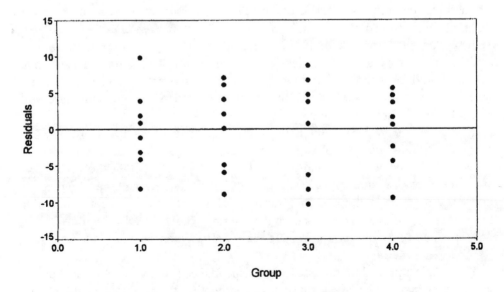

FIG. 3.2   Residual plots by group.

violation of the homogeneity assumption is the use of formal statistical tests. Each of the major statistical packages includes one or more tests for homogeneity of variance. For the example data, the residual plot of Fig. 3.2 shows a similar variance across the groups.

Several solutions are available for dealing with a violation of the homogeneity assumption. These include the use of variance stabilizing transformations (such as $\sqrt{Y}$, $1/Y$, or $\log Y$), or other ANOVA models that are less sensitive to unequal variances, such as the nonparametric equivalent Kruskal–Wallis procedure (see later discussion), or modifications of the parametric F test as described in Wilcox (1987) (such as the Welch, Brown-Forsythe, χ^2, and James tests).

Normality

The third and final part of the assumption states that the conditional distributions of the residual errors are normal in shape. That is, for all values of X, the residual errors are normally distributed. The F test is relatively robust to moderate violations of this assumption (i.e., in terms of Type I and II error rates). A violation of the normality assumption is also less severe with large ns (say more than 25 individuals per group), with equal ns, and/or with population distributions that are homogeneous in shape. Skewness has very little effect on the Type I and II error rates, whereas excessive *leptokurtosis* (i.e., sharp peak) or excessive *platykurtosis* (i.e., flat distribution) does affect these error rates somewhat. Violation of the normality assumption may be a result of outliers discussed in chapter 1. The simplest outlier detection procedure is to look for observations that are more than two or three standard errors from their respective group mean. Formal procedures for the detection of outliers in the analysis of variance context are described in Dunn and Clark (1987).

The following graphical techniques can be used to detect violations of the normality assumption: (a) the frequency distributions of the residuals for each group (through stem-and-leaf plots, box plots, or histograms), (b) the normal probability plot of deviations of each observation from its respective group mean, or (c) a plot of group means versus group variances. There are also several statistical procedures available for the detection of nonnormality (e.g., the Shapiro–Wilk test, 1965).

Transformations can be used to normalize the data, as previously discussed in chapters 1 and 2. For instance, a nonlinear relationship between X and Y may result in violations of the normality and/or homoscedasticity assumptions. In addition, moderate departures from *both* the normality and homogeneity assumptions will have little effect on the Type I and II error rates with equal or nearly equal ns.

In the example data, the residuals shown in Fig. 3.2 appear to be somewhat normal in shape, especially considering the groups have fairly small ns. In addition, the kurtosis statistic for the residuals overall is -1.0191, indicating a slightly platykurtic or flat distribution.

Now we have a complete assumption about the distributions of the residual errors. The distribution of the ε_{ij} for each group consists of random and independent (I) values that are normally (N) distributed with a mean of zero, and a variance of σ_{res}^2. In statistical notation, the assumption is written as $\varepsilon_{ij} \sim NI(0, \sigma_{res}^2)$. The definitive summary of assumption violations in the fixed-effects analysis of variance model is described by Glass et al. (1972).

For the statistics lab example, although sample size is quite small in terms of looking at conditional distributions, it would appear that all of our assumptions have been satisfied. All of the residuals are within two standard errors of zero (where $s_e = 6.0093$), and there does not seem to be any systematic pattern in the residuals. The distribution of the residuals is nearly symmetric and appears to be normal in shape. The more sophisticated statistical software have implemented various procedures to assist the researcher in the evaluation of these assumptions.

A summary of the assumptions and the effects of their violation for the one-factor analysis of variance design is presented in Table 3.6.

THE UNEQUAL *n*s OR UNBALANCED PROCEDURE

Up to this point in the chapter, we have only considered the equal *n*s or balanced case. That is, the model used was where the number of observations in each group was equal. This served to make the formulas and equations much easier to deal with. However, we need not assume that the *n*s must be equal (as some textbooks incorrectly do). This section provides the computational equivalents for the *unequal ns or unbalanced case.*

The minor changes for the unequal *n*s or unbalanced case are as follows. The side condition becomes

$$\sum_{j=1}^{J} n_j \alpha_j = 0$$

The expected value of mean square between, assuming H_0 is false, is

$$E(MS_{\text{betw}}) = \sigma_\varepsilon^2 + \frac{\sum_{j=1}^{J} n_j \alpha_j^2}{J-1}$$

The computational formula for the sum of squares within is

TABLE 3.6
Assumptions and Effects of Violations: One-Factor Design

Assumption	Effect of Assumption Violation
Independence of residuals	Increased likelihood of a Type I and/or Type II error in the F statistic; influences standard errors of means and thus inferences about those means
Homogeneity of variance	Bias in SS_{with}; increased likelihood of a Type I and/or Type II error; small effect with equal or nearly equal *n*s; effect decreases as *n* increases
Normality of residuals	Minimal effect with moderate violation; effect less severe with large *n*s, with equal or nearly equal *n*s, and/or with homogeneously shaped distributions

$$SS_{with} = \sum_{i=1}^{n_j} \sum_{j=1}^{J} Y_{ij}^2 - \sum_{j=1}^{J} \frac{\left(\sum_{i=1}^{n_j} Y_{ij}\right)^2}{n_j}$$

whereas the computational formula for the sum of squares between is

$$SS_{betw} = \sum_{j=1}^{J} \frac{\left(\sum_{i=1}^{n_j} Y_{ij}\right)^2}{n_j} - \frac{\left(\sum_{i=1}^{n_j} \sum_{j=1}^{J} Y_{ij}\right)^2}{N}$$

The remainder of the analysis, assumptions, and so forth are the same as with the equal ns case.

As an example, suppose that we take the statistics lab data and delete the first observation of the first group (i.e., $Y_{11} = 15$ is deleted). This will serve to create an unequal ns or unbalanced case. A summary of the analysis is shown in Table 3.7. As we can see, the procedure works almost the same as in the equal ns case. Most of the major statistical packages automatically deal with the unequal ns case for the one-factor model. As described in chapter 5, things become a bit more complicated for the unequal ns or unbalanced case when there is more than one independent variable (or factor).

THE KRUSKAL–WALLIS ONE-FACTOR ANALYSIS OF VARIANCE

As previously mentioned, there is a nonparametric equivalent to the parametric one-factor fixed-effects ANOVA, the Kruskal–Wallis (1952) one-factor ANOVA. The Kruskal–Wallis test is based on ranked data, makes no normality assumption about the population distributions, yet still assumes equal population variances across the groups (although violation has less of an effect with the Kruskal–Wallis test than with the parametric ANOVA). When the normality assumption is met, or nearly so (i.e., with mild nonnormality), the parametric ANOVA is more powerful than the

TABLE 3.7
Unequal ns Case: Statistics Lab Example

$\Sigma_i \Sigma_j Y_{ij}^2 = 12,366$

$(\Sigma_i \Sigma_j Y_{ij})^2 = (574)^2 = 329,476$

$\Sigma_j [(\Sigma_i Y_{ij})^2/n_j] = (74)^2/7 + (143)^2/8 + (162)^2/8 + (195)^2/8 = 11,372.0357$

$SS_{total} = \Sigma_i \Sigma_j Y_{ij}^2 - (\Sigma_i \Sigma_j Y_{ij})^2/N = 12,366 - (329,476/31) = 1,737.7419$

$SS_{betw} = \Sigma_j [(\Sigma_i Y_{ij})^2/n_j] - (\Sigma_i \Sigma_j Y_{ij})^2/N = 11,372.0357 - (329,476/31) = 743.7776$

$SS_{with} = \Sigma_i \Sigma_j Y_{ij}^2 - \Sigma_j [(\Sigma_i Y_{ij})^2/n_j] = 12,366 - 11,372.0357 = 993.9643$

Source	SS	df	MS	F
Between groups	743.7776	3	247.9259	6.7346*
Within groups	993.9643	27	36.8135	
Total	1,737.7419	30		

*${}_{.95}F_{3,27} = 2.96$.

Kruskal–Wallis test (i.e., less likelihood of a Type II error). Otherwise, the Kruskal–Wallis test is more powerful.

The Kruskal–Wallis procedure is carried out as follows. First, the observations on the dependent measure are ranked, regardless of group assignment. That is, the observations are ranked from first through last, disregarding group membership. The procedure essentially tests whether the average of the ranks are different across the groups such that they are unlikely to represent random samples from the same population. Thus, according to the null hypothesis, the mean rank is the same for each group, whereas for the alternative hypothesis the mean rank is not the same across groups. Note that the average of all of the ranks is equal to

$$\textbf{Mean rank} = (1 + 2 + \dots + N)/N = (N + 1)/2$$

The test statistic is

$$H = \left[\frac{12}{N(N+1)}\right] \sum_{j=1}^{J}\left[\frac{\left(\sum_{i=1}^{n_j} R_{ij}\right)^2}{n_j}\right] - [3(N+1)]$$

where R_{ij} is the overall rank of observation i in group j, n_j is the number of observations in group j, and N is the total number of observations. The value of H is compared to the critical value $_{1-\alpha}\chi^2_{J-1}$. The null hypothesis is rejected if the test statistic H exceeds the χ^2 critical value.

There are two situations of which you may want to be aware. First, the χ^2 critical value is really only appropriate when there are at least three groups and at least five observations per group (i.e., the χ^2 is not an exact sampling distribution of H). For those situations where you are only comparing two groups, the nonparametric equivalent to the independent t test is the Mann–Whitney–Wilcoxon U test.

The second situation is when there are tied ranks. Tied observations affect the sampling distribution of H. Typically a midranks procedure is used, where the rank assigned to a set of tied observations is the average of the available ranks. For example, if there is a two-way tie for the rank of 2, the available ranks would be 2 and 3, and both observations are given a rank of 2.5. Using the midranks procedure results in an overly conservative Kruskal–Wallis test. A correction for ties is commonly used where the test statistic becomes

$$H^* = \frac{H}{C}$$

where the correction factor C is equal to

$$C = 1 - \left[\frac{\sum_{k=1}^{K}(t_k^3 - t_k)}{N^3 - N}\right]$$

and where t_k is the number of ties in a set of ties, and the summation is taken over $k = 1$, ..., K sets of ties. Unless the number of ties is relatively large for any rank, the effect of the correction is minimal.

Using the statistics lab data as an example, rank order the observations, and perform the Kruskal–Wallis analysis of variance. Table 3.8 includes a summary of the preliminary analysis. There are numerous tied ranks, so the test statistic $H*$ is used in order to correct for the ties. First, the uncorrected test statistic H is computed to be

$$H = \left[\frac{12}{N(N+1)} \right] \left[\sum_{j=1}^{J} \frac{\left(\sum_{i=1}^{n_j} R_{ij} \right)^2}{n_j} \right] - [3(N+1)]$$

$$= \left[\frac{12}{32(33)} \right] (9{,}858) - [3(33)] = 13.0224$$

Next the correction for ties C is calculated as

$$C = 1 - \left[\frac{\sum_{k=1}^{K} (t_k^3 - t_k)}{N^3 - N} \right]$$

$$= 1 - \left[\frac{96}{32768 - 32} \right] = .9971$$

Finally the corrected test statistic $H*$ is computed as

$$H* = \frac{H}{C} = \frac{13.0224}{0.9971} = 13.0603$$

The number of observations tied for any one rank is small (i.e., either two or three); thus there is almost no effect of the correction on the test statistic. The test statistic $H*$ is then compared with the critical value $_{.95}\chi^2_3 = 7.81$, from Appendix Table 3, and the result is that H_0 is rejected. Thus the Kruskal–Wallis result agrees with the result of the parametric analysis of variance. This should not be surprising because the normality assumption apparently was met. Thus, in reality, one would probably not even have done the Kruskal–Wallis test for the example data. We merely provide it for purposes of explanation and comparison.

In summary, the Kruskal–Wallis test can be used as an alternative to the parametric one-factor analysis of variance. The Kruskal–Wallis procedure is based on ranked scores on the dependent measure and does not make an assumption of normality. When the data are ordinal and/or nonnormal in shape, we recommend that the Kruskal–Wallis test be considered and, at a minimum, compared to the parametric

TABLE 3.8
Kruskal–Wallis Test: Data and Summary Statistics for the Statistics Lab Example

	Rank of Number of Statistics Labs Attended by Group			
	Group 1	*Group 2*	*Group 3*	*Group 4*
	13.5	16.5	5.5	32
	5.5	10.5	22.5	20.5
	8	4	30.5	27
	3	20.5	8	16.5
	18.5	22.5	28	30.5
	2	25	18.5	29
	10.5	15	25	25
	1	8	12	13.5
$\Sigma_i R_{ij}$	62	122	150	194
$(\Sigma_i R_{ij})^2/n_j$	480.5	1,860.5	2,812.5	4,704.5

	Ties	t_k	$t_k^3 - t_k$	
	5.5	2	6	
	8	3	24	
	10.5	2	6	
	13.5	2	6	
	16.5	2	6	
	18.5	2	6	
	20.5	2	6	
	22.5	2	6	
	25	3	24	
	30.5	2	6	
			$\Sigma = 96$	

ANOVA. When these assumptions are met, the parametric ANOVA is more powerful than the Kruskal–Wallis test, and thus is the preferred method.

THE RELATIONSHIP OF ANOVA TO REGRESSION ANALYSIS

The analysis of variance and regression analysis are both forms of the same general linear model (GLM). In a fashion the analysis of variance can be viewed as a special case of multiple linear regression. In regression analysis, the independent variables are referred to as *predictors*. These regression independent variables are usually *continuous quantitative* variables used to predict the dependent variable. In conducting ANOVA through the regression approach, the independent variables contain information about group membership as there are no predictors in the regression sense. These ANOVA through regression analysis independent variables are *dichotomous qualitative* variables coded to represent group membership, and used to predict the dependent variable. Thus the major distinction between the two models is in the form of the independent variables. There are several methods of coding used to form these grouping-independent variables, including dummy variable coding, indicator variable coding, contrast coding, and reference cell coding. The details of these methods are beyond the scope of this text (cf. Cohen & Cohen, 1983; Keppel & Zedeck, 1989; Kirk, 1982; Myers & Well, 1995; Pedhazur, 1997). Suffice it to say that both the traditional ANOVA and the ANOVA through regression procedures give precisely the same results, as they are both forms of the same general linear model.

SUMMARY

In this chapter, methods involving the comparison of multiple group means for a single independent variable were considered. The chapter began with a look at the characteristics of the analysis of variance, including:

1. Control of the experiment-wise error rate through an omnibus test.
2. One independent variable with two or more fixed levels.
3. Individuals are randomly assigned to groups and then exposed to only one level of the independent variable.
4. The dependent variable is at least measured at the interval level.

Next, a discussion of the theory underlying ANOVA was conducted. Here we examined the concepts of between- and within-groups variability, sources of variation, and partitioning the sums of squares. The ANOVA model was examined and, later on, its relationship to the multiple linear regression model through the general linear model. The expected mean squares concept was also introduced. Some discussion was also devoted to the ANOVA assumptions, their assessment, and how to deal with assumption violations. Finally, the nonparametric Kruskal–Wallis ANOVA model was described for situations where the scores on the dependent variable are ranked. The Kruskal–Wallis test is particularly useful when the normality assumption of the parametric ANOVA is violated. At this point you should have met the following objectives: (a) be able to understand the characteristics and concepts underlying the one-factor ANOVA (balanced, unbalanced, nonparametric), (b) be able to compute and interpret the results of a one-factor ANOVA (balanced, unbalanced, nonparametric), and (c) be able to understand and evaluate the assumptions of the one-factor ANOVA (balanced, unbalanced, nonparametric). Chapter 4 considers a number of multiple comparison procedures for further examination of sets of means. Chapter 5 returns to the analysis of variance and discusses models for which there are more than one independent variable.

PROBLEMS

Conceptual Problems

1. Data for three independent random samples each of size four are analyzed by a one-factor analysis of variance fixed-effects model. If the values of the sample means are all equal, what is the value of MS_{betw}?

    a. 0
    b. 1
    c. 2
    d. 3

2. For a one-factor analysis of variance fixed effects model, which of the following is always true?

    a. $df_{betw} + df_{with} = df_{tot}$
    b. $SS_{betw} + SS_{with} = SS_{tot}$
    c. $MS_{betw} + MS_{with} = MS_{tot}$
    d. all of the above
    e. both a and b

3. Suppose that $n_1 = 19, n_2 = 21$, and $n_3 = 23$. For a one-factor ANOVA, the df_{with} would be

    a. 2
    b. 3
    c. 60
    d. 63

4. In a one-factor ANOVA, H_0 asserts that

    a. all of the population means are equal.
    b. the between-groups variance estimate and the within-groups variance estimate are both estimates of the same population variance.
    c. the within-group sum of squares is equal to the between-group sum of squares.
    d. both a and b

5. In a one-factor ANOVA with two groups and five observations per group, and the sample mean for group 1 = 20 and the sample mean for group 2 = 24, SS_{betw} is equal to

    a. 4
    b. 10
    c. 20
    d. 22
    e. 40

6. Which of the following statements is most appropriate?

    a. When H_0 is true, MS_{betw} overestimates the population residual variance.

    b.   When H_0 is true, MS_{with} overestimates the population residual variance.

    c.   When H_0 is false, MS_{betw} overestimates the population residual variance.

    d.   When H_0 is false, MS_{with} overestimates the population residual variance.

7.   The population means in each of the four groups is 100, the four population variances each equals 16, and the number of observations in each population is 100. In the one-factor fixed effects ANOVA, $E(MS_{betw})$ is equal to

    a.   4

    b.   16

    c.   100

    d.   256

8.   For a one-factor ANOVA comparing three groups with $n = 10$ in each group, the F ratio would have degrees of freedom equal to

    a.   2, 27

    b.   2, 29

    c.   3, 27

    d.   3, 29

9.   Which of the following is not an ANOVA assumption?

    a.   Observations are from random and independent samples.

    b.   The dependent variable is measured on at least the interval scale.

    c.   Populations have equal variances.

    d.   Equal sample sizes are necessary.

10.   If you find an F ratio of 1.0 in a one factor ANOVA, it means that

    a.   between-group variation exceeds within-group variation.

    b.   within-group variation exceeds between-group variation.

    c.   between-group variation is equal to within-group variation.

    d.   between-group variation exceeds total variation.

11.   Suppose students in Grades 7, 8, 9, 10, 11, and 12 were compared on absenteeism. If ANOVA were used rather than multiple t tests, the probability of a Type I error would be less. True or false?

12.   In ANOVA, if H_0 is true, then the expected values of MS_{betw} and MS_{with} are both equal to the population variance. True or false?

13.   In ANOVA, if H_0 is false, then the expected value of MS_{betw} represents the variance due to the treatment and random error. True or false?

14.   Mean square is another name for variance or variance estimate. True or false?

15.   In ANOVA each independent variable is known as a level. True or false?

16. A negative F ratio is impossible. True or false?

17. Suppose that for a one-factor ANOVA with $J = 4$ and $n = 10$ the four sample means all equal 15. I assert that the value of MS_{with} is necessarily equal to zero. Am I correct?

18. With $J = 3$ groups, I assert that if you reject H_0 in the one-factor ANOVA; you will necessarily conclude that all three group means are different. Am I correct?

Computational Problems

1. Complete the following summary table for a one-factor analysis of variance, where there are four groups each with 16 observations and $\alpha = .05$.

Source	SS	df	MS	F	Critical Value and Decision
Between	9.75	—	—	—	—
Within	—	—	—		
Total	18.75	—			

2. A social psychologist wants to determine if type of music has any effect on the number of beers consumed by people in a tavern. Four taverns are selected that have different musical formats. Five people are randomly sampled in each tavern and their beer consumption monitored for 3 hours. Complete the following ANOVA summary table using $\alpha = .05$.

Source	SS	df	MS	F	Critical Value and Decision
Between	—	—	7.52	5.01	—
Within	—	—	—		
Total	—	—			

3. A psychologist would like to know whether the season (fall, winter, spring, summer) has any consistent effect on people's sexual activity. In the middle of each season a psychologist selects a random sample of $n = 25$ students. Each individual is given a sexual activity questionnaire. A one-factor ANOVA was used to analyze these data. Complete the following ANOVA summary table ($\alpha = .05$).

Source	SS	df	MS	F	Critical Value and Decision
Between	—	—	—	5.00	—
Within	960	—	—		
Total	—	—			

4. The following five independent random samples are obtained from five normally distributed populations with equal variances.

Group 1	Group 2	Group 3	Group 4	Group 5
16	16	2	5	7
5	10	9	8	12
11	7	11	1	14
23	12	13	5	16
18	7	10	8	11
12	4	13	11	9
12	23	9	9	19
19	13	9	9	24

Conduct a one-factor analysis of variance to determine if the group means are equal ($\alpha = .05$).

4

MULTIPLE-COMPARISON PROCEDURES

Chapter Outline

1. Concepts of multiple-comparison procedures
   Contrasts
   Planned versus post hoc comparisons
   The Type I error rate
   Orthogonal contrasts
2. Selected multiple-comparison procedures
   Trend analysis
   Planned orthogonal contrasts
   Dunnett's method
   Dunn's method (Bonferroni)
   Scheffé's method
   Fisher's LSD test
   Tukey's HSD test
   The Tukey–Kramer test
   Newman–Keuls procedure
   Duncan's new multiple range test
   Follow-up tests to Kruskal–Wallis

Key Concepts

1. Contrast
2. Simple and complex contrasts
3. Planned and post hoc comparisons
4. Contrast and family-based Type I error rates
5. Orthogonal contrasts

In this chapter our concern is with multiple-comparison procedures that involve comparisons among the group means. Recall from chapter 3 the one-factor analysis of variance where the means from two or more samples were compared. What do we do if the omnibus F test leads us to reject H_0? First, consider the situation where there are only two samples (e.g., assessing the effectiveness of two types of medication) and H_0 has already been rejected in the omnibus test. Why was H_0 rejected? The answer should be obvious. Those two sample means must be significantly different, as there is no other way that the omnibus H_0 could have been rejected (e.g., one type of medication is more effective than the other).

Second, consider the situation where there are more than two samples (e.g., three types of medication) and H_0 has already been rejected in the omnibus test. Why was H_0 rejected? The answer is not so obvious. This situation is one where a *multiple-comparison procedure* (MCP) would be quite informative. Thus for situations where there are at least three groups and the analysis of variance (ANOVA) H_0 has been rejected, some sort of MCP is necessary to determine which means or combination of means are different. Third, consider the situation where the researcher is not even interested in the ANOVA omnibus test, but is only interested in comparisons involving particular means (e.g., certain medications are more effective than a placebo). This is also a situation where an MCP is of value for the evaluation of those specific comparisons.

If the ANOVA omnibus H_0 has been rejected, why not do all possible independent t tests? First return to a similar question from chapter 3. There we asked about doing all possible pairwise independent t tests rather than an ANOVA. The answer there was to do an omnibus F test. The reason was related to the probability of making a Type I error (i.e., α), where the researcher incorrectly rejects a true null hypothesis. Although the α level for each t test can be controlled at a specified nominal level, say .05, what would happen to the overall α level for the set of tests? The overall α level for the set of tests, often called the family-wise Type I error rate, would be larger than the α level for each of the individual t tests. The optimal solution, in terms of maintaining control over our overall α level as well as maximizing power, is to conduct one overall omnibus test. The omnibus test assesses the equality of all of the means simultaneously.

The same concept can be applied to the multiple comparison situation. Rather than doing all possible pairwise independent t tests, where the family-wise error could be quite large, one should use a procedure that controls the family-wise error in some way. This can be done with multiple-comparison procedures. As pointed out later in the chapter, there are two main methods for taking the Type I error rate into account.

This chapter is concerned with several important new concepts, such as the definition of a contrast, planned or a priori versus post hoc comparisons, dealing with the Type I error rate, and orthogonal contrasts. The remainder of the chapter consists of a discussion of the major multiple-comparison procedures, including when and how to apply them. The terms *comparison* and *contrast* are used here synonymously. Also, MCPs are only applicable for comparing levels of an independent variable that are fixed, in other words, for fixed-effects independent variables, and not for random-effects independent variables. Our objectives are that by the end of this chapter, you will be able to (a) understand the concepts underlying the MCPs, (b) select the appropriate MCP for a given research situation, and (c) compute and interpret the results of MCPs.

CONCEPTS OF MULTIPLE-COMPARISON PROCEDURES

This section describes the most important characteristics of the multiple-comparison procedures. We begin by defining a contrast, and then move into planned versus post hoc contrasts, the Type I error rates, and orthogonal contrasts.

Contrasts

A *contrast* is a weighted combination of the means. For example, one might wish to contrast the following means: (a) group 1 with group 2, or (b) the combination of groups 1 and 2 with group 3. Statistically a contrast is defined as

$$\psi = c_1 \mu_{.1} + c_2 \mu_{.2} + \dots + c_J \mu_{.J}$$

where the c_j are known as contrast coefficients (or weights), which are positive and negative values and define a particular contrast ψ_i. In other words, a contrast is simply a particular combination of the group means, depending on which means the researcher is interested in comparing. A contrast can also be written in a more compact (yet more complex) form as

$$\psi_i = \sum_{j=1}^{J} (c_j \mu_{.j})$$

where we see that each group mean $\mu_{.j}$ is weighted (or multiplied) by its contrast coefficient c_j, and then these are summed across the $j = 1, \dots, J$ groups. It should also be noted that to form a legitimate contrast, $\Sigma_j c_j = 0$ for the equal ns or balanced case, and $\Sigma_j (n_j c_j) = 0$ for the unequal ns or unbalanced case.

For example, suppose you want to compare the means of groups 1 and 3 for $J = 4$, and call this contrast 1. The contrast would be written as

$$\psi_1 = \sum_{j=1}^{J} (c_j \mu_{.j})$$

$$= c_1 \mu_{.1} + c_2 \mu_{.2} + \dots + c_4 \mu_{.4}$$

$$= (+1)\mu_{.1} + (0)\mu_{.2} + (-1)\mu_{.3} + (0)\mu_{.4}$$

$$= \mu_{.1} - \mu_{.3}$$

What hypotheses are we testing when we evaluate a contrast? The null and alternate hypotheses of any specific contrast can be written simply as

$$H_0: \psi_i = 0$$

and

$$H_1: \psi_i \neq 0$$

respectively. Thus we are testing whether a particular combination of means, as defined by the contrast coefficients, are different. How does this relate back to the omnibus F test? The null and alternate hypotheses for the omnibus F test can be written in terms of contrasts as

$$H_0: \text{all } \psi_i = 0$$

and

$$H_1: \text{at least one } \psi_i \neq 0$$

respectively. Here the omnibus test is determining whether any contrast that could be formulated for the set of J means is significant.

Before we get into the types of contrasts, let us relate the concept of a contrast back to the concept of a linear model. Recall the equation for the ANOVA linear model from chapter 3 as

$$Y_{ij} = \mu + \alpha_j + \varepsilon_{ij}$$

where $\alpha_j = (\mu_{.j} - \mu)$. As already stated, a contrast can be shown as

$$\psi_i = \sum_{j=1}^{J} (c_j \mu_{.j})$$

Because $\mu_{.j} = (\mu + \alpha_j)$, then a contrast can be rewritten as

$$\psi_i = \sum_{j=1}^{J} [c_j (\mu + \alpha_j)] = \mu \sum_{j=1}^{J} c_j + \sum_{j=1}^{J} (c_j \alpha_j) = \mu(0) + \sum_{j=1}^{J} (c_j \alpha_j) = \sum_{j=1}^{J} (c_j \alpha_j)$$

because $\Sigma_j c_j = 0$ as previously noted. From this reformulation of a contrast, two things are obvious. First, a contrast does not directly involve the overall mean μ; it only directly involves c_j and α_j. Second, a comparison among the means is also a comparison of the group effects, the α_j. Conceptually speaking, it is a comparison of the group effects that we are really interested in.

Contrasts can be divided into simple or pairwise contrasts, and complex or nonpairwise contrasts. A simple or pairwise contrast is a comparison involving only two means. Let us take as an example the situation where there are $J = 3$ groups. There are three possible distinct pairwise contrasts that could be formed: (a) $\mu_{.1} - \mu_{.2} = 0$, (b) $\mu_{.1} - \mu_{.3} = 0$, and (c) $\mu_{.2} - \mu_{.3} = 0$. It should be obvious that a pairwise contrast involving groups 1 and 2 is the same contrast whether it is written as $\mu_{.1} - \mu_{.2} = 0$, or as $\mu_{.2} - \mu_{.1} = 0$. In terms of contrast coefficients, these three contrasts could be written in the form of a table as

	c_1	c_2	c_3
$\psi_1: \mu_{.1} - \mu_{.2} = 0$	+1	−1	0
$\psi_2: \mu_{.1} - \mu_{.3} = 0$	+1	0	−1
$\psi_3: \mu_{.2} - \mu_{.3} = 0$	0	+1	−1

where each contrast is read across the table to determine its contrast coefficients. For example, the first contrast ψ_1 does not involve Group 3 because its contrast coefficient is zero, but does involve Groups 1 and 2 because their contrast coefficients are not zero. The coefficients are $+1$ for Group 1 and -1 for Group 2; consequently we are interested in examining the difference between Groups 1 and 2. Written in long form so that we can see where the contrast coefficients come from, the three contrasts are as follows:

$$\psi_1 = (+1)\mu_{.1} + (-1)\mu_{.2} + (0)\mu_{.3} = \mu_{.1} - \mu_{.2}$$

$$\psi_2 = (+1)\mu_{.1} + (0)\mu_{.2} + (-1)\mu_{.3} = \mu_{.1} - \mu_{.3}$$

$$\psi_3 = (0)\,\mu_{.1} + (+1)\mu_{.2} + (-1)\mu_{.3} = \mu_{.2} - \mu_{.3}$$

An easy way to remember the number of possible unique pairwise contrasts that could be written is $\frac{1}{2}[J(J-1)]$. Thus for $J = 3$ the number of possible unique pairwise contrasts is 3, whereas for $J = 4$ the number of such contrasts is 6.

A complex contrast is a comparison involving more than two means. Continuing with the example of $J = 3$ groups, we might be interested in testing the contrast $\mu_{.1} - \frac{1}{2}(\mu_{.2} + \mu_{.3})$. This contrast is a comparison of the mean for group 1 with the average of the means for groups 2 and 3. In terms of contrast coefficients, this contrast would be written as Written in long form so that we can see where the contrast coefficients come from, this complex contrast is as follows:

$$
\begin{array}{cccc}
 & c_1 & c_2 & c_3 \\
\end{array}
$$

$$\psi_4\colon \mu_{.1} - \tfrac{1}{2}\mu_{.2} - \tfrac{1}{2}\mu_{.3} = 0 \qquad 1 \qquad -\tfrac{1}{2} \qquad -\tfrac{1}{2}$$

$$\psi_4 = (+1)\mu_{.1} + (-\tfrac{1}{2})\mu_{.2} + (-\tfrac{1}{2})\mu_{.3} = \mu_{.1} - \tfrac{1}{2}\mu_{.2} - \tfrac{1}{2}\mu_{.3}$$

The number of unique complex contrasts is greater than $\frac{1}{2}[J(J-1)]$ when J is at least 4; in other words, the number of such contrasts that could be formed is quite large when there are more than three groups. Note that the total number of unique pairwise and complex contrasts is $[1 + \frac{1}{2}(3^J - 1) - 2^J]$ (Keppel, 1982). Thus for $J = 4$, one could form 25 total contrasts.

Many of the multiple comparison procedures are based on the same test statistic, which I introduce here as the "standard t." The standard t ratio for a contrast is given as

$$t = \frac{\psi'}{s_{\psi'}}$$

where $s_{\psi'}$ represents the standard error of the contrast as

$$s_{\psi'} = \sqrt{MS_{\text{error}} \sum_{j=1}^{J}\left(\frac{c_j^2}{n_j}\right)}$$

where the prime (i.e., $'$) indicates that the contrast is based on sample means, and n_j refers to the number of observations in group j. If the number of observations per group is a constant, which is the equal ns or balanced situation, then the general form of the standard error of a contrast can be simplified a bit as

$$s_{\psi'} = \sqrt{\frac{MS_{error}}{n}\left(\sum_{j=1}^{J} c_j^2\right)}$$

For pairwise contrasts the standard error of a contrast can be further simplified into

$$s_{\psi'} = \sqrt{MS_{error}\left(\frac{1}{n_1} + \frac{1}{n_2}\right)}$$

in general, or into the following for the equal ns pairwise case:

$$s_{\psi'} = \sqrt{\frac{2\,MS_{error}}{n}}$$

If you do not want to be bothered with special cases, then just use the general form.

Planned Versus Post Hoc Comparisons

This section examines specific types of contrasts or comparisons. One way of classifying contrasts is whether the contrasts are formulated prior to the research or following a significant omnibus F test. *Planned contrasts* (also known as specific or a priori contrasts) involve particular comparisons that the researcher is interested in examining prior to data collection. These planned contrasts are generally based on theory, previous research, and/or hypotheses. Here the researcher is interested in certain specific contrasts a priori, where the number of such contrasts is usually small. Planned contrasts are done without regard to the result of the omnibus F test. In other words, the researcher is interested in *certain specific contrasts*, but not in the omnibus F test that examines all possible contrasts. In this situation the researcher could care less about the multitude of possible contrasts and need not even examine the F test; but rather the concern is only with a few contrasts of substantive interest. In addition, the researcher may not be as concerned with the family-wise error rate for planned comparisons because only a few of them will actually be carried out. Fewer planned comparisons are usually conducted (due to their specificity) than post hoc comparisons (due to their generality), so planned contrasts generally yield narrower confidence intervals, are more powerful, and have a higher likelihood of a Type I error than post hoc comparisons.

Post hoc contrasts are formulated such that the researcher provides no advance specification of the actual contrasts to be tested. This type of contrast is only done following a significant omnibus F test. *Post hoc* is Latin for "after the fact"; thus this refers to contrasts tested after a significant F in the ANOVA. Here the researcher may want to take the family-wise error rate into account somehow for purposes of overall protection. Post hoc contrasts are also known as unplanned, a posteriori, or postmortem contrasts.

An interesting way of thinking about contrasts was suggested by Rosenthal and Rosnow (1985). They defined a contrast as a method for the researcher to ask focused questions about differences among the group means. The omnibus F test was defined by Rosenthal and Rosnow as a method for the researcher to ask unfocused or diffuse questions about overall differences among the group means. Many statisticians believe that MCPs do not have to be conditional on a significant F ratio. That is, the results of the omnibus F test are not relevant as far as testing contrasts are concerned. Wilcox (1987) pointed out that the derivation of most MCPs is not based on the assumption of a significant F test. In fact, Bernhardson (1975) showed that if you conduct MCPs only after a significant F, the Type I error rate will be smaller (perhaps smaller than the nominal) and there will be less power than if you conduct MCPs without regard to the F test. These preliminary results also suggest that the Scheffé MCP is unaffected by whether or not the F test is carried out.

Although the issue of whether or not a significant F-test is relevant for MCPs is a bit controversial, I follow the path of traditional statisticians where the F ratio is tested and rejected prior to doing post hoc comparisons. However, I do expect that over time many more statisticians will be sympathetic to the ouster of the F ratio as a necessary prelude to multiple comparisons.

The Type I Error Rate

How does the researcher deal with the family-wise Type I error rate? Depending on the multiple comparison procedure selected, one may either set α for each contrast or set α for a family of contrasts. In the former category, α is set for each individual contrast. The MCPs in this category are known as *contrast based*. We designate the α level for contrast-based procedures as α_{pc}, as it represents the *per contrast* Type I error rate. Thus α_{pc} represents the probability of making a Type I error for that particular contrast. In the latter category, α is set for a family or set of contrasts. The MCPs in this category are known as *family-wise*. We designate the α level for family-wise procedures as α_{fw}, as it represents the *family-wise* Type I error rate. Thus α_{fw} represents the probability of making at least one Type I error in the family or set of contrasts. For orthogonal (or independent) contrasts, the following property holds:

$$\alpha_{fw} = 1 - (1 - \alpha_{pc})^c$$

where c is the number of orthogonal contrasts and $c = J - 1$. Orthogonal contrasts are formally defined in the next section. For nonorthogonal contrasts, this property is more complicated in that

$$\alpha_{fw} \leq c\,\alpha_{pc}$$

These properties should be familiar from the discussion in chapter 3, where we were looking at the probability of a Type I error in the use of multiple independent t tests.

Orthogonal Contrasts

Let us begin this section by defining orthogonal contrasts. A set of contrasts is orthogonal if they represent nonredundant and independent (if the usual ANOVA assumptions are met) sources of variation. In other words, the information contained in and the outcome of each contrast is nonredundant and independent (if the assumptions are met). For J groups, you will only be able to construct $J - 1$ orthogonal contrasts. However, more than one set of orthogonal contrasts may exist; although the contrasts within each set are orthogonal, contrasts across such sets may not be orthogonal.

For purposes of simplicity, I would like to first consider the equal ns or balanced case. With equal observations per group, two contrasts are defined to be orthogonal if the products of their contrast coefficients sum to zero. In more formal terms, two contrasts are orthogonal if

$$\sum_{j=1}^{J} (c_j c_{j'}) = c_1 c_{1'} + c_2 c_{2'} + \ldots + c_J c_{J'} = 0$$

where j and j' represent two distinct contrasts. Thus we see that orthogonality depends on the contrast coefficients, the c_j, and not the group means, the μ_j. For example, if $J = 3$, then we can form a set of two orthogonal contrasts. One such set is

	c_1	c_2	c_3
$\psi_1: \mu_{.1} - \mu_{.2} = 0$	$+1$	-1	0
$\psi_2: \tfrac{1}{2}\mu_{.1} + \tfrac{1}{2}\mu_{.2} - \mu_{.3} = 0$	$+\tfrac{1}{2}$	$+\tfrac{1}{2}$	-1
	$+\tfrac{1}{2}$ +	$-\tfrac{1}{2}$ +	$0 = 0$

If the sum of the contrast coefficient products for a set of contrasts is equal to zero, then we define this as a *mutually orthogonal set of contrasts*.

A set of two contrasts that are not orthogonal is

	c_1	c_2	c_3
$\psi_3: \mu_{.1} - \mu_{.2} = 0$	$+1$	-1	0
$\psi_4: \mu_{.1} - \mu_{.3} = 0$	$+1$	0	-1
	$+1$ +	0 +	$0 = +1$

Consider for a moment a situation where there are three groups and we decide to form three pairwise contrasts, knowing full well that they cannot all be mutually orthogonal. The contrasts we form are

	c_1	c_2	c_3
$\psi_1: \mu_{.1} - \mu_{.2} = 0$	$+1$	-1	0
$\psi_2: \mu_{.2} - \mu_{.3} = 0$	0	$+1$	-1
$\psi_3: \mu_{.1} - \mu_{.3} = 0$	$+1$	0	-1

Say that the group means are $\mu_{.1} = 30$, $\mu_{.2} = 24$, and $\mu_{.3} = 20$. We find $\psi_1 = 6$ for the first contrast, and $\psi_2 = 4$ for the second contrast. Because these three contrasts are not orthogonal and contain totally redundant information about the means, $\psi_3 = 10$ for the third contrast by definition. Thus the third contrast contains no information additional to that contained in the first two contrasts.

Finally, consider the unequal ns or unbalanced case. Here, two contrasts are orthogonal if

$$\sum_{j=1}^{J} \left[\frac{(c_j c_{j'})}{n_j} \right] = 0$$

The denominator n_j makes it more difficult to find an orthogonal set of contrasts that is of any interest to the researcher (see Pedhazur, 1997, for an example).

SELECTED MULTIPLE–COMPARISON PROCEDURES

This section considers a selection of multiple-comparison procedures (MCP). These represent the "best" procedures in some sense, in terms of ease of utility, popularity, and control of Type I and II error rates. Other procedures are briefly mentioned. In the interest of consistency, each procedure is discussed in the hypothesis testing situation based on a test statistic. Most, but not all, of the procedures can also be formulated as confidence intervals (sometimes called a *critical difference*), although not discussed here. The first few procedures discussed are for planned comparisons, whereas the remainder of the section is devoted to posthoc comparisons. For each MCP, I describe its major characteristics, present the test statistic with an example using the data from chapter 3, and discuss the pros and cons with respect to other MCPs.

Unless otherwise specified, each MCP makes the standard assumptions of normality, homogeneity of variance, and independence of observations. Some of the procedures do make additional assumptions, as I point out (e.g., equal ns per group). Throughout this section I also assume that a two-tailed alternative hypothesis is of interest, although some of the MCPs can also be used with a one-tailed alternative. In general, the MCPs are fairly robust to nonnormality (but not for extreme cases), but are not as robust to departures from homogeneity of variance or from independence (see Pavur, 1988).

New procedures are seemingly devised each year with no end in sight. Of the topics considered in this text, it is clear that more research is being done on multiple comparisons than any other topic.

Trend Analysis

Trend analysis is a planned MCP useful when the groups represent different quantitative levels of a factor (i.e., an interval or ratio level independent variable). Examples of such a factor might be age, drug dosage, and different amounts of instruction, practice, or trials. Here the researcher is interested in whether the sample means vary with a change in the amount of the independent variable. Recall the concept of polynomials from chapter 2. For purposes of this chapter we define *trend analysis* in the form of orthogonal polynomials, and assume that the levels of the independent variable are equally spaced and the number of observations per group are equal. Although this is the standard case, other cases are briefly discussed at the end of this section.

Orthogonal polynomial contrasts use the standard t-test statistic, which is compared to the critical values of $\pm_{1-\alpha/2}t_{df(error)}$ obtained from the t table in Appendix Table 2. The form of the contrasts is a bit different and requires a bit of discussion. Orthogonal polynomial contrasts incorporate two concepts that we are already familiar with, namely, orthogonal contrasts and polynomial regression. For J groups, there can be only $J-1$ mutually orthogonal contrasts in the set. In polynomial regression, we have terms in the model for a linear trend, a quadratic trend, a cubic trend, and so on. In regression form, the linear model of the sample means would be

$$\overline{Y}_j = b_0 + b_1 X + b_2 X^2 + \ldots + b_{J-1} X^{J-1}$$

where b_0 represents the Y intercept, and the other bs represent the various coefficients for trend (e.g., linear, quadratic, etc.). To see what some of the simpler trends look like, I suggest you return to chapter 2 and examine Fig. 2.3.

Now put those two ideas together. A set of orthogonal contrasts can be formed where the first contrast evaluates a linear trend, the second a quadratic trend, the third a cubic trend, and so forth. Thus for J groups, the highest order polynomial that could be formed is $J-1$. With four groups, for example, one could form a set of orthogonal contrasts to assess linear, quadratic, and cubic trend. Trend analysis provides another connection between the analysis of variance and regression analysis.

You may be wondering just how these contrasts are formed. For $J=4$ groups, the contrast coefficients for the linear, quadratic, and cubic trends are

	c_1	c_2	c_3	c_4
ψ_{linear}	-3	-1	$+1$	$+3$
$\psi_{quadratic}$	$+1$	-1	-1	$+1$
ψ_{cubic}	-1	$+3$	-3	$+1$

where the contrasts can be written out as

$$\psi_{linear} = (-3)\mu_{.1} + (-1)\mu_{.2} + (+1)\mu_{.3} + (+3)\mu_{.4}$$
$$\psi_{quadratic} = (+1)\mu_{.1} + (-1)\mu_{.2} + (-1)\mu_{.3} + (+1)\mu_{.4}$$
$$\psi_{cubic} = (-1)\mu_{.1} + (+3)\mu_{.2} + (-3)\mu_{.3} + (+1)\mu_{.4}$$

These contrast coefficients can be found in Appendix Table 6, for a number of different values of J. If you look in the table of contrast coefficients for values of J greater than 6, you see that the coefficients for the higher-order polynomials are not included. As an example, for $J=7$, coefficients only up through a quintic trend are included. Although they could easily be derived and tested, these higher order polynomials are usually not of interest to the researcher. In fact, it is rare to find anyone interested in polynomials beyond the cubic because they are difficult to understand and interpret (although statistically sophisticated, they say little to the applied researcher). The contrasts are typically tested sequentially beginning with the linear trend and proceeding to higher order trends.

It may help you to remember that the degree of the polynomial is the number of times the sign changes for that particular contrast. In the linear contrast presented earlier, this is a first-degree polynomial (i.e., using X^1 or X), and the signs change only once. In the quadratic contrast, which is a second-degree polynomial (i.e., using X^2), the signs change twice. In the cubic contrast, the order is the third-degree (i.e., using X^3), where the signs change three times.

Using again the example data on the attractiveness of the lab instructors from chapter 3, let us test for linear, quadratic, and cubic trends. Trend analysis may be relevant for this data because the groups do represent different quantitative levels of an attractiveness factor (whether interval level or not is a question for attractiveness researchers). Because $J = 4$, we can use the contrast coefficients given previously. The following are the computations:

Critical values:

$$\pm_{1 - \alpha/2} \, t_{\text{df(error)}} = \pm_{.975} t_{28} = \pm 2.048$$

Standard error for linear trend:

$$s_\psi' = \sqrt{MS_{\text{error}} \sum_{j=1}^{J} \left(\frac{c_j^2}{n_j} \right)} = \sqrt{36.1116(9/8 + 1/8 + 1/8 + 9/8)} = 9.5015$$

Standard error for quadratic trend:

$$s_\psi' = \sqrt{MS_{\text{error}} \sum_{j=1}^{J} \left(\frac{c_j^2}{n_j} \right)} = \sqrt{36.1116(1/8 + 1/8 + 1/8 + 1/8)} = 4.2492$$

Standard error for cubic trend:

$$s_\psi' = \sqrt{MS_{\text{error}} \sum_{j=1}^{J} \left(\frac{c_j^2}{n_j} \right)} = \sqrt{36.1116(1/8 + 9/8 + 9/8 + 1/8)} = 9.5015$$

Test statistics:

$$t_{\text{linear}} = \frac{-3\overline{Y}_{.1} - 1\overline{Y}_{.2} + 1\overline{Y}_{.3} + 3\overline{Y}_{.4}}{s_{\psi'}}$$

$$= \frac{-3(11.1250) - 1(17.8750) + 1(20.2500) + 3(24.3750)}{9.5015} = 4.4335 \text{ (significant)}$$

$$t_{\text{quadratic}} = \frac{+1\overline{Y}_{.1} - 1\overline{Y}_{.2} - 1\overline{Y}_{.3} + 1\overline{Y}_{.4}}{s_{\psi'}}$$

$$= \frac{+1(11.1250) - 1(17.8750) - 1(20.2500) + 1(24.3750)}{4.2492} = -0.6178 \text{ (nonsignificant)}$$

$$t_{cubic} = \frac{-1\overline{Y}_{.1} + 3\overline{Y}_{.2} - 3\overline{Y}_{.3} + 1\overline{Y}_{.4}}{s_{\psi'}}$$

$$= \frac{-1(11.1250) + 3(17.8750) - 3(20.2500) + 1(24.3750)}{9.5015} = 0.6446 \text{ (nonsignificant)}$$

Thus we see that there is a significant linear trend in the means, but no higher order trend. This should not be surprising when we plot the means, as shown in Fig. 4.1. It is obvious from the figure that there is a very strong linear trend, and that is about it. In other words, there is a steady increase in mean attendance as the level of attractiveness of the instructor increases. Always plot the means so that you can interpret the results of the contrasts.

Let me make some final points about orthogonal polynomial contrasts. First, as in regression analysis, be particularly careful about extrapolating beyond the range of the levels investigated. The trend may or may not be the same outside of this range; given only those sample means, we have no way of knowing what the trend is outside of the range. We do not have to be quite as careful with interpolating between two levels of the independent variable because some supporting data do exist. Again, these points have already been made in the regression chapters and apply in this case as well. Second, what happens in the unequal ns or unbalanced case? In this case it becomes difficult to formulate a set of orthogonal contrasts that make any sense to the researcher. See the discussion in the next section on planned orthogonal contrasts, as well as Kirk (1982). Third, what happens when the levels are not equally spaced? The obvious solution is to use contrast coefficients that are not equally spaced. For further discussion, see Kirk (1982).

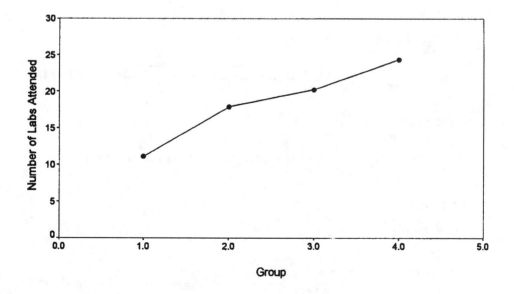

FIG. 4.1 Plot of group means.

Planned Orthogonal Contrasts

Planned orthogonal contrasts (POC) are an MCP where the contrasts are defined ahead of time by the researcher (i.e., planned) and the set of contrasts are mutually orthogonal. The POC method is a contrast-based procedure where the researcher is not concerned with control of the family-wise error rate. The set of contrasts are mutually orthogonal, so the number of contrasts should be small.

Computationally, planned orthogonal contrasts use the standard t-test statistic that is compared to the critical values of $\pm_{1-\alpha/2}t_{df(error)}$ obtained from the t table in Appendix Table 2. Using the example data set from chapter 3, let us find a set of orthogonal contrasts and complete the computations. Since $J = 4$, we can find at most a set of three (or $J - 1$) mutually orthogonal contrasts. One orthogonal set that seems reasonable for these data is

	c_1	c_2	c_3	c_4
ψ_1:	$+\frac{1}{2}$	$+\frac{1}{2}$	$-\frac{1}{2}$	$-\frac{1}{2}$
ψ_2:	$+1$	-1	0	0
ψ_3:	0	0	$+1$	-1

Show yourself that these contrasts are mutually orthogonal (i.e., the following pairs of contrasts are orthogonal: 1 and 2; 1 and 3; and 2 and 3).

Here we see that the first contrast compares the average of the two least attractive groups with the average of the two most attractive groups, the second contrast compares the two least attractive groups with one another, and the third contrast compares the two most attractive groups with one another. Note that the design is balanced (i.e., the equal ns case). The following are the computations:

Critical values:

$$\pm_{1-\alpha/2}t_{df(error)} = \pm_{.975}t_{28} = \pm2.048$$

Standard error for contrast 1:

$$s_{\psi}' = \sqrt{MS_{error} \sum_{j=1}^{J}\left(\frac{c_j^2}{n_j}\right)} = \sqrt{36.1116(.25/8 + .25/8 + .25/8 + .25/8)} = 2.2146$$

Standard error for contrasts 2 and 3:

$$s_{\psi}' = \sqrt{MS_{error}\left[\frac{1}{n_j} + \frac{1}{n_{j'}}\right]} = \sqrt{36.1116(1/8 + 1/8)} = 3.0046$$

Test statistics:

$$t_1 = \frac{+\frac{1}{2}\,\overline{Y}_{.1} + \frac{1}{2}\,\overline{Y}_{.2} - \frac{1}{2}\,\overline{Y}_{.3} - \frac{1}{2}\,\overline{Y}_{.4}}{s_{\psi'}}$$

$$= \frac{+\frac{1}{2}(11.1250) + \frac{1}{2}(17.8750) - \frac{1}{2}(20.2500) - \frac{1}{2}(24.3750)}{2.1246} = -3.6772 \text{ (significant)}$$

$$t_2 = \frac{\overline{Y}_{.1} - \overline{Y}_{.2}}{s_{\psi'}} = \frac{11.1250 - 17.8750}{3.0046} = -2.2466 \text{ (significant)}$$

$$t_3 = \frac{\overline{Y}_{.3} - \overline{Y}_{.4}}{s_{\psi'}} = \frac{20.2500 - 24.3750}{3.0046} = -1.3729 \text{ (nonsignificant)}$$

These results indicate that the less attractive groups have significantly lower attendance means than the more attractive groups, the two less attractive groups are different from one another, but the two more attractive groups are not different.

There is a practical problem with this procedure because the contrasts of interest may not be orthogonal, or the researcher may not be interested in all of the contrasts of an orthogonal set. Another problem already mentioned occurs when the design is unbalanced, where an orthogonal set of contrasts may be constructed at the expense of meaningful contrasts. My advice is simple. If the contrasts you are interested in are not orthogonal, then use another MCP. If you are not interested in all of the contrasts of an orthogonal set, then use another MCP. If your design is not balanced and the orthogonal contrasts formed are not meaningful, then use another MCP. In each case, if you desire a planned MCP, then I recommend either the Dunnett or Dunn (Bonferroni) procedure.

We defined the POC as a contrast-based procedure. One could also consider an alternative family-wise method where the α_{pc} level is divided among the contrasts in the set. This procedure is defined by $\alpha_{pc} = \alpha_{fw}/c$, where c is the number of orthogonal contrasts in the set (i.e., $c = J - 1$). As shown earlier, this borrows a concept from the Dunn (Bonferroni) procedure. There is some debate about using POC with this alternative definition (e.g., Games, 1971; Myers, 1979). If the variances are not equal across the groups, several approximate solutions have been proposed that take the individual group variance estimators into account (see Kirk, 1982).

Dunnett's Method

A third method of planned comparisons is due to Dunnett (1955). It is designed to test pairwise contrasts where a reference group (e.g., a control or baseline group) is compared to each of the other $J - 1$ groups. Thus a family of prespecified pairwise contrasts is to be evaluated. The Dunnett method is a family-wise MCP and is slightly more powerful than the Dunn procedure (another planned family-wise MCP). The test statistic is the standard t except that the standard error is simplified as follows:

$$s_{\psi'} = \sqrt{MS_{error}\left(\frac{1}{n_j} + \frac{1}{n_c}\right)}$$

where c is the reference group and j is the group to which it is being compared. The test statistic is compared to the critical values $\pm_{1-\alpha/2}\, t_{df(error),\, J-1}$ obtained from the Dunnett table located in Appendix Table 7.

Using the example data set, compare the unattractive group (used as a reference or baseline group) to each of the other three groups. The following are the computations:

Critical values:

$$\pm_{1-\alpha/2}\,t_{df(error),J-1} = \pm_{.975}t_{28,3} \approx \pm\,2.48$$

Standard error:

$$s_{\psi'} = \sqrt{MS_{error}\left(\frac{1}{n_j} + \frac{1}{n_c}\right)} = \sqrt{36.1116(1/8 + 1/8)} = 3.0046$$

Test statistics:

$$t_1 = \frac{\overline{Y}_{.1} - \overline{Y}_{.2}}{s_{\psi'}} = \frac{11.1250 - 17.8750}{3.0046} = -2.2466 \text{ (nonsignificant)}$$

$$t_2 = \frac{\overline{Y}_{.1} - \overline{Y}_{.3}}{s_{\psi'}} = \frac{11.1250 - 20.2500}{3.0046} = -3.0370 \text{ (significant)}$$

$$t_3 = \frac{\overline{Y}_{.1} - \overline{Y}_{.4}}{s_{\psi'}} = \frac{11.1250 - 24.3750}{3.0046} = -4.4099 \text{ (significant)}$$

Here we see that the second group (i.e., slightly attractive) is not significantly different from the baseline group (i.e., unattractive), but the third and fourth more attractive groups do differ from the baseline.

If the variance of the reference group is different from the variances of the other $J-1$ groups, a modification of this method is described in Dunnett (1964). For related procedures that are less sensitive to unequal group variances, see Wilcox (1987).

Dunn's Method (Bonferroni)

The Dunn (1961) procedure (commonly attributed to Dunn as the developer is unknown), also known as the Bonferroni procedure (because it is based on the Bonferroni inequality), is a planned family-wise MCP. It is designed to test either pairwise or complex contrasts for balanced or unbalanced designs. Thus this MCP is very flexible and may be used to test any planned contrast of interest. Dunn's method uses the standard t-test statistic with one important exception. The α level is split up among the set of planned contrasts. Typically the per contrast α level is set at α/c, where c is the number of contrasts. That is, $\alpha_{pc} = \alpha_{fw}/c$. According to this rationale, the family-wise Type I error rate will be maintained at α. For example, if $\alpha_{fw} = .05$ is desired and there are five contrasts to be tested, then each contrast would be tested at the .01 level of significance. Rosenthal and Rosnow (1985) reminded us that α need not be distributed equally among the set of contrasts, as long as the sum of the individual α_{pc} terms is equal to α_{fw}.

Computationally, the Dunn method uses the standard t-test statistic, which is compared to the critical values of $\pm_{1-\alpha/c}t_{df(error)}$ for a two-tailed test obtained from the table in

Appendix Table 8. The table takes the number of contrasts into account without requiring you to split up the α. Using the example data set from chapter 3, for comparison purposes let us test the same set of three orthogonal contrasts that we evaluated with the POC method. These contrasts are

	c_1	c_2	c_3	c_4
ψ_1:	$+\frac{1}{2}$	$+\frac{1}{2}$	$-\frac{1}{2}$	$-\frac{1}{2}$
ψ_2:	$+1$	-1	0	0
ψ_3:	0	0	$+1$	-1

The following are the computations:

Critical values:

$$\pm_{1-\alpha/c}\, t \;_{df(error)} = \pm_{1-.05/3} t_{28} = \pm 2.539$$

Standard error for contrast 1:

$$s_\psi' = \sqrt{MS_{error}\sum_{j=1}^{J}\left(\frac{c_j^2}{n_j}\right)} = \sqrt{36.1116(.25/8+.25/8+.25/8+.25/8)} = 2.1246$$

Standard error for contrasts 2 and 3:

$$s_\psi' = \sqrt{MS_{error}\left[\frac{1}{n_j}+\frac{1}{n_{j'}}\right]} = \sqrt{36.1116(1/8+1/8)} = 3.0046$$

Test statistics:

$$t_1 = \frac{+\frac{1}{2}\,\bar{Y}_{.1}+\frac{1}{2}\,\bar{Y}_{.2}-\frac{1}{2}\,\bar{Y}_{.3}-\frac{1}{2}\,\bar{Y}_{.4}}{s_{\psi'}}$$

$$= \frac{+\frac{1}{2}\,(11.1250)+\frac{1}{2}\,(17.8750)-\frac{1}{2}\,(20.2500)-\frac{1}{2}\,(24.3750)}{2.1246} = -3.6772 \text{ (significant)}$$

$$t_2 = \frac{\bar{Y}_{.1}-\bar{Y}_{.2}}{s_{\psi'}} = \frac{11.1250-17.8750}{3.0046} = -2.2466 \text{ (nonsignificant)}$$

$$t_3 = \frac{\bar{Y}_{.3}-\bar{Y}_{.4}}{s_{\psi'}} = \frac{20.2500-24.3750}{3.0046} = -1.3729 \text{ (nonsignificant)}$$

For this set of contrasts then, we see the same results as were obtained via the POC procedure with the exception of contrast 2, which is now nonsignificant. The reason for this difference lies in the critical values used, which were ± 2.048 for the POC method and ± 2.539 for the Dunn method. Here we see the conservative nature of the

Dunn procedure because the critical value is larger than with the POC method, thus making it a bit more difficult to reject H_0.

The Dunn procedure is slightly conservative (i.e., not as powerful) in that the true α_{fw} may be less than the specified nominal α level. A less conservative (i.e., more powerful) modification is known as the Dunn–Sidak procedure (Dunn, 1974; Sidák, 1967) and uses slightly different critical values. For more information see Kirk (1982) and Wilcox (1987).

Scheffé's Method

Another early MCP due to Scheffé (1953) is quite versatile. The Scheffé procedure can be used for any possible type of comparison, orthogonal or nonorthogonal, pairwise or complex, planned or post hoc, where the family-wise error rate is controlled. In general, the Scheffé method is usually recommended for post hoc comparisons or when the number of a priori contrasts is large. The Scheffé method is so general that the tests are quite conservative (i.e., less powerful), particularly for the pairwise contrasts. This is so because the family of contrasts for the Scheffé method consists of all possible linear comparisons. Thus, to control the Type I error rate for such a large family, the procedure has to be conservative.

The Scheffé procedure is the only MCP that is necessarily consistent with the results of the F ratio in the analysis of variance. If the F is significant, then at least one contrast from the family of linear contrasts, when tested by the Scheffé method, will also be significant. Do not forget, however, that this family is infinitely large and you may not even be interested in the significant contrasts. If the F is not significant, then none of the contrasts in the family, when tested by the Scheffé method, will be significant.

The test statistic for the Scheffé method is the standard t again. This is compared to the critical value $\sqrt{(J-1)_{1-\alpha} F_{J-1, df (error)}}$ taken from the F table in Appendix Table 4. In other words, the square root of the F critical value is adjusted by $J-1$, which serves to increase the Scheffé critical value and make the procedure a more conservative one.

Consider a few example contrasts with the Scheffé method. Using the example data set from chapter 3, for comparison purposes test the same set of three orthogonal contrasts that were evaluated with the POC method. These contrasts are again as follows:

	c_1	c_2	c_3	c_4
ψ_1:	$+\frac{1}{2}$	$+\frac{1}{2}$	$-\frac{1}{2}$	$-\frac{1}{2}$
ψ_2:	$+1$	-1	0	0
ψ_3:	0	0	$+1$	-1

The following are the computations:

Critical value:

$$\sqrt{(J-1)_{1-\alpha} F_{J-1, df\,(error)}} = \sqrt{(3)_{.95} F_{3, 28}} = \sqrt{(3)2.95} = 2.97$$

Standard error for contrast 1:

$$s_{\psi'} = \sqrt{MS_{error} \sum_{j=1}^{J} \left(\frac{c_j^2}{n_j} \right)} = \sqrt{36.1116(.25\,/\,8 + .25\,/\,8 + .25\,/\,8 + .25\,/\,8)} = 2.1246$$

Standard error for contrasts 2 and 3:

$$s_{\psi'} = \sqrt{MS_{error} \left[\frac{1}{n_j} + \frac{1}{n_{j'}} \right]} = \sqrt{36.1116(1\,/\,8 + 1\,/\,8)} = 3.0046$$

Test statistics:

$$t_1 = \frac{+\,{}^1\!/_2\,\overline{Y}_{.1} + {}^1\!/_2\,\overline{Y}_{.2} - {}^1\!/_2\,\overline{Y}_{.3} - {}^1\!/_2\,\overline{Y}_{.4}}{s_{\psi'}}$$

$$= \frac{+\,{}^1\!/_2\,(11.1250) + {}^1\!/_2\,(17.8750) - {}^1\!/_2\,(20.2500) - {}^1\!/_2\,(24.3750)}{2.1246} = -3.6772 \text{ (significant)}$$

$$t_2 = \frac{\overline{Y}_{.1} - \overline{Y}_{.2}}{s_{\psi'}} = \frac{11.1250 - 17.8750}{3.0046} = -2.2466 \text{ (nonsignificant)}$$

$$t_3 = \frac{\overline{Y}_{.3} - \overline{Y}_{.4}}{s_{\psi'}} = \frac{20.2500 - 24.3750}{3.0046} = -1.3729 \text{ (nonsignificant)}$$

Using the Scheffé method, these results are precisely the same as those obtained via the Dunn procedure. There is somewhat of a difference in the critical values, which were 2.97 for the Scheffé method, 2.539 for the Dunn method, and 2.048 for the POC method. Here we see that the Scheffé procedure is even more conservative than the Dunn procedure, thus making it a bit more difficult to reject H_0.

For situations where the group variances are unequal, a modification of the Scheffé method that is less sensitive to unequal variances has been proposed by Brown and Forsythe (1974). Kaiser and Bowden (1983) found that the Brown–Forsythe procedure may cause the actual α level to exceed the nominal α level. They suggest a modification that seems to be better in that regard. For more information on these modifications, see Kirk (1982) and Wilcox (1987).

Fisher's LSD Test

Fisher's (1949) least significant difference (LSD) test, also known as the protected t test, was the first MCP developed and is a pairwise post hoc procedure. After a significant F ratio in the analysis of variance, all (or perhaps some) pairwise t tests are examined. Here the standard t-test statistic is compared with the critical values of $\pm_{1-\alpha/2} t_{df(error)}$. There is a problem with this MCP because the family-wise error rate increases as the number of contrasts increases. The only control or protection the researcher has is the fact that the F ratio must be significant. There is less control of the Type I error rate here than with any other MCP. For this reason, Fisher's LSD procedure is not recommended and is not discussed further.

Tukey's HSD Test

Tukey's honestly significant difference (HSD) test is one of the most popular post hoc MCPs. Developed by John Tukey in 1953, the HSD test is a family-wise procedure and is most appropriate for considering all pairwise contrasts with equal ns per group (i.e., a balanced design). The next section discusses modifications for the unequal ns case. In the situation where complex contrasts are necessary, the HSD is not recommended.

The HSD test is sometimes referred to as the *studentized range test* because it is based on the sampling distribution of the studentized range statistic developed by William Sealy Gossett (he was forced to use the pseudonym "Student" by his employer, the Guinness brewery). For one approach, the first step in the analysis is to rank order the means from largest ($\overline{Y}_{.1}$) to smallest ($\overline{Y}_{.J}$). The test statistic, or studentized range statistic, is

$$q_i = \frac{\overline{Y}_{.j} - \overline{Y}_{.j'}}{s_\psi'}$$

where

$$s_\psi' = \sqrt{\frac{MS_{error}}{n}}$$

and i identifies the specific contrast, j and j' designate the two means to be compared, and n represents the number of observations per group (do not forget that equal ns per group is assumed). The test statistic is compared to the critical value $_{1-\alpha}q_{df(error),J}$, where df_{error} is equal to $J(n-1)$. A table for these critical values is given in Appendix Table 9.

The first contrast involves a test of the largest pairwise difference in the set of J means (q_1). If these means are not significantly different, then the analysis stops because no other pairwise difference would be significant. If these means are different, then we proceed to test the second pairwise difference involving group 1 (i.e., q_2). Contrasts involving the largest mean are continued until a nonsignificant difference is found. Then the analysis picks up with the second largest mean and compares it with the smallest mean. Contrasts involving the second largest mean are continued until a nonsignificant difference is detected. The analysis continues with the next largest mean and the smallest mean, and so on, until it is obvious that no other pairwise contrast would be significant.

Finally, consider an example using the HSD procedure with the attractiveness data. The following are the computations:

Critical value:

$$_{1-\alpha}q_{df(error),J} = {_{.95}}q_{28,4} \approx \mathbf{3.87}$$

Standard error:

$$s_{\psi}' = \sqrt{\frac{MS_{\text{error}}}{n}} = \sqrt{\frac{36.1116}{8}} = 2.1246$$

Test statistics:

$$q_1 = \frac{\overline{Y}_{.4} - \overline{Y}_{.1}}{s_{\psi'}} = \frac{24.3750 - 11.1250}{2.1246} = 6.2365 \text{ (significant)}$$

$$q_2 = \frac{\overline{Y}_{.4} - \overline{Y}_{.2}}{s_{\psi'}} = \frac{24.3750 - 17.8750}{2.1246} = 3.0594 \text{ (nonsignificant)}$$

$$q_3 = \frac{\overline{Y}_{.3} - \overline{Y}_{.1}}{s_{\psi'}} = \frac{20.2500 - 11.1250}{2.1246} = 4.2949 \text{ (significant)}$$

$$q_4 = \frac{\overline{Y}_{.3} - \overline{Y}_{.2}}{s_{\psi'}} = \frac{20.2500 - 17.8750}{2.1246} = 1.1179 \text{ (nonsignificant)}$$

$$q_5 = \frac{\overline{Y}_{.2} - \overline{Y}_{.1}}{s_{\psi'}} = \frac{17.8750 - 11.1250}{2.1246} = 3.1771 \text{ (nonsignificant)}$$

These results indicate that the group means are significantly different for Groups 1 and 4, and for Groups 1 and 3. Just for the heck of it, let us examine the final possible pairwise contrast involving Groups 3 and 4. However, we already know from the results of previous contrasts that these means cannot possibly be significantly different. The results for this contrast are as follows:

$$q_6 = \frac{\overline{Y}_{.4} - \overline{Y}_{.3}}{s_{\psi'}} = \frac{24.3750 - 20.2500}{2.1246} = 1.9415 \text{ (nonsignificant)}$$

Occasionally, researchers need to summarize the results of their pairwise comparisons. Table 4.1 shows the results of Tukey's HSD contrasts for the example data. For ease of interpretation, the means are ordered from lowest to highest. The first row consists of the results for those contrasts that involve Group 1. Thus the mean for Group 1

TABLE 4.1
Test Statistics and Results of Tukey HSD Contrasts

	Group 1	Group 2	Group 3	Group 4
Group 1 (mean = 11.1250)	—	3.1771	4.2949*	6.2365*
Group 2 (mean = 17.8750)		—	1.1179	3.0594
Group 3 (mean = 20.2500)			—	1.9415
Group 4 (mean = 24.3750)				—

[*]$p < .05$; $_{.95}q_{28,4} \approx 3.87$.

is different from those of Groups 3 and 4 only. None of the other pairwise contrasts were shown to be significant.

The HSD test is more conservative than the Newman–Keuls procedure, in that it has a lower family-wise Type I error rate, a higher Type II error rate, and therefore less power. The HSD procedure is more powerful than the Dunn and Scheffé comparisons for testing all possible pairwise contrasts, but for less than all possible pairwise contrasts the Dunn is more powerful than the HSD or Scheffé MCPs. The HSD test provides better control over the Type I error rate than either the Dunn or the Dunn–Sidak procedure as the family-wise error rate is exactly held at α. The HSD test is more powerful than the Scheffé test for pairwise contrasts and, occasionally, even more powerful for complex contrasts (Spjotvoll & Stoline, 1973). The HSD technique is the preferred MCP as a pairwise method in the equal ns situation (e.g., Hochberg & Tamhane, 1987), even over the Newman–Keuls procedure, which does not have as adequate control over the family-wise error rate as does the HSD test. The HSD test is reasonably robust to nonnormality, but not in extreme cases and not as robust as the Scheffé MCP.

The Tukey–Kramer Test

There are several alternatives to the HSD for the unequal ns case. These include the Tukey–Kramer modification (Tukey, 1953; Kramer, 1956), as well as other modifications. At this time the Tukey–Kramer MCP seems to be optimal in terms of computational simplicity as well as having the narrowest interval width.

The Tukey–Kramer test statistic is the same as the Tukey HSD except that

$$s_{\psi'} = \sqrt{MS_{\text{error}}\left[\frac{1}{2}\left(\frac{1}{n_1}+\frac{1}{n_2}\right)\right]}$$

The critical value is the same as with the Tukey HSD procedure.

When the group variances are unequal or both the variances and the ns are unequal, several procedures are available. These include the Games–Howell procedure (1976), Dunnett's T3 and C procedures (1980), and the Tamhane procedure (1979). For further details on these methods, see Kirk (1982) and Wilcox (1987).

Newman–Keuls Procedure

The Newman–Keuls (NK) MCP (Newman, 1939; rediscovered by Keuls, 1952) is quite similar to Tukey's HSD test with several notable exceptions. The NK is based on a per contrast Type I error rate rather than the family-wise error rate of the HSD test. Thus the NK procedure is a contrast-based method. The NK procedure is more liberal than the HSD test as it has a higher family-wise error rate, a lower Type II error rate, and therefore more power. The NK and HSD are post hoc procedures used for testing pairwise contrasts with equal observations per group.

The procedure follows the HSD exactly except in terms of the critical values used. The NK critical value used is $_{1-\alpha}q_{df(\text{error}),r}$, where r is equal to the number of means in the range of means being compared. Thus the critical value varies depending on the contrast. For a study consisting of 10 means, a contrast involving the largest and smallest means would have 10 as a value of r, whereas a contrast involving the largest and second smallest means would have 9 as a value of r. As you can see from the table of critical values shown in Appendix Table 9, when the number of means in the set decreases, so too does the critical value. Everything else is exactly the same as the HSD test.

Let us use the example data to illustrate the NK procedure. The results are shown here: Critical values:

$$_{1-\alpha}q_{df(\text{error}),r} = {}_{.95}q_{28,4} \approx 3.87$$

$$_{1-\alpha}q_{df(\text{error}),r} = {}_{.95}q_{28,3} \approx 3.50$$

$$_{1-\alpha}q_{df(\text{error}),r} = {}_{.95}q_{28,2} \approx 2.90$$

Standard error:

$$s_{\psi}' = \sqrt{\frac{MS_{\text{error}}}{n}} = \sqrt{\frac{36.1116}{8}} = 2.1246$$

Test statistics:

$$q_1 = \frac{\overline{Y}_{.4} - \overline{Y}_{.1}}{s_{\psi'}} = \frac{24.3750 - 11.1250}{2.1246} = 6.2365 \text{ (significant)}$$

$$q_2 = \frac{\overline{Y}_{.4} - \overline{Y}_{.2}}{s_{\psi'}} = \frac{24.3750 - 17.8750}{2.1246} = 3.0594 \text{ (nonsignificant)}$$

$$q_3 = \frac{\overline{Y}_{.3} - \overline{Y}_{.1}}{s_{\psi'}} = \frac{20.2500 - 11.1250}{2.1246} = 4.2949 \text{ (significant)}$$

TABLE 4.2
Test Statistics and Results of Newman–Keuls Contrasts

	Group 1	Group 2	Group 3	Group 4
Group 1 (mean = 11.1250)	—	3.1771*	4.2949*	6.2365*
Group 2 (mean = 17.8750)		—	1.1179	3.0594
Group 3 (mean = 20.2500)			—	1.9415
Group 4 (mean = 24.3750)				—

*$p < .05$; $_{.95}q_{28,4} \approx 3.87$; $_{.95}q_{28,3} \approx 3.50$; $_{.95}q_{28,2} \approx 2.90$

$$q_4 = \frac{\overline{Y}_{.3} - \overline{Y}_{.2}}{s_{\psi'}} = \frac{20.2500 - 17.8750}{2.1246} = 1.1179 \text{ (nonsignificant)}$$

$$q_5 = \frac{\overline{Y}_{.2} - \overline{Y}_{.1}}{s_{\psi'}} = \frac{17.8750 - 11.1250}{2.1246} = 3.1771 \text{ (significant)}$$

These results are the same as we obtained with the HSD method except for the fifth contrast. Here there is a significant difference with the NK procedure, whereas there was no significant difference with the HSD test. The results are summarized in Table 4.2.

For the unequal ns case, a number of alternatives are available including those described in the Tukey–Kramer section. When the group variances are unequal, a modification is suggested by Hochberg and Tamhane (1987).

Duncan's New Multiple Range Test

Duncan's new multiple range test (1955) was developed as a post hoc pairwise equal ns MCP. Duncan's test, like the Newman–Keuls, is a contrast-based method rather than a family-wise method. Duncan's test is more liberal than the Newman–Keuls in terms of the Type I error rate, but has a lower Type II error rate and thus is more powerful. The significance level of Duncan's test is computed as $1 - (1 - \alpha)^{r-1}$, where r is the number of means in the range. At $\alpha = .05$, the significance level changes as r increases, such as

$$\textbf{2 means in range: } 1 - (1 - .05)^1 = .0500$$

$$\textbf{3 means in range: } 1 - (1 - .05)^2 = .0975$$

$$\textbf{4 means in range: } 1 - (1 - .05)^3 = .1426$$

$$\textbf{5 means in range: } 1 - (1 - .05)^4 = .1855$$

Computationally, the procedure is exactly the same as with the Newman–Keuls procedure where the means are rank ordered and a stepwise approach is taken for testing the contrasts. The test statistic for each contrast is compared to the critical value $_{1-\alpha}q_{df(\text{error}),r}$ taken from the table in Appendix Table 10.

Consider the following example of Duncan's new multiple range test using the attractiveness data:

Critical values:

$$_{1-\alpha}q_{df(\text{error}),r} = {}_{.95}q_{28,4} = 3.13$$

$$_{1-\alpha}q_{df(\text{error}),r} = {}_{.95}q_{28,3} = 3.04$$

$$_{1-\alpha}q_{df(\text{error}),r} = {}_{.95}q_{28,2} = 2.90$$

Standard error:

$$s_{\psi'} = \sqrt{\frac{MS_{error}}{n}} = \sqrt{\frac{36.1116}{8}} = 2.1246$$

Test statistics:

$$q_1 = \frac{\overline{Y}_{.4} - \overline{Y}_{.1}}{s_{\psi'}} = \frac{24.3750 - 11.1250}{2.1246} = 6.2365 \text{ (significant)}$$

$$q_2 = \frac{\overline{Y}_{.4} - \overline{Y}_{.2}}{s_{\psi'}} = \frac{24.3750 - 17.8750}{2.1246} = 3.0594 \text{ (significant)}$$

$$q_{2'} = \frac{\overline{Y}_{.4} - \overline{Y}_{.3}}{s_{\psi'}} = \frac{24.3750 - 20.2500}{2.1246} = 1.9415 \text{ (nonsignificant)}$$

$$q_3 = \frac{\overline{Y}_{.3} - \overline{Y}_{.1}}{s_{\psi'}} = \frac{20.2500 - 11.1250}{2.1246} = 4.2949 \text{ (significant)}$$

$$q_4 = \frac{\overline{Y}_{.3} - \overline{Y}_{.2}}{s_{\psi'}} = \frac{20.2500 - 17.8750}{2.1246} = 1.1179 \text{ (nonsignificant)}$$

$$q_5 = \frac{\overline{Y}_{.2} - \overline{Y}_{.1}}{s_{\psi'}} = \frac{17.8750 - 11.1250}{2.1246} = 3.1771 \text{ (significant)}$$

Thus we find the same results as with the NK except for the second contrast, which was significant with Duncan's procedure. This led us to an additional contrast, denoted by $q_{2'}$, that was not significant with Duncan's procedure. Comparing the critical values for the same value of r, we see that Duncan's test is more powerful than Newman–Keuls except for the initial contrast, which is equally powerful. These results are shown in Table 4.3.

TABLE 4.3
Test Statistics and Results of Duncan's New Multiple Range Contrasts

	Group 1	Group 2	Group 3	Group 4
Group 1 (mean = 11.1250)	—	3.1771*	4.2949*	6.2365*
Group 2 (mean = 17.8750)		—	1.1179	3.0594*
Group 3 (mean = 20.2500)			—	1.9415
Group 4 (mean = 24.3750)				—

[*] $p < .05$; $_{.95}q_{28,4} = 3.13$; $_{.95}q_{28,3} = 3.04$; $_{.95}q_{28,2} = 2.90$

If one is concerned with maintaining the family-wise Type I error rate at α, then I do not recommend either the Newman–Keuls or the Duncan procedures. For these procedures the family-wise error rate can exceed α (e.g., Hartley, 1955; Ramsey, 1981). For unbalanced designs, see the discussion in Hochberg and Tamhane (1987).

Follow-up Tests to Kruskal–Wallis

In the nonparametric equivalent to the analysis of variance, the Kruskal–Wallis test would be conducted when the normality assumption is violated, based on the ranked data. Following a significant Kruskal–Wallis test statistic, how does one determine which groups are different with respect to the average ranks? One could do several protected Mann–Whitney U tests along the same lines as Fisher's protected t test. As in the parametric case, there is a problem because there is no control over the family-wise Type I error rate. Thus, the use of multiple protected Mann–Whitney U tests is not recommended, just as the use of multiple Fisher's protected t tests was not recommended earlier in the chapter.

There are several post hoc procedures available to follow up a significant Kruskal–Wallis test. The procedures discussed here are the nonparametric equivalents to the Scheffé and Tukey HSD methods. However, we need to define a few things. First, let us define a contrast as

$$\psi_i = \sum_{j=1}^{J} c_j \mu_{.j} = c_1 \mu_{.1} + c_2 \mu_{.2} + \ldots + c_J \mu_{.J}$$

where the c_j are the contrast coefficients as before and the $\mu_{.j}$ are the group rank means. One may form pairwise or complex contrasts as in the parametric case. The test statistic is Z and given as

$$Z = \frac{\psi_{i'}}{s_\psi}$$

where

$$s_\psi = \sqrt{\frac{N(N+1)}{12} \sum_{j=1}^{J} \left(\frac{c_j^2}{n_j} \right)}$$

and where N is the total number of observations. For the Scheffé method, the test statistic Z is compared to the critical value $\sqrt{_{1-\alpha}\chi^2_{J-1}}$ obtained from the χ^2 table in Appendix Table 3. For the Tukey procedure, the test statistic Z is compared to the critical value $[_{1-\alpha} q_{df(error),J}]/\sqrt{2}$ obtained from the table of critical values for the studentized range statistic in Appendix Table 9.

Let us use the attractiveness data to illustrate. Do not forget that we use the ranked data as described in chapter 3. The rank means for the groups are as follows: Group 1 = 7.7500; Group 2 = 15.2500; Group 3 = 18.7500; Group 4 = 24.2500. Here I only examine two contrasts and then compare the results for both the Scheffé and Tukey methods. The first contrast compares the two low-attractiveness groups (i.e., Groups 1 and 2), whereas the second contrast compares the two low-attractiveness groups with the two high-attractiveness groups (i.e., Groups 3 and 4). In other words, we examine a pairwise contrast and a complex contrast, respectively. The results are given here.

Critical values:

$$\textbf{Scheffé } \sqrt{_{1-\alpha}\chi^2_{J-1}} = \sqrt{_{.95}\chi^2_3} = \sqrt{7.8147} = 2.7955$$

$$\textbf{Tukey } \left[_{1-\alpha}q_{df\,(error),J}\right] / \sqrt{2} = _{.95}q_{28,4} / \sqrt{2} \approx 3.87 / \sqrt{2} \approx 2.7365$$

Standard error for contrast 1:

$$s_{\psi'} = \sqrt{\frac{N(N+1)}{12} \sum_{j=1}^{J}\left(\frac{c_j^2}{n_j}\right)} = \sqrt{\left[\frac{32(33)}{12}\right]\left[\frac{1}{8}+\frac{1}{8}\right]} = 4.6904$$

Standard error for contrast 2:

$$s_{\psi'} = \sqrt{\frac{N(N+1)}{12} \sum_{j=1}^{J}\left(\frac{c_j^2}{n_j}\right)} = \sqrt{\left[\frac{32(33)}{12}\right]\left[\frac{.25}{8}+\frac{.25}{8}+\frac{.25}{8}+\frac{.25}{8}\right]} = 3.3166$$

Test statistics:

$$Z_1 = \frac{\overline{Y}_{.1} - \overline{Y}_{.2}}{s_{\psi'}} = \frac{7.7500 - 15.2500}{4.6904} = -1.5990 \textbf{ (nonsignificant for either procedure)}$$

$$Z_2 =$$
$$\frac{\frac{1}{2}\overline{Y}_{.1} + \frac{1}{2}\overline{Y}_{.2} - \frac{1}{2}\overline{Y}_{.3} - \frac{1}{2}\overline{Y}_{.4}}{s_{\psi'}} = \frac{\frac{1}{2}(7.7500) + \frac{1}{2}(15.2500) - \frac{1}{2}(18.75) - \frac{1}{2}(24.25)}{3.3166}$$

$$= -3.0151 \textbf{ (significant for both procedures)}$$

These results agree with most of the other parametric procedures for these particular contrasts. That is, the less attractive groups are not significantly different (of the nine MCPs used to test this contrast, it was only significant with POC, NK, and Duncan), whereas the two less attractive groups are significantly different from the two more attractive groups (significant with all procedures). One could conceivably devise nonparametric equivalent MCPs for methods other than the Scheffé and Tukey procedures.

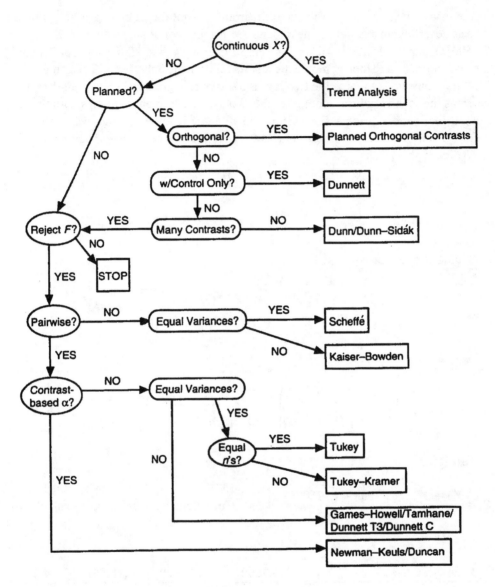

FIG. 4.2   Flowchart of multiple-comparison procedures.

SUMMARY

In this chapter methods involving the comparison of multiple group means for a single independent variable were considered. The chapter began with a look at the characteristics of multiple comparisons, including: (a) the definition of a contrast, (b) planned and post hoc comparisons, (c) contrast-based and family-wise Type I error rates, and (d) orthogonal contrasts. Next, we moved into a lengthy discussion of the major multiple comparison procedures, including examples, how to deal with assumption violations, and suggestions for their appropriate use.

Figure 4.2 is a flowchart to assist you in making decisions about which MCP to use. Several other such flowcharts exist in much simpler form, and I have found them to be quite useful (e.g., Games, 1971). Not every statistician will agree with every decision on the flowchart. This is because there is not a consensus among statisticians about which MCP is appropriate in every single situation. Nonetheless, this is simply a guide. But whether you use it in its present form, or adapt it for you own needs, I hope that you find the figure to be useful in conducting your own research.

At this point you should have met the following objectives: (a) be able to understand the concepts underlying the MCPs, (b) be able to select the appropriate MCP for a given research situation, and (c) be able to compute and interpret the results of MCPs. Chapter 5 returns to the analysis of variance again and discusses models for which there is more than one independent variable.

PROBLEMS

Conceptual Problems

1. Suppose I perform a one-factor analysis of variance fixed-effects model on data for five groups of equal size and reject H_0 at the .05 level of significance. I assert that, if I then use the Scheffé procedure also at the .05 level of significance to make all possible pairwise comparisons between the group means, I will find at least two means which differ significantly. Am I correct?

2. Which of the following linear combinations of population means is not a legitimate contrast?
   a. $(\mu_1 + \mu_2 + \mu_3)/3 - \mu_4$
   b. $\mu_1 - \mu_4$
   c. $(\mu_1 + \mu_2)/2 - (\mu_3 + \mu_4)$
   d. $\mu_1 - \mu_2 + \mu_3 - \mu_4$

3. When a one-factor ANOVA results in a significant F ratio for $J = 2$, one should follow the ANOVA with the
   a. Tukey method
   b. Scheffé method
   c. Newman–Keuls method
   d. none of the above

4. If a family-based error rate for α is desired, and hypotheses involving all pairs of means are to be tested, which method of multiple comparisons should be selected?
   a. Tukey
   b. Scheffé
   c. Duncan
   d. Newman–Keuls
   e. none of the above

5. A priori comparisons
    a. are planned in advance of the research.
    b. often arise out of theory and prior research.
    c. may be done without examining the F ratio.
    d. all of the above

6. Within a single study, the critical value of q changes from contrast to contrast in the
    a. t test for independent groups
    b. Tukey test
    c. Newman–Keuls test
    d. Scheffé test

7. Which is not a property of planned orthogonal contrasts?
    a. The contrasts are independent.
    b. The contrasts are post hoc.
    c. The sum of the cross-products of the contrast coefficients = 0.
    d. If there are J groups, there are $J - 1$ orthogonal contrasts.

8. Which multiple comparison procedure is most flexible in the contrasts that can be tested?
    a. planned orthogonal contrasts
    b. Newman–Keuls
    c. Dunnett
    d. Tukey
    e. Scheffé

9. Post hoc tests are necessary after an ANOVA whenever
    a. H_0 is rejected.
    b. there are more than two groups.
    c. H_0 is rejected and there are more than two groups.
    d. you should always do post hoc tests after an ANOVA.

10. Post hoc tests are done after ANOVA to determine why H_0 was not rejected. True or false?

11. Holding the α level and the number of groups constant, as the df_{with} increases, the critical value of the q decreases. True or false?

12. The Tukey procedure maintains the family Type I error rate at α. True or false?

13. The Dunnett procedure assumes equal numbers of observations per group. True or false?

14. I assert that the critical values for the Tukey and the Newman–Keuls multiple-comparison procedures will always be equal when there are more than two groups. Am I correct?

Computational Problems

1. A one-factor analysis of variance is performed on data for 10 groups of unequal sizes and H_0 is rejected at the .01 level of significance. Using the Scheffé procedure, test the contrast that

$$\overline{Y}_{.2} - \overline{Y}_{.5} = 0$$

at the .01 level of significance given the following information: $df_{with} = 40$, $\overline{Y}_{.2} = 10.8$, $n_2 = 8$, $\overline{Y}_{.5} = 15.8$, $n_5 = 8$, and $MS_{with} = 4$.

2. A one-factor fixed-effects ANOVA is performed on data from three groups of equal size ($n = 10$) and H_0 is rejected at the .01 level. The following values were computed: $MS_{with} = 40$, and the sample means are $\overline{Y}_{.1} = 4.5$, $\overline{Y}_{.2} = 12.5$, and $\overline{Y}_{.3} = 13.0$. Use the Tukey method to test all possible pairwise contrasts.

3. The following analysis is from an experiment in which three groups, each consisting of six persons, rated three different statistics software packages on a 10-point scale, where higher values indicate greater preference. The following values were computed: $MS_{with} = .83$, and the sample means are $\overline{Y}_{.1} = 4.8$, $\overline{Y}_{.2} = 6.0$, and $\overline{Y}_{.3} = 8.0$. Use the Tukey and Newman–Keuls methods to test all possible pairwise contrasts at the .05 level. Compare and contrast the results.

4. Using the data from chapter 3, Computational Problem 4, conduct a trend analysis at the .05 level.

5. Consider the situation where there are $J = 4$ groups of subjects. Answer the following questions:
   a. Construct a set of orthogonal contrasts and show that they are orthogonal.
   b. Is the following contrast legitimate? Why or why not?

$$H_0: \mu_1 - (\mu_2 + \mu_3 + \mu_4).$$

   c. How might the contrast in part (b) be altered to yield a legitimate contrast?

5

FACTORIAL ANALYSIS OF VARIANCE— FIXED-EFFECTS MODEL

Chapter Outline

Key Concepts

1. Main effects
2. Interaction effects
3. Partitioning the sums of squares
4. The ANOVA model
5. Expected mean squares
6. Main effects contrasts, simple and complex interaction contrasts
7. Nonorthogonal designs

The last two chapters have dealt with the one-factor analysis of variance (ANOVA) model and various multiple-comparison procedures (MCPs) for that model. In this chapter we continue our discussion of analysis of variance models by extending the one-factor case to the two- and three-factor models. This chapter seeks an answer to the question, what should we do if we have multiple factors for which we want to make comparisons of the means? In other words, the researcher is interested in the effect of two or more independent variables or factors on the dependent (or criterion) variable. In regression terminology, we have moved from one independent variable in the one-factor ANOVA model to multiple independent variables in the multiple-factor ANOVA model. This chapter is most concerned with two- and three-factor models, but the extension to more than three factors, when warranted, is fairly easy to transfer.

For example, suppose that a researcher is interested in the effects of textbook choice and time of day on statistics achievement. Thus one independent variable would be the textbook selected for the course, and the second independent variable would be the time of day the course was offered. The researcher hypothesizes that certain texts may be more effective in terms of achievement than others, and student learning may be greater at certain times of the day. For the time-of-day variable, one might expect, for example, that students would not do as well in an early-morning section or a late-evening section. In the example study, say that the researcher is interested in comparing three textbooks (A, B, and C) and three times of the day (early-morning, mid-afternoon, and evening sections). Students would be randomly assigned to sections of statistics based on a combination of textbook and time of day. One group of students might be assigned to the section offered in the evening using textbook A. These results would be of interest to statistics instructors for selecting a textbook and optimal time of the day for the course.

Most of the concepts used in this chapter are the same as those covered in chapters 3 and 4. In addition, new concepts include main effects, interaction effects, multiple comparison procedures for main and interaction effects, and nonorthogonal designs. Our objectives are that by the end of this chapter, you will be able to (a) understand the characteristics and concepts underlying factorial ANOVA, (b) compute and interpret the results of factorial ANOVA (balanced and unbalanced), and (c) understand and evaluate the assumptions of factorial ANOVA (balanced and unbalanced).

THE TWO-FACTOR ANOVA MODEL

This section describes the distinguishing characteristics of the two-factor ANOVA model, the layout of the data, the linear model, main effects and interactions, assumptions of the model and their violation, computation of the sums of squares, the ANOVA summary table, expected mean squares, multiple comparison procedures, measures of association, the relationship between ANOVA and regression analysis, and an example.

Characteristics of the Model

The first characteristic of the two-factor ANOVA model should be obvious by now, the notion of considering the effect of two factors or independent variables on a dependent variable. Each factor consists of two or more levels. This yields what we call a *factorial design* because more than a single factor is included. We see then that the two-factor ANOVA is an extension of the one-factor ANOVA. Why would a researcher want to complicate things by considering a second factor? Three reasons immediately come to mind. First, the researcher may have a genuine interest in studying the second factor. Rather than studying each factor separately in two analyses, the researcher includes both factors in the same analysis. This allows a test not only of the effect of each individual factor, but of the effect of both factors collectively. This latter effect is known as an *interaction* effect and provides information about whether the two factors are operating independent of one another (i.e., no interaction exists) or whether the two factors are operating simultaneously to produce some additional impact (i.e., an interaction exists). If two separate analyses were conducted, one for each independent variable, no information would be obtained about the interaction effect. As becomes evident, the researcher will test three hypotheses, one for each factor individually and a third for the interaction between the factors. This chapter spends considerable time discussing interactions.

A second reason for including an additional factor is an attempt to reduce the error (or within-groups) variation, which is variation that is unexplained by the first factor. This is precisely the same rationale used in multiple regression analysis for the inclusion of more than one independent variable (i.e., to reduce error variance, which will increase R^2). The use of a second factor provides a more precise estimate of error variance. For this reason, a two-factor design is generally more powerful than two one-factor designs, as the second factor serves to control for additional extraneous variability. A third reason for considering two factors simultaneously is to provide greater generalizability of results and to provide a more efficient and economical use of observations and resources. Thus the results can be generalized to more situations, and the study will be more cost-efficient in terms of time and money.

In addition, with the two-factor ANOVA every level of the first factor (hereafter known as factor A) is paired with every level of the second factor (hereafter known as factor B). In other words, every combination of factors A and B is included in the design of the study, yielding what is referred to as a *fully crossed design*. If some combinations are not included, then the design is not fully crossed and may form some sort of a nested design (see chap. 8). Individuals (or objects or subjects) are randomly assigned to one combination of the two factors. In other words, each individual responds to only one combination of the factors. If individuals respond to more than one combination of the factors, this would be some sort of repeated measures design, which we examine in chapter 7. It is assumed throughout this chapter that all factors under consideration represent fixed-effects factors. Thus the overall design is known as a fixed-effects model. If one or both factors are random, then the design is not a fixed-effects model, which we discuss in chapter 7. It is also assumed that the dependent variable is measured at least at the interval level.

In this section of the chapter, we assume the number of observations made in each factor combination is the same. This yields what is known as an orthogonal design, where the effects due to the factors (separately and collectively) are independent. We leave the discussion of the unequal ns factorial ANOVA until later in this chapter. In addition, we assume there are at least two observations per factor combination so as to have an error term (due to within-groups variation).

In summary, the characteristics of the two-factor analysis of variance fixed-effects model are as follows:

1. Two independent variables each with two or more levels.
2. The levels of both independent variables are fixed by the researcher.
3. Subjects are randomly assigned to only one combination of these levels.
4. The two factors are fully crossed.
5. The dependent variable is measured at least at the interval level.

In the context of experimental design, the two-factor analysis of variance is referred to as the *completely randomized factorial design*.

The Layout of the Data

Before we get into the theory and subsequent analysis of the data, let us examine the form in which the data is typically placed, known as the layout of the data. We designate each observation as Y_{ijk}, where the j subscript tells us what level of factor A (e.g., textbook) the observation belongs to, the k subscript tells us what level of factor B (e.g., time of day) the observation belongs to, and the i subscript tells us the observation or identification number within that combination of factor A and factor B. For instance, Y_{321} would mean that this is the third observation in the second level of factor A and the first level of factor B. The first subscript ranges over $i = 1, \ldots, n$, the second subscript ranges over $j = 1, \ldots, J$, and the third subscript ranges over $k = 1, \ldots, K$. Note also that the latter

TABLE 5.1
Layout for the Two-Factor ANOVA

Level of Factor A	Level of Factor B				Row Mean
	1	2	...	K	
1	Y_{111}	Y_{112}	...	Y_{11K}	$\overline{Y}_{.1.}$
	.	.	.	.	
	.	.	.	.	
	Y_{n11}	Y_{n12}	...	Y_{n1K}	
	$\overline{Y}_{.11}$	$\overline{Y}_{.12}$	...	$\overline{Y}_{.1K}$	
2	Y_{121}	Y_{122}	...	Y_{12K}	$\overline{Y}_{.2.}$
	.	.	.	.	
	.	.	.	.	
	Y_{n21}	Y_{n22}	...	Y_{n2K}	
	$\overline{Y}_{.21}$	$\overline{Y}_{.22}$	...	$\overline{Y}_{.2K}$	
J	Y_{1J1}	Y_{1J2}	...	Y_{1JK}	$\overline{Y}_{.J.}$
	.	.	.	.	
	.	.	.	.	
	Y_{nJ1}	Y_{nJ2}	...	Y_{nJK}	
	$\overline{Y}_{.J1}$	$\overline{Y}_{.J2}$	...	$\overline{Y}_{.JK}$	
Column Mean	$\overline{Y}_{..1}$	$\overline{Y}_{..2}$	...	$\overline{Y}_{..K}$	$\overline{Y}_{...}$

two subscripts denote the cell that an observation is in. Using the same example, we are referring to the third observation in the 21 cell. Thus there are J levels of factor A, K levels of factor B, and n subjects in each cell, for a total of $JKn = N$ observations. For now we assume there are n subjects in each cell in order to greatly simplify matters; this is referred to as the equal ns case. Later in this chapter we consider the unequal ns cases.

The layout of the sample data is shown in Table 5.1. Here we see that each row represents the observations for a particular level of factor A (textbook), and that each column represents the observations for a particular level of factor B (time). At the bottom of each column are the column means ($\overline{Y}_{..k}$), to the right of each row are the row means ($\overline{Y}_{.j.}$), and in the lower right-hand corner is the overall mean ($\overline{Y}_{...}$). We also need to compute cell means ($\overline{Y}_{.jk}$), which are shown at the bottom of each cell. In conclusion, the layout of the data is the form in which the researcher can place the data for purposes of setting up the analysis.

The ANOVA Model

This section introduces the analysis of variance linear model, as well as estimation of the parameters of the model. The two-factor analysis of variance model is a form of the general linear model like the simple and multiple regression models of chapters 1 and 2, and the one-factor ANOVA model of chapter 3. The two-factor ANOVA fixed-effects model can be written in terms of population parameters as

$$Y_{ijk} = \mu + \alpha_j + \beta_k + (\alpha\beta)_{jk} + \varepsilon_{ijk}$$

where Y_{ijk} is the observed score on the criterion variable for individual i in level j of factor A (text) and level k of factor B (time) (or in the jk cell), μ is the overall or grand population mean (i.e., regardless of cell designation), α_j is the effect for level j of factor A (row or text effect), β_k is the effect for level k of factor B (column or time effect), $(\alpha\beta)_{jk}$ is the interaction effect for the combination of level j of factor A and level k of factor B, and ε_{ijk} is the random residual error for individual i in cell jk. The residual error can be due to individual differences, measurement error, and/or other factors not under investigation. The population effects and residual error are computed as

$$\alpha_j = \mu_{.j.} - \mu$$

$$\beta_k = \mu_{..k} - \mu$$

$$(\alpha\beta)_{jk} = \mu_{.jk} - (\mu_{.j.} + \mu_{..k} - \mu)$$

and

$$\varepsilon_{ijk} = Y_{ijk} - \mu_{.jk}$$

That is, the row effect is equal to the difference between the population mean of level j of factor A (a particular text) and the overall population mean, the column effect is equal to the difference between the population mean of level k of factor B (a particular time) and the overall population mean, and the interaction effect is the effect of being in a certain combination of the levels of factor A and B (a particular text used at a particular time), whereas the residual error is equal to the difference between an individual's observed score and the population mean of cell jk. The row, column, and interaction effects can also be thought of as the average effect of being a member of a particular row, column, or cell, respectively. The residual error in the analysis of variance is similar to the residual error in regression analysis, which in both cases represents that portion of the dependent variable not accounted for by the independent variables.

You may be wondering why the interaction effect looks a little different from the other two effects. I have given you the version that is solely a function of population means. A more intuitively convincing conceptual version of this effect is

$$(\alpha\beta)_{jk} = \mu_{.jk} - \alpha_j - \beta_k - \mu$$

which is written in similar fashion to the row and column effects. Here we see that the interaction effect is equal to the population cell mean minus (a) the row effect, (b) the column effect, and (c) the overall population mean. In other words, the interaction is solely a function of cell means without regard to its row effect, column effect, or the overall mean. We can move from the conceptual version of the interaction effect back to the original version by

$$(\alpha\beta)_{jk} = \mu_{.jk} - \alpha_j - \beta_k - \mu$$

$$= \mu_{.jk} - (\mu_{.j.} - \mu) - (\mu_{..k} - \mu) - \mu$$

$$= \mu_{.jk} - (\mu_{.j.} + \mu_{..k} - \mu) \, .$$

There are special conditions of the model, known as side conditions. For the equal ns model being considered here, the side conditions are as follows:

$$\sum_{j=1}^{J} \alpha_j = 0$$

$$\sum_{k=1}^{K} \beta_k = 0$$

$$\sum_{j=1}^{J} (\alpha\beta)_{jk} = 0$$

$$\sum_{k=1}^{K} (\alpha\beta)_{jk} = 0$$

Thus the sum of the row effects is equal to zero, the sum of the column effects is equal to zero, and the sum of the interaction effects is equal to zero, both across rows and across columns. This implies, for example, that if there are any nonzero row effects, then the row effects will balance out around zero with some positive and some negative effects.

To estimate the parameters of the model μ, α_j, β_k, $(\alpha\beta)_{jk}$, and ε_{ijk}, the least squares method of estimation is used, as the least squares method is most appropriate for general linear models (regression, ANOVA). These sample estimates are represented as $\overline{Y}_{...}$, a_j, b_k, $(ab)_{jk}$, and e_{ijk}, respectively, where the latter four are computed as follows, respectively:

$$a_j = \overline{Y}_{.j.} - \overline{Y}_{...}$$

$$b_k = \overline{Y}_{..k} - \overline{Y}_{...}$$

$$(ab)_{jk} = \overline{Y}_{.jk} - (\overline{Y}_{.j.} + \overline{Y}_{..k} - \overline{Y}_{...})$$

$$e_{ijk} = Y_{ijk} - \overline{Y}_{.jk}$$

Note that $\overline{Y}_{...}$ represents the overall sample mean, $\overline{Y}_{.j.}$ represents the sample mean for level j of factor A (a particular text), $\overline{Y}_{..k}$ represents the sample mean for level k of factor B (a particular time), and $\overline{Y}_{.jk}$ represents the sample mean for cell jk (a particular text at a particular time), where the dot subscripts indicate whether we have averaged across the i, j and/or k subscripts.

In the case of the two-factor ANOVA model, there are three sets of hypotheses, one for each of the main effects and one for the interaction effect. The null and alternative hypotheses, respectively, for testing the effect of factor A (text) are

$$H_{01}: \mu_{.1.} = \mu_{.2.} = \mu_{.3.} = \ldots = \mu_{.J.}$$

$$H_{11}: \textbf{not all the } \mu_{.j.} \textbf{ are equal}$$

The hypotheses for testing the effect of factor B (time) are

$$H_{02}: \mu_{..1} = \mu_{..2} = \mu_{..3} = \ldots = \mu_{..K}$$

$$H_{12}: \textbf{not all the } \mu_{..k} \textbf{ are equal.}$$

Finally, the hypotheses for testing the interaction effect (text with time) are

$$H_{03}: (\mu_{.jk} - \mu_{.j.} - \mu_{..k} + \mu) = 0 \textbf{ for all } j \textbf{ and } k$$

$$H_{13}: \textbf{not all the } (\mu_{.jk} - \mu_{.j.} - \mu_{..k} + \mu) = 0$$

The null hypotheses can also be written in terms of row, column, and interaction effects (which may make more intuitive sense) as

$$H_{01}: \alpha_1 = \alpha_2 = \alpha_3 = \ldots = \alpha_J = 0$$

$$H_{02}: \beta_1 = \beta_2 = \beta_3 = \ldots = \beta_K = 0$$

$$H_{03}: (\alpha\beta)_{jk} = 0 \textbf{ for all } j \textbf{ and } k$$

As in the one-factor model, all of the alternative hypotheses are written in a general form to cover the multitude of possible mean differences that could arise. These range from only two of the means being different to all of the means being different from one another. Also, because of the way the alternative hypotheses have been written, only a nondirectional alternative is appropriate. If one of the null hypotheses is rejected, then the researcher may want to consider a multiple comparison procedure so as to determine which means or combination of means are significantly different (discussed later).

Main Effects and Interaction Effects

Finally we come to a formal discussion of main effects and interaction effects. A *main effect* of factor A (text) is defined as the effect of factor A, averaged across the levels of factor B (time), on the dependent variable Y (achievement). More precisely, it represents the unique effect of factor A on Y, controlling statistically for factor B. A similar statement may be made for the main effect of factor B.

As far as the concept of interaction is concerned, things are a bit more complex. Recall from chapter 2 on multiple regression a discussion of the interaction of two independent variables as an additional predictor. Let us build on that notion. An *interaction* can be defined in any of the following ways: An interaction is said to exist if (a) certain combinations of the two factors produce effects beyond the effects of the two factors when considered separately; (b) the mean differences among the levels of factor A are not constant across (and thus depend on) the levels of factor B; (c) there is a joint effect of factors A and B on Y; or (d) there is a unique effect that could not be predicted from knowledge of only the main effects. Let me mention two fairly common examples of interaction effects. The first is known as an aptitude–treatment interaction (ATI). This means that the effectiveness of a particular treatment depends on the aptitude of the individual. In other words, some treatments are particularly effective for individuals with a high aptitude, and other treatments are more effective for those with a low aptitude. A second example is an interaction between treatment and gender. Here some treatments may be more effective for males and others may be more effective for females. This is often considered in gender differences research.

For some graphical examples of main and interaction effects, take a look at the various plots in Fig. 5.1. Each plot represents the graph of a particular set of cell means, sometimes referred to as a *profile plot*. On the X axis are the levels of factor A (text), the Y axis provides the cell means on the dependent variable Y (achievement), and the lines in the body of the plot represent the levels of factor B (time) (although the specific placement of the two factors here is arbitrary; i.e., alternatively factor B could be plotted on the X axis and factor A as the lines). Profile plots provide information about the possible existence of a main effect for A, a main effect for B, and/or an interaction effect. A main effect for factor A, for example, can be examined by taking the means for each level of A and averaging them across the levels of B. If these marginal means for the levels of A are the same or nearly so, this would be indicative of no main effect for factor A. A main effect for factor B would be assessed by taking the means for each level of B and averaging them across the levels of A. If these marginal means for the levels of B are the same or nearly so, then we would conclude that there is no main effect for factor B. An interaction effect is determined by whether the cell means for the levels of A are constant across the levels of B (or vice versa). This is easily viewed in a profile plot by checking to see whether or not the lines are parallel. Parallel lines indicate no interaction, whereas nonparallel lines suggest that an interaction may exist. Of course the statistical significance of the main and interaction effects is a matter to be determined by the F ratios. The profile plots only give you a rough idea as to the possible existence of the effects. For instance, lines that are nearly parallel will probably not show up as a significant interaction. As a suggestion, the plot is simplified somewhat if the factor with the most levels is shown on the X axis. This cuts down on the number of lines drawn.

The plots shown in Fig. 5.1 represent the eight general patterns that may possibly result for a two-factor design. To simplify matters, only two levels of each factor are

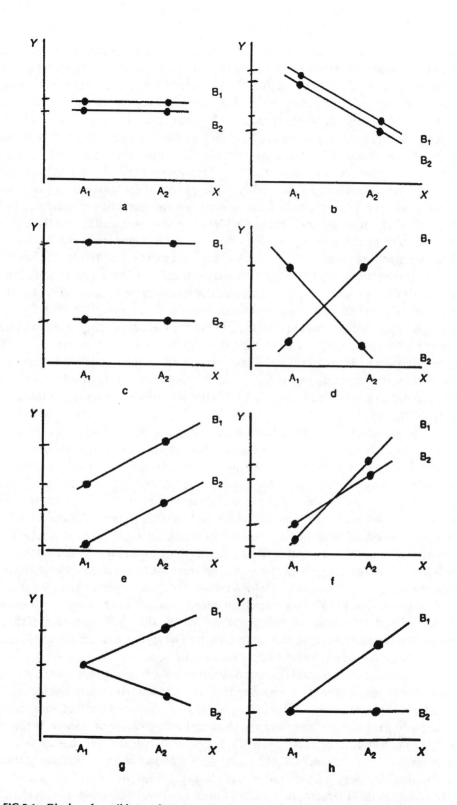

FIG.5.1   Display of possible two-factor ANOVA effects.

used. Figure 5.1(a) indicates that there is no main effect either for factor A or B and there is no interaction effect. The lines are horizontal (no A effect), lie nearly on top of one another (no B effect), and are parallel (no interaction effect). Figure 5.1(b) suggests the presence of an effect due to factor A only (the lines are not horizontal because the mean for A_1 is higher than the mean for A_2), but are nearly on top of one another (no B effect), and are parallel (no interaction). In Fig. 5.1(c) we see a separation between the lines for the levels of B (B_1 being higher than B_2); thus a main effect for B is likely, but the lines are horizontal (no A effect), and are parallel (no interaction).

For Fig. 5.1(d) there are no main effects (the means for the levels of A are the same, and the means for the levels of B are the same), but an interaction is indicated by the lack of parallelism of the lines. Figure 5.1(e) suggests a main effect for both factors as shown by mean differences (A_1 lower than A_2, and B_1 higher than B_2), but no interaction (the lines are parallel). In Fig. 5.1(f) we see a main effect for A (A_1 lower than A_2) and an interaction are likely, but no main effect for B (little separation between the lines for factor B). For Fig. 5.1(g) there appears to be a main effect for B (B_1 higher than B_2) and an interaction, but no main effect for A. Finally, in Fig. 5.1(h) we see the likelihood of two main effects (A_1 lower than A_2, and B_1 higher than B_2), and an interaction. Although these are clearly the only possible outcomes from a two-factor design, the precise pattern will differ depending on the obtained cell means. In other words, if your study yields a significant effect only for factor A, your profile plot need not look exactly like Fig. 5.1(b), but it will retain the same general pattern and interpretation.

In many statistics texts, the authors make a big deal about the type of interaction shown in the profile plot. They make a distinction between an ordinal interaction and a disordinal interaction. An ordinal interaction is said to exist when the lines are not parallel and they do not cross; ordinal here means the same relative order of the cell means is maintained across the levels of one of the factors. For example, the means for level 1 of factor B are always larger than the means for level 2 of B, regardless of the level of factor A. A disordinal interaction is said to exist when the lines are not parallel and they do cross. For example, the mean for B_1 is larger than the mean for B_2 at A_1, but the opposite is true at A_2. Dwelling on the distinction between the two types of interaction is not recommended, as it can depend on which factor is plotted on the X axis. That is, when factor A is plotted on the X axis a disordinal interaction may be shown, and when factor B is plotted on the X axis an ordinal interaction may be shown. The purpose of the profile plot is to simplify interpretation of the results; worrying about the type of interaction as drawn may merely serve to confuse the interpretation.

Now for a Lomax commercial about dealing with the interaction effect. Let us consider two possible situations, one where there is a significant interaction effect and one where there is no such effect. If there is no significant interaction effect, then the findings regarding the main effects can be generalized with greater confidence. In this situation, the main effects are known as *additive effects* and an additive linear model with no interaction term could actually be used to describe the data (if somehow you knew ahead of time that there is no interaction, say from previous research). For example, the results might be that for factor A, the level 1 means always exceed those of level 2 by 10 points, across all levels of factor B. Thus we can make a blanket statement about the constant added benefits of A_1 over A_2, regardless of the level of factor B. In addition, for the no-interaction situation, the main effects are statistically independent of one another; that is, each of the main effects serve as an independent predictor of Y.

If there is a significant interaction effect, then the findings regarding the main effects cannot be generalized with such confidence. In this situation, the main effects are not additive and the interaction term must be included in the linear model. For example, the results might be that (a) the mean for A_1 is greater than A_2 when considering B_1, but (b) the mean for A_1 is less than A_2 when considering B_2. Thus we cannot make a blanket statement about the constant added benefits of A_1 over A_2, because it depends on the level of factor B. In addition, for the interaction situation, the main effects are not statistically independent of one another; that is, each of the main effects does not serve as an independent predictor of Y. In order to predict Y well, information is necessary about the levels of factors A and B. Thus in the presence of a significant interaction, generalizations about the main effects must be qualified. A profile plot should be examined so that a proper graphical interpretation of the interaction and main effects can be made. A significant interaction serves as a warning that one cannot generalize statements about a main effect for A over all levels of B. If you obtain a significant interaction, this is an important result. Do not ignore it and go ahead to interpret the main effects.

Assumptions and Violation of Assumptions

In chapter 3 we described the assumptions for the one-factor analysis of variance. The assumptions are the same for the two-factor model and we need not devote much attention to them here. Again the assumptions are concerned with the distribution of the residual errors. In the two-factor case, we are concerned with the residuals at the cell level, that is, the residuals within each cell of the design.

The assumption of the distribution of the residual errors is actually a set of three statements about the form of the residual errors, the ε_{ijk}. First, the residual errors are assumed to be random and independent errors. That is, there is no systematic pattern about the errors and the errors are independent across individuals. An example of a systematic pattern would be where for one cell the residuals tended to be small whereas for another cell the residuals tended to be large. Thus there would be a relationship between the cell and the ε_{ijk}.

The use of independent random samples is crucial in the analysis of variance. The F ratio is very sensitive to violation of the independence assumption in terms of increased likelihood of a Type I and/or Type II error. A violation of the independence assumption may affect the standard errors of the sample means and thus influence any inferences made about those means. One purpose of random assignment of individuals to groups is to achieve independence of the ε_{ijk} terms. If each individual is only observed once and individuals are randomly assigned to cells, then the independence assumption is usually met (but not guaranteed).

The simplest procedure for assessing independence is to examine residual plots by cell. If the independence assumption is satisfied, then the residuals should fall into a random display of points for each cell. If the assumption is violated, then the residuals will fall into some type of cyclical pattern. As discussed in chapter 1, the Durbin–Watson statistic (1950, 1951, 1971) can be used to test for autocorrelation. Violations of the independence assumption generally occur in the three situations we mentioned in chapter 1: time-series data, observations within blocks, or replication. For severe violations of the independence assumption, there is no simple "fix" such as the use of transformations or nonparametric tests. As an example, in a serious violation with time-series data, an autocorrelation between rows may affect a test of columns, and vice versa (e.g., Box, 1954). If the violation is due to some extraneous or nuisance factor, one solution is to include it as a third factor in the model.

The second part of the assumption holds that the distributions of the residual errors for each cell have a constant variance, σ_{res}^2. Often this is referred to as the assumption of homogeneity of variance or homoscedasticity. In other words, for all cells, the conditional distributions of the residual errors will have the same variance. If the first two parts of the assumption are satisfied, then s_{res}^2 is an unbiased estimator of the population error variance (i.e., σ_{res}^2) for each cell.

A violation of the homogeneity assumption may lead to bias in the SS_{with} term, as well as an increase in the Type I error rate and possibly an increase in the Type II error rate. The effect of the violation seems to be small with balanced or nearly balanced designs, whereas the effect increases as the design becomes less balanced. In addition, as n increases, the effect decreases. Thus to minimize the problem, use a balanced design (or nearly so), or if this is not possible, use as many observations per cell as possible. There is very little research on this problem, except for the classic Box (1954) article for a no-interaction model with one observation per cell. In general, the effects of nonnormality are thought not to be severe except for extreme violations.

In a plot of cell means versus cell variances, the consistency of the variance of the conditional residual distributions may be examined. No formal statistical test can be recommended. There are unfortunately no wonderful solutions for dealing with a violation of the homogeneity assumption. Transformations are not usually used, as they may destroy an additive linear model and create interactions that did not previously exist. Nonparametric techniques are not commonly used with the two-factor model, unless one wants to assume no interaction or to only analyze the cell means. For additional information on such violations, see Miller (1997).

The third and final part of the assumption states that the conditional distributions of the residual errors are normal in shape. That is, for all cells, the residual errors are normally distributed. The F test is relatively robust to moderate violations of this assumption (i.e., in terms of Type I and II error rates). The effect of the violation seems to be the same as with the homogeneity assumption. To detect a violation of the normality assumption one can graphically look at the distribution of the residuals for each of the cells, although no statistical test can be recommended (see Miller, 1997). Solutions for dealing with nonnormality are the same as with variance heterogeneity. For additional information on such violations, see Miller (1997).

A summary of the assumptions and the effects of their violation for the two-factor model is presented in Table 5.2.

TABLE 5.2
Assumptions and Effects of Violations—Two-Factor Design

Assumption	Effect of Assumption Violation
1. Independence of residuals	Increased likelihood of a Type I and/or Type II error in the F statistic; influences standard errors of means and thus inferences about those means
2. Homogeneity of variance	Bias in SS_{with}; increased likelihood of a Type I and/or Type II error; small effect with balanced or nearly balanced design; effect decreases as n increases
3. Normality of residuals	Minimal effect with balanced or nearly balanced design; effect decreases as n increases

Computation of Sums of Squares

As pointed out in chapters 1 to 3, the partitioning of the sums of squares is an important concept in both regression analysis and the analysis of variance. Let us begin with the total sum of squares in Y, denoted here as SS_{total}. The term SS_{total} represents the amount of total variation among all of the observations without regard to cell membership. The next step is to partition the total variation into variation between the levels of factor A (denoted by SS_A), variation between the levels of factor B (denoted by SS_B), variation due to the interaction of the levels of factors A and B (denoted by SS_{AB}), and variation within the cells combined across cells (denoted by SS_{with}). In the two-factor analysis of variance, then, we can partition SS_{total} into

$$SS_{\text{total}} = SS_A + SS_B + SS_{AB} + SS_{\text{with}}$$

or in terms of population parameters by

$$\sum_{i=1}^{n}\sum_{j=1}^{J}\sum_{k=1}^{K}\left(Y_{ijk}-\mu_{...}\right)^2 = nK\sum_{j=1}^{J}\alpha_j^2 + nJ\sum_{k=1}^{K}\beta_k^2 + n\sum_{j=1}^{J}\sum_{k=1}^{K}(\alpha\beta)_{jk}^2 + \sum_{i=1}^{n}\sum_{j=1}^{J}\sum_{k=1}^{K}\varepsilon_{ijk}^2$$

We refer to this particular formulation of the partitioned sums of squares as the *definitional formula*, because each term literally defines a form of variation.

Due to computational complexity and the likelihood of computational error, the definitional formula is rarely used with real data. Instead, a computational formula for the partitioning of the sums of squares is used for hand computations, which is

$$SS_{\text{total}} = \sum_{i=1}^{n}\sum_{j=1}^{J}\sum_{k=1}^{K}Y_{ijk}^2 - \frac{\left(\sum_{i=1}^{n}\sum_{j=1}^{J}\sum_{k=1}^{K}Y_{ijk}\right)^2}{N}$$

$$SS_A = \sum_{j=1}^{J}\frac{\left(\sum_{i=1}^{n}\sum_{k=1}^{K}Y_{ijk}\right)^2}{nK} - \frac{\left(\sum_{i=1}^{n}\sum_{j=1}^{J}\sum_{k=1}^{K}Y_{ijk}\right)^2}{N}$$

$$SS_{\text{B}} = \sum_{k=1}^{K} \frac{\left(\sum_{i=1}^{n}\sum_{j=1}^{J} Y_{ijk}\right)^{2}}{nJ} - \frac{\left(\sum_{i=1}^{n}\sum_{j=1}^{J}\sum_{k=1}^{K} Y_{ijk}\right)^{2}}{N}$$

$$SS_{AB} = \sum_{j=1}^{J}\sum_{k=1}^{K} \frac{\left(\sum_{i=1}^{n} Y_{ijk}\right)^{2}}{n} - \sum_{j=1}^{J} \frac{\left(\sum_{i=1}^{n}\sum_{k=1}^{K} Y_{ijk}\right)^{2}}{nK} - \sum_{k=1}^{K} \frac{\left(\sum_{i=1}^{n}\sum_{j=1}^{J} Y_{ijk}\right)^{2}}{nJ} + \frac{\left(\sum_{i=1}^{n}\sum_{j=1}^{J}\sum_{k=1}^{K} Y_{ijk}\right)^{2}}{N}$$

$$SS_{\text{with}} = \sum_{i=1}^{n}\sum_{j=1}^{J}\sum_{k=1}^{K} Y_{ijk}^{2} - \sum_{j=1}^{J}\sum_{k=1}^{K} \frac{\left(\sum_{i=1}^{n} Y_{ijk}\right)^{2}}{n}$$

Granted, this case is somewhat more complicated than the one-factor case where there were three different terms to compute. As you can see from the previous series of equations, there are five different terms to compute. Once each of these terms has been computed, calculating the various sums of squares is simply a matter of arranging the proper terms.

The ANOVA Summary Table

Now that we have computed the sums of squares, the next step is to assemble the ANOVA summary table. The purpose of the summary table is to simply summarize the analysis of variance. A general form of the summary table for the two-factor case is shown in Table 5.3. However, the summary tables presented by statistical packages do not always take this precise form, although all of the same components are included (e.g., SPSS also includes "corrected" sources for some models, which can be ignored). The first column lists the sources of variation in the model. We note that the total variation is divided into a within-groups source, and a general between groups source, which is subdivided into the sources due to A, B, and the interaction between A and B. This is in keeping with the spirit of the one-factor model, where total variation was divided into a between-groups source (just one because there is only one factor and no interaction terms) and a within-groups source. The second column provides the sums of squares obtained from the computational formulas given in the previous subsection.

The third column gives the degrees of freedom for each source. As always, degrees of freedom have to do with the number of observations that are free to vary in a particular context. Because there are J levels of factor A, then the number of degrees of freedom for the A source is equal to $J - 1$. As there are J means and we know the overall mean, then only $J - 1$ of the means are free to vary. This is the same rationale we have been using all along, and I promise not to repeat it again in this text. As there are K levels of factor B, there are then $K - 1$ degrees of freedom for the B source. For the interaction between A and B source, we take the product of the degrees of freedom for the main effects. Thus we have as degrees of freedom for AB the product $(J - 1)(K - 1)$.

TABLE 5.3
Two-Factor Analysis of Variance Summary Table

Source	SS	df	MS	F
Between:				
A	SS_A	$J-1$	MS_A	MS_A/MS_{with}
B	SS_B	$K-1$	MS_B	MS_B/MS_{with}
AB	SS_{AB}	$(J-1)(K-1)$	MS_{AB}	MS_{AB}/MS_{with}
Within	SS_{with}	$N-JK$	MS_{with}	
Total	SS_{total}	$N-1$		

The within groups source is equal to the total number of observations minus the number of cells in the model; thus we have $N-JK$ as the degrees of freedom within. Finally, the degrees of freedom total can be written simply as $N-1$.

Next, the sum of squares terms are weighted by the appropriate degrees of freedom to arrive at the mean squares terms. Thus, for instance, $MS_A = SS_A / df_A$. Finally, in the last column of the ANOVA summary table, we have the F values, which represent the summary statistics for the analysis of variance. There are three hypotheses that we are interested in testing, so there will be three F-test statistics, for the two main effects and the interaction effect. For the factorial fixed-effects model, each F value is computed by taking the MS for the source that you are interested in testing and dividing it by MS_{with}. Thus for each hypothesis to be tested, the same error term is used in forming the F ratio (i.e., MS_{with}). We return to the two-factor model for cases where the effects are not fixed in chapter 7.

Each of the F-test statistics is then compared with the appropriate F critical value so as to make a decision about the relevant null hypothesis. The critical value for the test of factor A is found in the F table as $_{1-\alpha}F_{J-1,N-JK}$. The critical value for the test of factor B is found in the F table as $_{1-\alpha}F_{K-1,N-JK}$. The critical value for the test of the interaction is found in the F table as $_{1-\alpha}F_{(J-1)(K-1),N-JK}$. Each significance test is a one-tailed test so as to be consistent with the alternative hypothesis. The null hypothesis is rejected if the F-test statistic exceeds the F critical value. The critical values are found in the F table of Appendix Table 4.

If the F-test statistic does exceed the F critical value, and there is more than one degree of freedom for the source being tested, then it is not clear precisely why the null hypothesis was rejected. For example, if there are three levels of factor A and the null hypothesis for A is rejected, then we are not sure where the mean differences lie among the levels of A. In this case, some multiple-comparison procedure should be used to determine where the mean differences are; this is the topic of a later subsection.

Expected Mean Squares

The concept of expected mean squares was previously introduced in chapter 3. To refresh your memory, the notion of expected mean squares provides the basis for determining what the appropriate error term is when forming an F ratio. In other words, when forming an F ratio to test a certain hypothesis, how do we know which source of variation to use as the error term in the denominator? In the two-factor fixed-effects ANOVA model, how did we know to use MS_{with} as the error term in testing each of the three hypotheses of interest?

An expected mean square for a particular source of variation represents the average mean square value for that source obtained if the same study were to be repeated an infinite number of times. For instance the expected value of mean square for factor A, represented by $E(MS_A)$, is the average value of MS_A over repeated samplings. Now we are ready to see what the expected mean squares look like for the two-factor model. Consider the alternative situations of H_0 actually being true and H_0 actually being false. If H_0 is actually true for all three tests, then the expected mean squares are

$$E(MS_A) = \sigma_\varepsilon^2$$

$$E(MS_B) = \sigma_\varepsilon^2$$

$$E(MS_{AB}) = \sigma_\varepsilon^2$$

and

$$E(MS_{\text{with}}) = \sigma_\varepsilon^2$$

where σ_ε^2 is the population variance of the residual errors. Thus, for example, $E(MS_A)$ $/E(MS_{\text{with}}) = 1$. If H_0 is actually true for A, then each of the J samples for the levels of factor A actually come from the same population with mean μ. Similar statements may be made for factor B and the interaction effect.

If H_0 is actually false for all three tests, then the expected mean squares are

$$E(MS_A) = \sigma_\varepsilon^2 + \frac{nK\sum_{j=1}^{J}\alpha_j^2}{J-1}$$

$$E(MS_B) = \sigma_\varepsilon^2 + \frac{nJ\sum_{k=1}^{K}\beta_k^2}{K-1}$$

$$E(MS_{AB}) = \sigma_\varepsilon^2 + \frac{n\sum_{j=1}^{J}\sum_{k=1}^{K}(\alpha\beta)_{jk}^2}{(J-1)(K-1)}$$

$$E(MS_{\text{with}}) = \sigma_\varepsilon^2$$

From a conceptual perspective, the $E(MS)$ values for A, B, and AB all consist of two terms. The first term consists of the now familiar population variance of the residuals. The second term consists of variation either due to the main effect for A, the main effect for B, or the interaction between A and B, respectively. Do not be overly concerned with the specifics of each $E(MS)$ yet, but just be aware that they consist of error variability due to the residuals plus systematic variability due to the effect of interest (i.e., A, B, or AB).

In forming the F ratios, we see when H_0 is false that, for example, $E(MS_A) / E(MS_{with})$ > 1. If H_0 is actually false for A, then the J samples for the levels of factor A do actually come from different populations with different means $\mu_{.j}$. There is a difference in $E(MS_A)$ when H_0 is actually true as compared to when H_0 is actually false because in the latter situation there is a second term. The size of the second term determines the outcome of the test.

In summary, the F ratio represents

$$F = \frac{\text{systematic variability} + \text{error variability}}{\text{error variability}}$$

where for the two-factor fixed-effects model, systematic variability is variability between the levels of factor A, or factor B, or the interaction between factors A and B, and error variability is variability within the groups. As always, we want to isolate the systematic variability in the numerator. For this model, the only appropriate F ratio is to use MS_{with} in the denominator, because it does serve to isolate the systematic variability. In other words, the appropriate error term for testing a particular effect (e.g., A) is the mean square that is identical to the mean square of that effect, except that it lacks a term due to the effect of interest (α). For this model, MS_{with} is the appropriate error term to use for testing each of the three hypotheses. As discussed in chapter 7, this is not the case when one or both factors are random.

Multiple-Comparison Procedures

In this section, we extend the concepts related to multiple-comparison procedures (MCPs) covered in chapter 4 to the two-factor ANOVA model. This model includes main and interaction effects; consequently you can examine contrasts of both main and interaction effects. In general, the procedures described in chapter 4 can be applied to the two-factor situation. Things become a bit more complicated in that we have row and column means (or marginal means) as well as cell means. Thus we have to be careful so that it is clear which means are indicated. We also have to be careful about which n is used based on the particular means we are comparing (e.g., whether to use the n based on a cell mean or a marginal mean).

Let us begin with contrasts of the main effects. If the effect for factor A is significant, and there are more than two levels of factor A, we can form contrasts that compare the levels of factor A ignoring factor B. Here we would be comparing the means for the levels of factor A, which are marginal means as opposed to cell means. In addition, the ns that would be in effect are those on which the marginal means are based, rather than the number of observations per cell. Thus for contrasts involving factor A, the number of observations would be nK (denoted by n_j), and for contrasts involving factor B, the number of observations would be nJ (denoted by n_k). Considering each factor separately is strongly advised; considering the factors simultaneously is to be avoided. Some statistics texts suggest that you consider the design as a one-factor model with JK levels when using MCPs to examine main effects. This is inconsistent with the design and the intent of separating effects, and is not recommended.

For contrasts involving the interaction, things get a bit more complicated. My recommendation is to begin with a complex interaction contrast if there are more than four cells in the model. Thus for a 4×4 design that consists of four levels of A (method of instruction) and four levels of B (instructor), one possibility is to test both 4×2 complex interaction contrasts. An example of one such contrast is

$$\psi' = \frac{(\overline{Y}_{.11} + \overline{Y}_{.21} + \overline{Y}_{.31} + \overline{Y}_{.41})}{4} - \frac{(\overline{Y}_{.12} + \overline{Y}_{.22} + \overline{Y}_{.32} + \overline{Y}_{.42})}{4}$$

with a standard error of

$$s_{\psi'} = \sqrt{MS_{\text{with}} \left(\sum_{j=1}^{J} \sum_{k=1}^{K} \frac{c_{jk}^2}{n_{jk}} \right)}$$

where n_{jk} is the number of observations in cell jk. This contrast would examine the interaction between the four methods of instruction and the first two instructors. The second complex interaction contrast would consider the interaction between the four methods of instruction and the other two instructors.

If the complex interaction contrast is significant, then follow this up with a simple interaction contrast that involves only four cell means. This is a single degree of freedom contrast because it involves only two levels of each factor (also known as a *tetrad difference*). An example of such a contrast is

$$\psi' = (\overline{Y}_{.11} - \overline{Y}_{.21}) - (\overline{Y}_{.12} - \overline{Y}_{.22})$$

with a similar standard error term. Using the same example, this contrast would examine the interaction between the first two methods of instruction and the first two instructors.

Other statistics texts suggest the use of simple main effects in testing a significant interaction. These involve comparing, for example, the levels of factor A at a particular level of factor B, and are generally conducted by a further partitioning of the sums of squares. However, the simple effects sums of squares represent a portion of a main effect plus the interaction effect. Despite the wonderful claims that some statisticians make, the simple main effect does not really help us to understand the interaction and is not recommended here.

Most of the MCPs previously discussed in chapter 4 can be used for testing main effects and interaction effects. Just be sure to insert the appropriate cell or marginal means with the right number of observations and the right degrees of freedom. There is considerable debate about the appropriate use of interaction contrasts (e.g., Boik, 1979; Marascuilo & Levin, 1970, 1976).

Measures of Association

Various measures of the strength of association between the effects and Y have been proposed. Let us examine briefly two of these measures, which assume equal variances across the cells. First we have η^2, known as the correlation ratio, which represents the proportion of variation in Y explained by the effect of interest (i.e., by factor A, or factor B or the AB interaction). We can compute η^2 as

$$\eta_A^2 = SS_A / SS_{total}$$

$$\eta_B^2 = SS_B / SS_{total}$$

$$\eta_{AB}^2 = SS_{AB} / SS_{total}$$

As discussed previously in chapter 3, this statistic is conceptually similar to the R^2 statistic used in regression analysis, and like R^2 is a biased statistic.

Another measure of the strength of the association between the effects and Y is the statistic ω^2. We can compute ω^2 as

$$\omega_A^2 = \frac{SS_A - (J-1)MS_{with}}{SS_{total} + MS_{with}}$$

$$\omega_B^2 = \frac{SS_B - (K-1)MS_{with}}{SS_{total} + MS_{with}}$$

$$\omega_{AB}^2 = \frac{SS_{AB} - (J-1)(K-1)MS_{with}}{SS_{total} + MS_{with}}$$

depending again on the effect of interest.

Each of these measures does have limitations having to do with equal group variances, and/or equal ns. Thus it is difficult to make a recommendation as to the use of these measures (Keppel, 1982; O'Grady, 1982; Wilcox, 1987). In addition, there is no magical rule of thumb for interpreting the size of these statistics, only that they are scaled theoretically from zero (no association) to one (perfect association). It is up to researchers in the particular substantive area of research to interpret the magnitude of these measures by comparing their results to the results of other similar studies.

The Relationship Between ANOVA and Regression Analysis

It is possible to extend the previous discussion from chapter 3 on the relationship between the analysis of variance and regression analysis (i.e., the general linear model). We do not, however, because there is nothing really new to add to a conceptual discussion. Computationally, things get a bit more complicated in terms of dealing with two independent variables as well as their interaction. Suffice it to say, using regression analysis to do ANOVA would necessitate a set of qualitatively coded variables for the levels of factor A, a set for the levels of factor B, and a set for the levels of the interaction between factors A and B. This type regression model was previously covered in chapters 2 and 3; for the two-factor ANOVA model in regression see Kirk (1982), Pedhazur (1997), and Kleinbaum et al. (1998).

An Example

Consider the following illustration of the two-factor design. Here we expand on the example presented in chapter 3 by adding a second factor to the model. Our dependent variable will again be the number of times a student attends statistics lab during one semester (or quarter), factor A is the attractiveness of the lab instructor (assuming each instructor is of the same gender and is equally competent), and factor B is the time of day the lab is offered. Thus the researcher is interested in whether the attractiveness of the instructor, the time of day, or the interaction of attractiveness and time influences student attendance in the statistics lab. The attractiveness levels are defined as (a) unattractive, (b) slightly attractive, (c) moderately attractive, and (d) very attractive. The time of day levels are defined as (a) afternoon lab and (b) evening lab. Students were randomly assigned to a combination of lab instructor and lab time at the beginning of the semester, and attendance was taken by the instructor. There were four students in each cell and eight cells (combinations of instructor and time) for a total of 32 observations. Students could attend a maximum of 30 lab sessions. In Table 5.4 we see the data and sample means for each cell (given beneath each cell), column, row, and overall.

Let us begin the ANOVA computations. First we compute the sums of squares.

$$SS_{total} = \sum_{i=1}^{n}\sum_{j=1}^{J}\sum_{k=1}^{K} Y_{ijk}^2 - \frac{\left(\sum_{i=1}^{n}\sum_{j=1}^{J}\sum_{k=1}^{K} Y_{ijk}\right)^2}{N} = 1{,}749.7188$$

$$SS_{A} = \sum_{j=1}^{J} \frac{\left(\sum_{i=1}^{n}\sum_{k=1}^{K} Y_{ijk}\right)^2}{nK} - \frac{\left(\sum_{i=1}^{n}\sum_{j=1}^{J}\sum_{k=1}^{K} Y_{ijk}\right)^2}{N} = 738.5938$$

$$SS_{B} = \sum_{k=1}^{K} \frac{\left(\sum_{i=1}^{n}\sum_{j=1}^{J} Y_{ijk}\right)^2}{nJ} - \frac{\left(\sum_{i=1}^{n}\sum_{j=1}^{J}\sum_{k=1}^{K} Y_{ijk}\right)^2}{N} = 712.5313$$

$$SS_{AB} = \sum_{j=1}^{J}\sum_{k=1}^{K} \frac{\left(\sum_{i=1}^{n} Y_{ijk}\right)^2}{n} - \sum_{j=1}^{J} \frac{\left(\sum_{i=1}^{n}\sum_{k=1}^{K} Y_{ijk}\right)^2}{nK} - \sum_{k=1}^{K} \frac{\left(\sum_{i=1}^{n}\sum_{j=1}^{J} Y_{ijk}\right)^2}{nJ} + \frac{\left(\sum_{i=1}^{n}\sum_{j=1}^{J}\sum_{k=1}^{K} Y_{ijk}\right)^2}{N}$$

$$= 21.8438$$

$$SS_{with} = \sum_{i=1}^{n}\sum_{j=1}^{J}\sum_{k=1}^{K} Y_{ijk}^2 - \sum_{j=1}^{J}\sum_{k=1}^{K} \frac{\left(\sum_{i=1}^{n} Y_{ijk}\right)^2}{n} = 276.7500$$

[handwritten: 8 groups (4×2)]
[handwritten: $n = 4$]
[handwritten: $N = 32$]

TABLE 5.4

Data for the Statistics Lab Example: Number of Statistics Labs Attended,
by Level of Attractiveness and Time of Day

[handwritten: Factor A] *[handwritten: Factor B]*

Level of Attractiveness	Time of Day		Row Mean
	Time 1	Time 2	
Attractiveness 1	15	10	11.1250
	12	8	
	21	7	
	13	3	
	15.2500	7.0000	
Attractiveness 2	20	13	17.8750
	22	9	
	24	18	
	25	12	
	22.7500	13.0000	
Attractiveness 3	24	10	20.2500
	29	12	
	27	21	
	25	14	
	26.2500	14.2500	
Attractiveness 4	30	22	24.3750
	26	20	
	29	25	
	28	15	
	28.2500	20.2500	
Column mean	23.1250	13.6875	18.4063 (Overall mean)

[handwritten annotations on Attractiveness 1: $\Sigma y^2 = 979$, $\Sigma = 61$, $61^2 = 3721$; $28^2 = 784$, $\Sigma = 28$, $\Sigma y^2 = 222$; $\Sigma Row = 89$]

[handwritten annotations on Attractiveness 2: $\Sigma y^2 = 2085$, $\Sigma = 91$, $91^2 = 8281$; $52^2 = 2704$, $\Sigma = 52$, $\Sigma y^2 = 718$; $\Sigma Row = 143$]

[handwritten annotations on Attractiveness 3: $\Sigma y^2 = 2771$, $\Sigma = 105$, $105^2 = 11025$; $57^2 = 3249$, $\Sigma = 57$, $\Sigma y^2 = 881$; $\Sigma Row = 162$]

[handwritten annotations on Attractiveness 4: $\Sigma y^2 = 3201$, $\Sigma = 113$, $113^2 = 12769$; $82^2 = 6724$, $\Sigma = 82$, $\Sigma y^2 = 1734$; $\Sigma Row = 195$]

[handwritten: Σ column = 370, $\Sigma Y..1 = 136900$, Σ Column = 219, $\Sigma y..2 = 47961$, $\Sigma y^2_{TOT} = 12591$]

Next we compute the mean squares:

$$MS_A = \frac{SS_A}{df_A} = \frac{738.5938}{3} = 246.1979$$

$$MS_B = \frac{SS_B}{df_B} = \frac{712.5313}{1} = 712.5313$$

$$MS_{AB} = \frac{SS_{AB}}{df_{AB}} = \frac{21.8438}{3} = 7.2813$$

$$MS_{with} = \frac{SS_{with}}{df_{with}} = \frac{276.7500}{24} = 11.5313$$

[handwritten: $\Sigma y_{TOTAL} = 589$, $\frac{(\Sigma y)^2}{32} = 10841.28125$]

Finally we compute the F-test statistics:

$$F_A = \frac{MS_A}{MS_{with}} = \frac{246.1979}{11.5313} = 21.3504$$

$$F_B = \frac{MS_B}{MS_{with}} = \frac{712.5313}{11.5313} = 61.7911$$

$$F_{AB} = \frac{MS_{AB}}{MS_{with}} = \frac{7.2813}{11.5313} = 0.6314$$

The test statistics are compared to the critical values $_{.95}F_{3,24} = 3.01$ for the A and AB effects and $_{.95}F_{1,24} = 4.26$ for the B effect, obtained from Appendix Table 4, using the .05 level of significance. The test statistics exceed the critical values for the A and B effects only, so we reject these H_0 and conclude that both the level of attractiveness and time of day are related to mean differences in statistics lab attendance. The interaction was shown not to be a significant effect. These results are summarized in the ANOVA summary table as shown in Table 5.5. If you would like to see an example of a two-factor design where the interaction is significant, take a look at the fifth section in chapter 7.

Let us next estimate the main and interaction effects. The main effects for the levels of A are estimated to be:

$$a_1 = \overline{Y}_{.1.} - \overline{Y}_{...} = 11.1250 - 18.4063 = -7.2813$$

$$a_2 = \overline{Y}_{.2.} - \overline{Y}_{...} = 17.8750 - 18.4063 = -0.5313$$

$$a_3 = \overline{Y}_{.3.} - \overline{Y}_{...} = 20.2500 - 18.4063 = 1.8437$$

$$a_4 = \overline{Y}_{.4.} - \overline{Y}_{...} = 24.3750 - 18.4063 = 5.9687$$

TABLE 5.5
Two-Factor Analysis of Variance Summary Table—Statistics Lab Example

Source	SS	df	MS	F
Between				
A	738.5938	3	246.1979	21.3504*
B	712.5313	1	712.5313	61.7911**
AB	21.8438	3	7.2813	0.6314*
Within	276.7500	24	11.5313	
Total	1749.7188	31		

*$_{.95}F_{3,24} = 3.01$.
**$_{.95}F_{1,24} = 4.26$.

The main effects for the levels of B are estimated to be:

$$b_1 = \overline{Y}_{.1} - \overline{Y}_{...} = 23.1250 - 18.4063 = 4.7187$$

$$b_2 = \overline{Y}_{.2} - \overline{Y}_{...} = 13.6875 - 18.4063 = -4.7188$$

Finally, the interaction effects for the various combinations of the levels of factors A and B are estimated to be:

$$(ab)_{11} = \overline{Y}_{.11} - (\overline{Y}_{.1.} + \overline{Y}_{.1} - \overline{Y}_{...}) = 15.2500 - (11.1250 + 23.1250 - 18.4063) = -0.5937$$

$$(ab)_{12} = \overline{Y}_{.12} - (\overline{Y}_{.1.} + \overline{Y}_{.2} - \overline{Y}_{...}) = 7.0000 - (11.1250 + 13.6875 - 18.4063) = 0.5938$$

$$(ab)_{21} = \overline{Y}_{.21} - (\overline{Y}_{.2.} + \overline{Y}_{.1} - \overline{Y}_{...}) = 22.7500 - (17.8750 + 23.1250 - 18.4063) = 0.1563$$

$$(ab)_{22} = \overline{Y}_{.22} - (\overline{Y}_{.2.} + \overline{Y}_{.2} - \overline{Y}_{...}) = 13.0000 - (17.8750 + 13.6875 - 18.4063) = -0.1562$$

$$(ab)_{31} = \overline{Y}_{.31} - (\overline{Y}_{.3.} + \overline{Y}_{.1} - \overline{Y}_{...}) = 26.2500 - (20.2500 + 23.1250 - 18.4063) = 1.2813$$

$$(ab)_{32} = \overline{Y}_{.32} - (\overline{Y}_{.3.} + \overline{Y}_{.2} - \overline{Y}_{...}) = 14.2500 - (20.2500 + 13.6875 - 18.4063) = -1.2812$$

$$(ab)_{41} = \overline{Y}_{.41} - (\overline{Y}_{.4.} + \overline{Y}_{.1} - \overline{Y}_{...}) = 28.2500 - (24.3750 + 23.1250 - 18.4063) = -0.8437$$

$$(ab)_{42} = \overline{Y}_{.42} - (\overline{Y}_{.4.} + \overline{Y}_{.2} - \overline{Y}_{...}) = 20.5000 - (24.3750 + 13.6875 - 18.4063) = 0.8438$$

The profile plot shown in Fig. 5.2 graphically depicts these effects. The A effect was significant and has more than two levels, so let us consider one example of a multiple comparison procedure, Tukey's HSD test. Recall from chapter 4 that the HSD test is a family-wise procedure most appropriate for considering all pairwise contrasts with a balanced design (which is the case for these data). The following are the computations:

Critical value (obtained from Appendix Table 9):

$$_{1-\alpha}q_{df(\text{with}), J} = {}_{.95}q_{24,4} = 3.901$$

Standard error:

$$s_{\psi'} = \sqrt{\frac{MS_{\text{with}}}{n_j}} = \sqrt{\frac{11.5313}{8}} = 1.2006$$

Test statistics:

$$q_1 = \frac{\overline{Y}_{.4.} - \overline{Y}_{.1.}}{s_{\psi'}} = \frac{24.3750 - 11.1250}{1.2006} = 11.0361 \text{ (significant)}$$

$$q_2 = \frac{\overline{Y}_{.4.} - \overline{Y}_{.2.}}{s_{\psi'}} = \frac{24.3750 - 17.8750}{1.2006} = 5.4140 \text{ (significant)}$$

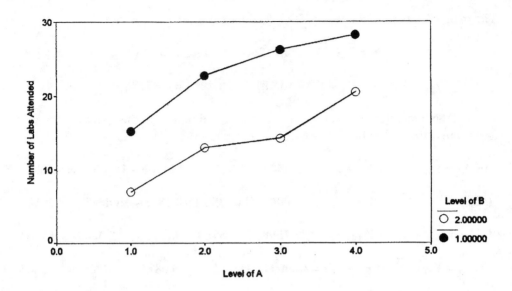

FIG. 5.2   Profile plot for example data.

$$q_3 = \frac{\overline{Y}_{.4.} - \overline{Y}_{.3.}}{s_{\psi'}} = \frac{24.3750 - 20.2500}{1.2006} = 3.4358 \text{ (nonsignificant)}$$

$$q_4 = \frac{\overline{Y}_{.3.} - \overline{Y}_{.1.}}{s_{\psi'}} = \frac{20.2500 - 11.1250}{1.2006} = 7.6004 \text{ (significant)}$$

$$q_5 = \frac{\overline{Y}_{.3.} - \overline{Y}_{.2.}}{s_{\psi'}} = \frac{20.2500 - 17.8750}{1.2006} = 1.9782 \text{ (nonsignificant)}$$

$$q_6 = \frac{\overline{Y}_{.2.} - \overline{Y}_{.1.}}{s_{\psi'}} = \frac{17.8750 - 11.1250}{1.2006} = 5.6222 \text{ (significant)}$$

These results indicate that the means for the levels of factor A are significantly different for levels 1 and 4, 2 and 4, 1 and 3, and 1 and 2. Thus, level 1 (unattractive) is significantly different from the other three levels of attractiveness, and levels 2 and 4 (slightly unattractive vs. very attractive) are also significantly different. These results are somewhat different than those found with the one-factor model in chapter 4 for one main reason (where levels 1 and 4 as well as 1 and 3 were different). The MS_{with} has been reduced with the introduction of the second factor from 36.1116 to 11.5313. You should recall that this is one of the benefits we mentioned earlier about the use of additional factors in the model. Finally, although the B effect was significant, there are only two levels of the B factor, and thus we need not carry out any additional multiple comparisons (attendance is better in the afternoon section).

Finally we can estimate the measures of association. The correlation ratios η^2 are calculated to be

$$\eta_A^2 = \frac{SS_A}{SS_{total}} = \frac{738.5938}{1,749.7188} = 0.4221$$

$$\eta_B^2 = \frac{SS_B}{SS_{total}} = \frac{712.5313}{1,749.7188} = 0.4072$$

$$\eta_{AB}^2 = \frac{SS_{AB}}{SS_{total}} = \frac{21.8438}{1,749.7188} = 0.0125$$

We calculate the ω^2 to be

$$\omega_A^2 = \frac{SS_A - (J-1)MS_{with}}{SS_{total} + MS_{with}} = \frac{738.5938 - (3)11.5313}{1,749.7188 + 11.5313} = 0.3997$$

$$\omega_B^2 = \frac{SS_B - (K-1)MS_{with}}{SS_{total} + MS_{with}} = \frac{712.5313 - (1)11.5313}{1,749.7188 + 11.5313} = 0.3980$$

$$\omega_{AB}^2 = \frac{SS_{AB} - (J-1)(K-1)MS_{with}}{SS_{total} + MS_{with}} = \frac{21.8438 - (3)11.5313}{1,749.7188 + 11.5313} = -0.0072$$

Based on the measures of association, and without knowledge of other research on instructor attractiveness and time of day, one would conclude that there is a moderate relationship between instructor attractiveness and lab attendance, a moderate relationship between time of day and lab attendance, but no relationship between the time–attractiveness interaction and lab attendance.

THREE-FACTOR AND HIGHER ORDER ANOVA

Characteristics of the Model

All of the characteristics that we discussed for the two-factor model apply to the three-factor model, with one obvious exception. There are three factors rather than two. This will result in three main effects (one for each factor known as A, B, and C), three two-way interactions (known as AB, AC, and BC), and one three-way interaction (known as ABC). Here the only new concept is the three-way interaction, which may be stated as follows: Is the AB interaction constant across all levels of factor C? This may also be stated as "AC across the levels of B" or as "BC across the levels of A," where the choice of statements has no impact on the test itself (i.e., there is only one way of testing the three-way interaction no matter how it is stated).

We do not explicitly consider models with more than three factors (cf. Marascuilo & Serlin, 1988). However, be warned that such models do exist, and that they will necessarily result in more main effects, more two-way interactions, more three-way interactions, as well as higher order interactions. Conceptually, the only change is to add these additional terms to the model. Computationally, one would do well to use a computer especially for factorial models, although I strongly recommend the use of computers for all general linear models.

The ANOVA Model

The model for the three factor design is

$$Y_{ijkl} = \mu + \alpha_j + \beta_k + \gamma_l + (\alpha\beta)_{jk} + (\alpha\gamma)_{jl} + (\beta\gamma)_{kl} + (\alpha\beta\gamma)_{jkl} + \varepsilon_{ijkl}$$

where Y_{ijkl} is the observed score on the criterion variable for individual i in level j of factor A, level k of factor B, and level l of factor C (or in the jkl cell), μ is the overall or grand population mean (i.e., regardless of cell designation), α_j is the effect for level j of factor A, β_k is the effect for level k of factor B, γ_l is the effect for level l of factor C, $(\alpha\beta)_{jk}$ is the interaction effect for the combination of level j of factor A and level k of factor B, $(\alpha\gamma)_{jl}$ is the interaction effect for the combination of level j of factor A and level l of factor C, $(\beta\gamma)_{kl}$ is the interaction effect for the combination of level k of factor B and level l of factor C, $(\alpha\beta\gamma)_{jkl}$ is the interaction effect for the combination of level j of factor A, level k of factor B, and level l of factor C, and ε_{ijkl} is the random residual error for individual i in cell jkl. The population effects and residual error are computed, in simplest form, as

$$\alpha_j = \mu_{.j..} - \mu$$

$$\beta_k = \mu_{..k.} - \mu$$

$$\gamma_l = \mu_{...l} - \mu$$

$$(\alpha\beta)_{jk} = \mu_{.jk.} - (\mu + \alpha_j + \beta_k)$$

$$(\alpha\gamma)_{jl} = \mu_{.j.l} - (\mu + \alpha_j + \gamma_l)$$

$$(\beta\gamma)_{kl} = \mu_{..kl} - (\mu + \beta_k + \gamma_l)$$

$$(\alpha\beta\gamma)_{jkl} = \mu_{.jkl} - [\mu + \alpha_j + \beta_k + \gamma_l + (\alpha\beta)_{jk} + (\alpha\gamma)_{jl} + (\beta\gamma)_{kl}]$$

$$\varepsilon_{ijkl} = Y_{ijkl} - \mu_{.jkl}$$

These effects may be estimated, of course, through the use of sample means along the lines discussed earlier in this chapter. Given that there are three main effects, three two-way interactions, and a three-way interaction, there will be an accompanying null and alternative hypothesis for each of these effects. At this point in your statistics career, the hypotheses should be obvious (simply expand on the hypotheses in the first section if you need help).

The ANOVA Summary Table

The ANOVA summary table for the three-factor model is shown in Table 5.6. As always, there are columns for the sources of variation, sums of squares, degrees of freedom, mean squares, and F values. It would be ludicrous to conduct a three-factor ANOVA by hand, so I do not provide the computational formulas for the sums-of-squares terms. If you are not already using computer software to do your statistical analyses, now is a good time to begin.

The Triple Interaction

Everything else about the three-factor design follows an expanded version of the two-factor model. The assumptions are the same. The expected mean squares are conceptually the same, such that MS_{with} is the error term used for testing each of the hypotheses in the fixed-effects model. The multiple comparison procedures discussed in the preceding section can be expanded fairly easily. Just remember to use the appropriate ns on which the sample means being compared are based. The main new feature is the three-way interaction. If this interaction is significant, then interpretation of the two-way interactions is difficult. Remember what we said about having a significant two-factor interaction before with the two-factor model? The same goes here with the three-factor interaction, except here the other interactions are confounded.

Although the inclusion of additional factors in the design should result in a reduction in error variation, there is a price to pay for the study of additional factors. Several things can get out of hand. Each additional factor requires more cells and usually more observations, which result in additional costs in terms of time and money. Although the analysis is no big deal with the use of the computer, one should be concerned with the higher order interactions. If you find, for example, that the four-factor interaction is significant, how do you deal with it? First you have to interpret this interaction (which is sometimes difficult if it is unexpected and/or has not previously been de-

TABLE 5.6
Three-Factor Analysis of Variance Summary Table

Source	SS	df	MS	F
Between				
A	SS_A	$J-1$	MS_A	MS_A/MS_{with}
B	SS_B	$K-1$	MS_B	MS_B/MS_{with}
C	SS_C	$L-1$	MS_C	MS_C/MS_{with}
AB	SS_{AB}	$(J-1)(K-1)$	MS_{AB}	MS_{AB}/MS_{with}
AC	SS_{AC}	$(J-1)(L-1)$	MS_{AC}	MS_{AC}/MS_{with}
BC	SS_{BC}	$(K-1)(L-1)$	MS_{BC}	MS_{BC}/MS_{with}
ABC	SS_{ABC}	$(J-1)(K-1)(L-1)$	MS_{ABC}	MS_{ABC}/MS_{with}
Within	SS_{with}	$N-JKL$	MS_{with}	
Total	SS_{total}	$N-1$		

tected in other research); then you have trouble in dealing with the interpretation of your other effects. My advice is simple. Do not include additional factors just because they sound interesting. Only include those factors that are theoretically and empirically important and interpretable. Then if a significant higher order interaction occurs, you will be in a better position to understand it because you have already thought about its consequences. Reporting that an interaction is significant but not interpretable is not sound research.

FACTORIAL ANOVA WITH UNEQUAL *n*s

Up to this point in the chapter, we have only considered the equal *n*s or balanced case. That is, the model used was where the number of observations in each cell was equal. This served to make the formulas and equations easier to deal with. However, we need not assume that the *n*s are equal. In this section we discuss ways to deal with the unequal *n*s (or unbalanced) case for the two-factor model, although these notions can be transferred to higher order models as well.

First, let us make a distinction between those designs with equal *n*s, with proportional *n*s and with disproportional *n*s. The equal *n*s case has already been covered in this chapter. Proportional cell *n*s are such that the number of observations in each cell is equal to

$$n_{jk} = \frac{n_j n_k}{N}$$

for all *j* and *k*, where n_{jk} is the number of observations in cell *jk*, n_j is the number of observations in level *j* of factor A, n_k is the number of observations in level *k* of factor B, and *N* is the total number of observations. Some examples of proportional *n*s are shown in Table 5.7 (check out the proportionality on your own). The traditional equal *n*s ANOVA can be used for the proportional *n*'s case with minor modifications. The computations of the sums of squares are (note the minor modifications)

$$SS_{total} = \sum_{i=1}^{n_{jk}} \sum_{j=1}^{J} \sum_{k=1}^{K} Y_{ijk}^2 - \frac{\left(\sum_{i=1}^{n_{jk}} \sum_{j=1}^{J} \sum_{k=1}^{K} Y_{ijk} \right)^2}{N}$$

$$SS_{A} = \sum_{j=1}^{J} \left[\frac{\left(\sum_{i=1}^{n_{jk}} \sum_{k=1}^{K} Y_{ijk} \right)^2}{n_j} \right] - \frac{\left(\sum_{i=1}^{n_{jk}} \sum_{j=1}^{J} \sum_{k=1}^{K} Y_{ijk} \right)^2}{N}$$

$$SS_{B} = \sum_{k=1}^{K} \left[\frac{\left(\sum_{i=1}^{n_{jk}} \sum_{j=1}^{J} Y_{ijk} \right)^2}{n_k} \right] - \frac{\left(\sum_{i=1}^{n_{jk}} \sum_{j=1}^{J} \sum_{k=1}^{K} Y_{ijk} \right)^2}{N}$$

$$SS_{AB} = \sum_{j=1}^{J}\sum_{k=1}^{K}\left[\frac{\left(\sum_{i=1}^{n_{jk}} Y_{ijk}\right)^2}{n_{jk}}\right] - \sum_{j=1}^{J}\left[\frac{\left(\sum_{i=1}^{n_{jk}}\sum_{k=1}^{K} Y_{ijk}\right)^2}{n_{j}}\right] - \sum_{k=1}^{K}\left[\frac{\left(\sum_{i=1}^{n_{jk}}\sum_{j=1}^{J} Y_{ijk}\right)^2}{n_{k}}\right] + \frac{\left(\sum_{i=1}^{n_{jk}}\sum_{j=1}^{J}\sum_{k=1}^{K} Y_{ijk}\right)^2}{N}$$

$$SS_{with} = \sum_{i=1}^{n_{jk}}\sum_{j=1}^{J}\sum_{k=1}^{K} Y_{ijk}^2 - \sum_{j=1}^{J}\sum_{k=1}^{K}\left[\frac{\left(\sum_{i=1}^{n_{jk}} Y_{ijk}\right)^2}{n_{jk}}\right]$$

The disproportional ns case occurs when the ns are unequal and do not follow the proportionality rule previously stated. This is the tricky case because the main effects and the interaction effect are not orthogonal. In other words, the sums of squares cannot be partitioned into independent effects. As a result, there are several computational approaches that attempt to deal with the disproportionality. In the old days, prior to the wide availability of high-speed computing, the standard approach to this problem was to use unweighted means analysis. This is essentially an analysis of means, rather than raw scores, which are unweighted by cell size. This approach is only an approximate procedure in terms of the F-test statistic being distributed as F. Due to the availability of quality statistical software for dealing with this problem, the unweighted means approach is no longer necessary. Another silly approach is to delete enough data until you have either a proportional ns model or an equal ns model.

TABLE 5.7
Proportional ns Examples

Example 1

	b_1	b_2	b_3	
a_1	$n_{11} = 5$	$n_{12} = 5$	$n_{13} = 5$	$n_{1.} = 15$
a_2	$n_{21} = 7$	$n_{22} = 7$	$n_{23} = 7$	$n_{2.} = 21$
	$n_{.1} = 12$	$n_{.2} = 12$	$n_{.3} = 12$	$N = 36$

Example 2

	b_1	b_2	b_3	
a_1	$n_{11} = 4$	$n_{12} = 6$	$n_{13} = 8$	$n_{1.} = 18$
a_2	$n_{21} = 4$	$n_{22} = 6$	$n_{23} = 8$	$n_{2.} = 18$
	$n_{.1} = 8$	$n_{.2} = 12$	$n_{.3} = 16$	$N = 36$

Example 3

	b_1	b_2	b_3	
a_1	$n_{11} = 2$	$n_{12} = 4$	$n_{13} = 6$	$n_{1.} = 12$
a_2	$n_{21} = 4$	$n_{22} = 8$	$n_{23} = 12$	$n_{2.} = 24$
	$n_{.1} = 6$	$n_{.2} = 12$	$n_{.3} = 18$	$N = 36$

There are three other approaches to the disproportional *ns* case. Each of these approaches really tests different hypotheses and thus may result in different conclusions: (a) the *sequential approach* (also known as the hierarchical sums of squares approach), (b) the *partially sequential approach* (also known as the partially hierarchical, or experimental design or method of fitting constants approach), and (c) the *regression approach* (also known as the marginal means or unique approach). There has been considerable debate over the past three decades about the relative merits of each approach (e.g., Applebaum & Cramer, 1974; Carlson & Timm, 1974; Cramer & Applebaum, 1980; Overall, Lee, & Hornick, 1981; Overall & Spiegel, 1969; Timm & Carlson, 1975).

Briefly, here is what each approach is testing. In the sequential approach, the effects being tested are:

$$\alpha \mid \mu$$

$$\beta \mid \mu, \alpha$$

$$\alpha\beta \mid \mu, \alpha, \beta$$

This indicates, for example, that the effect for factor B is adjusted for (as denoted by the vertical line) the overall mean (μ) and the effect due to factor A (α). Thus, each effect is adjusted for prior effects in the sequential order given. Here the α effect is given theoretical or practical priority over the β effect. In SAS PROC GLM and in SPSS, this is the Type I sum of squares method.

In the partially sequential approach, the effects being tested are:

$$\alpha \mid \mu, \beta$$

$$\beta \mid \mu, \alpha$$

$$\alpha\beta \mid \mu, \alpha, \beta$$

There is difference here because each main effect controls for the other main effect, but not for the interaction effect. In SAS PROC GLM and in SPSS, this is the Type II sum of squares method. This is the only one of the three methods where the sums of squares add up to the total sum of squares. Notice in the sequential and partially sequential approaches that the interaction is not taken into account in estimating the main effects. This is fine if there is no interaction effect, but is problematic if the interaction is significant.

In the regression approach, the effects being tested are:

$$\alpha \mid \mu, \beta, \alpha\beta$$

$$\beta \mid \mu, \alpha, \alpha\beta$$

$$\alpha\beta \mid \mu, \alpha, \beta$$

In this case each effect controls for each of the other effects. In SAS PROC GLM and in SPSS, this is the Type III sum of squares method. Many statisticians, including myself, recommend exclusive use of the regression approach because each effect is estimated taking the other effects into account. The hypotheses tested in the sequential and partially sequential methods are seldom of interest and are difficult to interpret (Carlson & Timm, 1974; Kirk, 1982; Overall et al., 1981; Timm & Carlson, 1975). The regression method seems to be conceptually closest to the traditional analysis of variance. When the *ns* are equal, each of these three methods tests the same hypotheses and yields the same results.

SUMMARY

This chapter considered methods involving the comparison of means for multiple independent variables. The chapter began with a look at the characteristics of the factorial analysis of variance, including:

1. Two or more independent variables each with two or more fixed levels.
2. Subjects are randomly assigned to cells and then exposed to only one combination of the independent variables.
3. The factors are fully crossed such that all possible combinations of the factors' levels are included in the design.
4. The dependent variable is at least measured at the interval level.

The ANOVA model was examined and followed by a discussion of main effects and, in particular, the interaction effect. Some discussion was also devoted to the ANOVA assumptions, their assessment, and how to deal with assumption violations. The ANOVA summary table was shown, as well as the computational formulas for the sums of squares. The expected mean squares were given for the two-factor case. The notion of multiple comparisons provided in chapter 4 was then extended to factorial models. Finally, several procedures were given for dealing with the unequal *ns* case for factorial models. At this point you should have met the following objectives: (a) be able to understand the characteristics and concepts underlying factorial ANOVA, (b) be able to compute and interpret the results of factorial ANOVA (balanced and unbalanced), and (c) be able to understand and evaluate the assumptions of factorial ANOVA (balanced and unbalanced). In chapter 6 we consider an introduction to the analysis of covariance.

PROBLEMS

Conceptual Problems

1. You are given a two-factor design with the following cell means (cell 11 = 25; cell 12 = 75; cell 21 = 50; cell 22 = 50; cell 31 = 75; cell 32 = 25). Assume that the within cell variation is small. Which one of the following conclusions seems most probable?

   a. The row means are significantly different.

    b.   The column means are significantly different.

    c.   The interaction is significant.

    d.   All of the above.

2.   In a two-factor ANOVA, one independent variable has five levels and the second has four levels. If each cell has seven observations, what is df_{with}?

    a.   20

    b.   120

    c.   139

    d.   140

3.   Which of the following conclusions would result in the greatest generalizability of the main effect for factor A across the levels of factor B? The interaction between the independent variables A and B was

    a.   not significant at the .25 level.

    b.   significant at the .10 level.

    c.   significant at the .05 level.

    d.   significant at the .01 level.

    e.   significant at the .001 level.

4.   In a two-factor fixed-effects ANOVA, $F_A = 2$, $df_A = 3$, $df_B = 6$, $df_{AB} = 18$, $df_{with} = 56$. The null hypothesis for factor A can be rejected

    a.   at the .01 level.

    b.   at the .05 level but not at the .01 level.

    c.   at the .10 level but not at the .05 level.

    d.   none of the above.

5.   In ANOVA the interaction of two factors is certainly present when

    a.   the two factors are positively correlated.

    b.   the two factors are negatively correlated.

    c.   row effects are not consistent across columns.

    d.   main effects do not account for all of the variation in Y.

    e.   main effects do account for all of the variation in Y.

Questions 6 through 9 are based on the following ANOVA summary table (fixed effects):

Source	df	MS	F
A	2	45	4.5
B	1	70	7.0
AB	2	170	17.0
Within	60	10	

6. For which source of variation is the null hypothesis rejected at the .01 level of significance?
       a. A
       b. B
       c. AB
       d. all of the above

7. How many cells are there in the design?
       a. 1
       b. 2
       c. 3
       d. 5
       e. none of the above

8. The total sample size for the design is
       a. 66
       b. 68
       c. 70
       d. none of the above

9. SS_{AB} is equal to
       a. 170
       b. 340
       c. 510
       d. 1,020
       e. none of the above

10. In a design with four factors, how many interactions will there be?
        a. 4
        b. 8
        c. 11
        d. 12
        e. 16

11. Degrees of freedom for the AB interaction are equal to
        a. $df_A - df_B$
        b. $(df_A)(df_B)$
        c. $df_{with} - (df_A + df_B)$
        d. $df_{tot} - df_{with}$

12. A two-factor experiment means that the design includes
        a. two independent variables.
        b. two dependent variables.

      c.   an interaction between independent and dependent variables.

      d.   exactly two separate groups of subjects.

13.   Two independent variables are said to interact when
      a.   both variables are equally influenced by a third variable.
      b.   the variables are differentially affected by a third variable.
      c.   both factors produce a change in the subjects' scores.
      d.   the effect of one variable depends on the second variable.

14.   If there is an interaction between the independent variables textbook and time of day, this means that the textbook used has the same effect at different times of the day. True or false?

15.   If the AB interaction is significant, then at least one of the two main effects must be significant. True or false?

16.   If all three null hypotheses are true in a two factor model, I assert that each of the following is an estimate of population residual variance: $MS_A, MS_B, MS_{AB}, MS_{with}$. Am I correct?

17.   I assert that a two-factor experiment (using factors A and B) yields no more information than two single factor experiments (using factor A in experiment 1 and factor B in experiment 2). Am I correct?

18.   For a two-factor fixed-effects model, if the degrees of freedom for the test of factor A = 2,24, then I assert that the degrees of freedom for the test of factor B will necessarily be = 2,24. Am I correct?

Computational Problems

1.   Complete the following summary table for a two-factor analysis of variance, where there are two levels of factor A and three levels of factor B. In each cell of the design there are 26 students. Complete the following summary table below where $\alpha = .05$.

Source	SS	df	MS	F	Critical Value	Decision
A	6.15	—	—	—	—	—
B	10.60	—	—	—	—	—
AB	9.10	—	—	—	—	—
Within	—	—	—			
Total	250.85	—				

2.   Complete the following summary table for a two-factor analysis of variance, where there are three levels of factor A and two levels of factor B. In each cell of the design there are four students. Complete the following summary table where $\alpha = .01$.

Source	SS	df	MS	F	Critical Value	Decision
A	3.64	—	—	—	—	—
B	.57	—	—	—	—	—
AB	2.07	—	—	—	—	—
Within	—	—	—			
Total	8.18	—				

3. The following independent random samples are obtained from populations assumed to be normally distributed with equal variances:

A_1B_1: 41, 39, 25, 25, 37, 51, 39, 101
A_1B_2: 46, 54, 97, 93, 51, 36, 29, 69
A_1B_3: 113, 135, 109, 96, 47, 49, 68, 38
A_2B_1: 86, 38, 45, 45, 60, 106, 106, 31
A_2B_2: 74, 96, 101, 124, 48, 113, 139, 131
A_2B_3: 152, 79, 135, 144, 52, 102, 166, 155

Conduct a two-factor ANOVA to determine if there are any effects due to A, B or the AB interaction ($\alpha = .01$). Conduct Scheffé post hoc comparisons if necessary.

4. An experimenter is interested in the effects of strength of reinforcement (factor A), type of reinforcement (factor B), and sex of the adult administering the reinforcement (factor C) on children's behavior. Each factor consists of two levels. Thirty-two children are randomly assigned to 8 cells (i.e., 4 per cell), one for each of the factor combinations. Using the data that follow, conduct an analysis of variance ($\alpha = .05$). If there are any significant interactions, graph the interactions and interpret them.

$A_1B_1C_1$: 3, 6, 3, 3
$A_1B_1C_2$: 4, 5, 4, 3
$A_1B_2C_1$: 7, 8, 7, 6
$A_1B_2C_2$: 7, 8, 9, 8
$A_2B_1C_1$: 1, 2, 2, 2
$A_2B_1C_2$: 2, 3, 4, 3
$A_2B_2C_1$: 5, 6, 5, 6
$A_2B_2C_2$: 10, 10, 9, 11

6

INTRODUCTION TO ANALYSIS OF COVARIANCE: THE ONE-FACTOR FIXED-EFFECTS MODEL WITH A SINGLE COVARIATE

Chapter Outline

10. Using statistical packages
11. ANCOVA without randomization
12. More complex ANCOVA models
13. Nonparametric ANCOVA procedures

Key Concepts

1. Statistical adjustment
2. Covariate
3. Adjusted means
4. Homogeneity of regression slopes
5. Independence of the independent variable and the covariate

We have now considered several different analysis of variance (ANOVA) models. As we moved through chapter 5, we saw that the inclusion of additional factors helped to reduce the residual or uncontrolled variation. These additional factors served as "experimental design controls" in that their inclusion in the design helped to reduce the uncontrolled variation. For example, this could be the reason an additional factor is included in a factorial design.

In this chapter we take our knowledge of the analysis of variance and combine it with our knowledge of regression analysis. This combined model is known as the analysis of covariance (ANCOVA) model, where an additional variable, known as the covariate, is incorporated into the analysis. Rather than serving as an "experimental design control," the covariate serves as a "statistical control" where uncontrolled variation is reduced statistically in the analysis. Thus a model where a covariate is used is known as an *analysis of covariance design*. We are most concerned with the one-factor fixed-effects model, although this model can be generalized to any of the other ANOVA designs considered in this text. That is, any of the ANOVA models discussed in the text can also include a covariate, and thus become an ANCOVA model.

Most of the concepts used in this chapter have already been covered in the text. In addition, new concepts include statistical adjustment, covariate, adjusted means, and two new assumptions, homogeneity of regression slopes and independence of the independent variable and the covariate. Our objectives are that by the end of this chapter, you will be able to (a) understand the characteristics and concepts underlying ANCOVA; (b) compute and interpret the results of ANCOVA, including adjusted means and multiple comparison procedures; and (c) understand and evaluate the assumptions of ANCOVA.

CHARACTERISTICS OF THE MODEL

In this section, we describe the distinguishing characteristics of the one-factor fixed-effects ANCOVA model. However, before we begin an extended discussion of these characteristics, consider the following example. Imagine a situation where a statistics professor is scheduled to teach two sections of introductory statistics. The professor, being a cunning researcher, decides to perform a little experiment where Section 1 is taught using the traditional lecture method and Section 2 is taught using extensive graphics overheads, computer simulations, and computer-assisted and calculator-based instruction, using mostly small-group and self-directed instruction. The professor is interested in which section performs better.

Before the study/course begins, the professor thinks about whether there are other variables related to statistics performance that should somehow be taken into account. An obvious one is ability in quantitative methods. From previous research and experience, the professor knows that ability in quantitative methods is highly correlated with performance in statistics and decides to give a measure of quantitative ability in the first class and use that as a covariate in the analysis. A *covariate* (i.e, quantitative ability) is defined as a source of variation not controlled for in the design of the experiment, but that the researcher believes to affect the dependent variable (i.e., course performance). The covariate is used to statistically adjust the dependent variable. For instance, if Section 1 has higher quantitative ability than Section 2, it would be wise to take this into account in the analysis. This is precisely what happens in the analysis of covariance. Some of the more typical examples of covariates in the social and behavioral sciences are pretest (where the dependent variable is the posttest), prior achievement, weight, IQ, aptitude, age, experience, previous training, motivation, and grade point average.

Let us now begin with the characteristics of the ANCOVA model. The first set of characteristics is obvious because they carry over from the one-factor fixed-effects ANOVA model. There is a single independent variable or factor with two or more levels. The levels are fixed by the researcher rather than randomly sampled from a population of levels. Once the levels of the independent variable are selected, subjects or individuals are somehow assigned to these levels or groups. Each subject is then exposed to only one level of the independent variable (although ANCOVA with repeated measures is also possible, but is not discussed here). In our example, method of statistics instruction is the independent variable with two levels or groups, the traditional lecture method and the cutting-edge method.

Situations where the researcher is able to randomly assign subjects to groups are known as *true experimental designs*. Situations where the researcher does not have control over which level a subject is assigned to are known as *quasi-experimental designs*. This lack of control may occur for one of two reasons. First, the groups may be already in place when the researcher arrives on the scene, and these groups are referred to as *intact groups* (e.g., based on classroom assignments). Second, it may be theoretically impossible for the researcher to assign subjects to groups (e.g., income level). Thus a distinction is typically made about whether or not the researcher can control the assignment of subjects to groups. The distinction about the use of ANCOVA in true and quasi-experimental situations has been quite controversial over the past 35 years; we look at it in more detail later in this chapter. For further information on true experimental designs and quasi-experimental designs, see Campbell and Stanley (1966) and Cook and Campbell (1979). In our example again, if assignment of students to sections is random, then we have a true experimental design. If assignment of students to sections is not random, perhaps already assigned at registration, then we have a quasi-experimental design.

One final item in the first set of characteristics has to do with the measurement scales of the variables. In the analysis of covariance, it is assumed the dependent variable is measured at the interval level or better. If the dependent variable is measured at the ordinal level, then alternative nonparametric procedures as in the last section of this chapter should be considered. It is also assumed the covariate is measured at the interval level or better. No assumptions need be made about the independent variable because it is a grouping or categorical variable.

The remaining characteristics have to do with the uniqueness of the analysis of covariance, which as we see represents a combination of the analysis of variance and linear regression analysis. As already mentioned, the analysis of covariance is a form of statistical control developed specifically to reduce unexplained error variation. The covariate (sometimes known as a concomitant variable) is a source of variation not controlled for in the design of the experiment but believed to affect the dependent variable. In a factorial design, for example, one factor could also be used to reduce error variation. However, this represents an experimental design form of control as it is included as a factor in the model.

In ANCOVA, the dependent variable is adjusted statistically to remove the effects of the portion of uncontrolled variation represented by the covariate. The group means on the dependent variable are adjusted so that they represent groups with the same means on the covariate. The analysis of covariance is essentially an analysis of variance on these "adjusted means." This needs further explanation. Consider first the situation of the true experiment involving randomization where there are two groups. Here it is unlikely that the two groups will be statistically different on any variable related to the dependent measure. The two groups should have roughly equivalent means on the covariate, although 5% of the time we would expect a significant difference due to chance at $\alpha = .05$. Thus we typically do not see preexisting differences between the two groups on the covariate in a true experiment. However, the relationship between the covariate and the dependent variable is important. If these variables are linearly related (discussed later), then the use of the covariate in the analysis will serve to reduce the unexplained variation in the model. The greater the magnitude of the correlation, the more uncontrolled variation can be removed, as shown by a reduction in mean square error.

Consider next the situation of the quasi-experiment, that is, without randomization. Here it is more likely that the two groups will be statistically different on the covariate as well as other variables related to the dependent variable. Thus there may indeed be a preexisting difference between the two groups on the covariate. If the groups do differ on the covariate and we ignore it by conducting an ANOVA, our ability to get a precise estimate of the group effects will be reduced as the group effect will be confounded with the effect of the covariate. For instance, if a significant group difference is revealed by the ANOVA, we would not be certain if there was truly a group effect or whether the effect was due to preexisting differences on the covariate, or some combination of group and covariate effects. The analysis of covariance takes the covariate mean difference into account as well as the linear relationship between the covariate and the dependent variable.

Thus, the covariate is used to (a) reduce error variance, (b) take any preexisting mean group difference on the covariate into account, (c) take into account the relationship between the covariate and the dependent variable, and (d) yield a more precise and less biased estimate of the group effects. If error variance is reduced, the analysis of covariance will be more powerful than the analysis of variance. If error variance is not reduced, the analysis of variance is more powerful. A more extensive comparison of ANOVA versus ANCOVA is given in chapter 8. In addition, as also shown later, one degree of freedom is lost from the error term for each covariate used. This results in a larger critical value for the F test and makes it a bit more difficult to find a significant F-test statistic. This is the major cost of using a covariate. If the covariate is not effective in reducing error variance, then we are worse off than if we had just ignored the covariate. Note two importance references on ANCOVA, Elashoff (1969) and Huitema (1980).

THE LAYOUT OF THE DATA

Before we get into the theory and subsequent analysis of the data, let us examine the layout of the data. We designate each observation on the dependent or criterion variable as Y_{ij}, where the j subscript tells us what group or level the observation belongs to and the i subscript tells us the observation or identification number within that group. The first subscript ranges over $i = 1, ..., n_j$ and the second subscript ranges over $j = 1, ..., J$. Thus there are J levels of the independent variable and n_j subjects in group j. We designate each observation on the covariate or concomitant variable as X_{ij}, where the subscripts have the same meaning.

The layout of the data is shown in Table 6.1. Here we see that each pair of columns represents the observations for a particular group or level of the independent variable on the dependent variable and the covariate. At the bottom of the pair of columns for each group j are the sums of the observations ($\Sigma Y_{.j}, \Sigma X_{.j}$), the group means ($\overline{Y}_{.j}, \overline{X}_{.j}$), the sums of the squared observations ($\Sigma Y_{.j}^2, \Sigma X_{.j}^2$), the variances for Y and X (s_Y^2, s_X^2), the covariance of X and Y (s_{XY}), the slope of the regression of Y on X (b_{YX}), and the correlation between X and Y (r_{XY}). Although the table shows there are n observations for each group, we need not make such a restriction, as this was done only for purposes of simplifying the table.

THE ANCOVA MODEL

The analysis of covariance model is a form of the general linear model much like the models shown in the last few chapters of this text. However, the ANCOVA model represents a combination of an analysis of variance model and a simple linear regression model. The one-factor ANCOVA fixed-effects model can be written in terms of population parameters as

TABLE 6.1

Layout for the One-Factor ANCOVA

Level of the Independent Variable						
1		2		...	J	
Y_{11}	X_{11}	Y_{12}	X_{12}	...	Y_{1J}	X_{1J}
Y_{21}	X_{21}	Y_{22}	X_{22}	...	Y_{2J}	X_{2J}
...	...	...	...	...	...	...
Y_{n1}	X_{n1}	Y_{n2}	X_{n2}	...	Y_{nJ}	X_{nJ}
$\overline{Y}_{.1}$	$\overline{X}_{.1}$	$\overline{Y}_{.2}$	$\overline{X}_{.2}$	...	$\overline{Y}_{.J}$	$\overline{X}_{.J}$
$\Sigma Y_{.1}$	$\Sigma X_{.1}$	$\Sigma Y_{.2}$	$\Sigma X_{.2}$	...	$\Sigma Y_{.J}$	$\Sigma X_{.J}$
$\Sigma Y_{.1}^{2}$	$\Sigma X_{.1}^{2}$	$\Sigma Y_{.2}^{2}$	$\Sigma X_{.2}^{2}$	...	$\Sigma Y_{.J}^{2}$	$\Sigma X_{.J}^{2}$
s_{Y1}^{2}	s_{X1}^{2}	s_{Y2}^{2}	s_{X2}^{2}	...	s_{YJ}^{2}	s_{XJ}^{2}
s_{XY1}		s_{XY2}		...	s_{XYJ}	
b_{YX1}		b_{YX2}		...	b_{YXJ}	
r_{XY1}		r_{XY2}		...	r_{XYJ}	

$$Y_{ij} = \mu_Y + \alpha_j + \beta_w(X_{ij} - \mu_X) + \varepsilon_{ij}$$

where Y_{ij} is the observed score on the criterion variable for individual i in group j, μ_y is the overall or grand population mean (i.e., regardless of group designation) for the dependent variable Y, α_j is the group effect for group j, β_w is the within-groups regression slope from the regression of Y on X, X_{ij} is the observed score on the covariate for individual i in group j, μ_x is the overall or grand population mean (i.e., regardless of group designation) for the independent variable X, and ε_{ij} is the random residual error for individual i in group j. The residual error can be due to individual differences, measurement error, and/or other factors not under investigation. As you would expect, the least squares estimators for each of these parameters are as follows: $\overline{Y}$ for μ_y, $\overline{X}$ for μ_x, a_j for α_j, b_w for β_w, and e_{ij} for ε_{ij}.

There is a side condition of the model, which, for the equal ns or balanced case, is $\sum_{j=1}^{J} \alpha_j = 0$, and for the unequal ns or unbalanced case is $\sum_{j=1}^{J} n_j \alpha_j = 0$. Thus the sum of the group effects is equal to zero. This implies that if there are any nonzero group effects, then the group effects will balance out around zero with some positive and some negative effects. As always, a positive group effect implies a group mean greater than the overall mean, whereas a negative group effect implies a group mean less than the overall mean (i.e., $a_j = \overline{Y}_{.j} - \overline{Y}_{..}$).

The hypotheses consist of testing the equality of the adjusted means (defined by μ'_j and discussed later) as follows:

$$H_0: \mu'_{.1} = \mu'_{.2} = \dots = \mu'_{.J}$$

$$H_1: \text{not all the } \mu'_{.j} \text{ are equal}$$

THE ANCOVA SUMMARY TABLE

We turn our attention to the familiar summary table, this time for the one-factor ANCOVA model. A general form of the summary table is shown in Table 6.2. Under the first column you see the following sources: adjusted between-groups variation, adjusted within-groups variation, variation due to the covariate, and total variation. You should know that only some textbooks and computer packages include the covariate explicitly as a source. Whether it is included explicitly or not, the covariate does represent a source of variation. The second column notes the sums of squares terms for each source (i.e., $SS_{\text{betw(adj)}}$, $SS_{\text{with(adj)}}$, SS_{cov}, and SS_{total}).

The third column gives the degrees of freedom for each source. For the adjusted between groups source, because there are J group means, the $df_{\text{betw(adj)}}$ is $J-1$, the same as in the one-factor ANOVA model. For the adjusted within-groups source, because there are N total observations and J groups, we would expect the degrees of freedom within to be $N-J$, because this was the case in the one-factor ANOVA model. However, as we pointed out in the characteristics of the ANCOVA model, a price is paid for the use of a covariate. There is a price here because we lose one degree of freedom from the within term for the covariate, so that $df_{\text{with(adj)}}$ is $N-J-1$. For multiple covariates, we lose one degree of freedom for each covariate used (see later discussion). This degree of freedom has gone to the covariate source such that df_{cov} is equal to 1. Finally, for the total source, because there are N total observations, the df_{total} is $N-1$.

The fourth column gives the mean squares for each source of variation. As always, the mean squares represent the sum of squares weighted by their respective degrees of freedom. Thus $MS_{\text{betw(adj)}} = SS_{\text{betw(adj)}}/(J-1)$, $MS_{\text{with(adj)}} = SS_{\text{with(adj)}}/(N-J-1)$, and $MS_{\text{cov}} = SS_{\text{cov}}/1$. The last column in the ANCOVA summary table is for the F values. Thus for the one-factor ANCOVA fixed-effects model, the F value to test for differences between the adjusted means is computed as $F = MS_{\text{betw(adj)}}/MS_{\text{with(adj)}}$. A second F value, which is obviously not included in the ANOVA model, is the test of the covariate. To be specific, this F is actually testing the hypothesis of $H_0: \beta_w = 0$. If the slope is equal to zero, then the covariate and the dependent variable are uncorrelated. This F value is equal to $F = MS_{\text{cov}}/MS_{\text{with(adj)}}$.

TABLE 6.2
One-Factor Analysis of Covariance Summary Table

Source	SS	df	MS	F
Adjusted between	$SS_{\text{betw(adj)}}$	$J-1$	$MS_{\text{betw(adj)}}$	$MS_{\text{betw(adj)}}/MS_{\text{with(adj)}}$
Adjusted within	$SS_{\text{with(adj)}}$	$N-J-1$	$MS_{\text{with(adj)}}$	—
Covariate	SS_{cov}	1	MS_{cov}	$MS_{\text{cov}}/MS_{\text{with(adj)}}$
Total	SS_{total}	$N-1$		

The critical value for the test of differences between the adjusted means is $_{1-\alpha}F_{J-1,N-J-1}$. The critical value for the test of the covariate is $_{1-\alpha}F_{1,N-J-1}$. The null hypotheses in each case are rejected if the F-test statistic exceeds the F critical value. The critical values are found in the F table of Appendix Table 4.

If the F-test statistic for the adjusted means exceeds the F critical value, and there are more than two groups, then it is not clear exactly how the means are different. In this case, some multiple-comparison procedure may be used to determine where the mean differences are (see later discussion). For the test of the covariate (or within groups regression slope), we hope that the F- test statistic does exceed the F critical value. Otherwise, the power and precision of the test of the adjusted means in ANCOVA will be lower than the test of the unadjusted means in ANOVA because the covariate is not significantly related to the dependent variable.

COMPUTATION OF SUMS OF SQUARES

As seen already, the partitioning of the sums of squares is the backbone of all general linear models, whether we are dealing with an ANOVA model, a linear regression model, or an ANCOVA model. As always, the first step is to partition the total variation into its relevant sources of variation. As we have learned from the previous section, the sources of variation for the one-factor ANCOVA model are between-groups adjusted, within-groups adjusted, and the covariate. This is written as

$$SS_{total} = SS_{betw(adj)} + SS_{with(adj)} + SS_{cov}$$

There are several different ways to represent the sum of squares computationally. If we choose to write them in the same way we did for the one-factor ANOVA model, the computations become quite outrageous as various sums of squares are required for X, Y, and the XY cross-product. This method is extremely heavy in a computational sense, so I do not give further details. In its place, let us use a simpler method where the sums of squares are computed as follows:

$$SS_{with(adj)} = SS_{with(Y)} - b_w^2 SS_{with(X)}$$

$$SS_{cov} = b_{total}^2 SS_{total(X)}$$

$$SS_{betw(adj)} = SS_{total(Y)} - SS_{cov} - SS_{with(adj)}$$

Here $SS_{total(Y)}$ and $SS_{with(Y)}$ are the unadjusted SS due to total and within from the ANOVA on Y (i.e., where Y is the dependent variable, group is the independent variable, and there is no covariate), the $SS_{total(X)}$ and $SS_{with(X)}$ are the SS due to total and within from the ANOVA on the covariate X (i.e., where X is the dependent variable and group is the independent variable), b_{total}^2 is the square of the regression slope from the regression of Y on X for all J groups in total (i.e., the slope resulting from the regression for the total collection of observations, regardless of group membership), and b_w^2 is the square of the within-groups regression slope from the regression of Y on X within each of the J groups combined (i.e., the slopes resulting from the regression for each of the J groups, which are then statistically combined).

Let us take a closer look at the computations involved here. First, the computation of the sums of squares should be familiar by now. However, they are presented here as a reminder.

$$SS_{\text{with}(Y)} = \sum_{i=1}^{n_j} \sum_{j=1}^{J} Y_{ij}^2 - \sum_{j=1}^{J} \frac{\left(\sum_{i=1}^{n_j} Y_{ij}\right)^2}{n_j}$$

$$SS_{\text{with}(X)} = \sum_{i=1}^{n_j} \sum_{j=1}^{J} X_{ij}^2 - \sum_{j=1}^{J} \frac{\left(\sum_{i=1}^{n_j} X_{ij}\right)^2}{n_j}$$

$$SS_{\text{total}(Y)} = \sum_{i=1}^{n_j} \sum_{j=1}^{J} Y_{ij}^2 - \frac{\left(\sum_{i=1}^{n_j} \sum_{j=1}^{J} Y_{ij}\right)^2}{N}$$

$$SS_{\text{total}(X)} = \sum_{i=1}^{n_j} \sum_{j=1}^{J} X_{ij}^2 - \frac{\left(\sum_{i=1}^{n_j} \sum_{j=1}^{J} X_{ij}\right)^2}{N}$$

The new components for the computations involve b_{total} and b_{w}. The computational formula for b_{total} is

$$b_{\text{total}} = \frac{s_{XY\,(\text{total})}}{s_{X\,(\text{total})}^2}$$

where $s_{XY(\text{total})}$ and $s_{X\,(\text{total})}^2$ represent the covariance and variance of X, respectively, for the total collection of observations irrespective of group membership. The computational formula for b_{w} is

$$b_{\text{w}} = \frac{\sum_{j=1}^{J} s_{XY\,(\text{with})}}{\sum_{j=1}^{J} s_{X\,(\text{with})}^2}$$

where $s_{XY(\text{with})}$ and $s_{X\,(\text{with})}^2$ represent the covariance and the variance of X, respectively, for each of the J groups, which are then summed over the J groups.

ADJUSTED MEANS AND MULTIPLE-COMPARISON PROCEDURES

In this section we define the adjusted mean statistically, and examine the more popular multiple-comparison procedures for the one-factor ANCOVA model.

Adjusted Means

We have spent considerable time already discussing the analysis of the adjusted means. Now it is time to define them. The adjusted mean is denoted by $\overline{Y}'_j$ and estimated by

$$\overline{Y}'_j = \overline{Y}_j - b_w (\overline{X}_j - \overline{X}_{..})$$

Here it should be noted that the adjusted mean is equal to the unadjusted mean minus the adjustment. The adjustment is a function of the within-groups regression slope and the difference between the group mean and the overall mean for the covariate. No adjustment will be made if (a) $b_w = 0$ (i.e., X and Y are unrelated) or (b) the group means on the covariate are all the same. Thus, in both of these cases $\overline{Y}_j = \overline{Y}'_j$. In all other cases, at least some adjustment will be made for some of the group means (although not necessarily for all of the group means).

You may be wondering how this adjustment actually works. Let us assume the covariate and the dependent variable are positively correlated such that b_w is also positive, and there are two treatment groups with equal ns that differ on the covariate. If Group 1 has a higher mean on both the covariate and the dependent variable than Group 2, the adjusted means will be closer together than the unadjusted means. For our first example, if $b_w = 1$, $\overline{Y}_{.1} = 50$, $\overline{Y}_{.2} = 30$, $\overline{X}_{.1} = 20$, $\overline{X}_{.2} = 10$, then the adjusted means are equal to

$$\overline{Y}'_{.1} = \overline{Y}_{.1} - b_w (\overline{X}_{.1} - \overline{X}_{..}) = 50 - 1 (20 - 15) = 45$$

and

$$\overline{Y}'_{.2} = \overline{Y}_{.2} - b_w (\overline{X}_{.2} - \overline{X}_{..}) = 30 - 1 (10 - 15) = 35$$

This is shown graphically in Fig. 6.1 (a). In looking at the covariate X, we see that Group 1 has a higher mean ($\overline{X}_{.1} = 20$) than Group 2 ($\overline{X}_{.2} = 10$) by 10 points. The vertical line represents the overall mean on the covariate ($\overline{X} = 15$). In looking at the dependent variable Y, we see that Group 1 has a higher mean ($\overline{Y}_{.1} = 50$) than Group 2 ($\overline{Y}_{.2} = 30$) by 20 points. The diagonal lines represent the regression lines for each group with $b_w = 1.0$. The points at which the regression lines intersect (or cross) the vertical line (*i.e.*, $\overline{X} = 15$) represent on the Y scale the values of the adjusted means. Here we see that the adjusted mean for group 1 ($\overline{Y}'_{.1} = 45$) is larger than the adjusted mean for group 2 ($\overline{Y}'_{.2} = 35$) by 10 points. Thus, because of the preexisting difference on the covariate, the adjusted means here are somewhat closer together than the unadjusted means (10 points vs. 20 points, respectively).

If Group 1 has a higher mean on the covariate and a lower mean on the dependent variable than Group 2, then the adjusted means will be further apart than the unadjusted means. For our second example, if $b_w = 1$, $\overline{Y}_{.1} = 30$, $\overline{Y}_{.2} = 50$, $\overline{X}_{.1} = 20$, $\overline{X}_{.2} = 10$, then the adjusted means are

$$\overline{Y}'_{.1} = \overline{Y}_{.1} - b_w(\overline{X}_{.1} - \overline{X}_{..}) = 30 - 1(20 - 15) = 25$$

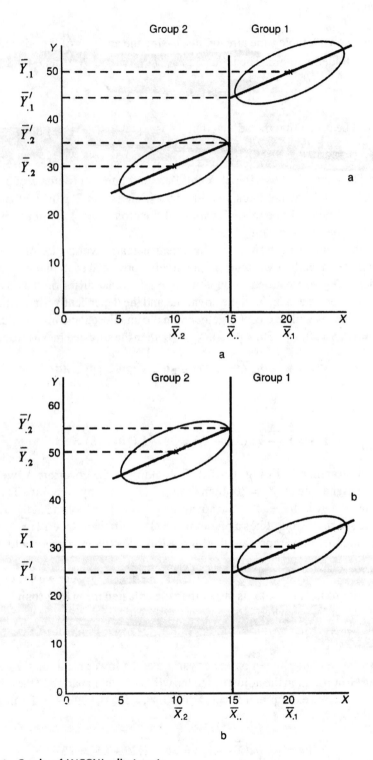

FIG. 6.1 Graphs of ANCOVA adjustments.

and

$$\overline{Y}'_{.2} = \overline{Y}_{.2} - b_w(\overline{X}_{.2} - \overline{X}_{..}) = 50 - 1(10 - 15) = 55$$

This is shown graphically in Fig. 6.1(b), where the unadjusted means differ by 20 points and the adjusted means differ by 30 points. There are obviously other possibilities, but those two examples cover the basics.

As discussed later in this chapter, the ANCOVA model assumes that the regression slopes are equal for each of the J groups. If the assumption is not met and the slopes are unequal, then the adjusted means are not accurate (and can be downright misleading). This occurs because the size of the group effect will depend on the value of the covariate X.

Multiple Comparison Procedures

Let us examine three multiple comparison procedures (MCPs) for use in the analysis of covariance situation. Most of the procedures described in chapter 4 can be adapted for use with a covariate, although a few procedures are not mentioned here as critical values do not currently exist. The adapted procedures involve a different form of the standard error of a contrast. The contrasts are formed based on adjusted means, of course. Let me briefly outline just a few procedures. Each of the test statistics has as its numerator the contrast ψ' (e.g., $\psi' = \overline{Y}'_{.1} - \overline{Y}'_{.2}$). The denominators, or standard errors, do differ somewhat.

Dunn's Method (Bonferroni).   You may recall from chapter 4 (see Fig. 4.2) that Dunn's method is appropriate for a small number of planned contrasts, and the same goes for the analysis of covariance. The test statistic for a randomized design is

$$t = \frac{\psi'}{\sqrt{MS_{\text{with(adj)}}\left(1 + \frac{MS_{\text{betw}(X)}}{SS_{\text{with}(X)}}\right)\left(\sum_{j=1}^{J}\frac{c_j^2}{n_j}\right)}}$$

where c_j are the contrast coefficients (everything else should be familiar). The test statistic for a nonrandomized design is

$$t = \frac{\psi'}{\sqrt{MS_{\text{with(adj)}}\left[\frac{\left(\sum_{j=1}^{J}c_j\overline{X}_{.j}\right)^2}{SS_{\text{with}(X)}}\right]\left(\sum_{j=1}^{J}\frac{c_j^2}{n_j}\right)}}$$

where the middle term in the denominator must be computed separately for each contrast because it is based on the difference between the group means on the covariate X. The test statistic is compared to the critical value $_{1-\alpha/c}t_{df(\text{error})}$, where df_{error} is $N - J - 1$ for the single covariate case, c is the number of planned contrasts, and is taken from the table in Appendix Table 8.

Scheffé's Method. In ANOVA, Scheffé's method is appropriate for unplanned complex contrasts with equal group variances. This is also true for ANCOVA. The test statistic is precisely the same as in Dunn's method and is compared to the critical value $\sqrt{(J-1)}_{1-\alpha} F_{J-1, df\,(error)}$ and taken from the F table in Appendix Table 4.

Tukey's HSD Test and the Bryant–Paulson Procedure. Tukey's HSD test is appropriate in ANOVA for unplanned pairwise contrasts with equal ns per group. There has been some discussion in the literature about the appropriateness of this test in ANCOVA. Most statisticians currently argue that the procedure is only appropriate when the covariate is fixed, when in fact it is almost always random. As a result, the Bryant–Paulson (1976) generalization of the Tukey procedure has been developed for the random covariate case. The Bryant–Paulson test statistic for a randomized design is

$$t = \frac{\psi'}{\sqrt{MS_{with(adj)}\left(1 + \dfrac{MS_{betw(X)}}{SS_{with(X)}}\right)\left(\dfrac{1}{n}\right)}}$$

The test statistic for a nonrandomized design is

$$t = \frac{\psi'}{\sqrt{MS_{with(adj)}\left[\dfrac{2}{n} + \dfrac{\left(\overline{X}_{.j} - \overline{X}_{.j'}\right)^2}{SS_{with(X)}}\right]\left(\frac{1}{2}\right)}}$$

where the middle term in the denominator must be computed separately for each contrast because it is based on the difference between the group means on the covariate X (e.g., $\overline{X}_{.1} - \overline{X}_{.2}$). The test statistic is compared to the critical value $_{1-\alpha}\,q_{X, df(error), J}$ taken from Appendix Table 11, where X is the number of covariates.

If the group sizes are unequal, the harmonic mean can be used in ANCOVA (Huitema, 1980). A generalization of the Tukey–Bryant procedure for unequal ns ANCOVA was developed by Hochberg and Varon-Salomon (1984) (also see Hochberg & Tamhane, 1987; Miller, 1997).

ASSUMPTIONS AND VIOLATION OF ASSUMPTIONS

For the most part, the assumptions of the one-factor analysis of covariance are a combination of the assumptions of simple linear regression and the one-factor analysis of variance. For the familiar assumptions, the discussion is kept to a minimum as these have already been described in chapters 1 and 3. There are three additional assumptions we have not yet encountered, the covariate being measured without error, homogeneity of the regression slopes, and independence of the independent variable and the covariate. In this section, we describe each assumption, how each assumption can be evaluated, the effects that a violation of the assumption might have, and how one might deal with a serious violation.

Random and Independent Errors

First, the residual errors are assumed to be random and independent errors. That is, there is no systematic pattern about the errors and the errors are independent across individuals. An example of a systematic pattern would be where for one group the residuals tended to be small, whereas for another group the residuals tended to be large.

The use of independent random samples is crucial in the analysis of covariance. The F ratio is very sensitive to violation of the independence assumption in terms of increased likelihood of a Type I and/or Type II error. A violation of the independence assumption may affect the standard errors of the sample adjusted means and thus influence any inferences made about those means. One purpose of random assignment of individuals to groups is to achieve independence of the ε_{ij} terms. If each individual is only observed once and individuals are randomly assigned to groups, then the independence assumption is usually met. Random assignment is important for valid interpretation of the F test and of multiple comparison procedures. Otherwise, the F test and adjusted means may be biased.

The simplest procedure for assessing independence is to examine residual plots by group. If the independence assumption is satisfied, then the residuals should fall into a random display of points for each group. If the assumption is violated, then the residuals will fall into some type of cyclical pattern. As discussed in chapter 1, the Durbin–Watson statistic (1950, 1951, 1971) can be used to test for autocorrelation. Violations of the independence assumption generally occur in the three situations we mentioned in chapter 1: time-series data, observations within blocks, or replication. For severe violations of the independence assumption, there is no simple "fix" such as the use of transformations or nonparametric tests (see Scariano & Davenport, 1987).

Homogeneity of Variance

According to the second assumption, the conditional distributions of Y given X ($Y|X$) have a constant variance, both across groups and for all values of X. As before, this is referred to as the homogeneity of variance or homoscedasticity assumption. A violation of the homogeneity assumption may lead to bias in the SS_{with} term, as well as an increase in the Type I error rate and possibly an increase in the Type II error rate. The effect of the violation seems to be small with equal or nearly equal ns across the groups (e.g., one suggestion is a maximum ratio of largest n_j to smallest n_j of 1.5 as being safe). There is a more serious problem if the larger ns are associated with the smaller variances (actual α > nominal α, which is a liberal result), or if the larger ns are associated with the larger variances (actual α < nominal α, which is a conservative result).

In a plot of Y versus the covariate X for each group, the consistency of the variance of the conditional residual distributions may be examined. Another method for detecting violation of the homogeneity assumption is the use of formal statistical tests, as discussed in chapter 1. Several solutions are available for dealing with a violation of the homogeneity assumption. These include the use of variance-stabilizing transformations, or other ANCOVA models that are less sensitive to unequal variances, such as nonparametric ANCOVA procedures. Some rank ANCOVA procedures have been proposed by Quade (1967), Puri and Sen (1969), and Conover and Iman (1982). For a thorough description of such procedures, see these references as well as Huitema (1980, which includes computational examples as well).

Normality

The third assumption states that the conditional distributions are normal in shape. That is, for all values of X, Y is normally distributed for all groups. If X is normally distributed, then the F test is relatively robust to nonnormality in Y. If Y is normally distributed, then the F test is not very robust to nonnormality in X. These results are attributed to Box and Anderson (1962) and Atiqullah (1964). Violation of the normality assumption may be a result of outliers as discussed in chapter 1. The simplest outlier detection procedure is to look for observations that are more than two or three standard errors from their respective group mean. Formal procedures for the detection of outliers in this context are described in Dunn and Clark (1987).

The following graphical techniques can be used to detect violation of the normality assumption: (a) frequency distributions (such as stem-and-leaf plots, box plots, or histograms), or (b) normal probability plots. There are also several statistical procedures available for the detection of nonnormality (such as the Shapiro–Wilk test, 1965). Transformations can also be used to normalize the data, as previously discussed in chapters 1 and 2. In addition, one can use one of the rank ANCOVA procedures mentioned at the end of the preceding subsection.

Linearity

The next assumption holds that the regression of Y on X is linear. If the relationship between X and Y is not linear, the use of the usual ANCOVA procedure is not appropriate, just as linear regression would not be appropriate. In linear regression and ANCOVA, we fit a straight line to the data points. When the relationship is nonlinear, a straight line will not fit the data as well as a curved line. In addition, the magnitude of the linear correlation will be less than if we were to compute a nonlinear correlation coefficient. If the relationship is not linear, the estimate of the group effects will be biased, and the adjustments made in SS_{with} and SS_{betw} will be smaller.

Violations of the linearity assumption can generally be detected by looking at plots of Y versus X, overall and for each group. There are also formal statistical tests as given in chapter 1. Once a serious violation of the linearity assumption has been detected, there are two alternatives that one can use, transformations and nonlinear ANCOVA. As in chapter 1, transformations on one or both variables can be used to achieve linearity. The second option is to use nonlinear ANCOVA methods as described by Huitema (1980).

Fixed Independent Variable

The fifth assumption states that the levels of the independent variable are fixed by the researcher. This results in a fixed-effects model rather than a random-effects model. As in the one-factor ANOVA model, the one-factor ANCOVA model is the same computationally in the fixed- and random-effects cases. For factorial designs, visit the discussion about random and mixed effects for the formation of appropriate F ratios in chapter 7.

Independence of the Covariate and the Independent Variable

A condition of the ANCOVA model (although not an assumption) requires that the covariate and the independent variable be independent. That is, the covariate is not influenced by the independent or treatment variable. If the covariate is affected by the treatment itself, then the use of the covariate in the analysis either (a) may remove part of the treatment effect or produce a spurious (inflated) treatment effect, or (b) may alter the covariate scores as a result of the treatment being administered prior to obtaining the covariate data. The obvious solution to this potential problem is to obtain the covariate scores prior to the administration of the treatment. In other words, be alert prior to the study for possible covariate candidates.

Let us consider an example where this condition is obviously violated. A psychologist is interested in which of several hypnosis treatments is most successful in reducing or eliminating cigarette smoking. A group of heavy smokers is randomly assigned to the hypnosis treatments. After the treatments have been completed, the researcher suspects that some patients are more susceptible to hypnosis (i.e., more suggestible) than others. By using suggestibility as a covariate, the researcher would not be able to determine whether group differences were a result of hypnosis treatment, suggestibility, or some combination. Thus, the use of suggestibility after the hypnosis treatments have been administered would be ill advised. An extended discussion of this condition is given in Maxwell and Delaney (1990).

Covariate Measured Without Error

An assumption that we have not yet encountered in this text purports that the covariate is measured without error. This is of special concern in the social and behavioral sciences where variables are often measured with considerable measurement error. In randomized experiments, b_w will be underestimated so that less of the covariate effect is removed from the dependent variable (i.e., the adjustments will be smaller). In addition, the reduction in the unexplained variation will not be as great and the F test will not be as powerful. The F test is generally conservative in terms of Type I error (the actual α will be less than the nominal α). However, the treatment effects will not be biased. In quasi-experimental designs, b_w will also be underestimated with similar effects. However, the treatment effects may be seriously biased. A method by Porter (1967) is suggested for this situation.

There is considerable discussion about the effects of measurement error (e.g., Cohen & Cohen, 1983; Huitema, 1980; Lord, 1960, 1967, 1969; Pedhazur, 1997; Porter,

1967; Reichardt, 1979; Weisberg, 1979). Obvious violations of this assumption can be detected by computing the reliability of the covariate prior to the study or from previous research. This is the minimum that should be done. One may also want to consider the validity of the covariate as well, where validity is the extent to which an instrument measures what it was intended to measure.

Homogeneity of Regression Slopes

The final assumption, and a new one at that, puts forth that the slopes of the regression lines are the same for each group. Here we assume that $\beta_1 = \beta_2 = \ldots = \beta_J$. This is an important assumption because it allows us to use b_w, which is a sample estimator of β_w, as the within-groups regression slope. Assuming that the group slopes are parallel allows us to test for group intercept differences, which is all we are really doing when we test for differences among the adjusted means. Without this assumption, groups can differ on both the regression slope and intercept, and β_w cannot legitimately be used. If the slopes differ, then the regression lines interact in some way. As a result, the size of the group differences in Y will depend on the value of X. For example, Treatment 1 may be most effective for low values of the covariate, Treatment 2 may be most effective for middle values of the covariate, and Treatment 3 may be most effective for high values of the covariate. Thus, we do not have constant differences between the groups across the values of the covariate. A straightforward interpretation is not possible, which is the same situation in factorial ANOVA when the interaction between factor A and factor B is found to be significant.

What are the other potential outcomes if this assumption is violated? Without homogeneous regression slopes, the use of β_w will also yield biased adjusted means. In general, the F test is not as powerful with slope heterogeneity and is more conservative in terms of Type I error (F will be smaller or negatively biased). Earlier simulation studies by Peckham (1968) and Glass et al. (1972) suggest that for the one-factor fixed-effects model the effects will be minimal. However, more recent analytical research by Rogosa (1980) suggests that the F test is only appropriately distributed as F for mild heterogeneity. For this reason, some statistical test of this assumption is strongly recommended.

A formal statistical procedure is often conducted to test for homogeneity of slopes, although the eyeball method (i.e., see if the slopes look about the same) can be a good starting point. A test statistic for the test of parallelism is

$$F = \frac{(SS_{\text{with(adj)}} - SS_{\text{res}}) / (J-1)}{SS_{\text{res}} / (N-2J)}$$

where SS_{res} is the sum of squared residuals computed by

$$SS_{\text{res}} = \sum_{j=1}^{J} SS_j (1 - r_j^2)$$

such that r_j is the correlation between X and Y for each group j, computed by

$$r_j = \frac{s_{XY}}{s_X \, s_Y}$$

and where SS_j is the sum of squares in Y for each group j, computed by

$$SS_j = \sum_{i=1}^{n_j} Y_i^2 - \frac{\left(\sum_{i=1}^{n_j} Y_i \right)^2}{n_j}$$

The critical value for this test statistic is $_{1-\alpha}F_{J-1,N-2J}$, found in Appendix Table 4. To minimize the likelihood of a Type II error in this test, a larger α level than usual is suggested (e.g., .25 or .10). An alternative test for equality of slopes when the variances are unequal is provided by Tabatabai and Tan (1985) and described by Wilcox (1987).

What alternatives are there for the applied researcher if the homogeneity of slopes assumption is violated? There are several possibilities. The first is to use the concomitant variable not as a covariate but as a blocking variable. This will work because this assumption is not made for the randomized block design (see chap. 8). A second option, and not a very desirable one, is to analyze each group separately with its own β or subsets of the groups having equal βs. A third possibility is to use interaction terms between the covariate and the independent variable and conduct a regression analysis (see Agresti & Finlay, 1986). A fourth, and most desirable option, is to use the Johnson–Neyman (1936) technique, whose purpose is to determine the values of X that are related to significant group differences on Y. This procedure is beyond the scope of this text, and the interested reader is referred to Huitema (1980) or Wilcox (1987). A fifth option, a new approach, is to allow for heterogeneity of regression in the ANCOVA model (see Maxwell & Delaney, 1990).

A summary of the ANCOVA assumptions and the effects of their violation is presented in Table 6.3.

AN EXAMPLE

Consider the following illustration of what we have covered in this chapter. Our dependent variable is the score on a statistics quiz (with a maximum possible score of 6), the covariate is the score on an aptitude test for statistics taken at the beginning of the course (with a maximum possible score of 10), and the independent variable is the section of statistics taken (where Group 1 receives the traditional lecture method and Group 2 receives the computer-assisted instruction method). Thus the researcher is interested in whether the method of instruction influences student performance in statistics, controlling for statistics aptitude (assume we have developed a measure that is relatively error free). Students are randomly assigned to one of the two groups at the beginning of the semester when the measure of statistics aptitude is administered. There are six students in each group for a total of 12 (to keep the computations as simple as possible). The layout of the data is shown in Table 6.4, where we see the data, sample statistics (means, variances, covariances, slopes, and correlations) for each group and overall, and the other necessary summation terms for computing the sums of squares.

TABLE 6.3

Assumptions and Effects of Violations—One-Factor ANCOVA

Assumption	Effect of Assumption Violation
1. Independence of residuals	Increased likelihood of a Type I and/or Type II error in the F statistic; influences standard errors of means and thus inferences about those means
2. Homogeneity of variance	Bias in SS_{with}; increased likelihood of a Type I and/or Type II error; small effect with equal or nearly equal ns; otherwise more serious problem if the larger ns are associated with the smaller variances (increased α) or larger variances (decreased α)
3. Normality of residuals	If X is normal, then the F test is fairly robust to nonnormal Y; if Y is normal, then the F test is not very robust to nonnormal X
4. Linearity	Reduced magnitude of r_{XY}; straight line will not fit data well; estimate of group effects biased; adjustments made in SS will be smaller
5. Fixed X	Use random-effects model; computations the same
6. Independence of covariate and independent variable	May reduce or increase group effects; may alter covariate scores
7. Covariate measured without error	True experiment: b_w underestimated; adjustments smaller; reduction in unexplained variation smaller; F less powerful; reduced likelihood of Type I error. Quasi-experiment: b_w underestimated; adjustments smaller; treatment effects seriously biased
8. Homogeneity of slopes	Treatment effects depend on value of X; adjusted means biased; F less powerful, reduced likelihood of Type I error

TABLE 6.4

Data and Summary Statistics for the Statistics Instruction Example

Statistic	Group 1 Quiz (Y)	Group 1 Aptitude (X)	Group 2 Quiz (Y)	Group 2 Aptitude (X)	Overall Quiz (Y)	Overall Aptitude (X)
	1	4	1	1		
	2	3	2	3		
	3	5	4	2		
	4	6	5	4		
	5	7	6	5		
	6	9	6	7		
Σ_{ij}	21	34	24	22	45	56
Means	3.5000	5.6667	4.0000	3.6667	3.7500	4.6667
Σ_{ij}^2	91	216	118	104	209	320
Variances	3.5000	4.6667	4.4000	4.6667	3.6591	5.3333
ΣXY	138.0000		107.0000		245.0000	
s_{XY}	3.8000		3.8000		3.1818	
b_{YX}	0.8143		0.8143		0.5966	
r_{XY}	0.9403		0.8386		0.7203	

Let us begin the computations for the analysis of covariance. First we compute the sums of squares and slopes:

$$SS_{\text{with}(Y)} = \sum_{i=1}^{n_j} \sum_{j=1}^{J} Y_{ij}^2 - \sum_{j=1}^{J} \frac{\left(\sum_{i=1}^{n_j} Y_{ij}\right)^2}{n_j} = 209.0000 - 169.5000 = 39.5000$$

$$SS_{\text{with}(X)} = \sum_{i=1}^{n_j} \sum_{j=1}^{J} X_{ij}^2 - \sum_{j=1}^{J} \frac{\left(\sum_{i=1}^{n_j} X_{ij}\right)^2}{n_j} = 320.0000 - 273.3333 = 46.6667$$

$$SS_{\text{total}(Y)} = \sum_{i=1}^{n_j} \sum_{j=1}^{J} Y_{ij}^2 - \frac{\left(\sum_{i=1}^{n_j} \sum_{j=1}^{J} Y_{ij}\right)^2}{N} = 209.0000 - 168.7500 = 40.2500$$

$$SS_{\text{total}(X)} = \sum_{i=1}^{n_j} \sum_{j=1}^{J} X_{ij}^2 - \frac{\left(\sum_{i=1}^{n_j} \sum_{j=1}^{J} X_{ij}\right)^2}{N} = 320.0000 - 261.3333 = 58.6667$$

$$b_{\text{total}} = \frac{s_{XY\,(\text{total})}}{s_{X\,(\text{total})}^2} = \frac{3.1818}{5.3333} = 0.5966$$

$$b_w = \frac{\sum_{j=1}^{J} s_{XY\,(\text{with})}}{\sum_{j=1}^{J} s_{X\,(\text{with})}^2} = \frac{7.6000}{9.3334} = 0.8143$$

$$SS_{\text{with}(\text{adj})} = SS_{\text{with}(Y)} - b_w^2 SS_{\text{with}(X)} = 39.5000 - (.8143)^2 (46.6667) = 8.5560$$

$$SS_{\text{cov}} = b_{\text{total}}^2 SS_{\text{total}(X)} = (.5966)^2 (58.6667) = 20.8813$$

$$SS_{\text{betw}(\text{adj})} = SS_{\text{total}(Y)} - SS_{\text{cov}} - SS_{\text{with}(\text{adj})} = 40.2500 - 20.8813 - 8.5560 = 10.8127$$

Let us next compute the mean square terms:

$$MS_{\text{betw}(\text{adj})} = \frac{SS_{\text{betw}(\text{adj})}}{df_{\text{betw}(\text{adj})}} = \frac{10.8127}{1} = 10.8127$$

$$MS_{\text{with}(\text{adj})} = \frac{SS_{\text{with}(\text{adj})}}{df_{\text{with}(\text{adj})}} = \frac{8.5560}{9} = 0.9507$$

$$MS_{cov} = \frac{SS_{cov}}{df_{cov}} = \frac{20.8813}{1} = 20.8813$$

Finally, we compute the F-test statistics as follows:

$$F_{ANCOVA} = \frac{MS_{betw(adj)}}{MS_{with(adj)}} = \frac{10.8127}{0.9507} = 11.3734$$

$$F_{cov} = \frac{MS_{cov}}{MS_{with(adj)}} = \frac{20.8813}{0.9507} = 21.9641$$

The ANCOVA test statistics are compared to the critical value $_{.95}F_{1,9} = 5.12$ obtained from Appendix Table 4, using the .05 level of significance. Both test statistics exceed the critical value, so we reject H_0 in each case. We conclude that the quiz score means do differ for the two statistics groups when adjusted for aptitude in statistics, and the slope of the regression of Y on X is significantly different from zero (i.e., the test of the covariate). These results are summarized in the ANCOVA summary table as shown in the top section of Table 6.5. Just to be complete, the results for the analysis of variance on Y are shown in the bottom section of Table 6.5. We see that in the analysis of the unadjusted means (i.e., the ANOVA), there is no significant group difference, and in the analysis of the adjusted means (i.e., the ANCOVA), there is a significant group difference. Thus the adjustment yielded a different statistical result. The covariate also "did its thing" in that a reduction in MS_{with} resulted due to the strong relationship between the covariate and the dependent variable (i.e., $r_{XY} = 0.7203$ overall).

Let us next estimate the adjusted means and look at multiple comparison procedures. First the adjusted means are estimated:

$$\overline{Y}'_{.1} = \overline{Y}_{.1} - b_w(\overline{X}_{.1} - \overline{X}_{..}) = 3.5000 - 0.8143(5.6667 - 4.6667) = 2.6857$$

$$\overline{Y}'_{.2} = \overline{Y}_{.2} - b_w(\overline{X}_{.2} - \overline{X}_{..}) = 4.0000 - 0.8143(3.6667 - 4.6667) = 4.8143$$

Hence we see that with the unadjusted means, there is a 0.5000 point difference in favor of Group 2, whereas for the adjusted means there is a 2.1286 point difference in favor of Group 2. In other words, the adjustment in this case resulted in a greater difference between the adjusted means than between the unadjusted means.

Consider two forms of a multiple comparison procedure as an illustration, although we know already the adjusted means are statistically different. Remember that with two groups only one contrast can be formed (i.e., the difference between the two adjusted means). Before we begin, however, we need to compute $SS_{betw(X)}$ and $MS_{betw(X)}$ in order to proceed with the analysis. We have already computed $SS_{with(X)} = 46.6667$ and $SS_{total(X)} = 58.6667$, such that

$$SS_{betw(X)} = SS_{total(X)} - SS_{with(X)} = 58.6667 - 46.6667 = 12.0000$$

Finally we need to compute $MS_{betw(X)}$:

TABLE 6.5
Analysis of Covariance and Variance Summary Table—Statistics Instruction Example

Source	SS	df	MS	F
ANCOVA				
Adjusted between	10.8127	1	10.8127	11.3734*
Adjusted within	8.5560	9	0.9507	—
covariate	20.8813	1	20.8813	21.9641*
Total	40.2500	11		
ANOVA				
Between	0.7500	1	0.7500	0.1899**
Within	39.5000	10	3.9500	
Total	40.2500	11		

* $_{.95}F_{1,9} = 5.12$.
** $_{.95}F_{1,10} = 4.96$.

$$MS_{betw(X)} = \frac{SS_{betw(X)}}{df_{betw}} = \frac{12.0000}{1} = 12.000$$

Let us illustrate the use of the Bryant–Paulson generalization of Tukey's procedure. The Scheffé and Dunn methods are not really appropriate for the design being considered here. The test statistic of the Bryant–Paulson–Tukey procedure for a randomized design is as follows:

$$t = \frac{\psi'}{\sqrt{MS_{with(adj)}\left(1 + \frac{MS_{betw(X)}}{SS_{with(X)}}\right)\left(\frac{1}{n}\right)}} = \frac{2.1286}{\sqrt{0.9507\left(1 + \frac{12}{46.6667}\right)\frac{1}{6}}} = \frac{2.1286}{0.4463} = 4.7694$$

This test statistic is compared to the critical value $_{.95}q_{1,9,2} \approx 3.40$, so that the contrast is a significant one at the .05 level of significance. The test statistic of the Bryant–Paulson–Tukey method for a nonrandomized design is as follows:

$$t = \frac{\psi'}{\sqrt{[MS_{with(adj)}]\left[\frac{2}{n} + \frac{(\overline{X}_{.1} - \overline{X}_{.2})^2}{SS_{with(X)}}\right]\left(\frac{1}{2}\right)}} = \frac{2.1286}{\sqrt{0.9507\left[\frac{2}{6} + \frac{(5.6667 - 3.6667)^2}{46.6667}\right]\frac{1}{2}}} = \frac{2.1286}{0.4463} = 4.7694$$

The test statistics are equivalent here because there are only two groups in the design. Obviously, both contrasts are significant at the .05 level.

Finally, let us consider the assumptions of the model. We only take a close look at the homogeneity of slopes assumption, and leave the evaluation of the other assumptions to you. (Hint: Given the small sample size, the other assumptions seem to be met.) The computations for the test of the homogeneity of slopes assumption follow.

The r_j are the correlations between X and Y for each group j, computed by

$$r_j = \frac{s_{XY}}{s_X \, s_Y}$$

so that

$$r_1 = \frac{3.8000}{(1.8708)(2.1603)} = 0.9403$$

and

$$r_2 = \frac{3.8000}{(2.0976)(2.1603)} = 0.8386$$

The SS_j represent the sum of squares in Y for each group j, computed by

$$SS_j = \sum_{i=1}^{n_j} Y_i^2 - \frac{\left(\sum_{i=1}^{n_j} Y_i \right)^2}{n_j}$$

so that

$$SS_1 = 91.0000 - \frac{(21)^2}{6} = 17.5000$$

and

$$SS_2 = 118.0000 - \frac{(24)^2}{6} = 22.0000$$

We compute SS_{res} as

$$SS_{res} = \sum_{j=1}^{J} [SS_j(1 - r_j^2)] = [17.5000(1 - .9403^2)] + [22.000(1 - .8386^2)] = 8.5556$$

Finally, the test statistic for the homogeneity of slopes assumption is

$$F = \frac{(SS_{with(adj)} - SS_{res}) / (J-1)}{SS_{res} / (N - 2J)} = \frac{(8.5560 - 8.5556) / 1}{8.5556 / 8} = 0.0004$$

Just for the heck of it, the critical value for this test statistic is $_{.95}F_{1,8} = 5.32$ from Appendix Table 4, although the assumption of homogeneity of slopes is clearly upheld for these data.

RELATIONSHIP OF ANCOVA AND REGRESSION ANALYSIS

As in chapter 3, when we looked at the relationship of ANOVA to regression analysis, we can also examine the relationship of ANCOVA to regression analysis. By now it should be clear that ANCOVA involves a combination of simple linear regression and analysis of variance. One could also conduct an ANCOVA through the use of regression analysis. In fact, the analysis is greatly simplified for an ANCOVA model when using regression methods as compared to analysis of variance methods. For further information on the use of regression with ANCOVA models, see Huitema (1980), Kirk (1982), Pedhazur (1997), Cohen and Cohen (1983), or Kleinbaum et al. (1998).

USING STATISTICAL PACKAGES

The use of the major statistical packages for the analysis of covariance needs to be discussed. In SAS, PROC GLM will allow you to do the following:

1. Test for equality of the regression slopes through the use of an interaction term between the independent variable and the covariate.
2. Use multiple covariates.
3. Analyze complex designs.
4. Obtain unadjusted sums of squares (ANOVA on Y, known as Type I SS) and adjusted sums of squares (ANCOVA, known as Type III SS).
5. Compute adjusted means through the "LS MEANS" (least squares means) option and unadjusted means through the usual "MEANS" option.

In SPSS, the following options are available:

1. Test of equality of the regression slopes
2. Use of multiple covariates.
3. Analyze complex designs.
4. Options for the unique, hierarchical, and experimental methods.
5. Gives adjusted and unadjusted means as well as procedures for testing contrasts.

ANCOVA WITHOUT RANDOMIZATION

There is a great deal of discussion and controversy, particularly in the social and behavioral sciences, about the use of the analysis of covariance in situations where randomization is not conducted. *Randomization* is defined as an experiment where individuals are randomly assigned to groups (or cells in a factorial design). In the Campbell and Stanley (1966) system of experimental design, these designs are known as *true experiments*.

In certain situations, randomization either has not occurred or is not possible due to the circumstances. The best example is the situation where there are *intact groups*, which are groups that have been formed prior to the researcher arriving on the scene. Either the researcher chooses not to randomly assign these individuals to groups through a reassignment (e.g., it is just easier to keep the groups in their current form) or the researcher cannot randomly assign them (legally, ethically, or otherwise). When randomization does not occur, the resulting designs are known as *quasi-experimental*. For instance, in classroom research the researcher is almost never able to come into a school district and randomly assign students to groups. Once students are given their classroom assignments at the beginning of the year, that is that. On occasion, the researcher might be able to pull a few students out of several classrooms, randomly assign them to groups, and conduct a true experiment. In general, this is possible only on a very small scale and for short periods of time.

Let me briefly wade through the issues here because not all statisticians agree. In true experiments (i.e., with randomization), there is no cause for concern (except for dealing with the statistical assumptions). The analysis of covariance is more powerful and has greater precision for true experiments than for quasi-experiments. So if you have a choice, go with a true experimental situation (which is a big if). In a true experiment, the probability that the groups differ on the covariate or any other concomitant variable is equal to α. That is, the likelihood that the group means will be different on the covariate is small, and thus the adjustment in the group means may be small. The payoff is in the possibility that the error term will be greatly reduced.

In quasi-experiments, there are several possible causes for concern. Although this is the situation where the researcher needs the most help, this is also the situation where less help is available. Here it is more likely that there will be significant differences among the group means on the covariate. Thus the adjustment in the group means can be substantial (assuming that b_w is different from zero). Because there are significant mean differences on the covariate, any of the following may occur:

1. It is likely that the groups may be different on other important characteristics as well, which have not been controlled for either statistically or experimentally.

2. The homogeneity of regression slopes assumption is less likely to be met (which is a critical assumption).

3. Adjusting for the covariate may remove part of the treatment effect.

4. Equating groups on the covariate may be an extrapolation beyond the range of possible values that occur for a particular group (e.g., see the examples by Lord, 1967, 1969, on trying to equate men and women, or by Ferguson & Takane, 1989, on trying to equate mice and elephants; these groups should not be equated on the covariate because their distributions on the covariate do not overlap).

5. Although the slopes may be equal for the range of Xs obtained, when extrapolating beyond the range of scores the slopes may in reality not be equal.

6. The standard errors of the adjusted means may increase, making tests of the adjusted means not significant.

7. There may be differential growth in the groups confounding the results (e.g., adult and children groups).

Although one should be cautious about the use of ANCOVA in quasi-experiments, this is not to suggest that ANCOVA should never be used in such situations (as some suggest). Just be extra careful and do not go too far in terms of interpreting your results. If at all possible, replicate your study. For further discussion see Huitema (1980) or Porter and Raudenbush (1987).

MORE COMPLEX ANCOVA MODELS

The one-factor ANCOVA model can be extended to more complex models in much the same way as we expanded the one-factor ANOVA model. Thus one can evaluate ANCOVA designs that involve any of the following characteristics: (a) factorial designs (i.e., having more than one factor); (b) fixed-, random-, and mixed-effects designs; (c) repeated measures and split-plot (mixed) designs; (d) hierarchical designs; and (e) randomized block designs. Although the computations become difficult, conceptually there is nothing new for these types of ANCOVA designs, and you should have no trouble getting a statistical package to do such analyses. For further information on these designs see Huitema (1980), Keppel (1982), or Kirk (1982).

One can also utilize multiple covariates in an analysis of covariance design. Due to the adjustments that have to be made for each additional covariate, the computations are rough. Your best solution is to have a statistical package do the computations. For further information about the use of multiple covariates see Huitema (1980) or Kirk (1982).

NONPARAMETRIC ANCOVA PROCEDURES

In situations where the assumptions of normality, homogeneity of variance, and/or linearity have been seriously violated, an alternative is to consider nonparametric ANCOVA procedures. Some rank ANCOVA procedures have been proposed by Quade (1967), Puri and Sen (1969), and Conover and Iman (1982). For a thorough description of such procedures, see these references as well as Huitema (1980, which includes computational examples as well).

SUMMARY

In this chapter, methods involving the comparison of multiple-group adjusted means for a single independent variable were considered. The chapter began with a look at the unique characteristics of the analysis of covariance, including: (a) statistical control through the use of a covariate, (b) the dependent variable means adjusted by the covariate, (c) the covariate used to reduce error variance, (d) the relationship between the covariate and the dependent variable taken into account in the adjustment, and (e) the covariate measured at least at the interval level. The layout of the data was shown, followed by an examination of the ANCOVA model and the computations involved in deriving the ANCOVA summary table. Next the estimation of the adjusted means was considered along with several different multiple comparison procedures. Some discussion was also devoted to the ANCOVA assumptions, their assessment, and how to deal with assumption violations. We illustrated the use of the analysis of covariance by looking at an example. Finally, we finished off the chapter by briefly examining (a) the relationship of ANCOVA to regression analysis, (b) the use of the major statistical packages for conducting an analysis of covariance, (c) some cautions about the use of ANCOVA in situations without randomization, (d) ANCOVA for models having multiple factors and/or multiple covariates, and (e) nonparametric ANCOVA procedures. At this point you should have met the following objectives: (a) be able to understand the characteristics and concepts underlying ANCOVA; (b) be able to compute and interpret the results of ANCOVA, including adjusted means and multiple comparison procedures; and (c) be able to understand and evaluate the assumptions of ANCOVA. Chapter 7 goes beyond the fixed-effects models we have discussed thus far and considers random- and mixed-effects models.

PROBLEMS

Conceptual Problems

1. If the correlation between the covariate X and the dependent variable Y differs markedly in the two treatment groups, it seems likely that
   a. the assumption of normality is suspect.
   b. the assumption of parallel regression lines is suspect.
   c. a nonlinear relation exists between X and Y.
   d. the adjusted means for Y differ significantly.

2. If for both the treatment and control groups the correlation between the covariate X and the dependent variable Y is substantial but negative, the error variation for ANCOVA as compared to that for ANOVA is
   a. less.
   b. about the same.
   c. greater.
   d. unpredictably different.

3. An experiment was conducted to compare three different instructional strategies. Fifteen subjects were included in each group. The same test was administered prior to and after the treatments. If both pretest and IQ are used as covariates, what is the degrees of freedom for the error term?
   a. 2
   b. 40
   c. 41
   d. 42

4. The effects of a training program concerned with educating heart attack patients to the benefits of moderate exercise was examined. A group of recent heart attack patients was randomly divided into two groups; one group received the training program and the other did not. The dependent variable was the amount of time taken to jog three laps, with the weight of the patient used as a covariate. Examination of the data after the study revealed that the covariate means of the two groups differed. Which of the following assumptions is most clearly violated?
   a. linearity
   b. homogeneity of regression coefficients
   c. independence of the treatment and the covariate
   d. normality

5. In ANCOVA, the covariate is a variable that should have a
   a. low positive correlation with the dependent variable.
   b. high positive correlation with the independent variable.
   c. high positive correlation with the dependent variable.
   d. zero correlation with the dependent variable.

6. In ANCOVA, how will the correlation of zero between the covariate and the dependent variable appear?
   a. unequal group means on the dependent variable.
   b. unequal group means on the covariate.
   c. regression of the dependent variable on the covariate with $b = 0$.
   d. regression of the dependent variable on the covariate with $b = 1$.

7. Which of the following is not a necessary requirement for using ANCOVA?
   a. Covariate scores are not affected by the treatment.
   b. There is a linear relationship between the covariate and the dependent variable.
   c. The covariate variable is the same measure as the dependent variable.
   d. Regression coefficients for the groups are similar.

8. Which of the following is the most desirable situation to use ANCOVA?
   a. The slope of the regression line equals zero.
   b. The variance of the dependent variable for a specific covariate score is relatively large.
   c. The correlation between the covariate and the dependent variable is $-.95$.
   d. The correlation between the covariate and the dependent variable is .60.

9. A group of students was randomly assigned to one of three instructional strategies. Data from the study indicated an interaction between slope and treatment group. It seems likely that
   a. the assumption of normality is suspect.
   b. the assumption of homogeneity of regression lines is suspect.
   c. a nonlinear relation exists between X and Y.
   d. the covariate is not independent of the treatment.

10. If the mean on the dependent variable GPA (Y) for persons of middle social class (X) is higher than for persons of lower and higher social classes, one would expect that
    a. the relationship between X and Y is curvilinear.
    b. the covariate X contains substantial measurement error.
    c. GPA is not normally distributed.
    d. social class is not related to GPA.

11. If both the covariate and the dependent variable are assessed after the treatment has been concluded, and if both are affected by the treatment, the use of ANCOVA for these data would likely result in
    a. an inflated F ratio for the treatment effect.
    b. an exaggerated difference in the adjusted means.
    c. an underestimate of the treatment effect.
    d. an inflated value of the correlation r_w.

12. When the covariate correlates $+.5$ with the dependent variable, I assert that the adjusted MS_{with} from the ANCOVA will be less than the MS_{with} from the ANOVA. Am I correct?

13. For each of two groups, the correlation between the covariate and the dependent variable is substantial, but negative in direction. I assert that the error variance for ANCOVA, as compared to that for ANOVA, is greater. Am I correct?

Computational Problems

1. Consider the analysis of covariance situation where the dependent variable Y is the posttest of an achievement test and the covariate X is the pretest of the same test. Given the data that follow where there are three groups, (a) calculate the adjusted Y values assuming that $b_w = 1.00$, and (b) determine what effects the adjustment had on the posttest results.

Group	X	$\overline{X}$	Y	$\overline{Y}$
	40		120	
1	50	50	125	125
	60		130	
	70		140	
2	75	75	150	150
	80		160	
	90		160	
3	100	100	175	175
	110		190	

2. Here are four independent random samples of paired values of the covariate (X) and the dependent variable (Y). Conduct an analysis of variance on Y, an analysis of covariance on Y using X as a covariate, and compare the results ($\alpha = .05$). Compute the unadjusted and adjusted means.

Group 1		Group 2		Group 3		Group 4	
X	Y	X	Y	X	Y	X	Y
94	14	80	38	92	55	94	24
96	19	84	34	96	53	94	37
98	17	90	43	99	55	98	22
100	38	97	43	101	52	100	43
102	40	97	61	102	35	103	49
105	26	112	63	104	46	104	24
109	41	115	93	107	57	104	41
110	28	118	74	110	55	108	26
111	36	120	76	111	42	113	70
130	66	120	79	118	81	115	63

7

RANDOM- AND MIXED-EFFECTS ANALYSIS OF VARIANCE MODELS

Chapter Outline

1. The one-factor random-effects model
   Characteristics of the model
   The ANOVA model
   ANOVA summary table
   Assumptions and violation of assumptions
   Expected mean squares
   Measures of association
   Multiple-comparison procedures
2. The two-factor random-effects model
   Characteristics of the model
   The ANOVA model
   ANOVA summary table
   Assumptions and violation of assumptions
   Expected mean squares
   Measures of association
   Multiple-comparison procedures
3. The two-factor mixed-effects model
   Characteristics of the model
   The ANOVA model
   ANOVA summary table
   Assumptions and violation of assumptions
   Expected mean squares

Measures of association
Multiple-comparison procedures
4. The one-factor repeated measures design
Characteristics of the model
The layout of the data
The ANOVA model
Assumptions and violation of assumptions
ANOVA summary table
Expected mean squares
Multiple-comparison procedures
The Friedman test
An example
5. The two-factor split-plot or mixed design
Characteristics of the model
The layout of the data
The ANOVA model
Assumptions and violation of assumptions
ANOVA summary table
Expected mean squares
Multiple-comparison procedures
An example

Key Concepts

1. Fixed- and random-effects models
2. Intraclass correlation coefficient
3. Components of variance
4. Mixed-effects models
5. Repeated measures models
6. Homogeneity of covariance assumption
7. Friedman repeated measures test based on ranks
8. Split-plot or mixed designs (i.e., both between and within subjects factors)

In this chapter we continue our discussion of the analysis of variance (ANOVA) by considering models in which there is one or more random-effects factors, previously discussed in chapter 3. These models include the one-factor and factorial designs, as well as repeated measures designs. As becomes evident, repeated measures designs are used when there is at least one factor where each individual is exposed to all levels of that factor. This factor is referred to as a *repeated factor*, for obvious reasons. This chapter is most concerned with one- and two-factor random-effects models, the two-factor mixed-effects model, and one- and two-factor repeated measures designs.

Many of the concepts used in this chapter are the same as those covered in chapters 3 through 6. In addition, the following new concepts are addressed: random- and mixed-effects factors, the interclass correlation coefficient, components of variance, repeated measures factors, the homogeneity of covariance assumption, and mixed designs. Our objectives are that by the end of this chapter, you will be able to (a) understand the characteristics and concepts underlying random- and mixed-effects ANOVA models, (b) compute and interpret the results of random- and mixed-effects ANOVA models, including measures of association and multiple comparison procedures, and (c) understand and evaluate the assumptions of random- and mixed-effects ANOVA models.

THE ONE-FACTOR RANDOM-EFFECTS MODEL

This section describes the distinguishing characteristics of the one-factor random-effects ANOVA model, the linear model, the ANOVA summary table, assumptions and their violation, expected mean squares, the intraclass correlation coefficient, and multiple-comparison procedures.

Characteristics of the Model

The characteristics of the one-factor fixed-effects ANOVA model have already been covered in chapter 3. These characteristics include (a) one factor (or independent variable) with two or more levels, (b) all levels of the factor of interest are included in the design (i.e., a fixed-effects factor), (c) subjects are randomly assigned to one level of the factor, and (d) the dependent variable is measured at least at the interval level. Thus the overall design is a fixed-effects model, where there is one factor and the individuals respond to only one level of the factor. If individuals respond to more than one level of the factor, then this would be some sort of repeated measures design, as shown later in this chapter.

The characteristics of the one-factor random-effects ANOVA model are the same with one obvious exception. This has to do with the selection of the levels of the factor. In the fixed-effects case, researchers select all of the levels of interest, because they are only interested in making generalizations (or inferences) about those particular levels. Thus in replications of the design, each replicate would use precisely the same levels. Examples of factors that are typically fixed include gender, treatment, marital status, method of instruction, and type of disease.

In the random-effects case, researchers randomly select levels from the population of levels, because they are interested in making generalizations (or inferences) about the entire population of levels, not merely those that have been sampled. Thus in replications of the design, each replicate need not have the same levels included. The concept of random selection of factor levels from the population of levels is the same as the random selection of subjects from the population. Here the researcher is making an inference from the sampled levels to the population of levels, instead of making an inference from the sample of individuals to the population of individuals. In a random-effects design then, a random sample of factor levels is selected in the same way as a random sample of individuals is selected.

For instance, a researcher interested in teacher effectiveness may have randomly sampled history teachers (i.e., the independent variable) from the population of history teachers in a particular school district. Generalizations can then be made about other history teachers in that school district not actually sampled. Other examples of factors that are typically random include classrooms, observers or raters, time (seconds, minutes, hours, days, weeks, etc.), animals, students, or schools. It should be noted that in educational settings, the researcher is often in a position where the random selection of schools, classes, teachers, and/or students is not possible. Here we would need to consider such factors as fixed rather than random effects.

We again assume that the number of observations made in each factor level is the same. If the number of observations across levels are not equal, then use the procedures discussed in chapter 3. In addition, we assume there are at least two observations per factor level so as to have an error term (due to within-groups variation) with which to test the hypothesis of interest.

The ANOVA Model

The one-factor ANOVA random-effects model is written in terms of population parameters as

$$Y_{ij} = \mu + a_j + \epsilon_{ij}$$

where Y_{ij} is the observed score on the criterion variable for individual i in level j of factor A, μ is the overall or grand population mean, a_j is the random effect for level j of factor A, and ϵ_{ij} is the random residual error for individual i for level j. The residual error can be due to individual differences, measurement error, and/or other factors not under investigation. Note that we use a_j to designate the random effects to differentiate them from the α_j in the fixed-effects model.

There are no side conditions for the random-effects model as there was for the fixed-effects model (i.e., $\Sigma \alpha_j = 0$). However, in the random-effects model only a sample of the effects from the population is included in the study. If the entire population of effects were examined, the sum of these effects would indeed be zero. Only a sample of effects is examined, so the sum of these effects need not be zero. For instance, we may select a sample having only positive effects. Thus this sample of effects would not sum to zero.

For the one-factor random-effects ANOVA model, the hypotheses for testing the effect of factor A are

$$H_0: \sigma_a{}^2 = 0$$

$$H_1: \sigma_a{}^2 > 0$$

Recall for the one-factor fixed-effects ANOVA model that the hypotheses for testing the effect of factor A are

$$H_0: \mu_{.1} = \mu_{.2} = \mu_{.3} = \ldots = \mu_{.J}$$

$$H_1: \text{not all the } \mu_{.j} \text{ are equal .}$$

This reflects the difference in the inferences made in the random- and fixed-effects models. In the fixed-effects case the null hypothesis is about means, whereas in the random-effects case the null hypothesis is about variance among the means. As becomes evident, the difference in the models is also reflected in the expected mean squares and in the multiple comparison procedures.

ANOVA Summary Table

The computations for the one-factor random-effects model are exactly the same as the one-factor fixed-effects model. The sources of variation are A (or between), within, and total. The sums of squares, degrees of freedom, mean squares, F-test statistic, and critical value are determined in the same way as in the fixed-effects case. Obviously then, the ANOVA summary table looks the same as well. Using the example from chapter 3, assuming the model is now a random-effects model, we again obtain a test statistic $F = 6.8177$, which is significant at the .05 level.

Assumptions and Violation of Assumptions

In chapter 3 we described the assumptions for the one-factor fixed-effects model. The assumptions are nearly the same for the one-factor random-effects model and we need not devote much attention to them here. The assumptions are again mainly concerned with the distribution of the residual errors.

The assumption of the distribution of the residual errors is actually a set of three statements about the form of the residual errors, the ε_{ij}. First, the residual errors are assumed to be random and independent errors. That is, there is no systematic pattern about the errors and the errors are independent across individuals. The use of independent random samples is crucial in the analysis of variance as the F ratio is very sensitive to such violations in terms of increased likelihood of a Type I and/or Type II error. A violation of the independence assumption may affect the standard errors of the sample means and thus influence any inferences made about those means. One purpose of random assignment of individuals to groups is to achieve independence of the ε_{ij} terms. If each individual is only observed once and individuals are randomly assigned to groups, then the independence assumption is usually met.

The simplest procedure for assessing independence is to examine residual plots by group. If the independence assumption is satisfied, then the residuals should fall into a random display of points for each group. If the assumption is violated, then the residuals will fall into some type of cyclical pattern. As discussed in chapter 1, the Durbin–Watson statistic (1950, 1951, 1971) can be used to test for serial correlation. For severe violations of the independence assumption, there is no simple "fix" such as the use of transformations or nonparametric tests.

According to the second part of the assumption, the distributions of the residual errors for each group have a constant variance, σ_ϵ^2. Often this is referred to as the assumption of homogeneity of variance or homoscedasticity. In other words, for all groups, the conditional distributions of the residual errors will have the same variance. A violation of the homogeneity assumption may lead to bias in the SS_{with} term, as well as an increase in the Type I error rate and possibly an increase in the Type II error rate. The effect of the violation seems to be small with balanced or nearly balanced designs, whereas the effect increases as the design becomes less balanced. In addition, as n increases, the effect decreases. Thus to minimize the problem, use a balanced design (or nearly so), or if this is not possible, use as many observations per group as possible. In general, the effects of heterogeneity are thought not to be severe except for extreme violations.

In a plot of group means versus group variances, the consistency of the variance of the conditional residual distributions may be examined. No formal statistical test is recommended. There are no wonderful solutions for dealing with a violation of the homogeneity assumption.

The third and final part of the assumption notes that the conditional distributions of the residual errors are normal in shape. That is, for all groups, the residual errors are normally distributed. The F test is relatively robust to moderate violations of this assumption (i.e., in terms of Type I and II error rates). The effect of the violation seems to be small with balanced or nearly balanced designs, whereas the effect increases as the design becomes less balanced. In addition, as n increases, the effect decreases. Thus to minimize the problem, use a balanced design (or nearly so), or if not possible, use as many observations per group as possible. In general, the effects of nonnormality are thought not to be severe except for extreme violations.

To detect a violation of the normality assumption one can graphically look at the distribution of the residuals for each group, although no statistical test can be recommended. As far as dealing with a violation of the normality assumption, transformations are often useful (see Miller, 1997). In summary, the assumptions about the residuals can be written as $\epsilon_{ij} \sim NI(0, \sigma_\epsilon^2)$.

Additional assumptions must be made for the random-effects model. These assumptions deal with the effects for the levels of the independent variable, the a_j. First, here are a few words about the a_j. The random group effects a_j are computed, in the population, by the following:

$$a_j = \mu_{.j} - \mu_{..}$$

For example, a_3 represents the effect for being a member of Group 3. If the overall mean $\mu_{..}$ is 60 and $\mu_{.3}$ is 100, then the group effect would be

$$a_3 = \mu_{.3} - \mu_{..} = 100 - 60 = 40$$

Thus, the effect for being a member of Group 3 would be an increase of 40 points over the population mean.

The assumptions about the a_j are similar to those for the ε_{ij}. In this case, the a_j group effects are randomly and independently sampled from the normally distributed population of group effects, with a population mean of zero and a population variance of σ_a^2. Stated another way, there is a population of group effects out there from which we are taking a random sample. For example, with teacher as the factor of interest, we are interested in examining the effectiveness of teachers. We take a random sample from the population of second-grade teachers. For these teachers we measure their effectiveness in the classroom and generate an effect for each teacher (i.e., the a_j). These effects indicate the extent to which a particular teacher is more or less effective than the population of teachers. Their effects are known as random effects because the teachers are randomly selected. In the selection of teachers, each teacher is selected independently of all other teachers to prevent a biased sample. The population of teacher effects is represented by a normal distribution with variance equal to σ_a^2 (i.e., a measure of the variability of the teacher effects). Thus the assumptions for a_j can be written as $a_j \sim NI(0,\sigma_a^2)$.

In addition, it is assumed that the a_j terms are independent of the ε_{ij} terms. The effects of the violation of the assumptions about the a_j are the same as with the residuals. The F test is quite robust to nonnormality of the a_j terms, and unequal variances of the a_j terms. However, the F test is quite sensitive to nonindependence among the a_j terms and between the a_j and the ε_{ij} terms, with no known solutions. A summary of the assumptions and the effects of their violation for the one-factor random-effects model is presented in Table 7.1.

Expected Mean Squares

Recall from previous chapters that the notion of expected mean squares provides the basis for determining what the appropriate error term is when forming an F ratio. An expected mean square for a particular source of variation represents the average mean square value for that source obtained if the same study were to be repeated an infinite number of times. For instance the expected value of mean square for factor A, represented by $E(MS_A)$, is the average value of MS_A over repeated samplings. Consider the alternative situations of H_0 actually being true and H_0 actually being false. If H_0 is actually true, then the expected mean squares are

$$E(MS_A) = \sigma_\varepsilon^2$$

and

$$E(MS_{with}) = \sigma_\varepsilon^2$$

where σ_ε^2 is the population variance of the residual errors. Thus $E(MS_A)/E(MS_{with}) = 1$.

If H_0 is actually false, then the expected mean squares are

$$E(MS_A) = \sigma_\varepsilon^2 + n\sigma_a^2$$

TABLE 7.1

Assumptions and Effects of Violations—One-Factor Random-Effects Model

Assumption	Effect of Assumption Violation
1. Independence of (a) residuals; (b) random effects	Increased likelihood of a Type I and/or Type II error in the F statistic; influences standard errors of means and thus inferences about those means
2. Homogeneity of variance for (a) residuals; (b) random effects	Bias in SS_{with}; increased likelihood of a Type I and/or Type II error; small effect with equal or nearly equal ns; otherwise effect decreases as n increases
3. Normality of (a) residuals; (b) random effects	Minimal effect with equal or nearly equal ns

for the equal ns or balanced case, and

$$E(MS_{with}) = \sigma_\varepsilon^2$$

Thus $E(MS_A)/E(MS_{with}) > 1$. There is a difference in $E(MS_A)$ when H_0 is actually true as compared to when H_0 is actually false because in the latter situation there is a second term that represents systematic variability among the levels of Factor A. The size of the second term determines the outcome of the test. In general, the F ratio represents

$$F = \frac{\text{systematic variability} + \text{error variability}}{\text{error variability}}$$

As always, we want to isolate the systematic variability in the numerator. For this model, the only appropriate F ratio is to use MS_{with} in the denominator as it isolates the systematic variability.

Measures of Association

Measures of association provide us with quantitative information about the relationship between the independent and dependent variables. Recall from chapter 3 for fixed-effects models that ω^2 is a measure of association indicating the proportion of variation in Y that is accounted for by X. The conceptual equivalent for the random-effects model is the intraclass correlation coefficient ρ_I which measures association in terms of proportion of variation as well. The intraclass correlation coefficient is essentially a within population correlation coefficient, and is computed by

$$\rho_I = \frac{MS_{betw} - MS_{with}}{MS_{betw} + (n-1)MS_{with}}$$

Using the example from chapter 3, and assuming the model is now a random-effects model, we compute the intraclass correlation coefficient as

$$\rho_I = \frac{MS_{betw} - MS_{with}}{MS_{betw} + (n-1)MS_{with}} = \frac{246.1979 - 36.1116}{246.1979 + (7)36.1116} = 0.4210$$

which is comparable to $\omega^2 = .3529$ obtained for the fixed-effects model. The intraclass correlation coefficient can also be represented as

$$\rho_I = \frac{\sigma_a^2}{\sigma_a^2 + \sigma_\varepsilon^2}$$

where σ_a^2 and σ_ε^2 are known as *variance components* and can be estimated by

$$\sigma_a^2 = \frac{MS_{betw} - MS_{with}}{n}$$

for the equal ns or balanced case, and

$$\sigma_\varepsilon^2 = MS_{with}$$

This definition of ρ_I is conceptually more like the $E(MS)$ and hypotheses of the random-effects model than the initial definition. Note that if MS_{betw} is smaller than MS_{with}, which occasionally happens, then the estimate of σ_ε^2 would be negative. However, because a variance can never be negative, the usual procedure is to set σ_ε^2 equal to zero.

There is no magical rule of thumb for interpreting the size of ρ_I, only that it is scaled theoretically from zero (no association) to one (perfect association). It is up to researchers in the particular substantive area of research to interpret the magnitude of these measures by comparing their results to the results of other similar studies.

Using the data from chapter 3 as a random-effects model, the variance components are estimated as follows:

$$\sigma_a^2 = \frac{MS_{betw} - MS_{with}}{n} = \frac{246.1979 - 36.1116}{8} = 26.2608$$

$$\sigma_\varepsilon^2 = MS_{with} = 36.1116$$

Multiple-Comparison Procedures

Let us think for a moment about the use of multiple-comparison procedures for the random-effects model. In general, the researcher is not usually interested in making inferences about just the levels of A that were sampled. Thus, estimation of the a_j terms does not provide us with any information about the a_j terms that were not sampled. Also, the a_j terms cannot be summarized by their mean, because it will not necessarily be equal to zero for the levels sampled, only for the population of levels. Thus rather than looking at comparisons among the means of the a_j levels, the researcher is interested in looking at σ_a^2 and ρ_I as shown earlier.

THE TWO-FACTOR RANDOM-EFFECTS MODEL

In this section, we describe the distinguishing characteristics of the two-factor random-effects ANOVA model, the linear model, the ANOVA summary table, assumptions of the model and their violation, expected mean squares, the intraclass correlation coefficient, and multiple-comparison procedures.

Characteristics of the Model

The characteristics of the one-factor random-effects ANOVA model have already been covered in the preceding section, and of the two-factor fixed-effects model in chapter 5. Here we extend and combine these characteristics to form the two-factor random-effects model. These characteristics include:

1. Two factors (or independent variables) each with two or more levels.
2. The levels of each of the factors are randomly sampled from the population of levels (i.e., two random-effects factors).
3. Subjects are randomly assigned to one combination of the levels of the two factors.
4. The dependent variable is measured at least at the interval level.

Thus the overall design is a random-effects model, with two factors, and the individuals respond to only one combination of the levels of the two factors. If individuals respond to more than one combination of the levels of the two factors, then this would be some sort of repeated measures design (discussed later in this chapter).

We again assume for simplicity that the number of observations in each factor level combination is the same. If the numbers of observations are not equal, then return to the procedures discussed in chapter 5. In addition, we assume there are at least two observations per factor level combination (i.e., per cell) so as to have a within cells source of variation.

The ANOVA Model

The two-factor ANOVA random-effects model is written in terms of population parameters as

$$Y_{ijk} = \mu + a_j + b_k + (ab)_{jk} + \varepsilon_{ijk}$$

where Y_{ijk} is the observed score on the criterion variable for individual i in level j of factor A and level k of factor B (or in the jk cell), μ is the overall or grand population mean (i.e., regardless of cell designation), a_j is the random effect for level j of factor A (row effect), b_k is the random effect for level k of factor B (column effect), $(ab)_{jk}$ is the interaction random effect for the combination of level j of factor A and level k of factor B, and ε_{ijk} is the random residual error for individual i in cell jk. The residual error can be due to individual differences, measurement error, and/or other factors not under investigation. Note that we use a_j, b_k, and $(ab)_{jk}$ to designate the random effects to differentiate them from the α_j, β_k, and $(\alpha\beta)_{jk}$ in the fixed-effects model.

There are no side conditions for the random-effects model about the main and interaction effects. Thus there is no requirement that the sum of the main or interaction effects is equal to zero because only a sample of these effects are taken from the population of effects.

There are three sets of hypotheses, one for each main effect and one for the interaction effect. The null and alternative hypotheses, respectively, for testing the effect of factor A are

$$H_{01}: \sigma_a^2 = 0$$

$$H_{11}: \sigma_a^2 > 0$$

The hypotheses for testing the effect of factor B are

$$H_{02}: \sigma_b^2 = 0$$

$$H_{12}: \sigma_b^2 > 0$$

Finally, the hypotheses for testing the interaction effect are

$$H_{03}: \sigma_{ab}^2 = 0$$

$$H_{13}: \sigma_{ab}^2 > 0$$

These hypotheses again reflect the difference in the inferences made in the random- and fixed-effects models. In the fixed-effects case the null hypotheses are about means, whereas in the random-effects case the null hypotheses are about variance among the means.

ANOVA Summary Table

There are very few differences between the two-factor fixed-effects and random-effects models. The computations are exactly the same for both models. The sources of variation are A, B, AB, within, and total. Thus, the sums of squares, degrees of freedom, and mean squares are calculated the same as we did in the fixed-effects case. However, the F-test statistics are different, as well as the critical values used. As put forth in the next section, this is due to how the expected mean squares are written. At this point, the F-test statistics are formed for the test of factor A as

$$F_A = \frac{MS_A}{MS_{AB}}$$

for the test of factor B as

$$F_B = \frac{MS_B}{MS_{AB}}$$

and for the test of the AB interaction as

$$F_{AB} = \frac{MS_{AB}}{MS_{with}}$$

Recall that in the fixed-effects model, the MS_{with} was used as the error term for all three hypotheses. However, in the random-effects model, the MS_{with} is used as the error term only for the test of the interaction. The MS_{AB} is used as the error term for the tests of the main effects. The critical values used are those based on the degrees of freedom for the numerator and denominator of each hypothesis tested. Thus using the example from chapter 5, assuming that the model is now a random-effects model, we obtain as our test statistic for the test of factor A

$$F_A = \frac{MS_A}{MS_{AB}} = \frac{246.1979}{7.2813} = 33.8124$$

for the test of factor B

$$F_B = \frac{MS_B}{MS_{AB}} = \frac{712.5313}{7.2813} = 97.8577$$

and for the test of the AB interaction

$$F_{AB} = \frac{MS_{AB}}{MS_{with}} = \frac{7.2813}{11.5313} = 0.6314$$

The critical value for the test of factor A is found in the F table of Appendix Table 4 as $_{1-\alpha}F_{J-1,(J-1)(K-1)}$, which for the example is $_{.95}F_{3,3} = 9.28$, and is significant at the .05 level. The critical value for the test of factor B is found in the F table as $_{1-\alpha}F_{K-1,(J-1)(K-1)}$, which for the example is $_{.95}F_{1,3} = 10.13$, and is significant at the .05 level. The critical value for the test of the interaction is found in the F table as $_{1-\alpha}F_{(J-1)(K-1),N-JK}$, which for the example is $_{.95}F_{3,24} = 3.01$, and is not significant at the .05 level. It just so happens for the example data that the results for the random- and fixed-effects models are the same. This will not always be the case.

Assumptions and Violation of Assumptions

In the preceding section we described the assumptions for the one-factor random-effects model. The assumptions are nearly the same for the two-factor random-effects model and we need not devote much attention to them here. As before, the assumptions are mainly concerned with the distribution of the residual errors. In the two-factor case, we are concerned with the residuals at the cell level, that is, the residuals within each cell of the design.

The assumption of the distribution of the residual errors is again a set of three statements about the form of the residual errors, the ε_{ijk} (i.e., normality, independence, homogeneity). A general statement of the assumptions about the residuals can be written as $\varepsilon_{ijk} \sim NI\ (0,\sigma^2_\varepsilon)$. Little is known about the effect of unequal variances (i.e., heteroscedasticity) or dependence for the random-effects model. For violation of the normality assumption, effects are known to be substantial. Detection is usually obtained via a plot of the residuals, but not much else is of value here. Under violation of the normality assumption, it is unlikely that a useful transformation can be found (see Miller, 1997, for suggestions).

Additional assumptions must be made in the random-effects model. These assumptions deal with the sampled levels of the independent variables, the a_j, b_k, and their interaction $(ab)_{jk}$. The assumptions about these effects are the same as with the ε_{ijk}. These assumptions are that the a_j, b_k, and $(ab)_{jk}$ are randomly and independently sampled from the normally distributed population of levels, with a population mean of zero and a population variance of σ_a^2, σ_b^2, and σ_{ab}^2, respectively. Thus the assumptions for the random effects can be written as $a_j \sim NI\ (0,\sigma^2_a)$, $b_k \sim NI\ (0,\sigma_b^2)$, and $(ab)_{jk} \sim NI\ (0,\sigma^2_{ab})$. In addition, it is assumed that the a_j, b_k, $(ab)_{jk}$, and ε_{ijk} terms are mutually independent. In general, statements about the violation of these assumptions are the same as with the residuals. A summary of the assumptions and the effects of their violation for the two-factor random-effects model are presented in Table 7.2.

Expected Mean Squares

Let us now provide a basis for determining the appropriate error terms for forming an F ratio in this model. Consider the alternative situations of H_0 actually being true and H_0 actually being false. If H_0 is actually true for all three tests, then the expected mean squares are as follows:

$$E(MS_A) = \sigma_\varepsilon^2$$
$$E(MS_B) = \sigma_\varepsilon^2$$
$$E(MS_{AB}) = \sigma_\varepsilon^2$$
$$E(MS_{with}) = \sigma_\varepsilon^2$$

TABLE 7.2
Assumptions and Effects of Violations—Two-Factor Random-Effects Model

Assumption	Effect of Assumption Violation
1. Independence of (a) residuals; (b) random effects	Little is known about the effects of dependence; however, based on the fixed-effects case we might expect the following: increased likelihood of a Type I and/or Type II error in the F statistic; influences standard errors of means and thus inferences about those means
2. Homogeneity of variance for (a) residuals; (b) random effects	Little is known about the effects of heteroscedasticity; however, based on the fixed-effects case we might expect the following: bias in SS_{with}; increased likelihood of a Type I and/or Type II error; small effect with equal or nearly equal ns; otherwise effect decreases as n increases
3. Normality of (a) residuals; (b) random effects	Minimal effect with equal or nearly equal ns; otherwise substantial effects

Here σ_ϵ^2 is the population variance of the residual errors.

If H_0 is actually false for all three tests, then the expected mean squares for the equal ns or balanced case are as follows.

$$E(MS_\text{A}) = \sigma_\epsilon^2 + n\sigma_{ab}^2 + Kn\sigma_a^2$$

$$E(MS_\text{B}) = \sigma_\epsilon^2 + n\sigma_{ab}^2 + Jn\sigma_b^2$$

$$E(MS_\text{AB}) = \sigma_\epsilon^2 + n\sigma_{ab}^2$$

$$E(MS_\text{with}) = \sigma_\epsilon^2$$

Thus, given that the F ratio represents

$$F = \frac{\text{systematic variability} + \text{error variability}}{\text{error variability}}$$

then the appropriate error term for the tests of the main effects is the interaction term, and the appropriate error term for the test of the interaction is the within term. This is the only way the main and interaction effects can be isolated and formulate a proper F ratio.

Measures of Association

The standard measure of association for the random-effects model is the intraclass correlation coefficient ρ, and is computed for the A effect by

$$\rho_a = \frac{\sigma_a^2}{\sigma_a^2 + \sigma_b^2 + \sigma_{ab}^2 + \sigma_\epsilon^2}$$

for the B effect by

$$\rho_b = \frac{\sigma_b^2}{\sigma_a^2 + \sigma_b^2 + \sigma_{ab}^2 + \sigma_\epsilon^2}$$

and for the AB interaction effect by

$$\rho_{ab} = \frac{\sigma_{ab}^2}{\sigma_a^2 + \sigma_b^2 + \sigma_{ab}^2 + \sigma_\epsilon^2}$$

The variance components can be estimated for the A effect as

$$\sigma_a^2 = \frac{MS_\text{A} - MS_\text{AB}}{Kn}$$

for the B effect by

$$\sigma_b^2 = \frac{MS_\text{B} - MS_\text{AB}}{Jn}$$

for the AB interaction effect by

$$\sigma_{ab}^{\,2} = \frac{MS_{AB} - MS_{with}}{n}$$

and, for the within cells effect by

$$\sigma_{\varepsilon}^{\,2} = MS_{with}$$

Using the example from chapter 5, assuming that the model is now a random-effects model, we estimate the variance component for the A effect as

$$\sigma_a^{\,2} = \frac{MS_A - MS_{AB}}{Kn} = \frac{246.1979 - 7.2813}{8} = 29.8646$$

for the B effect by

$$\sigma_b^{\,2} = \frac{MS_B - MS_{AB}}{Jn} = \frac{712.5313 - 7.2813}{16} = 44.0781$$

for the AB interaction effect by

$$\sigma_{ab}^{\,2} = \frac{MS_{AB} - MS_{with}}{n} = \frac{7.2813 - 11.5313}{4} = 0$$

substituting 0 for a negative variance, and for the within-cells effect by

$$\sigma_{\varepsilon}^{\,2} = MS_{with} = 11.5313$$

Thus, the intraclass correlation coefficient for the A effect is

$$\rho_a = \frac{\sigma_a^2}{\sigma_a^2 + \sigma_b^2 + \sigma_{ab}^2 + \sigma_{\varepsilon}^2} = \frac{29.8646}{29.8646 + 44.0781 + 0 + 11.5313} = .3494$$

for the B effect is

$$\rho_b = \frac{\sigma_b^2}{\sigma_a^2 + \sigma_b^2 + \sigma_{ab}^2 + \sigma_{\varepsilon}^2} = \frac{44.0781}{29.8646 + 44.0781 + 0 + 11.5313} = .5157$$

and for the AB interaction effect is

$$\rho_{ab} = \frac{\sigma_{ab}^2}{\sigma_a^2 + \sigma_b^2 + \sigma_{ab}^2 + \sigma_{\varepsilon}^2} = \frac{0}{29.8646 + 44.0781 + 0 + 11.5313} = 0$$

Again there is no magical rule of thumb for interpreting the size of ρ, only that it is scaled theoretically from zero (no association) to one (perfect association).

Multiple-Comparison Procedures

The story of multiple comparisons for the two-factor random-effects model is the same as that for the one-factor random-effects model. In general, the researcher is not usually interested in making inferences about just the levels of A, B, or AB that were sampled. Thus, estimation of the a_j, b_k, or $(ab)_{jk}$ terms does not provide us with any information about the a_j, b_k, or $(ab)_{jk}$ terms that were not sampled. Also, the a_j, b_k, or $(ab)_{jk}$ terms cannot be summarized by their means, because they will not necessarily be equal to zero for the levels sampled, only for the population of levels. Thus rather than looking at comparisons among the means of the a_j, b_k, or $(ab)_{jk}$ levels, the researcher is interested in looking at the variances and intraclass correlations of the a_j, b_k, or $(ab)_{jk}$ terms as previously shown.

THE TWO-FACTOR MIXED-EFFECTS MODEL

This section describes the distinguishing characteristics of the two-factor mixed-effects ANOVA model, the linear model, the ANOVA summary table, assumptions of the model and their violation, expected mean squares, measures of association, and multiple-comparison procedures.

Characteristics of the Model

The characteristics of the two-factor random-effects ANOVA model have already been covered in the preceding section, and of the two-factor fixed-effects model in chapter 5. Here we extend and combine these characteristics to form the two-factor mixed-effects model. These characteristics include:

1. Two factors (or independent variables) each with two or more levels.
2. The levels for one of the factors are randomly sampled from the population of levels (i.e., the random-effects factor) and all of the levels of interest for the second factor are included in the design (i.e., the fixed-effects factor).
3. Subjects are randomly selected and assigned to one combination of the levels of the two factors.
4. The dependent variable is measured at least at the interval level.

Thus the overall design is a mixed-effects model, with one fixed-effects factor and one random-effects factor, and individuals respond to only one combination of the levels of the two factors. If individuals respond to more than one combination, then this would be some sort of repeated measures design.

We again assume for simplicity that the number of observations in each factor level combination is the same. If the numbers of observations are not equal, return to the procedures as discussed in chapter 5. In addition, we assume there are at least two observations per factor level combination (i.e., per cell) so as to have a within-cells source of variation.

The ANOVA Model

There are actually two variations of the two-factor mixed-effects model, one where factor A is fixed and factor B is random, and the other where factor A is random and factor B is fixed. The labeling of a factor as A or B is arbitrary, so we only consider the former variation where A is fixed and B is random. For the latter variation merely switch the labels of the factors. The two-factor ANOVA mixed-effects model is written in terms of population parameters as

$$Y_{ijk} = \mu + \alpha_j + b_k + (\alpha b)_{jk} + \varepsilon_{ijk}$$

where Y_{ijk} is the observed score on the criterion variable for individual i in level j of factor A and level k of factor B (or in the jk cell), μ is the overall or grand population mean (i.e., regardless of cell designation), α_j is the fixed effect for level j of factor A (row effect), b_k is the random effect for level k of factor B (column effect), $(\alpha b)_{jk}$ is the interaction mixed effect for the combination of level j of factor A and level k of factor B, and ε_{ijk} is the random residual error for individual i in cell jk. The residual error can be due to individual differences, measurement error, and/or other factors not under investigation. Note that we use b_k and $(\alpha b)_{jk}$ to designate the random and mixed effects to differentiate them from β_k and $(\alpha\beta)_{jk}$ in the fixed-effects model.

There are two side conditions for the mixed-effects model about the main and interaction effects. For the equal ns model we are considering here, the side conditions are that $\Sigma_j \alpha_j = 0$, and $\Sigma_j (\alpha b)_{jk} = 0$, for each level k. Thus the sum of the row effects is equal to zero, and the sum of the interaction effects is equal to zero across rows for each column, as shown in Fig. 7.1.

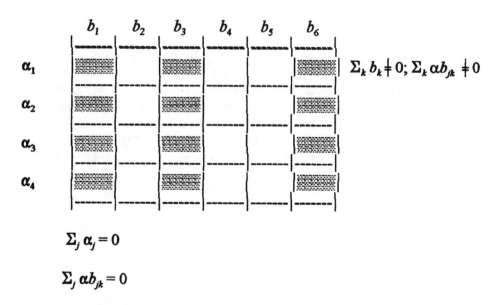

$$\Sigma_j \, \alpha_j = 0$$

$$\Sigma_j \, \alpha b_{jk} = 0$$

FIG. 7.1   Side conditions for the two-factor mixed-effects model. Although all four levels of factor A are selected by the researcher (A is fixed), only three of the six levels of factor B are selected (B is random). If the levels of B selected are 1, 3, and 6, then the design only consists of the shaded cells. In each cell of the design there are α_j, b_k, and αb_{jk} effects. If we sum these effects across rows and columns, we see that the sums are only equal to zero for each column, not for each row.

The null and alternative hypotheses, respectively, for testing the effect of factor A are

$$H_{01}: \mu_{.1.} = \mu_{.2.} = \mu_{.3.} = \ldots = \mu_{.J.}$$

$$H_{11}: \text{not all the } \mu_{j.} \text{ are equal}$$

The hypotheses for testing the effect of factor B are

$$H_{02}: \sigma_b^2 = 0$$

$$H_{12}: \sigma_b^2 > 0$$

Finally, the hypotheses for testing the interaction effect are

$$H_{03}: \sigma_{ab}^2 = 0$$

$$H_{13}: \sigma_{ab}^2 > 0$$

These hypotheses reflect the difference in the inferences made in the mixed-effects model. Here we see that the hypothesis about the fixed-effect A (the main effect of A) is about means, whereas the hypotheses involving the random-effect B (the main effect of B and the interaction effect AB) are about variances among the means.

ANOVA Summary Table

There are very few differences between the two-factor fixed-effects, random-effects, and mixed-effects models. The computations are exactly the same as the two-factor fixed-effects model. The sources of variation are again A, B, AB, within, and total. Thus, the sums of squares, degrees of freedom, and mean squares are calculated the same as we did in the fixed-effects case. However, the F-test statistics are different, as well as the critical values used. As put forth in the next section, this is due to how the expected mean squares are written. At this point the F-test statistics are formed for the test of factor A, the fixed effect, as

$$F_A = \frac{MS_A}{MS_{AB}}$$

for the test of factor B, the random effect, as

$$F_B = \frac{MS_B}{MS_{with}}$$

and for the test of the AB interaction, the mixed effect, as

$$F_{AB} = \frac{MS_{AB}}{MS_{with}}$$

Recall that in the fixed-effects model, the MS_{with} is used as the error term for all three hypotheses. However, in the random-effects model, the MS_{with} is used as the error term only for the test of the interaction, and the MS_{AB} is used as the error term for the tests of the main effects. Finally, in the mixed-effects model, the MS_{with} is used as the error term for the test of B and the interaction, whereas the MS_{AB} is used as the error term for the test of A. The critical values used are those based on the degrees of freedom for the numerator and denominator of each hypothesis tested.

Thus using the example from chapter 5, assuming the model is now a mixed-effects model, we obtain as our test statistic for the test of factor A

$$F_A = \frac{MS_A}{MS_{AB}} = \frac{246.1979}{7.2813} = 33.8124$$

for the test of factor B

$$F_B = \frac{MS_B}{MS_{with}} = \frac{712.5313}{11.5313} = 61.7911$$

and for the test of the AB interaction

$$F_{AB} = \frac{MS_{AB}}{MS_{with}} = \frac{7.2813}{11.5313} = 0.6314$$

The critical value for the test of factor A is found in the F table as $_{1-\alpha}F_{J-1,(J-1)(K-1)}$, which for the example is $_{.95}F_{3,3} = 9.28$, and is significant at the .05 level. The critical value for the test of factor B is found in the F table as $_{1-\alpha}F_{K-1,N-JK}$, which for the example is $_{.95}F_{1,24} = 4.26$, and is significant at the .05 level. The critical value for the test of the interaction is found in the F table as $_{1-\alpha}F_{(J-1)(K-1),N-JK}$, which for the example is $_{.95}F_{3,24} = 3.01$, and is not significant at the .05 level. It just so happens for the example data that the results for the mixed-, random-, and fixed-effects models are the same. This is not always the case.

Assumptions and Violation of Assumptions

In the preceding section we described the assumptions for the two-factor random-effects model. The assumptions are nearly the same for the two-factor mixed-effects model and we need not devote much attention to them here. As always, the assumptions are mainly concerned with the distribution of the residual errors. In the two-factor case, we are concerned with the residuals at the cell level, that is, the residuals within each cell of the design.

A general statement of the assumptions about the residuals is written as $\varepsilon_{ijk} \sim NI(0, \sigma_\varepsilon^2)$. The effect of heteroscedasticity (unequal variances) is the same as in the fixed-effects model. That is, the effect of the violation seems small with balanced or nearly balanced designs, whereas the effect increases as the design becomes less balanced. In addition, as n increases, the effect decreases. Detection is usually done by looking at a plot of cell means versus cell variances. Transformations may be useful if they do not destroy the additive linear model. Not much is known about the effects of dependence for random effects, although we expect the effects are the same as for the fixed-effects case. For violation of the normality assumption, effects are known to be minimal with balanced or nearly balanced designs. For severe violations, transformations may be useful; otherwise, a nonparametric procedure can be used if a no interaction model can be assumed. Detection is usually obtained via a plot of the residuals (see Miller, 1997).

Additional assumptions must be made in the mixed-effects model. These assumptions deal with the sampled levels of the random independent variable, b_k, and its interaction with the fixed variable, $(\alpha b)_{jk}$. The assumptions about these effects are the same as with the ε_{ijk}; the b_k and $(\alpha b)_{jk}$ are randomly and independently sampled from the normally distributed population of levels, with a population mean of zero and a population variance of σ_b^2 and $\sigma_{\alpha b}^2$, respectively. Thus the assumptions for the random effects can be written as $b_k \sim NI(0, \sigma_b^2)$ and $(\alpha b)_{jk} \sim NI(0, \sigma_{\alpha b}^2)$. In addition it is assumed that the b_k and ε_{ijk} terms are independent, and the $(\alpha b)_{jk}$ and ε_{ijk} terms are independent. In general, statements about the violation of these assumptions are the same as with the residuals. A summary of the assumptions and the effects of their violation for the two-factor mixed-effects model is presented in Table 7.3.

Expected Mean Squares

Let us now provide a basis for determining the appropriate error terms for forming an F ratio in this model. Consider the alternative situations of H_0 actually being true and H_0 actually being false. If H_0 is actually true for all three tests, then the expected mean squares are as follows:

$$E(MS_A) = \sigma_\varepsilon^2$$

$$E(MS_B) = \sigma_\varepsilon^2$$

$$E(MS_{AB}) = \sigma_\varepsilon^2$$

TABLE 7.3
Assumptions and Effects of Violations—Two-Factor Mixed-Effects Model

Assumption	Effect of Assumption Violation
1. Independence of (a) residuals; (b) random effects	Little is known about the effects of dependence; however, based on the fixed-effects case we might expect the following: increased likelihood of a Type I and/or Type II error in the F statistic; influences standard errors of means and thus inferences about those means
2. Homogeneity of variance for (a) residuals; (b) random effects	Little is known about the effects of heteroscedasticity; however, based on the fixed-effects case we might expect the following: bias in SS_{with}; increased likelihood of a Type I and/or Type II error; small effect with equal or nearly equal ns; otherwise effect decreases as n increases
3. Normality of (a) residuals; (b) random effects	Minimal effect with equal or nearly equal ns; otherwise substantial effects

$$E(MS_{\text{with}}) = \sigma_\varepsilon^2$$

Again σ_ε^2 is the population variance of the residual errors.

If H_0 is actually false for all three tests, then the expected mean squares for the equal ns or balanced case are as follows:

$$E(MS_A) = \sigma_\varepsilon^2 + n\sigma_{ab}^2 + Kn\ [(\Sigma_j\alpha_j^2)/(J-1)]$$

$$E(MS_B) = \sigma_\varepsilon^2 + Jn\sigma_b^2$$

$$E(MS_{AB}) = \sigma_\varepsilon^2 + n\sigma_{ab}^2$$

$$E(MS_{\text{with}}) = \sigma_\varepsilon^2$$

Thus, given that the F ratio represents

$$F = \frac{\text{systematic variability} + \text{error variability}}{\text{error variability}}$$

then the appropriate error term for the test of A is the interaction term, and the appropriate error term for the test of B and the interaction is the within term. This is the only way the main and interaction effects can be isolated and formulate a proper F ratio.

Measures of Association

Two different measures of association are necessary for the mixed-effects model, ω^2 for the fixed effect and ρ for the random and interaction effects. The intraclass correlation coefficient ρ is computed for the B effect by

$$\rho_b = \frac{\sigma_b^2}{\sigma_b^2 + \sigma_{ab}^2 + \sigma_\varepsilon^2 + (\Sigma_j\ \alpha_j^2)\ /\ J}$$

and for the AB interaction effect by

$$\rho_{ab} = \frac{\sigma_{ab}^2}{\sigma_b^2 + \sigma_{ab}^2 + \sigma_\varepsilon^2 + (\Sigma_j\ \alpha_j^2)\ /\ J}$$

Strength of association for the fixed effect can be measured by

$$\omega_a^2 = \frac{(\Sigma_j\alpha_j^2)\ /\ J}{\sigma_b^2 + \sigma_{ab}^2 + \sigma_\varepsilon^2 + (\Sigma_j\ \alpha_j^2)\ /\ J}$$

These measures are modifications of the random- and fixed-effects cases due to Kirk (1982). The variance components can be estimated for the B effect as

$$\sigma_b^2 = \frac{MS_B - MS_{with}}{Jn}$$

for the AB interaction effect by

$$\sigma_{ab}^2 = \frac{MS_{AB} - MS_{with}}{n}$$

and for the within-cells effect by

$$\sigma_\varepsilon^2 = MS_{with}$$

The last term in the denominator for the fixed A effect can be estimated by

$$\Sigma_j \, \alpha_j^2 / J = \frac{(J-1)(MS_A - MS_{AB})}{JKn}$$

Using the example from chapter 5, assuming the model is now a mixed-effects model, we estimate the variance component for the B effect as

$$\sigma_b^2 = \frac{MS_B - MS_{with}}{Jn} = \frac{712.5313 - 11.5313}{16} = 43.8125$$

for the AB interaction effect by

$$\sigma_{ab}^2 = \frac{MS_{AB} - MS_{with}}{n} = \frac{7.2813 - 11.5313}{4} = 0$$

substituting 0 for a negative variance, and for the within-cells effect by

$$\sigma_\varepsilon^2 = MS_{with} = 11.5313$$

The last term in the denominator for the fixed effect is estimated by

$$\Sigma_j \, \alpha_j^2 / J = \frac{(J-1)(MS_A - MS_{AB})}{JKn} = \frac{(3)(246.1979 - 7.2813)}{32} = 22.3984$$

Thus, the intraclass correlation coefficient for the B effect is

$$\rho_b = \frac{\sigma_b^2}{\sigma_b^2 + \sigma_{ab}^2 + \sigma_\varepsilon^2 + (\Sigma_j \, \alpha_j^2)/J} = \frac{43.8125}{43.8125 + 0 + 11.5313 + 22.3984} = 0.5636$$

and for the AB interaction effect is

$$\rho_{ab} = \frac{\sigma_{ab}^2}{\sigma_b^2 + \sigma_{ab}^2 + \sigma_\varepsilon^2 + (\Sigma_j \, \alpha_j^2)/J} = \frac{0}{43.8125 + 0 + 11.5313 + 22.3984} = 0$$

Strength of association for the fixed effect can be measured by

$$\omega_a{}^2 = \frac{(\Sigma_j \, \alpha_j^2) \, / \, J}{\sigma_b^2 + \sigma_{\alpha b}^2 + \sigma_\varepsilon^2 + (\Sigma_j \, \alpha_j^2) \, / \, J} = \frac{22.3984}{43.8125 + 0 + 11.5313 + 22.3984} = 0.2881$$

As before, there is no magical rule of thumb for interpreting the size of these coefficients, only that they are scaled theoretically from zero (no association) to one (perfect association).

Multiple-Comparison Procedures

For multiple comparisons of the two-factor mixed-effects model, the researcher is not usually interested in making inferences about just the levels of B or AB that were randomly sampled. Thus, estimation of the b_k or $(\alpha b)_{jk}$ terms does not provide us with any information about the b_k or $(\alpha b)_{jk}$ terms not sampled. Also, the b_k or $(\alpha b)_{jk}$ terms cannot be summarized by their means as they will not necessarily be equal to zero for the levels sampled, only for the population of levels. Rather than looking at comparisons among the means of the b_k or $(\alpha b)_{jk}$ levels, we are interested in looking at the variances and intraclass correlations of the b_k and $(\alpha b)_{jk}$ terms as shown earlier.

However, inferences about the fixed-factor A can be made in the same way they were made for the two-factor fixed-effects model. However, the error term used for the multiple-comparison procedures is the interaction instead of the within-cells term (i.e., we use MS_{AB} instead of MS_{with} and df_{AB} instead of df_{with}). We have already used the example data to look at some multiple comparison procedures in chapter 5 (see the first section for an example).

This concludes our discussion of random- and mixed-effects models for the one- and two-factor designs. For three-factor designs see Keppel (1982). In the major statistical computer packages, the analysis of random effects is as follows: in SAS PROC GLM use the RANDOM statement to designate random effects; in SPSS, random effects can also be designated.

THE ONE-FACTOR REPEATED MEASURES DESIGN

In this section, we describe the distinguishing characteristics of the one-factor repeated measures ANOVA model, the layout of the data, the linear model, assumptions of the model and their violation, the ANOVA summary table, expected mean squares, multiple-comparison procedures, and the Friedman (1937) nonparametric test.

Characteristics of the Model

The characteristics of the one-factor repeated measures ANOVA model are somewhat similar to the one-factor fixed-effects model, yet there are a number of obvious exceptions. The first unique characteristic has to do with the fact that each subject responds to each level of factor A. This is in contrast to the nonrepeated case where each subject is exposed to only one level of factor A. The one-factor repeated measures model is the logical extension to the dependent *t* test. Although in the dependent *t* test there are only two levels of the independent variable, in the one-factor repeated measures model two or more levels of the independent variable are utilized.

This design is often referred to as a *within-subjects design,* as each subject responds to each level of factor A. Thus subjects serve as their own controls such that individual differences are taken into account. This was not the case in any of the previously discussed models. As a result, subjects' scores are not independent across the levels of factor A. Compare this design to the one-factor fixed-effects model where total variation was decomposed into variation due to A and due to the residual. In the one-factor repeated measures design, residual variation is further decomposed into variation due to subjects and variation due to the interaction between A and subjects. The reduction in the residual sum of squares yields a more powerful design and more precision in terms of estimating the effects of A. The repeated measures design is economical in that less subjects are necessary than in previously discussed models.

The one-factor repeated measures design is also a mixed model. The subjects factor is a random effect, whereas the A factor is almost always a fixed effect. If time is the fixed effect, then the researcher can examine phenomena over time. Finally, the one-factor repeated measures design is similar in many ways to the two-factor mixed-effects design except with one subject per cell. We again assume that the number of observations made in each factor level is the same. In other words, the one-factor repeated measures design is really a special case of the two-factor mixed-effects design with $n = 1$ per cell. Unequal ns can only happen when subjects miss the administration of one or more levels of factor A.

On the down side, the repeated measures design includes some risk of carry-over effects from one level of A to another because each subject responds to all levels of A. As examples of the carry-over effect, subjects' performance may be altered due to fatigue (decreased performance), practice (increased performance), and sensitization (increased performance) effects. These effects may be minimized by (a) counterbalancing the order of administration of the levels of A so that each subject does not receive the same order of the levels of A (this can also minimize problems with the heterogeneity of covariance; see later discussion), (b) allowing some time to pass between the administration of the levels of A, or (c) matching or blocking similar subjects with the assumption of subjects within a block being randomly assigned to a level of A. This last method would necessitate a randomized block design, considered in chapter 8.

The Layout of the Data

The layout of the data for the one-factor repeated measures model is shown in Table 7.4. Here we see the columns designated as the levels of factor A and the rows as the subjects. Row, column, and overall means are also shown, although the subject means are seldom of any utility (and thus are not reported). Here you see that the layout of the data looks the same as the two-factor model, only there is just a single observation per cell.

The ANOVA Model

The one-factor repeated measures ANOVA model is written in terms of population parameters as

$$Y_{ij} = \mu + \alpha_j + s_i + (s\alpha)_{ij} + \varepsilon_{ij}$$

where Y_{ij} is the observed score on the criterion variable for individual i responding to level j of factor A, μ is the overall or grand population mean, α_j is the fixed effect for level j of factor A, s_i is the random effect for subject i of the subject factor, $(s\alpha)_{ij}$ is the interaction between subject i and level j, and ε_{ij} is the random residual error for individual i in level j. The residual error can be due to measurement error and/or other factors not under investigation. From the model you can see this is similar to the two-factor model with one observation per cell. Also, the fixed effect is denoted by α and the random effect by s; thus we have a mixed-effects model.

There are two side conditions for the model about the main and interaction effects. For the equal ns model under consideration here, the side conditions are that $\Sigma_j \alpha_j = 0$, and $\Sigma_j (s\alpha)_{ij} = 0$ for each subject i. These side conditions are much the same as in the two-factor mixed-effects model described earlier.

The hypotheses for testing the effect of factor A are

$$H_{01}: \mu_{.1} = \mu_{.2} = \mu_{.3} = \dots = \mu_{.J}$$

$$H_{11}: \text{not all the } \mu_{.j} \text{ are equal}$$

The hypotheses are written in terms of means because factor A is a fixed effect.

Assumptions and Violation of Assumptions

In the preceding section we described the assumptions for the two-factor mixed-effects model. The assumptions are nearly the same for the one-factor repeated measures model and are again mainly concerned with the distribution of the residual errors.

TABLE 7.4
Layout for the One-Factor Repeated Measures ANOVA

Level of Factor S	Level of Factor A (Repeated Factor)				Row Mean
	1	2	...	J	
1	Y_{11}	Y_{12}	...	Y_{1J}	$\bar{Y}_{1.}$
2	Y_{21}	Y_{22}	...	Y_{2J}	$\bar{Y}_{2.}$
...	...	...	...	...	...
n	Y_{n1}	Y_{n2}	...	Y_{nJ}	$\bar{Y}_{n.}$
Column mean	$\bar{Y}_{.1}$	$\bar{Y}_{.2}$	...	$\bar{Y}_{.J}$	$\bar{Y}_{..}$

A general statement of the assumptions about the residuals are written as $\varepsilon_{ij} \sim NI(0, \sigma_{\varepsilon}^2)$. The effect of violation of these assumptions is thought to be about the same as in the two-factor mixed-effects design. In addition, there is a set of assumptions about the sampled levels of the random independent variable, the s_i. The assumptions about these effects are the same as with the ε_{ij}, where the s_i are randomly and independently sampled from the normally distributed population of subjects, with a population mean of zero and a population variance of σ_s^2, respectively. Thus the assumptions for the random effect can be written as $s_i \sim NI(0, \sigma_s^2)$. In addition it is assumed that the s_i and ε_{ij} terms are independent. In general, statements about the violation of these assumptions are the same as with the residuals.

A final assumption is known as *compound symmetry* (or homogeneity of covariance) and states that the covariances between the scores of the subjects across the levels of the repeated factor A are constant. In other words, the covariances for all pairs of levels of the fixed factor are constant across the population of random effects (i.e., the subjects). The analysis of variance is not particularly robust to a violation of this assumption. In particular, the assumption is often violated when factor A is time, as the relationship between adjacent levels of A is strongest. If the assumption is violated, three alternative procedures are available. The first is to limit the levels of factor A either to those that meet the assumption, or to two (in which case there would be only one covariance). The second, and more plausible, alternative is to use adjusted F tests. These are reported in the next subsection. The third is to use multivariate analysis of variance, which has no compound symmetry assumption but is slightly less powerful.

Huynh and Feldt (1970) showed that the compound symmetry assumption is a sufficient but not necessary condition for the validity of the F test. Thus the F test may also be valid under less stringent conditions. The necessary and sufficient condition for the validity of the F test is known as *circularity* (or *sphericity*). This assumes that the variance of the difference scores for each pair of factor levels is the same. Further discussion of circularity is beyond the scope of this text (see Keppel, 1982, or Kirk, 1982). A summary of the assumptions and the effects of their violation for the one-factor repeated measures design is presented in Table 7.5.

ANOVA Summary Table

The sources of variation for this model are similar to those for the two-factor model, except that there is no within-cell variation. The ANOVA summary table is shown in Table 7.6, where we see the following sources of variation: A, subjects (denoted by S), the SA interaction, and total. The test of subject differences is of no real interest. Quite naturally, we expect there to be differences between the subjects. Given our expected mean squares (in the next section), the subjects effect cannot be tested anyway. From the table we see that although three mean square terms can be computed, only one F ratio results for the test of factor A.

Next we need to consider the computation of the sums of squares for the one-factor repeated measures model. If we take the total sum of squares and decompose it, we have

$$SS_{tot} = SS_A + SS_S + SS_{SA}$$

TABLE 7.5
Assumptions and Effects of Violations—One-Factor Repeated Measures Design

Assumption	Effect of Assumption Violation
1. Independence of (a) residuals; (b) subject effects	Little is known about the effects of dependence; however, based on the fixed-effects case we might expect the following: increased likelihood of a Type I and/or Type II error in the F statistic; influences standard errors of means and thus inferences about those means
2. Homogeneity of variance for (a) residuals; (b) subject effects	Little is known about the effects of heteroscedasticity; however, based on the fixed-effects case we might expect the following: bias in SS_{SA}; increased likelihood of a Type I and/or Type II error; small effect with equal or nearly equal ns; otherwise effect decreases as n increases
3. Normality of (a) residuals; (b) subject effects	Minimal effect with equal or nearly equal ns; otherwise substantial effects
4. Compound symmetry	F test not particularly robust; conduct the usual F test, and continue with the Geisser–Greenhouse conservative F test, and then the adjusted (Box) F test, if necessary

These three terms can be computed by

$$SS_A = \sum_{j=1}^{J} \left[\frac{\left(\sum_{i=1}^{n} Y_{ij} \right)^2}{n} \right] - \frac{\left(\sum_{i=1}^{n} \sum_{j=1}^{J} Y_{ij} \right)^2}{N}$$

$$SS_S = \sum_{i=1}^{n} \left[\frac{\left(\sum_{j=1}^{J} Y_{ij} \right)^2}{J} \right] - \frac{\left(\sum_{i=1}^{n} \sum_{j=1}^{J} Y_{ij} \right)^2}{N}$$

$$SS_{SA} = \sum_{i=1}^{n} \sum_{j=1}^{J} Y_{ij}^2 - \sum_{i=1}^{n} \left[\frac{\left(\sum_{j=1}^{J} Y_{ij} \right)^2}{J} \right] - \sum_{j=1}^{J} \left[\frac{\left(\sum_{i=1}^{n} Y_{ij} \right)^2}{n} \right] + \frac{\left(\sum_{i=1}^{n} \sum_{j=1}^{J} Y_{ij} \right)^2}{N}$$

The degrees of freedom, mean squares, and F ratio are computed as shown in Table 7.6.

Earlier in the discussion on the one-factor repeated measures model, I mentioned that the F test is not very robust to violation of the compound symmetry assumption. This assumption is often violated; consequently, statisticians have spent considerable time studying this problem. Research currently suggests that the following sequential procedure be used in the test of factor A. First, do the usual F test that is quite liberal in terms of rejecting H_0 too often. If H_0 is not rejected, then stop. If H_0 is rejected, then continue with step 2, which is to use the Geisser–Greenhouse (1958) conservative F test. For the model being considered here, the degrees of freedom for the F critical value are adjusted to be 1 and $n - 1$. If H_0 is rejected then stop. This would indicate that both the liberal and conservative tests reached the same conclusion to reject H_0. If H_0 is not rejected, then the two

TABLE 7.6
One-Factor Repeated Measures ANOVA Summary Table

Source	SS	df	MS	F
A	SS_A	$J-1$	MS_A	MS_A/MS_{SA}
S	SS_S	$n-1$	MS_S	
SA	SS_{SA}	$(J-1)(n-1)$	MS_{SA}	
Total	SS_{total}	$N-1$		

tests did not reach the same conclusion, and a further test (a tie-breaker, so to speak) should be undertaken. Thus in step 3 an adjusted F test is conducted. The adjustment is known as Box's (1954) correction (sometimes referred to as the Huynh & Feldt [1970] procedure). Here the numerator degrees of freedom are $(J-1)\varepsilon$, and the denominator degrees of freedom are $(J-1)(n-1)\varepsilon$, where ε is the correction factor (not to be confused with the residual term ε). The correction factor is quite complex and is not shown here (see Myers, 1979, or Wilcox, 1987). Most major statistical computer packages conduct the Geisser–Greenhouse and Box (Huynh & Feldt) tests.

Expected Mean Squares

Consider the alternative situations of H_0 actually being true and H_0 actually being false. If H_0 is actually true, then the expected mean squares are as follows:

$$E(MS_A) = \sigma_\varepsilon^2$$

$$E(MS_S) = \sigma_\varepsilon^2$$

$$E(MS_{SA}) = \sigma_\varepsilon^2$$

Again σ_ε^2 is the population variance of the residual errors.

If H_0 is actually false, then the expected mean squares are as follows.

$$E(MS_A) = \sigma_\varepsilon^2 + \sigma_{s\alpha}^2 + n[\Sigma_j \alpha_j^2/(J-1)]$$

$$E(MS_S) = \sigma_\varepsilon^2 + J\sigma_s^2$$

$$E(MS_{SA}) = \sigma_\varepsilon^2 + \sigma_{s\alpha}^2$$

Thus we see that the error term for the proper test of factor A is the SA interaction. However, there is no error term for a proper test of the subjects factor or for a proper test of the interaction.

Multiple-Comparison Procedures

If the null hypothesis for the A factor is rejected and there are more than two levels of the factor, then the researcher may be interested in which means or combinations of means are different. This could be assessed, as we have seen in previous chapters, by the use of some multiple-comparison procedure (MCP). In general, most of the MCPs outlined in chapter 4 can be used in the one-factor repeated measures model. However, rather than using MS_{with} as the error term, MS_{SA} would be used.

It has been shown that these MCPs are seriously affected by a violation of the homogeneity of covariance assumption. In this situation two alternatives are recommended. The first alternative is, rather than using the same error term for each contrast (i.e., MS_{SA}), to use a separate error term for each contrast tested. Then many of the MCPs previously covered in chapter 4 can be used. This complicates matters considerably (see Keppel, 1982, or Kirk, 1982). A second alternative, recommended by Maxwell (1980) and Wilcox (1987), involves the use of multiple dependent t-tests where the α level is adjusted much like the Bonferroni procedure. Maxwell concluded that this procedure is better than many of the other MCPs. For other similar procedures, see Hochberg and Tamhane (1987).

The Friedman Test

There is a nonparametric equivalent to the one-factor repeated measures ANOVA model. The test was developed by Friedman (1937) and, like the Kruskal–Wallis test, is based on ranks. However, the Kruskal–Wallis test cannot be used in a repeated measures model as it assumes that the individual scores are independent. This is obviously not the case in the one-factor repeated measures model where each individual is exposed to all levels of factor A.

Let me outline how the Friedman test is conducted. First, scores are ranked within subject. For instance, if there are $J = 4$ levels of factor A, then each subjects' scores would be ranked from 1 to 4. From this, one can compute a mean ranking for each level of factor A. The null hypothesis essentially becomes one of testing whether the mean rankings for each of the levels of A are equal. The test statistic is computed as

$$\chi^2 = \left[\frac{12}{nJ(J+1)} \sum_{j=1}^{J} \left(\sum_{i=1}^{n} R_{ij} \right)^2 \right] - [3n(J+1)]$$

where R_{ij} is the ranking for subject i on level j of factor A. In the case of tied ranks, either the available ranks can be averaged, or a correction factor can be used as we did with the Kruskal– Wallis test (see chap. 3). The test statistic is compared to the critical value of $_{1-\alpha}\chi^2_{J-1}$ (see Appendix Table 3). The null hypothesis that the mean rankings are the same for the levels of factor A is rejected if the test statistic exceeds the critical value.

You may also recall from the Kruskal–Wallis test the problem with small ns in terms of the test statistic not being precisely a χ^2. The same problem exists with the Friedman test when $J < 6$ and $n < 6$, so I suggest you consult the table of critical values in Marascuilo and McSweeney (1977, Table A-22, p. 521). The Friedman test, like the Kruskal–Wallis test, assumes that the population distributions have the same shape (although not necessarily normal) and variability, and that the dependent measure is continuous. For a discussion of alternative nonparametric procedures, see Wilcox (1987).

Various multiple-comparison procedures (MCPs) can be used for the nonparametric one-factor repeated measures model. For the most part these MCPs are analogs to their parametric equivalents. In the case of planned (or a priori) pairwise comparisons, one may use multiple matched-pair Wilcoxon tests (i.e., a form of the Kruskal–Wallis test for two groups) in a Bonferroni form (i.e., taking the number of contrasts into account through an adjustment of the α level). Due to the nature of planned comparisons, these are more powerful than the Friedman test. For post hoc comparisons, two examples are the Tukey analog for pairwise contrasts, and the Scheffé analog for complex contrasts. For these methods, we first define a contrast as some combination of the group mean rankings. A contrast is equal to

$$\psi = \sum_{j=1}^{J} c_j (\overline{R}_j)$$

where $\overline{R}_j$ is the mean of R_j. The standard error of the constrast is defined as

$$se_{\psi} = \sqrt{\left[\frac{J(J+1)}{12} \right] \left(\sum_{j=1}^{J} \frac{c_j^{\,2}}{n_j} \right)}$$

A test statistic is formed as

$$q = \frac{\psi}{se_{\psi}}$$

For the Tukey analog, the test statistic is compared to the critical value of

$$T = \frac{\alpha q_{J,\infty}}{\sqrt{2}}$$

where the degrees of freedom are equal to J (the number of means) and ∞ (infinity), found in Appendix Table 9. For the Scheffé analog, the test statistic is compared to the critical value

$$S = \sqrt{1-\alpha \chi_{J-1}^{2}}$$

In both cases the test statistic must exceed the critical value in order to reject the null hypothesis. For additional discussion on MCPs for this model, see Marascuilo and McSweeney (1977).

An Example

Let us consider an example to illustrate the procedures used in this section. The data are shown in Table 7.7 where there are eight subjects, each of whom has been evaluated by four raters on a task of writing assessment. Table 7.7 also contains various sums for the raw scores, the ranked scores, and various sums for the ranked scores. First, let us take a look at the computations for the parametric ANOVA model. The sums of squares are computed as follows:

$$SS_A = \sum_{j=1}^{J} \left[\frac{\left(\sum_{i=1}^{n} Y_{ij} \right)^2}{n} \right] - \frac{\left(\sum_{i=1}^{n} \sum_{j=1}^{J} Y_{ij} \right)^2}{N} = 1{,}144.2500 - \left[\frac{(174)^2}{32} \right] = 198.1250$$

$$SS_S = \sum_{i=1}^{n} \left[\frac{\left(\sum_{i=1}^{J} Y_{ij} \right)^2}{J} \right] - \frac{\left(\sum_{i=1}^{n} \sum_{j=1}^{J} Y_{ij} \right)^2}{N} = 961.0000 - \left[\frac{(174)^2}{32} \right] = 14.8750$$

$$SS_{SA} = \sum_{i=1}^{n} \sum_{j=1}^{J} Y_{ij}^2 - \sum_{i=1}^{n} \left[\frac{\left(\sum_{i=1}^{J} Y_{ij} \right)^2}{J} \right] - \sum_{j=1}^{J} \left[\frac{\left(\sum_{i=1}^{n} Y_{ij} \right)^2}{n} \right] + \frac{\left(\sum_{i=1}^{n} \sum_{j=1}^{J} Y_{ij} \right)^2}{N}$$

$$= 1{,}178.0000 - 961.0000 - 1{,}144.2500 + \left[\frac{(174)^2}{32} \right] = 18.8750$$

TABLE 7.7

Data for the Writing Assessment Example—One-Factor Design: Raw Scores and Rank Scores on the Writing Assessment Task by Subject and Rater

Subject	Rater 1		Rater 2		Rater 3		Rater 4		Row Raw Sums
	Raw	Rank	Raw	Rank	Raw	Rank	Raw	Rank	
1	3	1	4	2	7	3	8	4	22
2	6	2	5	1	8	3	9	4	28
3	3	1	4	2	7	3	9	4	23
4	3	1	4	2	6	3	8	4	21
5	1	1	2	2	5	3	10	4	18
6	2	1	3	2	6	3	10	4	21
7	2	1	4	2	5	3	9	4	20
8	2	1	3	2	6	3	10	4	21
Column sums	22	9	29	15	50	24	73	32	174
									(Overall raw sum)

The mean squares are computed as follows:

$$MS_A = \frac{SS_A}{df_A} = \frac{198.1250}{3} = 66.0417$$

$$MS_S = \frac{SS_S}{df_S} = \frac{14.8750}{7} = 2.1250$$

$$MS_{SA} = \frac{SS_{SA}}{df_{SA}} = \frac{18.8750}{21} = 0.8988$$

Finally, the test statistic is computed to be

$$F = \frac{MS_A}{MS_{SA}} = \frac{66.0417}{0.8988} = 73.4776$$

The test statistic is compared to the usual F-test critical value of $_{.95}F_{3,21} = 3.07$, which is significant. For the Geisser–Greenhouse conservative procedure, the test statistic is compared to the critical value of $_{.95}F_{1,7} = 5.59$, which is also significant. The two procedures both yield a statistically significant result; thus we need not be concerned with a violation of the compound symmetry assumption.

As an example of a MCP, the Tukey procedure can be used to test for the equivalence of raters 1 and 4, where the contrast is written as $\overline{Y}_{.4} - \overline{Y}_{.1}$. The standard error is

$$s_{\psi'} = \sqrt{\frac{MS_{SA}}{n}} = \sqrt{\frac{0.8988}{8}} = 0.3352$$

the studentized range statistic (as the mean for rater 4 is 9.1250 and for rater 1 is 2.7500) is

$$q = \frac{\overline{Y}_{.4} - \overline{Y}_{.1}}{s_{\psi'}} = \frac{9.1250 - 2.7500}{0.3352} = 19.0185$$

and the critical value is $_{.95}q_{21,4} \approx 3.94$. The test statistic exceeds the critical value, so we conclude that the means for groups 1 and 4 are significantly different at the .05 level.

Finally, let us take a look at the computations for the Friedman test. The test statistic is computed as

$$\chi^2 = \left[\frac{12}{nJ(J+1)} \sum_{j=1}^{J} \left(\sum_{i=1}^{n} R_{ij} \right)^2 \right] - [3n(J+1)] = \left[\frac{12}{(32)(5)} 1906 \right] - (24)(5) = 22.9500$$

This test statistic is compared to the critical value $_{.95}\chi^2_3 = 7.8147$, which is significant. As an example of a MCP, the Tukey analog will be used to test for the equivalence of raters 1 and 4; that is, the contrast will be written in the same form as before. As the rank means for these raters are 1.1250 and 4.0000, respectively, then the contrast is equal to

$$\psi = \sum_{j=1}^{J} c_j (\overline{R}_j) = 4.0000 - 1.1250 = 2.8750$$

The standard error of the constrast is equal to

$$se_\psi = \sqrt{\left[\frac{J(J+1)}{12}\right]\left[\sum_{j=1}^{J} \frac{c_j^2}{n_j}\right]} = \sqrt{\left(\frac{20}{12}\right)\left(\frac{1}{8} + \frac{1}{8}\right)} = 0.6455$$

A test statistic is formed as

$$q = \frac{\psi}{se_\psi} = \frac{2.8750}{0.6455} = 4.4539$$

For the Tukey analog, the test statistic is compared to the critical value of

$$T = \frac{\alpha q_{J,\infty}}{\sqrt{2}} = \frac{.05 q_{4,\infty}}{\sqrt{2}} = \frac{3.633}{\sqrt{2}} = 2.5689$$

The test statistic exceeds the critical value; consequently we conclude that the means for groups 1 and 4 are significantly different at the .05 level. Thus the conclusions for the parametric ANOVA and the nonparametric Friedman test are the same for this data set. This will not always be the case, particularly when one or more ANOVA assumptions are violated.

THE TWO-FACTOR SPLIT-PLOT OR MIXED DESIGN

In this section, we describe the distinguishing characteristics of the two-factor split-plot or mixed ANOVA design, the layout of the data, the linear model, assumptions and their violation, the ANOVA summary table, expected mean squares, and multiple-comparison procedures.

Characteristics of the Model

The characteristics of the two-factor split-plot or mixed ANOVA design are a combination of the characteristics of the one-factor repeated measures and the two-factor fixed-effects models. It is unique because there are two factors, only one of which is repeated. For this reason the design is often called a *mixed design*. Thus, one of the factors is a between-subjects factor, the other is a within subjects factor, and the result is known as a *split-plot design* (from agricultural research). Each subject then responds to each level of the repeated factor, but to only one level of the nonrepeated factor. Subjects then serve as their own controls for the repeated factor, but not for the nonrepeated factor. The other characteristics carry over from the one-factor repeated measures model and the two-factor model.

The Layout of the Data

The layout of the data for the two-factor split-plot or mixed design is shown in Table 7.8. Here we see the rows designated as the levels of factor A, the between-subjects or nonrepeated factor, and the columns as the levels of factor B, the within-subjects or repeated factor. Within each factor level combination or cell are the subjects. Notice that the same subjects appear at all levels of factor B, but only at one level of factor A. Row, column, cell, and overall means are also shown. Here you see that the layout of the data looks the same as for the two-factor model.

The ANOVA Model

The two factor split-plot model can be written in terms of population parameters as

$$Y_{ijk} = \mu + \alpha_j + s_{i(j)} + \beta_k + (\alpha\beta)_{jk} + (\beta s)_{ki(j)} + \varepsilon_{ijk}$$

where Y_{ijk} is the observed score on the criterion variable for individual i in level j of factor A and level k of factor B (or in the jk cell), μ is the overall or grand population mean (i.e., regardless of cell designation), α_j is the effect for level j of factor A (row effect for the nonrepeated factor), $s_{i(j)}$ is the effect of subject i that is nested within level j of factor A (i.e., $i(j)$ denotes that i is nested within j), β_k is the effect for level k of factor B (column effect for the repeated factor), $(\alpha\beta)_{jk}$ is the interaction effect for the combination of level j of factor A and level k of factor B, $(\beta s)_{ki(j)}$ is the interaction effect for the combination of level k of factor B and subject i that is nested within level j of factor A, and ε_{ijk} is the random residual error for individual i in cell jk.

We use the terminology "subjects are nested within factor A" to indicate that a particular subject s_i is only exposed to one level of factor A, level j. This observation is then denoted in the subjects effect by $s_{i(j)}$ and in the interaction effect by $(\beta s)_{ki(j)}$. This is due to the fact that not all possible combinations of subject with the levels of factor A are included in the model. A more extended discussion of designs with nested factors is given in chapter 8. The residual error can be due to individual differences, measurement error, and/or other factors not under investigation. We assume for now that A and B are fixed-effects factors and that S is a random-effects factor.

There are special conditions of the model, known as *side conditions*, that should be pointed out. For the equal *ns* model, the side conditions are as follows:

$$\sum_{j=1}^{J} \alpha_j = 0$$

$$\sum_{k=1}^{K} \beta_k = 0$$

$$\sum_{j=1}^{J} (\alpha\beta)_{jk} = 0$$

$$\sum_{k=1}^{K} (\alpha\beta)_{jk} = 0$$

Thus the sum of the row effects is equal to zero, the sum of the column effects is equal to zero, and the sum of the interaction effects is equal to zero, both across rows and across

TABLE 7.8

Layout for the Two-Factor Split-Plot or Mixed Design

Level of Factor A (Nonrepeated Factor)	Level of Factor B (Repeated Factor)				Row Mean
	1	2	...	K	
1	Y_{111}	Y_{112}	...	Y_{11K}	$\overline{Y}_{.1.}$
	.	.	.	.	
	.	.	.	.	
	.	.	.	.	
	Y_{n11}	Y_{n12}		Y_{n1K}	
	$\overline{Y}_{.11}$	$\overline{Y}_{.12}$	...	$\overline{Y}_{.1K}$	
2	Y_{121}	Y_{122}	...	Y_{12K}	$\overline{Y}_{.2.}$
	.	.	.	.	
	.	.	.	.	
	Y_{n21}	Y_{n22}	...	Y_{n2K}	
	$\overline{Y}_{.21}$	$\overline{Y}_{.22}$	...	$\overline{Y}_{.2K}$	
	.	.	.	.	
	.	.	.	.	
	.	.	.	.	
J	Y_{1J1}	Y_{1J2}	...	Y_{1JK}	$\overline{Y}_{.J.}$
	.	.	.	.	
	.	.	.	.	
	.	.	.	.	
	Y_{nJ1}	Y_{nJ2}	...	Y_{nJK}	
	$\overline{Y}_{.J1}$	$\overline{Y}_{.J2}$	...	$\overline{Y}_{.JK}$	
Column mean	$\overline{Y}_{..1}$	$\overline{Y}_{..2}$	...	$\overline{Y}_{..K}$	$\overline{Y}_{...}$

Note. Each subject is measured at all levels of factor B, but at only one level of factor A.

columns. This implies, for example, that if there are any nonzero row effects, then the row effects will balance out around zero with some positive and some negative effects.

The hypotheses to be tested here are exactly the same as in the nonrepeated two-factor ANOVA model. The hypotheses for testing A, B, and AB, respectively, are as follows:

$$H_{01}: \mu_{.1.} = \mu_{.2.} = \mu_{.3.} = \dots = \mu_{.J.}$$

$$H_{11}: \text{ not all the } \mu_{.j.} \text{ are equal}$$

$$H_{02}: \mu_{..1} = \mu_{..2} = \mu_{..3} = \dots = \mu_{..K}$$

$$H_{12}: \text{ not all the } \mu_{..k} \text{ are equal}$$

$$H_{03}: (\mu_{.jk} - \mu_{.j.} - \mu_{..k} + \mu) = 0 \text{ for all } j \text{ and } k$$

$$H_{13}: \text{ not all the } (\mu_{.jk} - \mu_{.j.} - \mu_{..k} + \mu) = 0$$

If one of the null hypotheses is rejected, then the researcher may want to consider a multiple-comparison procedure so as to determine which means or combination of means are significantly different. We leave the discussion of multiple comparison procedures for a later subsection.

Assumptions and Violation of Assumptions

Previously we described the assumptions for the two-factor models and the one-factor repeated measures model. The assumptions for the two-factor split-plot or mixed design are actually a combination of these two sets of assumptions.

The assumptions can be divided into two sets of assumptions, one about the between-subjects factor, and one about the within-subjects factor. For the between-subjects factor, a general statement of the assumptions about the residuals is written as $\varepsilon_{ijk} \sim NI(0, \sigma_\varepsilon^2)$. Violation of these assumptions is the same as in the nonrepeated models. For the within-subjects factor, the assumption is the already familiar homogeneity of covariance (or compound symmetry) assumption. For this design, the assumption involves the population covariances for all pairs of the levels of the within-subjects factor (i.e., k and k') being equal, at each level of the between subjects factor (for all levels j). To deal with this assumption, we look at alternative F tests in the next section. A summary of the assumptions and the effects of their violation for the two-factor split-plot or mixed design are presented in Table 7.9.

ANOVA Summary Table

The ANOVA summary table is shown in Table 7.10, where we see the following sources of variation: A, S, B, AB, BS, and total. The table is divided into within subjects sources and between subjects sources. The between-subjects sources are A and S, where S will be used as the error term for the test of factor A. The within-subjects

TABLE 7.9
Assumptions and Effects of Violations—Two-Factor Split-Plot or Mixed Design

Assumption	Effect of Assumption Violation
1. Independence of residuals	Increased likelihood of a Type I and/or Type II error in the F statistic; influences standard errors of means and thus inferences about those means
2. Homogeneity of variance	Bias in SS_{error}; increased likelihood of a Type I and/or Type II error; small effect with equal or nearly equal ns; otherwise effect decreases as n increases
3. Normality of residuals	Minimal effect with equal or nearly equal ns
4. Compound symmetry	F test not particularly robust; conduct the usual F test, and continue with the Geisser–Greenhouse conservative F test, and then the adjusted (Box) F test, if necessary

TABLE 7.10
Two-Factor Split-Plot or Mixed Design ANOVA Summary Table

Source	SS	df	MS	F
Between subjects				
A	SS_A	$J-1$	MS_A	MS_A/MS_S
S	SS_S	$J(n-1)$	MS_S	
Within subjects				
B	SS_B	$K-1$	MS_B	MS_B/MS_{BS}
AB	SS_{AB}	$(J-1)(K-1)$	MS_{AB}	MS_{AB}/MS_{BS}
BS	SS_{BS}	$(K-1)J(n-1)$	MS_{BS}	
Total	SS_{total}	$N-1$		

sources are B, AB, and BS, where BS will be used as the error term for the test of factor B and of the AB interaction.

Next we need to consider the computation of the sums of squares for the two-factor mixed design. Taking the total sum of squares and decomposing it yields

$$SS_{tot} = SS_A + SS_S + SS_B + SS_{AB} + SS_{BS}$$

These five terms can be computed as follows.

$$SS_A = \sum_{j=1}^{J} \frac{\left(\sum_{i=1}^{n} \sum_{k=1}^{K} Y_{ijk} \right)^2}{nK} - \frac{\left(\sum_{i=1}^{n} \sum_{j=1}^{J} \sum_{k=1}^{K} Y_{ijk} \right)^2}{N}$$

$$SS_\text{B} = \sum_{k=1}^{K} \frac{\left(\sum_{i=1}^{n}\sum_{j=1}^{J} Y_{ijk}\right)^2}{nJ} - \frac{\left(\sum_{i=1}^{n}\sum_{j=1}^{J}\sum_{k=1}^{K} Y_{ijk}\right)^2}{N}$$

$$SS_\text{AB} = \sum_{j=1}^{J}\sum_{k=1}^{K} \frac{\left(\sum_{i=1}^{n} Y_{ijk}\right)^2}{n} - \sum_{j=1}^{J} \frac{\left(\sum_{i=1}^{n}\sum_{k=1}^{K} Y_{ijk}\right)^2}{nK} - \sum_{k=1}^{K} \frac{\left(\sum_{i=1}^{n}\sum_{j=1}^{J} Y_{ijk}\right)^2}{nJ} + \frac{\left(\sum_{i=1}^{n}\sum_{j=1}^{J}\sum_{k=1}^{K} Y_{ijk}\right)^2}{N}$$

$$SS_\text{S} = \sum_{j=1}^{J}\sum_{i=1}^{n} \frac{\left(\sum_{k=1}^{K} Y_{ijk}\right)^2}{K} - \sum_{j=1}^{J} \frac{\left(\sum_{i=1}^{n}\sum_{k=1}^{K} Y_{ijk}\right)^2}{nK}$$

$$SS_\text{BS} = \sum_{i=1}^{n}\sum_{j=1}^{J}\sum_{k=1}^{K} Y_{ijk}^2 - \sum_{j=1}^{J}\sum_{k=1}^{K} \frac{\left(\sum_{i=1}^{n} Y_{ijk}\right)^2}{n} - \sum_{j=1}^{J}\sum_{i=1}^{n} \frac{\left(\sum_{k=1}^{K} Y_{ijk}\right)^2}{K} + \sum_{j=1}^{J} \frac{\left(\sum_{i=1}^{n}\sum_{k=1}^{K} Y_{ijk}\right)^2}{nK}$$

The degrees of freedom, mean squares, and F ratios are computed as shown in Table 7.10.

As the compound symmetry assumption is often violated, we again suggest the following sequential procedure to test for B and for AB. First, do the usual F test, which is quite liberal in terms of rejecting H_0 too often. If H_0 is not rejected then stop. If H_0 is rejected, then continue with step 2, which is to use the Geisser–Greenhouse (1958) conservative F test. For the model under consideration here, the degrees of freedom for the F critical values are adjusted to be 1 and $J(n-1)$ for the test of B, and $J-1$ and $J(n-1)$ for the test of the AB interaction. There is no conservative test necessary for factor A, the nonrepeated factor. If H_0 is rejected, then stop. This would indicate that both the liberal and conservative tests reached the same conclusion to reject H_0. If H_0 is not rejected, then the two tests did not yield the same conclusion, and an adjusted F test is conducted. The adjustment is known as Box's (1954) correction (or the Huynh & Feldt [1970] procedure, see Kirk, 1982, Myers, 1979, or Wilcox, 1987). Most major statistical computer packages conduct the Geisser–Greenhouse and Box (Huynh & Feldt) tests.

Expected Mean Squares

Consider the alternative situations of H_0 actually being true and H_0 actually being false. If H_0 is actually true, then the expected mean squares are as follows:

$$E(MS_\text{A}) = \sigma_\varepsilon^2$$

$$E(MS_\text{S}) = \sigma_\varepsilon^2$$

$$E(MS_B) = \sigma_\varepsilon^2$$

$$E(MS_{AB}) = \sigma_\varepsilon^2$$

$$E(MS_{BS}) = \sigma_\varepsilon^2$$

Again, σ_ε^2 is the population variance of the residual errors.

If H_0 is actually false, then the expected mean squares are as follows:

$$E(MS_A) = \sigma_\varepsilon^2 + K\sigma_s^2 + nK[\Sigma_j \alpha_j^2/(J-1)]$$

$$E(MS_S) = \sigma_\varepsilon^2 + K\sigma_s^2$$

$$E(MS_B) = \sigma_\varepsilon^2 + \sigma_{\beta s}^2 + nJ[\Sigma_k \beta_k^2/(K-1)]$$

$$E(MS_{AB}) = \sigma_\varepsilon^2 + \sigma_{\beta s}^2 + n[\Sigma_{jk}(\alpha\beta)_{jk}^2/(J-1)(K-1)]$$

$$E(MS_{BS}) = \sigma_\varepsilon^2 + \sigma_{\beta s}^2$$

Thus we see that the error term for the proper test of factor A is the S term, whereas the error term for the proper tests of factor B and the AB interaction is the BS interaction. For models where A and B are not both fixed-effects factors, see Keppel (1982).

Multiple-Comparison Procedures

Consider the situation where the null hypothesis for any of the three hypotheses is rejected (i.e., for A, B, and/or AB). If there are sufficient degrees of freedom, then the researcher may be interested in which means or combinations of means are different. This could be assessed again by the use of some multiple-comparison procedure (MCP). Thus the procedures outlined in chapter 5 (i.e., main effects, simple and complex interaction contrasts) for the regular two-factor ANOVA model can be used here. However, make sure you use the appropriate error term in the computation of the MCPs (i.e., either MS_s or MS_{BS}). Do not forget that in the presence of a significant interaction, generalizations about the main effects must be qualified.

However, it has been shown that the MCPs involving the repeated factor are seriously affected by a violation of the homogeneity of covariance assumption. In this situation, two alternatives are recommended. The first alternative is, rather than using the same error term for each contrast involving the repeated factor (i.e., MS_B or MS_{AB}), to use a separate error term for each contrast tested. Then many of the MCPs previously covered in chapter 4 can be used. This complicates matters considerably (see Keppel, 1982, or Kirk, 1982). The second and simpler alternative is suggested by Shavelson (1988). He recommended that the appropriate error terms be used in MCPs involving the main effects, but for interaction contrasts both error terms be pooled together (this procedure is conservative, yet simpler than the first alternative). In the pooling procedure, the new pooled error term is

$$MS_{pooled} = \frac{SS_S + SS_{BS}}{J(n-1) + J(n-1)(K-1)}$$

with error degrees of freedom

$$df_{pooled} = df_S + df_{BS} = J(n-1) + J(n-1)(K-1)$$

An Example

Consider now an example problem to illustrate the two-factor mixed design. Here we expand on the example presented earlier in this chapter by adding a second factor to the model. The data are shown in Table 7.11 where there are eight subjects, each of whom has been evaluated by four raters on a task of writing assessment. The possible ratings range from 1 (lowest rating) to 10 (highest rating). Factor A represents the instructors of English composition, where the first four subjects are assigned to level 1 of factor A (i.e., instructor 1) and the last four to level 2 of factor A (i.e., instructor 2). Thus factor B (i.e., rater) is repeated and factor A (i.e., instructor) is not repeated. The ANOVA sums of squares are computed as follows:

$$SS_A = \sum_{j=1}^{J} \frac{\left(\sum_{i=1}^{n}\sum_{k=1}^{K} Y_{ijk}\right)^2}{nK} - \frac{\left(\sum_{i=1}^{n}\sum_{j=1}^{J}\sum_{k=1}^{K} Y_{ijk}\right)^2}{N} = 952.2500 - \frac{(174)^2}{32} = 6.1250$$

$$SS_B = \sum_{k=1}^{K} \frac{\left(\sum_{i=1}^{n}\sum_{j=1}^{J} Y_{ijk}\right)^2}{nJ} - \frac{\left(\sum_{i=1}^{n}\sum_{j=1}^{J}\sum_{k=1}^{K} Y_{ijk}\right)^2}{N} = 1{,}144.2500 - \frac{(174)^2}{32} = 198.1250$$

$$SS_{AB} = \sum_{j=1}^{J}\sum_{k=1}^{K} \frac{\left(\sum_{i=1}^{n} Y_{ijk}\right)^2}{n} - \sum_{j=1}^{J} \frac{\left(\sum_{i=1}^{n}\sum_{k=1}^{K} Y_{ijk}\right)^2}{nK} - \sum_{k=1}^{K} \frac{\left(\sum_{i=1}^{n}\sum_{j=1}^{J} Y_{ijk}\right)^2}{nJ} + \frac{\left(\sum_{i=1}^{n}\sum_{j=1}^{J}\sum_{k=1}^{K} Y_{ijk}\right)^2}{N}$$

$$= 1163.0000 - 952.2500 - 1{,}144.2500 + \frac{(174)^2}{32} = 12.6250$$

$$SS_S = \sum_{j=1}^{J}\sum_{i=1}^{n} \frac{\left(\sum_{k=1}^{K} Y_{ijk}\right)^2}{K} - \sum_{j=1}^{J} \frac{\left(\sum_{i=1}^{n}\sum_{k=1}^{K} Y_{ijk}\right)^2}{nK} = 961.000 - 952.2500 = 8.7500$$

$$SS_{BS} = \sum_{i=1}^{n}\sum_{j=1}^{J}\sum_{k=1}^{K} Y_{ijk}^2 - \sum_{j=1}^{J}\sum_{k=1}^{K} \frac{\left(\sum_{i=1}^{n} Y_{ijk}\right)^2}{n} - \sum_{j=1}^{J}\sum_{i=1}^{n} \frac{\left(\sum_{k=1}^{K} Y_{ijk}\right)^2}{K} + \sum_{j=1}^{J} \frac{\left(\sum_{i=1}^{n}\sum_{k=1}^{K} Y_{ijk}\right)^2}{nK}$$

$$= 1{,}178.000 - 1{,}163.0000 - 961.0000 + 952.2500 = 6.2500$$

TABLE 7.11

Data for the Writing Assessment Example—Two-Factor Design:
Raw Scores on the Writing Assessment Task by Instructor and Rater

Factor A (Nonrepeated Factor):		Factor B (Repeated Factor)			
Instructor	Subject	Rater 1	Rater 2	Rater 3	Rater 4
1	1	3	4	7	8
	2	6	5	8	9
	3	3	4	7	9
	4	3	4	6	8
2	5	1	2	5	10
	6	2	3	6	10
	7	2	4	5	9
	8	2	3	6	10
Column sums		22	29	50	73

The mean squares are computed as follows:

$$MS_A = SS_A/df_A \quad = 6.1250/1 \quad = 6.1250$$

$$MS_B = SS_B/df_B \quad = 198.1250/3 \quad = 66.0417$$

$$MS_{AB} = SS_{AB}/df_{AB} = 12.6250/3 \quad = 4.2083$$

$$MS_S = SS_S/df_S \quad = 8.7500/6 \quad = 1.4583$$

$$MS_{BS} = SS_{BS}/df_{BS} \quad = 6.2500/18 \quad = 0.3472$$

Finally, the test statistics are computed as follows:

$$F_A = \frac{MS_A}{MS_S} = \frac{6.1250}{1.4583} = 4.2001$$

$$F_B = \frac{MS_B}{MS_{BS}} = \frac{66.0417}{0.3472} = 190.2123$$

$$F_{AB} = \frac{MS_{AB}}{MS_{BS}} = \frac{4.2083}{0.3472} = 12.1207$$

The test statistics are compared to the following usual F-test critical values: for A, $_{.95}F_{1,6} = 5.99$, which is not significant; for B, $_{.95}F_{3,18} = 3.16$, which is significant; and for AB, $_{.95}F_{3,18} = 3.16$, which is significant. For the Geisser–Greenhouse conservative procedure, the test statistics are compared to the following critical values: for A no conservative procedure is necessary; for B, $_{.95}F_{1,6} = 5.99$, which is also significant; and for AB, $_{.95}F_{1,6} = 5.99$, which is also significant. The two procedures both yield a statistically significant result for B and for AB; thus we need not be concerned with a violation of the compound symmetry assumption. A profile plot of the interaction is shown in Fig. 7.2.

There is a significant AB interaction, so we should follow this up with simple interaction contrasts, each involving only four cell means. As an example of a MCP, consider the contrast

$$\psi' = \frac{(\overline{Y}_{.11} - \overline{Y}_{.21}) - (\overline{Y}_{.14} - \overline{Y}_{.24})}{4} = \frac{(3.7500 - 1.7500) - (8.5000 - 9.7500)}{4} = 0.8125$$

with a standard error of

$$se_{\psi'} = \sqrt{MS_{BS}\left(\frac{\sum_{j=1}^{J}\sum_{k=1}^{K}c_{jk}^2}{n_{jk}}\right)} = \sqrt{0.3472\frac{(\frac{1}{16} + \frac{1}{16} + \frac{1}{16} + \frac{1}{16})}{4}} = 0.1473$$

Using the Scheffé procedure we formulate as the test statistic

$$t = \frac{\psi'}{se_{\psi'}} = \frac{0.8125}{0.1473} = 5.5160$$

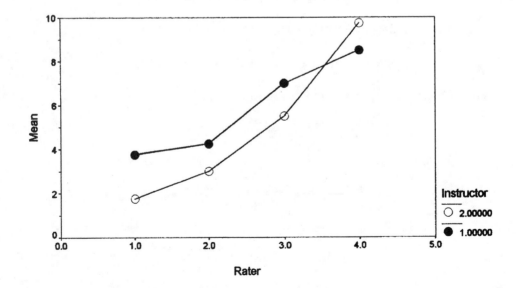

FIG. 7.2   Profile plot for mixed design example.

This is compared with the critical value of

$$\sqrt{(J-1)(K-1)_{1-\alpha} F_{(J-1)(K-1),(K-1)J(n-1)}} = \sqrt{3(_{.95} F_{3,18})} = \sqrt{3(3.16)} = 3.0790$$

Thus we may conclude that the tetrad difference between the first and second levels of factor A (instructor) and the first and fourth levels of factor B (rater) is significant. In other words, rater 1 finds better writing among the students of instructor 1 than instructor 2, whereas rater 4 finds better writing among the students of instructor 2 than instructor 1.

It should be obvious that more complex repeated measures designs exist. Here we have only concerned ourselves with the basic repeated measures designs. The intention was for these to serve as building blocks for more complicated designs. For further information about these types of designs see Myers (1979), Keppel (1982), or Kirk (1982). To analyze repeated measures designs in SAS, use the GLM procedure with the REPEATED statement, which gives the Box method. In SPSS, use the repeated measures program.

SUMMARY

In this chapter methods involving the comparision of means for random- and mixed-effects models were considered. Five different models were examined; these included the one-factor random-effects model, the two-factor random- and mixed-effects models, the one-factor repeated measures model, and the two-factor split-plot or mixed design. Included for each design were the usual topics of model characteristics, the linear model itself, assumptions of the model and dealing with their violation, the ANOVA summary table and its requisite computations, expected mean squares, and multiple-comparison procedures. Also included for particular designs was a discussion of the intraclass correlation coefficient, estimation of components of variance, the homogeneity of covariance assumption, and the Friedman repeated measures test based on ranks. At this point you should have met the following objectives: (a) be able to understand the characteristics and concepts underlying random- and mixed-effects ANOVA models, (b) be able to compute and interpret the results of random- and mixed-effects ANOVA models, including measures of association and multiple comparison procedures, and (c) be able to understand and evaluate the assumptions of random- and mixed-effects ANOVA models. In chapter 8, we continue our extended tour of the analysis of variance by looking at hierarchical designs that involve a factor nested within another factor, and randomized block designs, which we have very briefly introduced in this chapter.

PROBLEMS

Conceptual Problems

1. When an ANOVA design includes a random factor that is crossed with a fixed factor, the design illustrates which type of model?

    a.   fixed

    b.   mixed

    c.   random

    d.   crossed

2. The denominator of the F ratio used to test the interaction in a two factor ANOVA is MS_{with} in
    a. the fixed-effects model.
    b. the random-effects model.
    c. the mixed-effects model.
    d. All of the above.

3. A course consists of five units, the order of presentation of which is varied. A researcher used a 5×2 ANOVA design with order (five different randomly selected orders) and sex serving as factors. Which ANOVA model is illustrated by this design?
    a. the fixed-effects model
    b. the random-effects model
    c. the mixed-effects model
    d. the nested model

4. If a given set of data were analyzed with both a one-factor fixed-effects ANOVA and a one-factor random-effects ANOVA, the F ratio for the random effects model will be greater than the F ratio for the fixed effects model. True or false?

5. A repeated measures design is necessarily an example of the random-effects model. True or false?

6. Suppose researchers A and B perform a two-factor ANOVA on the same data, but that A assumes a fixed-effects model and B assumes a random-effects model. I assert that if A finds the interaction significant at the .05 level, B will also find the interaction significant at the .05 level. Am I correct?

7. I assert that MS_{with} should always be used as the denominator for all F ratios in the two-factor analysis of variance. Am I correct?

8. I assert that in a one-factor ANOVA and a one factor repeated measures ANOVA, the SS_{tot} is computed in exactly the same manner. Am I correct?

Computational Problems

1. Complete the following summary table for a two-factor analysis of variance, where there are three levels of factor A (a fixed effect) and two levels of factor B (a random effect). In each cell of the design there are four students. Complete the following summary table where $\alpha = .01$.

Source	SS	df	MS	F	Critical Value	Decision
A	3.64	—	—	—	—	—
B	.57	—	—	—	—	—
AB	2.07	—	—	—	—	—
Within	—	—	—			
Total	8.18	—				

2. A researcher randomly selected written essays from eight high school students who had participated in a state writing assessment. The essays were rated by four different raters. The raters were asked to develop an overall judgment based on clarity, composition, and creativity. Scores ranged on a scale from 1 to 12 points possible. The data are shown here. Conduct an ANOVA to determine whether the raters are consistent, where $\alpha = .05$. Use the Tukey and Newman–Keuls MCPs to detect exactly where the differences are among the raters (if they are different).

Subject	Rater 1	Rater 2	Rater 3	Rater 4
1	3	4	7	7
2	6	5	8	8
3	3	4	7	9
4	3	3	6	8
5	1	2	5	10
6	2	3	6	10
7	2	4	5	9
8	2	3	6	10

8

HIERARCHICAL AND RANDOMIZED BLOCK ANALYSIS OF VARIANCE MODELS

Chapter Outline

Key Concepts

1. Crossed designs
2. Nested designs
3. Confounding
4. Randomized block designs
5. Methods of blocking

In the last several chapters our discussion has dealt with different analysis of variance (ANOVA) models. In this chapter we complete our discussion of the analysis of variance by considering models in which there are multiple factors, but where at least one of the factors is either a nested factor or a blocking factor. As becomes evident when we define these models, this results in a nested or hierarchical design and a blocking design, respectively. In this chapter we are most concerned with the two-factor nested model and the two-factor randomized block model, although these models can be generalized to designs having more than two factors. Most of the concepts used in this chapter are the same as those covered in previous chapters. In addition, new concepts include crossed and nested factors, confounding, blocking factors, and methods of blocking. Our objectives are that by the end of this chapter, you will be able to (a) understand the characteristics and concepts underlying hierarchical and randomized block ANOVA models; (b) compute and interpret the results of hierarchical and randomized block ANOVA models, including measures of association and multiple comparison procedures; (c) understand and evaluate the assumptions of hierarchical and randomized block ANOVA models; and (d) compare different ANOVA models and select an appropriate model.

THE TWO-FACTOR HIERARCHICAL MODEL

In this section, we describe the distinguishing characteristics of the two-factor hierarchical ANOVA model, the layout of the data, the linear model, the ANOVA summary table, expected mean squares, and multiple-comparison procedures.

Characteristics of the Model

The characteristics of the two-factor fixed-, random-, and mixed-effects models have already been covered in chapters 5 and 7. Here we consider a special form of the two-factor model where one factor is nested within another factor. An example is the

best introduction to this model. Suppose you are interested in which of several different methods of instruction results in the highest level of achievement in mathematics
among fifth-grade students. Thus math achievement is the dependent variable and
method of instruction is one factor. A second factor is teacher. That is, you may also believe that some teachers are more effective than others, which results in different levels
of student achievement. However, each teacher has only one class of students and thus
can only be assigned to one method of instruction. In other words, all combinations of
the method (of instruction) and teacher factors are not possible. This design is known
as a *nested* or *hierarchical design* because the teacher factor is nested within the
method factor. This is in contrast to a two-factor *crossed design* where all possible
combinations of the two factors are included. The two-factor designs described in
chapters 5 and 7 were all crossed designs.

Let me give a more precise definition of crossed and nested designs. A two-factor
completely crossed design (or *complete factorial design*) is one where every level of
factor A occurs in combination with every level of factor B. A two-factor nested design
(or *incomplete factorial design*) of factor B being nested within factor A is one where
the levels of factor B occur for only one level of factor A. We denote this particular
nested design as B(A), which is read as factor B being nested within factor A (in other
references you may see this written as B:A or as B|A). To return to our example, the
teacher factor (factor B) is nested within the method factor (factor A) because each
teacher can only be assigned to one method of instruction.

These models are shown graphically in Fig. 8.1. In Fig. 8.1(a) a completely crossed
or complete factorial design is shown where there are 2 levels of factor A and 6 levels
of factor B. Thus, there are 12 possible factor combinations that would all be included
in a completely crossed design. The shaded region indicates the combinations that
might be included in a nested or incomplete factorial design where factor B is nested
within factor A. Although the number of levels of each factor remains the same, factor
B now has only three levels within each level of factor A. For A_1 we see only B_1, B_2,
and B_3, whereas for A_2 we see only B_4, B_5, and B_6. Thus, only 6 of the possible 12 factor combinations are included in the nested design. For example, level 1 of factor B occurs only with level 1 of factor A. In summary, Fig. 8.1(a) shows that the nested or
incomplete factorial design only consists of a portion of the completely crossed design
(the shaded regions). In Fig. 8.1(b) we see the nested design depicted in its more traditional form. Here you see that the 6 factor combinations not included are not even
shown (e.g., A_1 with B_4). Other examples of the two-factor nested design are where (a)
school is nested within school district, (b) faculty member is nested within department,
(c) individual is nested within gender, and (d) county is nested within state.

Thus with this design, one factor is nested within another factor, rather than the two
factors being crossed. As is shown in more detail later in this chapter, the nesting characteristic has some interesting and distinct outcomes. For now, some mention should
be made of these outcomes. *Nesting* is a particular type of confounding among the factors being investigated, where the AB interaction is part of the B effect (or is *confounded* with B) and therefore cannot be investigated. In the ANOVA model and the
ANOVA summary table, there will not be an interaction term or source of variation.
This is due to the fact that each level of factor B occurs in combination with only one

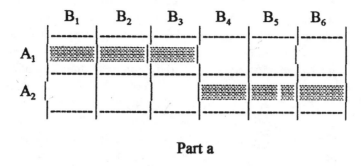

Part a

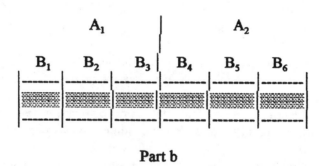

Part b

FIG. 8.1 Two-factor completely crossed versus nested designs. (a) the completely crossed design. The shaded region indicates the cells that would be included in a nested design where factor B is nested within factor A. In the nested design, factor A has two levels and factor B has three levels within each level of factor A. You see that only 6 of the 12 possible cells are filled in the nested design. (b) The same nested design in traditional form. The shaded region indicates the cells included in the nested design (i.e., the same 6 as shown in the first part).

level of factor A. We cannot compare for a particular level of B all levels of factor A, as a level of B only occurs with one level of A.

Confounding may occur for two reasons. First, the confounding may be intentional due to practical reasons, such as a reduction in the number of individuals to be observed. Fewer individuals would be necessary in a nested design as compared to a crossed design due to the fact that there are fewer cells in the model. Second, the confounding may be absolutely necessary because crossing may not be possible. For example, school is nested within school district because a particular school can only be a member of one school district. The nested factor (here factor B) may be a nuisance variable that the researcher wants to take into account in terms of explaining or predicting the dependent variable Y. An error commonly made is to ignore the nuisance variable B and to go with a one-factor design using only factor A. This design may result in a biased test of factor A such that the F ratio is inflated. Thus H_0 would be rejected more often than it should be, serving to increase the actual α level over that specified by the researcher and thereby increase the likelihood of a Type I error. The F test then would be too liberal.

Let me make one further point about this first characteristic. In the one-factor design discussed in chapter 3, we have already seen nesting going on in a different way. Here subjects were nested within factor A because each subject only responded to one level of factor A. It was only when we got to repeated measures designs in chapter 7 that individuals were allowed to respond to more than one level of a factor. For the repeated measures design we actually had a completely crossed design of subjects by factor A.

The remaining characteristics should be familiar. These include: two factors (or independent variables), each with two or more levels; the levels of each of the factors, which may be either randomly sampled from the population of levels or fixed by the researcher (i.e., the model may be fixed, mixed, or random); subjects who are randomly assigned to one combination of the levels of the two factors; and the dependent variable, which is measured at least at the interval level. If individuals respond to more than one combination of the levels of the two factors, then this would be some sort of repeated measures design (see chap. 7).

We again assume the design is balanced. For the two-factor nested design, a design is balanced if (a) the number of observations within each factor combination are equal and (b) the number of levels of the nested factor within each level of the other factor are equal. The first portion of this statement should be quite familiar, so no further explanation is necessary. The second portion of this statement is unique to this design and requires a brief explanation. As an example, say factor B is nested within factor A and factor A has two levels. On the one hand, factor B may have the same number of levels for each level of factor A. This occurs if there are three levels of factor B under level 1 of factor A (i.e., A_1) and also three levels of factor B under level 2 of factor A (i.e., A_2). On the other hand, factor B may not have the same number of levels for each level of factor A. This occurs if there are three levels of factor B under A_1 and only two levels of factor B under A_2. If the design is unbalanced, see the discussion in Kirk (1982) and Dunn and Clark (1987), although most statistical packages can deal with this type of unbalanced design (discussed later). In addition, we assume there are at least two observations per factor level combination (i.e., cell) so as to have a within cells source of variation.

The Layout of the Data

The layout of the data for the two-factor nested design is shown in Table 8.1. To simplify matters, I have limited the number of levels of the factors to two levels of factor A and three levels of factor B. This only serves as an example layout because many other possibilities obviously exist. Here we see the major set of columns designated as the levels of factor A, the nonnested factor, and for each level of A the minor set of columns are the levels of factor B, the nested factor. Within each factor level combination or cell are the subjects. Means are also shown for the levels of factor A, for each cell, and overall. Note that the means for the levels of factor B need not be shown, as they are the same as the cell means. For instance $\overline{Y}_{11}$ is the same as $\overline{Y}_{.1}$ (not shown) as B_1 only occurs once. This is another result of the nesting.

TABLE 8.1

Layout for the Two-Factor Nested Design

	A_1				A_2	
	B_1	B_2	B_3	B_4	B_5	B_6
	Y_{111}	Y_{112}	Y_{113}	Y_{124}	Y_{125}	Y_{126}
	.	.	.	.	.	.
	.	.	.	.	.	.
	.	.	.	.	.	.
	Y_{n11}	Y_{n12}	Y_{n13}	Y_{n24}	Y_{n25}	Y_{n26}
Cell means	$\overline{Y}_{.11}$	$\overline{Y}_{.12}$	$\overline{Y}_{.13}$	$\overline{Y}_{.24}$	$\overline{Y}_{.25}$	$\overline{Y}_{.26}$
A means		$\overline{Y}_{.1.}$			$\overline{Y}_{.2.}$	
Overall mean				$\overline{Y}_{...}$		

The ANOVA Model

The two-factor fixed-effects nested ANOVA model is written in terms of population parameters as

$$Y_{ijk} = \mu + \alpha_j + \beta_{k(j)} + \varepsilon_{ijk}$$

where Y_{ijk} is the observed score on the criterion variable for individual i in level j of factor A and level k of factor B (or in the jk cell), μ is the overall or grand population mean (i.e., regardless of cell designation), α_j is the fixed effect for level j of factor A, $\beta_{k(j)}$ is the fixed effect for level k of factor B, and ε_{ijk} is the random residual error for individual i in cell jk. Notice that there is no interaction term in the model, and also that the effect for factor B is denoted by $\beta_{k(j)}$. This tells us that factor B is nested within factor A. The residual error can be due to individual differences, measurement error, and/or other factors not under investigation. Note that we use α_j and $\beta_{k(j)}$ to designate the fixed effects. We consider the mixed- and random-effects cases later in this chapter. There are side conditions for the fixed-effects model about each of the main effects: $\sum_{j=1}^{J} \alpha_j = 0$ and $\sum_{k=1}^{K} \beta_{k(j)} = 0$.

For the two-factor fixed-effects nested ANOVA model, there are only two sets of hypotheses, one for each of the main effects, because there is no interaction effect. The null and alternative hypotheses, respectively, for testing the effect of factor A are

$$H_{01}: \mu_{.1.} = \mu_{.2.} = \mu_{.3.} = \ldots = \mu_{.J.}$$

$$H_{11}: \text{ not all the } \mu_{.j.} \text{ are equal}$$

The hypotheses for testing the effect of factor B are

$$H_{02}: \mu_{..1} = \mu_{..2} = \mu_{..3} = \ldots = \mu_{..K}$$

H_{12}: **not all the** $\mu_{..k}$ **are equal.**

These hypotheses reflect the inferences made in the fixed-, mixed-, and random-effects models (as fully described in chap. 7). For fixed main effects the null hypotheses are about means, whereas for random main effects the null hypotheses are about variance among the means. As we already know, the difference in the models is also reflected in the expected mean squares and in the multiple-comparison procedures. As before, we do need to pay particular attention to whether the model is fixed, mixed, or random. The assumptions about the two-factor nested model are exactly the same as with the two-factor crossed model, and thus we need not provide any additional discussion.

ANOVA Summary Table

The computations of the two-factor fixed-effects nested model are somewhat similar to those of the two-factor fixed-effects crossed model. The main difference lies in the fact that there is no interaction term. The ANOVA summary table is shown in Table 8.2, where we see the following sources of variation: A, B, within cells, and total. There we see that only two F ratios can be formed, one for each of the two main effects, because no interaction term is estimated.

If we take the total sum of squares and decompose it, we have

$$SS_{total} = SS_A + SS_{B(A)} + SS_{with}$$

These three terms can be computed as follows:

$$SS_A = \sum_{j=1}^{J} \frac{\left(\sum_{i=1}^{n}\sum_{k=1}^{K} Y_{ijk}\right)^2}{nK_{(j)}} - \frac{\left(\sum_{i=1}^{n}\sum_{j=1}^{J}\sum_{k=1}^{K} Y_{ijk}\right)^2}{nJK_{(j)}}$$

$$SS_{B(A)} = \sum_{j=1}^{J}\sum_{k=1}^{K} \frac{\left(\sum_{i=1}^{n} Y_{ijk}\right)^2}{n} - \sum_{j=1}^{J} \frac{\left(\sum_{i=1}^{n}\sum_{k=1}^{K} Y_{ijk}\right)^2}{nK_{(j)}}$$

$$SS_{with} = \sum_{i=1}^{n}\sum_{j=1}^{J}\sum_{k=1}^{K} Y_{ijk}^2 - \sum_{j=1}^{J}\sum_{k=1}^{K} \frac{\left(\sum_{i=1}^{n} Y_{ijk}\right)^2}{n}$$

Here $K_{(j)}$ denotes the number of levels of factor B that are nested within the jth level of factor A. The degrees of freedom, mean squares and F ratios are computed as shown in Table 8.2, assuming a fixed-effects model. The critical value for the test of factor A is $_{(1-\alpha)}F_{J-1, JK(j)(n-1)}$ and for the test of factor B is $_{(1-\alpha)}F_{J(K(j)-1), JK(j)(n-1)}$. Let me explain something about the degrees of freedom. The degrees of freedom for B(A) are equal to $J(K_{(j)} - 1)$. This means that for a design with two levels of factor A and three levels of

TABLE 8.2
Two-Factor Nested Design ANOVA Summary Table—Fixed Effects Model

Source	SS	df	MS	F
A	SS_A	$J - 1$	MS_A	MS_A/MS_{with}
B(A)	$SS_{B(A)}$	$J(K_{(j)} - 1)$	$MS_{B(A)}$	$MS_{B(A)}/MS_{with}$
Within	SS_{with}	$JK_{(j)}(n - 1)$	MS_{with}	
Total	SS_{total}	$N - 1$		

factor B within each level of A (for a total of six levels of B), the degrees of freedom are equal to $2(3 - 1) = 4$. This is not the same as the degrees of freedom for a completely crossed design where df_B would be 5. The degrees of freedom for within are equal to $JK_{(j)}(n - 1)$. For this same design with $n = 10$, then the degrees of freedom within are equal to $(2)(3)(10 - 1) = 54$.

Expected Mean Squares

Let us now provide a basis for determining the appropriate error terms for forming an F ratio in the fixed-, mixed-, and random-effects models. Consider the alternative situations of H_0 actually being true and H_0 actually being false. If H_0 is actually true for both tests, then the expected mean squares, regardless of model, are as follows:

$$E(MS_A) = \sigma_\varepsilon^2$$

$$E(MS_{B(A)}) = \sigma_\varepsilon^2$$

$$E(MS_{with}) = \sigma_\varepsilon^2$$

Again σ_ε^2 is the population variance of the residual errors.

If H_0 is actually false for both tests, then the expected mean squares for the *fixed-effects case* are as follows:

$$E(MS_A) = \sigma_\varepsilon^2 + \frac{nK_{(j)} \sum_{j=1}^{J} \alpha_j^2}{J - 1}$$

$$E(MS_{B(A)}) = \sigma_\varepsilon^2 + \frac{n \sum_{j=1}^{J} \sum_{k=1}^{K} \beta_{k(j)}^2}{J(K_{(j)} - 1)}$$

$$E(MS_{with}) = \sigma_\varepsilon^2$$

Thus, the appropriate F ratios both involve using the within source as the error term.

If H_0 is actually false for both tests, then the expected mean squares for the *random-effects case* are as follows:

$$E(MS_A) = \sigma_\varepsilon^2 + n\sigma_{b(a)}^2 + nK_{(j)}\sigma_a^2$$

$$E(MS_{B(A)}) = \sigma_\varepsilon^2 + n\sigma_{b(a)}^2$$

$$E(MS_{with}) = \sigma_\varepsilon^2$$

Thus, the appropriate error term for the test of A is $MS_{B(A)}$ and the appropriate error term for the test of B is MS_{with}.

If H_0 is actually false for both tests, then the expected mean squares for the *mixed-effects case where A is fixed and B is random* are as follows:

$$E(MS_A) = \sigma_\varepsilon^2 + n\sigma_{b(a)}^2 + \frac{nK_{(j)}\sum_{j=1}^{J}\alpha_j^2}{J-1}$$

$$E(MS_{B(A)}) = \sigma_\varepsilon^2 + n\sigma_{b(a)}^2$$

$$E(MS_{with}) = \sigma_\varepsilon^2$$

Thus, the appropriate error term for the test of A is $MS_{B(A)}$ and the appropriate error term for the test of B is MS_{with}. This model appears to the predominant model in the social and behavioral sciences.

If H_0 is actually false for both tests, then the expected mean squares for the *mixed-effects case where A is random and B is fixed* are as follows:

$$E(MS_A) = \sigma_\varepsilon^2 + nK_{(j)}\sigma_a^2$$

$$E(MS_{B(A)}) = \sigma_\varepsilon^2 + \frac{n\sum_{j=1}^{J}\sum_{k=1}^{K}\beta_{k(j)}^2}{J(K_{(j)} - 1)}$$

$$E(MS_{with}) = \sigma_\varepsilon^2$$

Thus, the appropriate F ratios both involve using the within source as the error term.

Multiple-Comparison Procedures

This section considers multiple-comparison procedures (MCPs) for the two-factor nested design. First of all, the researcher is usually not interested in making inferences about random effects. Second, for MCPs based on the levels of factor A (the nonnested factor), there is nothing new to say. Just be sure to use the appropriate error term and error degrees of freedom. Third, for MCPs based on the levels of factor B (the nested factor), this is a little different. The researcher is not always as interested in MCPs about the nested factor as compared to the nonnested factor because inferences about the levels of factor B are not even generalizable across the levels of factor A, due to the nesting. If you are nonetheless interested in MCPs for factor B, by necessity you have to look within a level of A to formulate your contrast. Otherwise MCPs can be conducted as before.

For measures of association and variance components, return to chapters 5 and 7 (also Dunn & Clark, 1987; Kirk, 1982). For three-factor designs see Myers (1979), Kirk (1982), or Dunn and Clark (1987). In the major statistical computer packages, the analysis of nested designs is as follows: in SAS, PROC NESTED can be used for balanced designs and PROC GLM for unbalanced designs using the B(A) notation; in SPSS, use the MANOVA program.

An Example

Let us consider an example to illustrate the procedures in this section. The data are shown in Table 8.3. Factor A is approach to the teaching of reading (basal vs. whole language approaches), and factor B is teacher. Thus there are two teachers using the basal approach and two different teachers using the whole language approach. The researcher is interested in the effects these factors have on student's reading comprehension in the second grade. Thus the dependent variable is a measure of reading comprehension. Six students are randomly assigned to each approach–teacher combination for small-group instruction. This particular example is a mixed model, where factor A (teaching method) is a fixed effect and factor B (teacher) is a random effect. Table 8.3 also contains various sums for the raw scores. First, the sums of squares are computed to be

$$SS_A = \sum_{j=1}^{J} \frac{\left(\sum_{i=1}^{n} \sum_{k=1}^{K} Y_{ijk} \right)^2}{nK_{(j)}} - \frac{\left(\sum_{i=1}^{n} \sum_{j=1}^{J} \sum_{k=1}^{K} Y_{ijk} \right)^2}{nJK_{(j)}} = 1,541.6667 - 1,204.1667 = 337.5000$$

$$SS_{B(A)} = \sum_{j=1}^{J} \sum_{k=1}^{K} \frac{\left(\sum_{i=1}^{n} Y_{ijk} \right)^2}{n} - \sum_{j=1}^{J} \frac{\left(\sum_{i=1}^{n} \sum_{k=1}^{K} Y_{ijk} \right)^2}{nK_{(j)}} = 1,553.0000 - 1,541.6667 = 11.3333$$

$$SS_{with} = \sum_{i=1}^{n} \sum_{j=1}^{J} \sum_{k=1}^{K} Y_{ijk}^2 - \sum_{j=1}^{J} \sum_{k=1}^{K} \frac{\left(\sum_{i=1}^{n} Y_{ijk} \right)^2}{n} = 1,672.0000 - 1,553.0000 = 119.0000$$

The mean squares are computed to be

$$MS_A = \frac{SS_A}{df_A} = \frac{337.5000}{1} = 337.5000$$

$$MS_{B(A)} = \frac{SS_{B(A)}}{df_{B(A)}} = \frac{11.3333}{2} = 5.6667$$

$$MS_{with} = \frac{SS_{with}}{df_{with}} = \frac{119.0000}{20} = 5.9500$$

Finally, for a mixed-effects model where A is fixed and B is random, the test statistics are

$$F_A = \frac{MS_A}{MS_{B(A)}} = \frac{337.5000}{5.6667} = 59.5585$$

$$F_{B(A)} = \frac{MS_{B(A)}}{MS_{with}} = \frac{5.6667}{5.9500} = 0.9524$$

From Appendix Table 4, the critical value for the test of factor A is $_{(1-\alpha)}F_{J-1,J(K(j)-1)} = _{.95}F_{1,2}$ = 18.51, and the critical value for the test of factor B is $_{(1-\alpha)}F_{J(K(j)-1),JK(j)(n-1)} = _{.95}F_{2,20} = 3.49$. Thus there is a significant difference between the two approaches to reading instruction at the .05 level of significance, and there is no significant difference between the teachers. When we look at the means for the levels of factor A, we see that the mean

TABLE 8.3

Data for the Teaching Reading Example—Two-Factor Nested Design:
Raw Scores on the Reading Achievement Test by Reading Approach and Teacher

	Reading Approaches:			
	A_1 *(Basal)*		A_2 *(Whole Language)*	
	Teacher B_1	*Teacher B_2*	*Teacher B_3*	*Teacher B_4*
	1	1	7	8
	1	3	8	9
	2	3	8	11
	4	4	10	13
	4	6	12	14
	5	6	15	15
Cell sums	17	23	60	70
Cell means	2.8333	3.8333	10.0000	11.6667
A sums		40		130
A means		3.3333		10.8333
Overall sum		170		
Overall mean		7.0833		

comprehension score for the whole language approach ($\overline{Y}_{.2} = 10.8333$) is greater than the mean for the basal approach ($\overline{Y}_{.1} = 3.3333$). No post hoc multiple comparisons are really necessary here, given the results obtained.

THE TWO-FACTOR RANDOMIZED BLOCK DESIGN FOR $n = 1$

In this section, we describe the distinguishing characteristics of the two-factor randomized block ANOVA model for one observation per cell, the layout of the data, the linear model, assumptions and their violation, the ANOVA summary table, expected mean squares, multiple-comparison procedures, measures of association, methods of block formation, and statistical packages.

Characteristics of the Model

The characteristics of the two-factor randomized block ANOVA model are quite similar to those of the regular two-factor model, as well as sharing a few characteristics with the one-factor repeated measures design. There is one obvious exception, which has to do with the nature of the factors being used. Here there are two factors, each with at least two levels. One factor is known as the *treatment factor* and is referred to as factor B (a treatment factor is what we have been considering in the last five chapters). The second factor is known as the *blocking factor* and is referred to as factor A. A blocking factor is a new concept and requires some discussion.

Take an ordinary one-factor design, where the single factor is a treatment factor (e.g., method of exercising) and the researcher is interested in its effect on some dependent variable (e.g., amount of body fat). Despite individuals being randomly assigned to a treatment group, the groups may be different due to a nuisance variable operating in a nonrandom way. For instance, Group 1 may have mostly older adults and Group 2 may have mostly younger adults. Thus, it is likely that Group 2 will be favored over Group 1 because age, the nuisance variable, has not been properly balanced out across the groups by randomization. One way to deal with this problem is to control the effect of the nuisance variable by incorporating it into the design of the study. Including the blocking or nuisance variable as a factor in the design will result in a reduction in residual variation (due to some portion of individual differences being explained) and an increase in power. The blocking factor is selected based on the strength of its relationship with the dependent variable, where an unrelated blocking variable would not reduce residual variation. It would be reasonable to expect, then, that variability among individuals within a block (e.g., within younger adults) should be less than variability among individuals between blocks (e.g., between younger and older adults). Thus each block represents the formation of a matched set of individuals, that is, matched on the blocking variable, but not necessarily matched on any other nuisance variable. Using our example, we expect that in general, adults within a particular age block (i.e., older or younger blocks) will be more similar in terms of variables related to body fat than adults across blocks.

Let us consider several examples of blocking factors. Some blocking factors are naturally occurring blocks such as siblings, friends, neighbors, plots of land, and time. Other blocking factors are not naturally occurring, but can be formed by the researcher. Examples of this type include grade point average, age, weight, aptitude test scores, intelligence test scores, socioeconomic status, and school or district size.

Let me make some summary statements about characteristics of blocking designs. First, designs that include one or more blocking factors are known as *randomized block designs*, also known as matching designs or treatment by block designs. The researcher's main interest is in the treatment factor. The purpose of the blocking factor is to reduce residual variation. Thus the researcher is not as much interested in the test of the blocking factor (possibly not at all) as compared to the treatment factor. Thus there is at least one blocking factor and one treatment factor, each with two or more levels. Second, each subject falls into only one block in the design and is subsequently randomly assigned to one level of the treatment factor within that block. Thus subjects within a block serve as their own controls such that some portion of their individual differences is taken into account. As a result, subjects' scores are not independent within a particular block. Third, for purposes of this section, we assume there is only one subject for each treatment–block level combination. As a result, the model does not include an interaction term. In the next section we consider the multiple observations case, where there is an interaction term in the model. Finally, the dependent variable is measured at least at the interval level.

The Layout of the Data

The layout of the data for the two-factor randomized block model is shown in Table 8.4. Here we see the columns designated as the levels of treatment factor B and the rows as the levels of blocking factor A. Row, column, and overall means are also shown. Here you see that the layout of the data looks the same as the two-factor model, but with a single observation per cell.

TABLE 8.4
Layout for the Two-Factor Randomized Block Design

Level of Factor A	Level of Factor B				Block Mean
	1	*2*	...	*K*	
1	Y_{11}	Y_{12}	...	Y_{1K}	$\overline{Y}_{1.}$
2	Y_{21}	Y_{22}	...	Y_{2K}	$\overline{Y}_{2.}$
.	.	.	.	.	.
.	.	.	.	.	.
.	.	.	.	.	.
J	Y_{J1}	Y_{J2}	...	Y_{JK}	$\overline{Y}_{J.}$
Column mean	$\overline{Y}_{.1}$	$\overline{Y}_{.2}$	...	$\overline{Y}_{.K}$	$\overline{Y}_{..}$

The ANOVA Model

The two-factor fixed-effects randomized block ANOVA model is written in terms of population parameters as

$$Y_{jk} = \mu + \alpha_j + \beta_k + \varepsilon_{jk}$$

where Y_{jk} is the observed score on the criterion variable for the individual responding to level j of block A and level k of factor B, μ is the overall or grand population mean, α_j is the fixed effect for level j of block A, β_k is the fixed effect for level k of the treatment factor B, and ε_{jk} is the random residual error for the individual in cell jk. The residual error can be due to measurement error, individual differences, and/or other factors not under investigation. You can see this is similar to the two-factor model with one observation per cell (i.e., $i = 1$ making the i subscript unnecessary), and there is no interaction term included. Also, the effects are denoted by α and β given we have a fixed-effects model.

There are two side conditions of the model for the main effects, $\sum_{j=1}^{J} \alpha_j = 0$ and $\sum_{k=1}^{K} \beta_k = 0$.

These side conditions are the same as in the regular two-factor fixed-effects model, although there is no side condition for the interaction because it is not a part of the model.

The hypotheses for testing the effect of factor A are

$$H_{01}: \mu_{1.} = \mu_{2.} = \mu_{3.} = \ldots = \mu_{J.}$$

$$H_{11}: \text{not all the } \mu_{j.} \text{ are equal}$$

and for testing the effect of factor B are

$$H_{02}: \mu_{.1} = \mu_{.2} = \mu_{.3} = \ldots = \mu_{.K}$$

$$H_{12}: \text{not all the } \mu_{.k} \text{ are equal}$$

The factors are both fixed effects, so the hypotheses are written in terms of means.

Assumptions and Violation of Assumptions

In chapter 7 we described the assumptions for the one-factor repeated measures model. The assumptions are nearly the same for the two-factor randomized block model and we need not devote much attention to them here. As before, the assumptions are mainly concerned with the distribution of the residual errors. A general statement of the assumptions about the residuals can be written as $\varepsilon_{jk} \sim NI(0,\sigma_\varepsilon^2)$.

A second assumption is *compound symmetry* (or homogeneity of covariance) and is necessary because the observations within a block are not independent. The assumption states that the population covariances for all pairs of the levels of the treatment factor B (i.e., k and k') are equal, at each level of the treatment factor B (for all levels k). The analysis of variance is not particularly robust to a violation of this assumption. If the assumption is violated, three alternative procedures are available. The first is to limit the levels of factor B either to those that meet the assumption or to two (in which case there would be only one covariance). The second, and more plausible alternative, is to use adjusted F tests. These are reported in the next subsection. The third is to use multivariate analysis of variance, which has no compound symmetry assumption, but is slightly less powerful.

Huynh and Feldt (1970) showed that the compound symmetry assumption is a sufficient but unnecessary condition for the test of treatment factor B to be F distributed. Thus the F test may also be valid under less stringent conditions. The necessary and sufficient condition for the validity of the F test of B is known as *circularity* (or sphericity). This assumes that the variance of the difference scores for each pair of factor levels is the same. Further discussion of circularity is beyond the scope of this text (see Keppel, 1982, or Kirk, 1982).

A third assumption purports that there is no interaction between the treatment and blocking factors. This is obviously an assumption of the model because no interaction term is included. Such a model is often referred to as an *additive model*. As was mentioned previously, in this model the interaction is confounded with the error term. Violation of the additivity assumption allows the test of factor B to be negatively biased; this means that we will reject too few false H_0s. In other words, if H_0 is rejected, then we are confident that H_0 is really false. If H_0 is not rejected, then our interpretation is ambiguous as H_0 may or may not be really true. Here you would not know whether H_0 was true or not, as there might really be a difference but the test may not be powerful enough to detect it. Also, the power of the test of factor B is reduced by a violation of the additivity assumption. The assumption may be tested by Tukey's (1949) test of additivity. The test statistic is

$$F = \frac{SS_N / 1}{(SS_{res} - SS_N) / [(J-1)(K-1)-1]}$$

where SS_N is the sum of squares due to nonadditivity and is computed by

$$SS_N = \frac{\left[\sum_{j=1}^{J} \sum_{k=1}^{K} Y_{jk} (\overline{Y}_{j.} - \overline{Y}_{..})(\overline{Y}_{.k} - \overline{Y}_{..}) \right]^2}{\left[\sum_{j=1}^{J} (\overline{Y}_{j.} - \overline{Y}_{..})^2 \right]\left[\sum_{k=1}^{K} (\overline{Y}_{.k} - \overline{Y}_{..})^2 \right]}$$

and the F test statistic is distributed as $F_{1,[(J-1)(K-1)-1]}$. If the test is nonsignificant, then the model is additive and the assumption has been met. If the test is significant, then the model is not additive and the assumption has not been met. A summary of the assumptions and the effects of their violation for this model is presented in Table 8.5.

ANOVA Summary Table

The sources of variation for this model are similar to those of the regular two-factor model, except there is no interaction term. The ANOVA summary table is shown in

TABLE 8.5

Assumptions and Effects of Violations—Two-Factor Randomized Block Design

Assumption	Effect of Assumption Violation
1. Homogeneity of variance	Small effect with equal or nearly equal ns; otherwise effect decreases as n increases
2. Independence of residuals	Increased likelihood of a Type I and/or Type II error in the F statistic; influences standard errors of means and thus inferences about those means
3. Normality of residuals	Minimal effect with equal or nearly equal ns
4. Compound symmetry	Fairly serious effect
5. No interaction between treatment and blocks	Increased likelihood of a Type II error for the test of factor B and thus reduced power

Table 8.6, where we see the following sources of variation: A (blocks), B (treatments), residual, and total. The test of block differences is usually of no real interest. In general, we expect there to be differences between the blocks. From the table we see that two F ratios can be formed.

If we take the total sum of squares and decompose it, we have

$$SS_{tot} = SS_A + SS_B + SS_{res}$$

These three terms can be computed as follows:

$$SS_A = \sum_{j=1}^{J} \left[\frac{\left(\sum_{k=1}^{K} Y_{jk} \right)^2}{K} \right] - \frac{\left(\sum_{j=1}^{J} \sum_{k=1}^{K} Y_{jk} \right)^2}{N}$$

$$SS_B = \sum_{k=1}^{K} \left[\frac{\left(\sum_{j=1}^{J} Y_{jk} \right)^2}{J} \right] - \frac{\left(\sum_{j=1}^{J} \sum_{k=1}^{K} Y_{jk} \right)^2}{N}$$

$$SS_{res} = \sum_{j=1}^{J} \sum_{k=1}^{K} Y_{jk}^2 - \sum_{j=1}^{J} \left[\frac{\left(\sum_{k=1}^{K} Y_{jk} \right)^2}{K} \right] - \sum_{k=1}^{K} \left[\frac{\left(\sum_{j=1}^{J} Y_{jk} \right)^2}{J} \right] + \frac{\left(\sum_{j=1}^{J} \sum_{k=1}^{K} Y_{jk} \right)^2}{N}$$

The degrees of freedom, mean squares, and F ratios are shown in Table 8.6.

Earlier in the discussion on the two-factor randomized block design, I mentioned that the F test is not very robust to a violation of the compound symmetry assumption. We again recommend the following sequential procedure be used in the test of factor B. First, do the usual F test, which is quite liberal in terms of rejecting H_0 too often, where the degrees of freedom are $K-1$ and $(J-1)(K-1)$. If H_0 is not rejected, then stop. If H_0 is rejected, then continue with step 2, which is to use the Geisser–Greenhouse (1958) conservative F test. For the model we are considering, the degrees of freedom for the F critical value are adjusted to be 1 and $J-1$. If H_0 is rejected then stop. This would indicate that both the liberal and conservative tests reached the same conclusion, that is, to reject H_0. If H_0 is not rejected, then the two tests did not reach the same conclusion, and a further test should be undertaken. Thus in step 3 an adjusted F test is conducted. The adjustment is known as Box's (1954) correction (the Huynh & Feldt [1970] procedure). Here the degrees of freedom are equal to $(K-1)\,\varepsilon$ and $(J-1)(K-1)\,\varepsilon$, where ε is the correction factor (see Kirk, 1982). It is now fairly routine for the major statistical computer packages to conduct the Geisser–Greenhouse and Box (Huynh & Feldt) tests.

Expected Mean Squares

For the two-factor randomized block model, the appropriate F ratios are the same regardless of whether we have a fixed-effects, random-effects, or mixed-effects model. The appropriate error term then for all such models is MS_{res}. Thus the residual is the proper error term for every model.

Multiple-Comparison Procedures

If the null hypothesis for either the A or B factor is rejected and there are more than two levels of the factor, then the researcher may be interested in which means or combinations of means are different. This could be assessed, as put forth in previous chapters, by the use of some multiple comparison procedure (MCP). In general, the use of the MCPs outlined in chapter 4 is straightforward if the circularity assumption is met. If the circularity assumption is not met, then MS_{res} is not the appropriate error term as the MCPs are seriously affected, and the two alternatives recommended in chapter 7 should be considered (also see Boik, 1981; Kirk, 1982; or Maxwell, 1980).

Measures of Association

One may also be interested in an assessment of the strength of association between the treatment factor B and the dependent variable Y (the association between the blocking

TABLE 8.6
Two-Factor Randomized Block Design ANOVA Summary Table

Source	SS	df	MS	F
A	SS_A	$J-1$	MS_A	MS_A / MS_{res}
B	SS_B	$K-1$	MS_B	MS_B / MS_{res}
Residual	SS_{res}	$(J-1)(K-1)$	MS_{res}	
Total	SS_{total}	$N-1$		

factor A and Y is usually not of interest, other than a simple bivariate correlation). In the fixed-effects model, strength of association is measured by ω^2, and computed by

$$\omega^2 = \frac{SS_B - (K-1)MS_{res}}{SS_{tot} + MS_{res}}$$

For the random-effects model, the intraclass correlation ρ^2 is the appropriate measure of association, and is computed by

$$\rho^2 = \frac{\sigma_b^2}{\sigma_b^2 + \sigma_a^2 + \sigma_{res}^2}$$

where

$$\sigma_b^2 = \frac{MS_B - MS_{res}}{J}$$

$$\sigma_a^2 = \frac{MS_A - MS_{res}}{K}$$

$$\sigma_{res}^2 = MS_{res}$$

For the mixed models, modifications of these measures as suggested by Kirk (1982) are as follows. If A is random and B is fixed, then the measure of association for B is ω^2 and is computed by

$$\omega^2 = \frac{[(K-1)/N](MS_B - MS_{res})}{[MS_{res} + (MS_A - MS_{res})/K] + [(K-1)/N](MS_B - MS_{res})}$$

If A is fixed and B is random, then the measure of association for B is ρ^2 and is computed by

$$\rho^2 = \frac{\sigma_b^2}{\sigma_b^2 + \sigma_{res}^2 + [(J-1)/N](MS_A - MS_{res})}$$

where

$$\sigma_b^2 = \frac{MS_B - MS_{res}}{J}$$

$$\sigma_{res}^2 = MS_{res}$$

Methods of Block Formation

There are different methods for the formation of blocks. This discussion borrows heavily from the work of Pingel (1969) in defining five such methods. The first method is the *predefined value blocking method*, where the blocking factor is an ordinal variable. Here the researcher specifies J different population values of the blocking variable. For each of these values (i.e., a fixed effect), individuals are randomly assigned to the levels of the treatment factor. Thus individuals within a block have the same value on the blocking variable. For example, if class rank is the blocking variable, the levels might be the top third, middle third, and bottom third of the class.

The second method is the *predefined range blocking method*, where the blocking factor is an interval variable. Here the researcher specifies J mutually exclusive ranges in the population distribution of the blocking variable, where the probability of obtaining a value of the blocking variable in each range may be specified as $1/J$. For each of these ranges (i.e., a fixed effect), individuals are randomly assigned to the levels of the treatment factor. Thus individuals within a block are in the same range on the blocking variable. For example, if the Graduate Record Exam–Verbal score is the blocking variable, the levels might be 200–400, 401–600, and 601–800.

The third method is the *sampled value blocking method*, where the blocking variable is an ordinal variable. Here the researcher randomly samples J population values of the blocking variable (i.e., a random effect). For each of these values, individuals are randomly assigned to the levels of the treatment factor. Thus individuals within a block have the same value on the blocking variable. For example, if class rank is again the blocking variable, only this time measured in tenths, the researcher might randomly select 3 levels from the population of 10.

The fourth method is the *sampled range blocking method*, where the blocking variable is an interval variable. Here the researcher randomly samples N individuals from the population, such that $N = JK$, where J is the number of blocks desired (i.e., a fixed effect) and K is the number of treatment groups. These individuals are ranked according to their values on the blocking variable from 1 to N. The first block consists of those individuals ranked from 1 to K, the second block of those ranked from $K + 1$ to $2K$, and so on. Finally, individuals within a block are randomly assigned to the K treatment groups. For example, consider the GRE–Verbal again as the blocking variable, where there are $J = 10$ blocks, $K = 4$ treatment groups, and thus $N = JK = 40$ individuals. The top 4 ranked individuals on the GRE–Verbal would constitute the first block and they would be randomly assigned to the four groups. The next 4 ranked individuals would constitute the second block, and so on.

The fifth method is the *post hoc blocking method*. Here the researcher has already designed the study and collected the data, without the benefit of a blocking variable. After the fact, a blocking variable is identified and incorporated into the analysis. It is possible to implement any of the four preceding procedures on a post hoc basis.

Based on the research of Pingel (1969), some statements can be made about the precision of these methods in terms of a reduction in residual variability and better estimation of the treatment effect. In general, for an ordinal blocking variable, the predefined value blocking method is more precise than the sampled value blocking method. Likewise, for an interval blocking variable, the predefined range blocking method is more precise than the sampled range blocking method. Finally, the post hoc blocking method is the least precise of the methods discussed. For a discussion of selecting the optimal number of blocks, see Feldt (1958) (highly recommended), as well as Myers (1979).

Statistical Packages

In the major statistical computer packages, the analysis of randomized block designs is as follows: in SAS, PROC ANOVA can be used for balanced designs and PROC GLM for unbalanced designs; in SPSS, use the MANOVA program where a DESIGN statement with the interaction term included will provide the Tukey test for $n = 1$. For a description of other randomized block designs, see Kirk (1982).

An Example

Let us consider an example to illustrate the procedures in this section. The data are shown in Table 8.7. The blocking factor is age (i.e., ages 50, 40, 30, and 20), the treatment factor is number of workouts per week (i.e., 1, 2, 3, and 4), and the dependent variable is amount of weight lost during the first month. Assume we have a fixed-effects model. Table 8.7 also contains various sums for the raw scores. The sums of squares are computed as follows:

$$SS_A = \sum_{j=1}^{J} \left[\frac{\left(\sum_{k=1}^{K} Y_{jk} \right)^2}{K} \right] - \frac{\left(\sum_{j=1}^{J} \sum_{k=1}^{K} Y_{jk} \right)^2}{N} = 473.2500 - \frac{(85)^2}{16} = 21.6875$$

$$SS_B = \sum_{k=1}^{K} \left[\frac{\left(\sum_{j=1}^{J} Y_{jk} \right)^2}{J} \right] - \frac{\left(\sum_{j=1}^{J} \sum_{k=1}^{K} Y_{jk} \right)^2}{N} = 561.7500 - \frac{(85)^2}{16} = 110.1875$$

$$SS_{res} = \sum_{j=1}^{J} \sum_{k=1}^{K} Y_{jk}^2 - \sum_{j=1}^{J} \left[\frac{\left(\sum_{k=1}^{K} Y_{jk} \right)^2}{K} \right] - \sum_{k=1}^{K} \left[\frac{\left(\sum_{j=1}^{J} Y_{jk} \right)^2}{J} \right] + \frac{\left(\sum_{j=1}^{J} \sum_{k=1}^{K} Y_{jk} \right)^2}{N}$$

$$= 587.0000 - 473.2500 - 561.7500 + \frac{(85)^2}{16} = 3.5625$$

The mean squares are computed as follows.

$$MS_A = SS_A/df_A \quad = 21.6875/3 \quad = 7.2292$$

$$MS_B = SS_B/df_B \quad = 110.1875/3 \quad = 36.7292$$

$$MS_{res} = SS_{res}/df_{res} = 3.5625/9 \quad = 0.3958$$

Finally the test statistics are computed as follows.

$$F_A = MS_A/MS_{res} = 7.2292/0.3958 = 18.2648$$

$$F_B = MS_B/MS_{res} = 36.7292/0.3958 = 92.7974$$

The test statistics are both compared with the usual F test critical value of $_{.95}F_{3,9} = 3.86$ (from Appendix Table 4), so that both tests are significant. The Geisser–Greenhouse conservative procedure is necessary for the test of factor B; here the test statistic is compared to the critical value of $_{.95}F_{1,3} = 10.13$, which is also significant. The two procedures both yield a statistically significant result, so we need not be concerned with a violation of the compound symmetry assumption for the test of B. In summary, the effects of amount of exercise undertaken and age on amount of weight lost are both statistically significant beyond the .05 level of significance.

Next we need to test the additivity assumption using Tukey's (1949) test of additivity. The sum of squares is

$$SS_N = \frac{\left[\sum_{j=1}^{J} \sum_{k=1}^{K} Y_{jk} (\bar{Y}_{j.} - \bar{Y}_{..})(\bar{Y}_{.k} - \bar{Y}_{..}) \right]^2}{\left[\sum_{j=1}^{J} (\bar{Y}_{j.} - \bar{Y}_{..})^2 \right] \left[\sum_{k=1}^{K} (\bar{Y}_{.k} - \bar{Y}_{..})^2 \right]} = \frac{(-2.5742)^2}{149.3557} = 0.0444$$

and the resultant F-test statistic is

$$F = \frac{SS_N / 1}{(SS_{res} - SS_N) / [(J-1)(K-1) - 1]} = \frac{0.0444 / 1}{(3.5625 - 0.0444) / 8} = 0.1010$$

The F-test statistic is compared with the critical value of $_{.95}F_{1,8} = 5.32$ from Appendix Table 4. The test is nonsignificant, so the model is additive and the assumption has been met.

TABLE 8.7

Data for the Exercise Example—Two-Factor Randomized Block Design:
Raw Scores on Weight Lost by Age and Exercise Program

	Exercise Program					
Age	1/week	2/week	3/week	4/week	Row Sums	Row Means
50	0	2	6	7	15	3.7500
40	1	4	7	8	20	5.0000
30	2	5	8	7	22	5.5000
20	3	6	10	9	28	7.0000
Column sums	6	17	31	31	85 (Overall sum)	
Column mean	1.5000	4.2500	7.7500	7.7500	5.3125 (Overall mean)	

In the fixed-effects model we have here, strength of association is measured by ω^2, and computed by

$$\omega^2 = \frac{SS_B - (K-1)MS_{res}}{SS_{tot} + MS_{res}} = \frac{110.1875 - (3)0.3958}{135.4375 + 0.3958} = 0.8025$$

Thus the relationship between the amount of exercise undertaken and the amount of weight lost is rather strong.

As an example of a MCP, the Tukey procedure will be used to test for the equivalence of exercising once a week ($k = 1$) and four times a week ($k = 4$), where the contrast is written as $\overline{Y}_{.4} - \overline{Y}_{.1}$. The means for these groups are 1.5000 for the once a week program and 7.7500 for the four times a week program. The standard error is

$$s_{\psi'} = \sqrt{\frac{MS_{res}}{K}} = \sqrt{\frac{0.3958}{4}} = 0.3146$$

and the studentized range statistic is

$$q = \frac{\overline{Y}_{.4} - \overline{Y}_{.1}}{s_{\psi'}} = \frac{7.7500 - 1.5000}{0.3146} = 19.8665$$

The critical value is $_{1-\alpha}q_{9,4} = 4.415$ (from Appendix Table 9). The test statistic exceeds the critical value; thus we conclude that the means for groups 1 and 4 are significantly different at the .05 level (i.e., more frequent exercise helps one to lose more weight).

THE TWO-FACTOR RANDOMIZED BLOCK DESIGN FOR $n > 1$

For two-factor randomized block designs where there is more than one observation per cell, there is little that we have not already covered. First, the characteristics are exactly the same as with the $n = 1$ model, with the obvious exception that when $n > 1$, an interaction term exists. Second, the layout of the data, the model, the ANOVA summary table, the expected mean squares, the measures of association, and the multiple-comparison procedures are the same as in the regular two-factor model. The assumptions are the same as with the $n = 1$ model, except the assumption of additivity is not necessary, because an interaction term exists. The circularity assumption is required for those tests that use MS_{AB} as the error term. That is all we really need to say about the $n > 1$ model (see chap. 5 for an example).

THE FRIEDMAN TEST

There is a nonparametric equivalent to the two-factor randomized block ANOVA model. The test was developed by Friedman (1937) and is based on ranks. For the case of $n = 1$, the procedure is precisely the same as the Friedman test in the one-factor repeated measures model (see chap. 7). For the case of $n > 1$, the procedure is slightly different. First, all of the scores within each block are ranked for that block. For instance, if there are $K = 4$ levels of factor B and $n = 10$ individuals per cell, then each block's scores would be ranked from 1 to 40. From this, one can compute a mean ranking for each level of factor B. The null hypothesis is one of testing whether the mean rankings for each of the levels of B are equal. The test statistic is computed as

$$\chi^2 = \left[\frac{12}{JKn^2(nK+1)} \sum_{k=1}^{K} \left(\sum_{i=1}^{n} \sum_{j=1}^{J} R_{ijk} \right)^2 \right] - [3J(nK+1)]$$

where R_{ijk} is the ranking for subject i in block j and level k of factor B. In the case of tied ranks, either the available ranks can be averaged, or a correction factor can be used (see chap. 3). The test statistic is compared to the critical value of $_{1-\alpha}\chi^2_{K-1}$ (see Appendix Table 3), and the null hypothesis is rejected if the test statistic exceeds the critical value. You may also recall the problem with small ns in terms of the test statistic not being precisely a χ^2. For situations where $K < 6$ and $n < 6$, consult the table of critical values in Marascuilo and McSweeney (1977, Table A-22, p. 521). The Friedman test assumes that the population distributions have the same shape (although not necessarily normal) and the same variability, and the dependent measure is continuous. For a discussion of alternative nonparametric procedures, see Wilcox (1987), and Marascuilo and McSweeney (1977).

Various multiple-comparison procedures (MCPs) can be used for the nonparametric two-factor randomized block model. For the most part these MCPs are analogs to their parametric equivalents. In the case of planned (or a priori) pairwise comparisons, one may use multiple matched-pair Wilcoxon tests in a Bonferroni form (i.e., taking the number of contrasts into account through an adjustment of the α level). Due to the nature of planned comparisons, these are more powerful than the Friedman test. For post hoc comparisons, two examples are the Tukey analog for pairwise contrasts, and the Scheffé analog for complex contrasts. For these methods, we first define a *contrast* as some combination of the group mean rankings. A contrast is equal to

$$\psi = \sum_{k=1}^{K} c_k \overline{R}_{..k}$$

The standard error of the contrast is defined as

$$se_{\psi} = \sqrt{\left[\frac{Kn(nK+1)}{12} \right] \left(\sum_{k=1}^{K} \frac{c_k^2}{Jn} \right)}$$

A test statistic is formed as $\dfrac{\psi}{se_{\psi}}$. For the Tukey analog, the test statistic is compared to the critical value of

$$T = \frac{_{\alpha}q_{k,\infty}}{\sqrt{2}}$$

where the degrees of freedom are equal to K (the number of treatment group means) and ∞ (infinity). The critical value ${}_\alpha q_{K,\infty}$ is found in Appendix Table 9. For the Scheffé analog, the test statistic is compared to the critical value of

$$S = \sqrt{{}_{1-\alpha}\chi^2_{K-1}}$$

In both cases the test statistic must exceed the critical value in order to reject the null hypothesis. For additional discussion about the use of MCPs for this model, see Marascuilo and McSweeney (1977). For an example of the Friedman test, I suggest another look at chapter 7. Finally, note that no mention has been made of MCPs for the blocking factor as they are usually of no interest to the researcher.

COMPARISON OF VARIOUS ANOVA MODELS

How do the various ANOVA models we have considered compare in terms of power and precision? Recall again that *power* is defined as the probability of rejecting H_0 when H_0 is false, and *precision* is defined as a measure of our ability to obtain a good estimate of the treatment effects. The classic literature on this topic revolves around the correlation between the dependent variable and the covariate or concomitant variable. First compare the one-factor ANOVA and one-factor ANCOVA models. If r_{xy} is not significantly different from zero, then the amount of unexplained variation will be the same in the two models, and no statistical adjustment will be made on the group means. In this situation, the ANOVA model is more powerful, as we lose one degree of freedom for each covariate used in the ANCOVA model. If r_{xy} is significantly different from zero, then the amount of unexplained variation will be smaller in the ANCOVA model as compared to the ANOVA model. Here the ANCOVA model is more powerful and is more precise as compared to the ANOVA model. According to one rule of thumb, if $r_{xy} < .2$, then ignore the covariate or concomitant variable and use the analysis of variance. Otherwise, take the concomitant variable into account somehow.

How might we take the concomitant variable into account if $r_{xy} > .2$? The two major possibilities are the analysis of covariance design (chap. 16) and the randomized block design. That is, the concomitant variable can be used either as a covariate through a statistical form of control on the dependent variable, or as a blocking factor through an experimental form of control on the dependent variable. As suggested by the classic work of Feldt (1958), if $.2 < r_{xy} < .4$, then use the concomitant variable as a blocking factor in a randomized block design as it is the most powerful and precise design. If $r_{xy} > .6$, then use the concomitant variable as a covariate in an ANCOVA design as it is the most powerful and precise design. If $.4 < r_{xy} < .6$, then the randomized block and ANCOVA designs are about equal in terms of power and precision.

However, Maxwell, Delaney, and Dill (1984) showed that the correlation between the covariate and dependent variable should not be the ultimate criterion in deciding whether to use an ANCOVA or randomized block design. These designs differ in two ways: (a) whether the concomitant variable is treated as continuous (ANCOVA) or categorical (randomized block), and (b) whether individuals are assigned to groups based on the concomitant variable (randomized blocks) or without regard to the concomitant variable (ANCOVA). Thus the Feldt (1958) comparison of these particular models is not a fair one in that the models differ in these two ways. The ANCOVA model makes full use of the information contained in the concomitant variable, whereas in the randomized block model some information is lost due to the categorization. In examining nine different models, Maxwell and colleagues suggest that r_{xy} should not be a factor in the choice of a design (given that r_{xy} is at least .3), but that two other factors be considered. The first factor is whether scores on the concomitant variable are available prior to the assignment of individuals to groups. If so, power will be increased by assigning individuals to groups based on the concomitant variable (i.e., blocking). The second factor is whether X and Y are linearly related. If so, the use of ANCOVA with a continuous concomitant variable is optimal because linearity is an assumption of the model. If not, either the concomitant variable should be used as a blocking variable, or some sort of nonlinear ANCOVA model should be used.

There are a few other decision criteria you may want to consider in choosing between the randomized block and ANCOVA designs. First, in some situations, blocking may be difficult to carry out. For instance, we may not be able to find enough homogeneous individuals to constitute a block. If the blocks formed are not relatively homogeneous, this defeats the whole purpose of blocking. Second, the interaction of the independent variable and the concomitant variable may be an important effect to study. In this case, use the randomized block design with multiple individuals per cell. If the interaction is significant, this violates the assumption of homogeneity of regression slopes in the analysis of covariance design, but does not violate any assumptions in the randomized block design. Third, it should be obvious by now that the assumptions of the ANCOVA design are much more restrictive than in the randomized block design. Thus when important assumptions are likely to be seriously violated, the randomized block design is preferable.

There are other alternative designs for incorporating the concomitant variable as a pretest, such as an analysis of variance on gain (the difference between posttest and pretest), or a mixed (split-plot) design where the pretest and posttest measures are treated as the levels of a repeated factor. Based on the research of Huck and McLean (1975) and Jennings (1988), the ANCOVA model is generally preferred over these other two models. For further discussion see Huitema (1980), Kirk (1982, p. 752), or Reichardt (1979).

SUMMARY

In this chapter, models involving nested and blocking factors for the two-factor case were considered. Three different models were examined; these included the two-factor nested design, the two-factor randomized block design with one observation per cell, and the two-factor randomized block design with multiple observations per cell. Included for each design were the usual topics of model characteristics, the layout of the data, the linear model, assumptions of the model and dealing with their violation, the ANOVA summary table and its requisite computations, expected mean squares (including the fixed-, random-, and mixed-effects cases), and multiple-comparison procedures. Also included for particular designs was a discussion of the intraclass correlation coefficient, estimation of components of variance, the homogeneity of covariance assumption, and the Friedman test based on ranks. We concluded with a comparison of various ANOVA models on precision and power. At this point you should have met the following objectives: (a) be able to understand the characteristics and concepts underlying hierarchical and randomized block ANOVA models; (b) be able to compute and interpret the results of hierarchical and randomized block ANOVA models, including measures of association and multiple comparison procedures; (c) be able to understand and evaluate the assumptions of hierarchical and randomized block ANOVA models; and (d) be able to compare different ANOVA models and select an appropriate model. This chapter concludes our extended discussion of ANOVA models, as well as our statistics course. Good luck in all of your future quantitative adventures.

PROBLEMS

Conceptual Problems

1. To study the effectiveness of three spelling methods, 45 subjects are randomly selected from the fourth graders in school X. Based on the order of their IQ scores, subjects are grouped into high, middle, and low IQ groups, 15 in each. Subjects in each group are randomly assigned to one of the three methods of spelling, 5 each. Which of the following methods of blocking is employed here?
    a. predefined value blocking
    b. predefined range blocking
    c. sampled value blocking
    d. sampled range blocking

2. If three teachers employ method A and three other teachers employ method B, then
    a. teachers are nested within method.
    b. teachers are crossed with methods.
    c. methods are nested within teacher.
    d. cannot be determined

3. The interaction of factors A and B can be assessed only if
    a. both factors are fixed.
    b. both factors are random.
    c. factor A is nested within factor B.
    d. factors A and B are crossed.

4. In a two-factor design, factor A is nested within factor B if
    a. at each level of A each level of B appears.
    b. at each level of A unique levels of B appear.
    c. at each level of B unique levels of A appear.
    d. cannot be determined

5. Five teachers use an experimental method of teaching statistics, and five other teachers use the traditional method. If factor M is method of teaching, and factor T is teacher, this design can be denoted by

    a. T(M)
    b. T×M
    c. M×T
    d. M(T)

6. If factor C is nested within factors A and B, this is denoted as AB:C. True or false?

7. A design in which all levels of each factor are found in combination with each level of every other factor is necessarily a mixed design. True or false?

8. To determine if counseling method E is uniformly superior to method C for the population of counselors, of which those in the study can be considered to be a random sample, one needs a nested design with a mixed model. True or false?

9. I assert that the predefined value method of block formation is more effective than the sampled value method in reducing unexplained variability. Am I correct?

Computational Problems

1. An experiment was conducted to compare three types of behavior modification in classrooms (1, 2, and 3) using age as a blocking variable (4-, 6-, and 8-year-old children). The mean scores on the dependent variable, number of instances of disruptive behavior, are listed here for each cell. The intention of the treatments is to minimize the number of disruptions. Use the mean for each cell to plot a graph of the interaction between type of behavior modification and age.

	Types of behavior modification		
Age	1	2	3
4	20	50	50
6	40	30	40
8	40	20	30

    a. Is there an interaction between type of behavior modification and age?
    b. What kind of recommendation would you make to teachers?

2. An experiment tested three types of perfume (or aftershave) (tame, sexy, and musk) when worn by light-haired and dark-haired women (or men). Thus hair color is a blocking variable. The dependent measure was attractiveness defined as the number of times during a 2-week period that other persons complimented a subject on their perfume (or after shave). There were five subjects in each cell. Complete the summary table, assuming a fixed-effects model, where $\alpha = .05$.

Source	SS	df	MS	F	Critical Value	Decision
Perfume (A)	200	—	—	—	—	—
Hair color (B)	100	—	—	—	—	—
Interaction (AB)	20	—	—	—	—	—
Within	240	—	—			
Total	—	—				

BIBLIOGRAPHY

Agresti, A., & Finlay, B. (1986). *Statistical methods for the social sciences* (2nd ed.). San Francisco: Dellen.

Algina, J., Blair, R. C., & Coombs, W. T. (1995). A maximum test for scale: Type I error rates and power. *Journal of Educational and Behavioral Statistics, 20,* 27–39.

Andrews, D. F. (1971). Significance tests based on residuals. *Biometrika, 58,* 139–148.

Andrews, D. F., & Pregibon, D. (1978). Finding the outliers that matter. *Journal of the Royal Statistical Society, Series B, 40,* 85–93.

Applebaum, M. I., & Cramer, E. M. (1974). Some problems in the nonorthogonal analysis of variance. *Psychological Bulletin, 81,* 335–343.

Atiqullah, M. (1964). The robustness of the covariance analysis of a one-way classification. *Biometrika, 51,* 365–373.

Atkinson, A. C. (1985). *Plots, transformations, and regression.* Oxford: Oxford University Press.

Barcikowski, R. S. (Ed.), (1983). *Computer packages & research design with annotations of input & output from the BMDP, SAS, SPSS & SPSSX statistical packages.* Lanham, MD: University Press of America.

Barnett, V., & Lewis, T. (1978). *Outliers in statistical data.* New York: Wiley.

Bates, D. M., & Watts, D. G. (1988). *Nonlinear regression analysis and its applications.* New York: Wiley.

Beal, S. L. (1987). Asymptotic confidence intervals for the difference between two binomial parameters for use with small samples. *Biometrics, 43,* 941–950.

Beckman, R., & Cook, R. D. (1983). Outliers ... s. *Technometrics,* 25, 119–149.

Belsley, D. A., Kuh, E., & Welsch, R. E. (1980). *Regression diagnostics.* New York: Wiley.

Bernhardson, C. (1975). Type I error rates when multiple comparison procedures follow a significant F test of ANOVA. *Biometrics, 31,* 229–232.

Berry, W. D., & Feldman, S. (1985). *Multiple regression in practice.* Beverly Hills, CA: Sage.

Boik, R. J. (1979). Interactions, partial interactions, and interaction contrasts in the analysis of variance. *Psychological Bulletin, 86,* 1084–1089.

Boik, R. J. (1981). A priori tests in repeated measures designs: Effects of nonsphericity. *Psychometrika, 46*, 241–255.

Box, G. E. P. (1954). Some theorems on quadratic forms applied in the study of analysis of variance problems, II: Effects of inequality of variance and of correlation between errors in the two-way classification. *Annals of Mathematical Statistics, 25*, 484–498.

Box, G. E. P., & Anderson, S. L. (1962). *Robust tests for variances and effect of non-normality and variance heterogeneity on standard tests* (Tech. Rep. No. 7). Ordinance Project No. TB 2-0001 (832), Department of Army Project No. 599-01-004.

Box, G. E. P., & Jenkins, G. M. (1976). *Time series analysis: Forecasting and control* (2nd ed.). San Francisco: Holden-Day.

Brown, M. B., & Forsythe, A. (1974). The ANOVA and multiple comparisons for data with heterogeneous variances. *Biometrics, 30*, 719–724.

Bryant, J. L., & Paulson, A. S. (1976). An extension of Tukey's method of multiple comparisons to experimental designs with random concomitant variables. *Biometrika, 63*, 631–638.

Campbell, D. T., & Stanley, J. C. (1966). *Experimental and quasi-experimental designs for research*. Chicago: Rand McNally.

Carlson, J. E., & Timm, N. H. (1974). Analysis of nonorthogonal fixed-effects designs. *Psychological Bulletin, 81*, 563–570.

Carroll, R. J., & Ruppert, D. (1982). Robust estimation in heteroscedastic linear models. *Annals of Statistics, 10*, 429–441.

Chambers, J. M., Cleveland, W. S., Kleiner, B., & Tukey, P. A. (1983). *Graphical methods for data analysis*. Belmont, CA: Wadsworth.

Chatterjee, S., & Price, B. (1977). *Regression analysis by example*. New York: Wiley.

Cleveland, W. S. (1993). *Elements of graphing data*. New York: Chapman & Hall.

Cody, R. P., & Smith, J. K. (1997). *Applied statistics and the SAS programming language*. Paramus, NJ: Prentice Hall.

Coe, P. R., & Tamhane, A. C. (1993). Small sample confidence intervals for the difference, ratio and odds ratio of two success probabilities. *Communications in Statistics—Simulation and Computation, 22*, 925–938.

Cohen, J. (1988). *Statistical power analysis for the behavioral sciences* (2nd ed.). Hillsdale, NJ: Lawrence Erlbaum Associates.

Cohen, J., & Cohen, P. (1983). *Applied multiple regression/correlation analysis for the behavioral sciences* (2nd ed.). Hillsdale, NJ: Lawrence Erlbaum Associates.

Conover, W., & Iman, R. (1981). Rank transformations as a bridge between parametric and nonparametric statistics. *The American Statistician, 35*, 124–129.

Conover, W., & Iman, R. (1982). Analysis of covariance using the rank transformation. *Biometrics, 38*, 715–724.

Cook, R. D. (1977). Detection of influential observations in linear regression. *Technometrics, 19*, 15–18.

Cook, R. D., & Weisberg, S. (1982). *Residuals and influence in regression*. London: Chapman and Hall.

Cook, T. D., & Campbell, D. T. (1979). *Quasi-experimentation: Design and analysis issues for field settings*. Chicago: Rand McNally.

Cramer, E. M., & Applebaum, M. I. (1980). Nonorthogonal analysis of variance—Once again. *Psychological Bulletin, 87*, 51–57.

D'Agostino, R. B. (1971). An omnibus test of normality for moderate and large size samples. *Biometrika, 58*, 341–348.

Duncan, D. B. (1955). Multiple range and multiple F tests. *Biometrics, 11*, 1–42.

Dunn, O. J. (1961). Multiple comparisons among means. *Journal of the American Statistical Association, 56*, 52–64.

Dunn, O. J. (1974). On multiple tests and confidence intervals. *Communications in Statistics, 3*, 101–103.

Dunn, O. J., & Clark, V. A. (1987). *Analysis of variance and regression* (2nd ed.). New York: Wiley.

Dunnett, C. W. (1955). A multiple comparison procedure for comparing several treatments with a control. *Journal of the American Statistical Association, 50*, 1096–1121.

Dunnett, C. W. (1964). New tables for multiple comparisons with a control. *Biometrics, 20*, 482–491.

Dunnett, C. W. (1980). Pairwise multiple comparisons in the unequal variance case. *Journal of the American Statistical Association, 75*, 796–800.

Durbin, J., & Watson, G. S. (1950). Testing for serial correlation in least squares regression, I. *Biometrika, 37*, 409–428.

Durbin, J., & Watson, G. S. (1951). Testing for serial correlation in least squares regression, II. *Biometrika, 38*, 159–178.

Durbin, J., & Watson, G. S. (1971). Testing for serial correlation in least squares regression, III. *Biometrika, 58*, 1–19.

Elashoff, J. D. (1969). Analysis of covariance: A delicate instrument. *American Educational Research Journal, 6*, 383–401.

Feldt, L. S. (1958). A comparison of the precision of three experimental designs employing a concomitant variable. *Psychometrika, 23*, 335–354.

Ferguson, G. A., & Takane, Y. (1989). *Statistical analysis in psychology and education* (6th ed.). New York: McGraw-Hill.

Fink, A. (1995). *How to sample in surveys*. Thousand Oaks, CA: Sage.

Fisher, R. A. (1949). *The design of experiments*. Edinburgh: Oliver & Boyd.

Friedman, M. (1937). The use of ranks to avoid the assumption of normality implicit in the analysis of variance. *Journal of the American Statistical Association, 32*, 675–701.

Games, P. A. (1971). Multiple comparisons of means. *American Educational Research Journal, 8*, 531–565.

Games, P. A., & Howell, J. F. (1976). Pairwise multiple comparison procedures with unequal n's and/or variances: A Monte Carlo study. *Journal of Educational Statistics, 1*, 113–125.

Geisser, S., & Greenhouse, S. (1958). Extension of Box's results on the use of the F distribution in multivariate analysis. *Annals of Mathematical Statistics, 29*, 855–891.

Ghosh, B. K. (1979). A comparison of some approximate confidence intervals for the binomial parameter. *Journal of the American Statistical Association, 74*, 894–900.

Glass, G. V, & Hopkins, K. D. (1996). *Statistical methods in education and psychology* (3rd ed.). Boston: Allyn & Bacon.

Glass, G. V, Peckham, P. D., & Sanders, J. R. (1972). Consequences of failure to meet assumptions underlying the fixed effects analyses of variance and covariance. *Review of Educational Research, 42*, 237–288.

Hartley, H. O. (1955). Some recent developments in analysis of variance. *Communications in Pure and Applied Mathematics, 8*, 47–72.

Hawkins, D. M. (1980). *Identification of outliers*. London: Chapman and Hall.

Hochberg, Y., & Tamhane, A. C. (1987). *Multiple comparison procedures*. New York: Wiley.

Hochberg, Y., & Varon-Salomon, Y. (1984). On simultaneous pairwise comparisons in analysis of covariance. *Journal of the American Statistical Association, 79*, 863–866.

Hocking, R. R. (1976). The analysis and selection of variables in linear regression. *Biometrics, 32*, 1–49.

Hoerl, A. E., & Kennard, R. W. (1970a). Ridge regression: Biased estimation for non-orthogonal models. *Technometrics, 12*, 55–67.

Hoerl, A. E., & Kennard, R. W. (1970b). Ridge regression: Application to non-orthogonal models. *Technometrics, 12*, 591–612.

Hogg, R. V., & Craig, A. T. (1970). *Introduction to mathematical statistics*. New York: Macmillan.

Huck, S. W., & McLean, R. A. (1975). Using a repeated measures ANOVA to analyze data from a pretest-posttest design: A potentially confusing task. *Psychological Bulletin, 82*, 511–518.

Huitema, B. E. (1980). *The analysis of covariance and alternatives*. New York: Wiley.

Huynh, H., & Feldt, L. S. (1970). Conditions under which mean square ratios in repeated measurement designs have exact F-distributions. *Journal of the American Statistical Association, 65*, 1582–1589.

Jaeger, R. M. (1984). *Sampling in education and the social sciences*. New York: Longman.

Jennings, E. (1988). Models for pretest-posttest data: Repeated measures ANOVA revisited. *Journal of Educational Statistics, 13*, 273–280.

Johnson, P. O., & Neyman, J. (1936). Tests of certain linear hypotheses and their application to some educational problems. *Statistical Research Memoirs, 1*, 57–93.

Kaiser, L., & Bowden, D. (1983). Simultaneous confidence intervals for all linear contrasts of means with heterogeneous variances. *Communications in Statistics—Theory and Methods, 12*, 73–88.

Keppel, G. (1982). *Design and analysis: A researcher's handbook* (2nd ed.). Englewood Cliffs, NJ: Prentice Hall.

Keppel, G., & Zedeck, S. (1989). *Data analysis for research designs: Analysis of variance and multiple regression/correlation approaches*. New York: Freeman.

Keuls, M. (1952). The use of studentized range in connection with an analysis of variance. *Euphytica, 1*, 112–122.

Kirk, R. E. (1982). *Experimental design: Procedures for the behavioral sciences* (2nd ed.). Monterey, CA: Brooks/Cole.

Kleinbaum, D. G., Kupper, L. L., Muller, K. E., & Nizam, A. (1998). *Applied regression analysis and other multivariable methods* (3rd ed.). Pacific Grove, CA: Duxbury.

Kramer, C. Y. (1956). Extension of multiple range test to group means with unequal numbers of replications. *Biometrics, 12*, 307–310.

Kruskal, W. H., & Wallis, W. A. (1952). Use of ranks on one-criterion variance analysis. *Journal of the American Statistical Association, 47*, 583–621. (with corrections in *48*, 907–911)

Lamb, G. S. (1984). What you always wanted to know about six but were afraid to ask. *The Journal of Irreproducible Results, 29*, 18–20.

Larsen, W. A., & McCleary, S. J. (1972). The use of partial residual plots in regression analysis. *Technometrics, 14*, 781–790.

Levine, G. (1991). *A guide to SPSS for analysis of variance*. Hillsdale, NJ: Lawrence Erlbaum Associates.

Lord, F. M. (1960). Large-sample covariance analysis when the control variable is fallible. *Journal of the American Statistical Association, 55*, 307–321.

Lord, F. M. (1967). A paradox in the interpretation of group comparisons. *Psychological Bulletin, 68*, 304–305.

Lord, F. M. (1969). Statistical adjustments when comparing preexisting groups. *Psychological Bulletin, 72*, 336–337.

Mallows, C. L. (1973). Some comments on C_p. *Technometrics, 15*, 661–675.

Mansfield, E. R., & Conerly, M. D. (1987). Diagnostic value of residual and partial residual plots. *The American Statistician, 41*, 107–116.

Marascuilo, L. A., & Levin, J. R. (1970). Appropriate post hoc comparisons for interactions and nested hypotheses in analysis of variance designs: The elimination of type IV errors. *American Educational Research Journal, 7*, 397–421.

Marascuilo, L. A., & Levin, J. R. (1976). The simultaneous investigation of interaction and nested hypotheses in two-factor analysis of variance designs. *American Educational Research Journal, 13*, 61–65.

Marascuilo, L. A., & McSweeney, M. (1977). *Nonparametric and distribution-free methods for the social sciences*. Monterey, CA: Brooks/Cole.

Marascuilo, L. A., & Serlin, R. C. (1988). *Statistical methods for the social and behavioral sciences*. New York: Freeman.

Marquardt, D. W., & Snee, R. D. (1975). Ridge regression in practice. *The American Statistician, 29*, 3–19.

Maxwell, S. E. (1980). Pairwise multiple comparisons in repeated measures designs. *Journal of Educational Statistics, 5*, 269–287.

Maxwell, S. E., & Delaney, H. D. (1990). *Designing experiments and analyzing data: A model comparison perspective*. Belmont, CA: Wadsworth.

Maxwell, S. E., Delaney, H. D., & Dill, C. A. (1984). Another look at ANOVA versus blocking. *Psychological Bulletin, 95*, 136–147.

Miller, A. J. (1990). *Subset selection in regression*. New York: Chapman and Hall.

Miller, R. G. (1997). *Beyond ANOVA, basics of applied statistics*. Boca Raton, FL: CRC Press.

Myers, J. L., & Well, A. D. (1995). *Research design and statistical analysis*. Hillsdale, NJ: Lawrence Erlbaum Associates.

Myers, R. H. (1979). *Fundamentals of experimental design* (3rd ed.). Boston: Allyn and Bacon.

Myers, R. H. (1986). *Classical and modern regression with applications*. Boston: Duxbury.

Newman, D. (1939). The distribution of the range in samples from a normal population, expressed in terms of an independent estimate of standard deviation. *Biometrika, 31*, 20–30.

Noreen, E. W. (1989). *Computer intensive methods for testing hypotheses*. New York: Wiley.

O'Grady, K. E. (1982). Measures of explained variance: Cautions and limitations. *Psychological Bulletin, 92*, 766–777.

Olejnik, S. F., & Algina, J. (1987). Type I error rates and power estimates of selected parametric and nonparametric tests of scale. *Journal of Educational Statistics, 21*, 45–61.

Overall, J. E., Lee, D. M., & Hornick, C. W. (1981). Comparison of two strategies for analysis of variance in nonorthogonal designs. *Psychological Bulletin, 90*, 367–375.

Overall, J. E., & Spiegel, D. K. (1969). Concerning least squares analysis of experimental data. *Psychological Bulletin, 72*, 311–322.

Pavur, R. (1988). Type I error rates for multiple comparison procedures with dependent data. *American Statistician, 42*, 171–173.

Pearson, E. S. (Ed.). (1978). *The history of statistics in the 17th and 18th centuries.* New York: Macmillan.

Peckham, P. D. (1968). *An investigation of the effects of non-homogeneity of regression slopes upon the F-test of analysis of covariance* (Rep. No. 16). Boulder, CO: Laboratory of Educational Research, University of Colorado.

Pedhazur, E. J. (1997). *Multiple regression in behavioral research* (3rd ed.). Fort Worth: Harcourt Brace.

Pingel, L. A. (1969). *A comparison of the effects of two methods of block formation on design precision.* Paper presented at the annual meeting of the American Educational Research Association, Los Angeles.

Porter, A. C. (1967). *The effects of using fallible variables in the analysis of covariance.* Unpublished doctoral dissertation, University of Wisconsin, Madison.

Porter, A. C., & Raudenbush, S. W. (1987). Analysis of covariance: Its model and use in psychological research. *Journal of Counseling Psychology, 34*, 383–392.

Puri, M. L., & Sen, P. K. (1969). Analysis of covariance based on general rank scores. *Annals of Mathematical Statistics, 40*, 610–618.

Quade, D. (1967). Rank analysis of covariance. *Journal of the American Statistical Association, 62*, 1187–1200.

Ramsey, P. H. (1981). Power of univariate pairwise multiple comparison procedures. *Psychological Bulletin, 90*, 352–366.

Ramsey, P. H. (1989). Critical values of Spearman's rank order correlation. *Journal of Educational Statistics, 14*, 245–253.

Ramsey, P. H. (1994). Testing variances in psychological and educational research. *Journal of Educational Statistics, 19*, 23–42.

Reichardt, C. S. (1979). The statistical analysis of data from nonequivalent control group designs. In T. D. Cook & D. T. Campbell (Eds.), *Quasi-experimentation: Design and analysis issues for field settings* (pp. 147–205). Chicago: Rand McNally.

Rogosa, D. R. (1980). Comparing non-parallel regression lines. *Psychological Bulletin, 88*, 307–321.

Rosenthal, R., & Rosnow, R. L. (1985). *Contrast analysis: Focused comparisons in the analysis of variance.* Cambridge: Cambridge University Press.

Rousseeuw, P. J., & Leroy, A. M. (1987). *Robust regression and outlier detection.* New York: Wiley.

Ruppert, D., & Carroll, R. J. (1980). Trimmed least squares estimation in the linear model. *Journal of the American Statistical Association, 75*, 828–838.

Sawilowsky, S. S., & Blair, R. C. (1992). A more realistic look at the robustness and type II error properties of the t-test to departures from population normality. *Psychological Bulletin, 111*, 352–360.

Scariano, S. M., & Davenport, J. M. (1987). The effects of violations of independence assumptions in the one-way ANOVA. *The American Statistician, 41*, 123–129.

Scheffé, H. (1953). A method for judging all contrasts in the analysis of variance. *Biometrika, 40*, 87–104.

Schmid, C. F. (1983). *Statistical graphics: Design principles and practices.* New York: Wiley.

Seber, G. A. F., & Wild, C. J. (1989). *Nonlinear regression.* New York: Wiley.

Shapiro, S. S., & Wilk, M. B. (1965). An analysis of variance test for normality (complete samples). *Biometrika, 52*, 591–611.

Shavelson, R. J. (1988). *Statistical reasoning for the behavioral sciences* (2nd ed.). Boston: Allyn and Bacon.

Sidak, Z. (1967). Rectangular confidence regions for the means of multivariate normal distributions. *Journal of the American Statistical Association, 62*, 626–633.

Spjotvoll, E., & Stoline, M. R. (1973). An extension of the T-method of multiple comparisons to include the case with unequal sample sizes. *Journal of the American Statistical Association, 68*, 975–978.

Stigler, S. M. (1986). *The history of statistics: The measurement of uncertainty before 1900.* Cambridge, MA: Harvard.

Storer, B. E., & Kim, C. (1990). Exact properties of some exact test statistics for comparing two binomial proportions. *Journal of the American Statistical Association, 85*, 146–155.

Sudman, S. (1976). *Applied sampling.* New York: Academic Press.

Tabatabai, M., & Tan, W. (1985). Some comparative studies on testing parallelism of several straight lines under heteroscedastic variances. *Communications in Statistics—Simulation and Computation, 14*, 837–844.

Tamhane, A. C. (1979). A comparison of procedures for multiple comparisons of means with unequal variances. *Journal of the American Statistical Association, 74*, 471–480.

Thompson, M. L. (1978). Selection of variables in multiple regression. Part I: A review and evaluation. Part II: Chosen procedures, computations and examples. *International Statistical Review, 46*, 1–19, 129–146.

Tiku, M. L., & Singh, M. (1981). Robust test for means when population variances are unequal. *Communications in Statistics—Theory and Methods, A10*, 2057–2071.

Timm, N. H., & Carlson, J. E. (1975). Analysis of variance through full rank models. *Multivariate Behavioral Research Monographs, 75–1*.

Tufte, E. R. (1992). *The visual display of quantitative information.* Cheshire, CT: Graphics Press.

Tukey, J. W. (1949). One degree of freedom for nonadditivity. *Biometrics, 5*, 232–242.

Tukey, J. W. (1953). *The problem of multiple comparisons.* Princeton, NJ: Princeton University.

Tukey, J. W. (1977). *Exploratory data analysis.* Reading, MA: Addison-Wesley.

Wainer, H. (1984). How to display data badly. *The American Statistician, 38*, 137–147.

Wainer, H. (1992). Understanding graphs and tables. *Educational Researcher, 21*, 14–23.

Wallgren, A., Wallgren, B., Persson, R., Jorner, U., & Haaland, J. A. (1996). *Graphing statistics & data.* Thousand Oaks, CA: Sage.

Weisberg, H. I. (1979). Statistical adjustments and uncontrolled studies. *Psychological Bulletin, 86*, 1149–1164.

Weisberg, S. (1985). *Applied linear regression* (2nd ed.). New York: Wiley.

Wetherill, G. B. (1986). *Regression analysis with applications.* London: Chapman and Hall.

Wilcox, R. R. (1987). *New statistical procedures for the social sciences: Modern solutions to basic problems.* Hillsdale, NJ: Lawrence Erlbaum Associates.

Wilcox, R. R. (1993). Comparing one-step M-estimators of location when there are more than two groups. *Psychometrika, 58*, 71–78.

Wilcox, R. R. (1996). *Statistics for the social sciences.* San Diego: Academic Press.

Wittink, D. R. (1988). *The application of regression analysis.* Boston: Allyn and Bacon.

Wonnacott, T. H., & Wonnacott, R. J. (1981). *Regression: A second course in statistics.* New
    York: Wiley.

Wu, L. L. (1985). Robust M-estimation of location and regression. In N. B. Tuma (Ed.), *Socio-
    logical methodology, 1985* (pp. 316–388). San Francisco: Jossey-Bass.

Yu, M. C., & Dunn, O. J. (1982). Robust tests for the equality of two correlation coefficients: A
    monte carlo study. *Educational and Psychological Measurement, 42*, 987–1004.

Appendix Tables

Standard Unit Normal Distribution

z	P(z)	z	P(z)	z	P(z)	z	P(z)
·00	·5000000	·50	·6914625	1·00	·8413447	1·50	·9331928
·01	·5039694	·51	·6949743	1·01	·8437524	1·51	·9344783
·02	·5079783	·52	·6984682	1·02	·8461358	1·52	·9357445
·03	·5119665	·53	·7019440	1·03	·8484950	1·53	·9369916
·04	·5159534	·54	·7054015	1·04	·8508300	1·54	·9382198
·05	·5199388	·55	·7088403	1·05	·8531409	1·55	·9394292
·06	·5239222	·56	·7122603	1·06	·8554277	1·56	·9406201
·07	·5279032	·57	·7156612	1·07	·8576903	1·57	·9417924
·08	·5318814	·58	·7190427	1·08	·8599289	1·58	·9429466
·09	·5358564	·59	·7224047	1·09	·8621434	1·59	·9440826
·10	·5398278	·60	·7257469	1·10	·8643339	1·60	·9452007
·11	·5437953	·61	·7290691	1·11	·8665005	1·61	·9463011
·12	·5477584	·62	·7323711	1·12	·8686431	1·62	·9473839
·13	·5517168	·63	·7356527	1·13	·8707619	1·63	·9484493
·14	·5556700	·64	·7389137	1·14	·8728568	1·64	·9494974
·15	·5596177	·65	·7421539	1·15	·8749281	1·65	·9505285
·16	·5635595	·66	·7453731	1·16	·8769756	1·66	·9515428
·17	·5674949	·67	·7485711	1·17	·8789995	1·67	·9525403
·18	·5714237	·68	·7517478	1·18	·8809999	1·68	·9535213
·19	·5753454	·69	·7549029	1·19	·8829768	1·69	·9544860
·20	·5792597	·70	·7580363	1·20	·8849303	1·70	·9554345
·21	·5831662	·71	·7611479	1·21	·8868606	1·71	·9563671
·22	·5870644	·72	·7642375	1·22	·8887676	1·72	·9572838
·23	·5909541	·73	·7673049	1·23	·8906514	1·73	·9581849
·24	·5948349	·74	·7703500	1·24	·8925123	1·74	·9590705
·25	·5987063	·75	·7733726	1·25	·8943502	1·75	·9599408
·26	·6025681	·76	·7763727	1·26	·8961653	1·76	·9607961
·27	·6064199	·77	·7793501	1·27	·8979577	1·77	·9616364
·28	·6102612	·78	·7823046	1·28	·8997274	1·78	·9624620
·29	·6140919	·79	·7852361	1·29	·9014747	1·79	·9632730
·30	·6179114	·80	·7881446	1·30	·9031995	1·80	·9640697
·31	·6217195	·81	·7910299	1·31	·9049021	1·81	·9648521
·32	·6255158	·82	·7938919	1·32	·9065825	1·82	·9656205
·33	·6293000	·83	·7967306	1·33	·9082409	1·83	·9663750
·34	·6330717	·84	·7995458	1·34	·9098773	1·84	·9671159
·35	·6368307	·85	·8023375	1·35	·9114920	1·85	·9678432
·36	·6405764	·86	·8051055	1·36	·9130850	1·86	·9685572
·37	·6443088	·87	·8078498	1·37	·9146565	1·87	·9692581
·38	·6480273	·88	·8105703	1·38	·9162067	1·88	·9699460
·39	·6517317	·89	·8132671	1·39	·9177356	1·89	·9706210
·40	·6554217	·90	·8159399	1·40	·9192433	1·90	·9712834
·41	·6590970	·91	·8185887	1·41	·9207302	1·91	·9719334
·42	·6627573	·92	·8212136	1·42	·9221962	1·92	·9725711
·43	·6664042	·93	·8238145	1·43	·9236415	1·93	·9731966
·44	·6700314	·94	·8263912	1·44	·9250663	1·94	·9738102
·45	·6736448	·95	·8289439	1·45	·9264707	1·95	·9744119
·46	·6772419	·96	·8314724	1·46	·9278550	1·96	·9750021
·47	·6808225	·97	·8339768	1·47	·9292191	1·97	·9755808
·48	·6843863	·98	·8364569	1·48	·9305634	1·98	·9761482
·49	·6879331	·99	·8389129	1·49	·9318879	1·99	·9767045
·50	·6914625	1·00	·8413447	1·50	·9331928	2·00	·9772499

P(z) represents the area below that value of z.

(continued)

The Standard Unit Normal Distribution

z	P(z)	z	P(z)	z	P(z)	z	P(z)
2·00	·9772499	2·50	·9937903	3·00	·9986501	3·50	·9997674
2·01	·9777844	2·51	·9939634	3·01	·9986938	3·51	·9997759
2·02	·9783083	2·52	·9941323	3·02	·9987361	3·52	·9997842
2·03	·9788217	2·53	·9942969	3·03	·9987772	3·53	·9997922
2·04	·9793248	2·54	·9944574	3·04	·9988171	3·54	·9997999
2·05	·9798178	2·55	·9946139	3·05	·9988558	3·55	·9998074
2·06	·9803007	2·56	·9947664	3·06	·9988933	3·56	·9998146
2·07	·9807738	2·57	·9949151	3·07	·9989297	3·57	·9998215
2·08	·9812372	2·58	·9950600	3·08	·9989650	3·58	·9998282
2·09	·9816911	2·59	·9952012	3·09	·9989992	3·59	·9998347
2·10	·9821356	2·60	·9953388	3·10	·9990324	3·60	·9998409
2·11	·9825708	2·61	·9954729	3·11	·9990646	3·61	·9998469
2·12	·9829970	2·62	·9956035	3·12	·9990957	3·62	·9998527
2·13	·9834142	2·63	·9957308	3·13	·9991260	3·63	·9998583
2·14	·9838226	2·64	·9958547	3·14	·9991553	3·64	·9998637
2·15	·9842224	2·65	·9959754	3·15	·9991836	3·65	·9998689
2·16	·9846137	2·66	·9960930	3·16	·9992112	3·66	·9998739
2·17	·9849966	2·67	·9962074	3·17	·9992378	3·67	·9998787
2·18	·9853713	2·68	·9963189	3·18	·9992636	3·68	·9998834
2·19	·9857379	2·69	·9964274	3·19	·9992886	3·69	·9998879
2·20	·9860966	2·70	·9965330	3·20	·9993129	3·70	·9998922
2·21	·9864474	2·71	·9966358	3·21	·9993363	3·71	·9998964
2·22	·9867906	2·72	·9967359	3·22	·9993590	3·72	·9999004
2·23	·9871263	2·73	·9968333	3·23	·9993810	3·73	·9999043
2·24	·9874545	2·74	·9969280	3·24	·9994024	3·74	·9999080
2·25	·9877755	2·75	·9970202	3·25	·9994230	3·75	·9999116
2·26	·9880894	2·76	·9971099	3·26	·9994429	3·76	·9999150
2·27	·9883962	2·77	·9971972	3·27	·9994623	3·77	·9999184
2·28	·9886962	2·78	·9972821	3·28	·9994810	3·78	·9999216
2·29	·9889893	2·79	·9973646	3·29	·9994991	3·79	·9999247
2·30	·9892759	2·80	·9974449	3·30	·9995166	3·80	·9999277
2·31	·9895559	2·81	·9975229	3·31	·9995335	3·81	·9999305
2·32	·9898296	2·82	·9975988	3·32	·9995499	3·82	·9999333
2·33	·9900969	2·83	·9976726	3·33	·9995658	3·83	·9999359
2·34	·9903581	2·84	·9977443	3·34	·9995811	3·84	·9999385
2·35	·9906133	2·85	·9978140	3·35	·9995959	3·85	·9999409
2·36	·9908625	2·86	·9978818	3·36	·9996103	3·86	·9999433
2·37	·9911060	2·87	·9979476	3·37	·9996242	3·87	·9999456
2·38	·9913437	2·88	·9980116	3·38	·9996376	3·88	·9999478
2·39	·9915758	2·89	·9980738	3·39	·9996505	3·89	·9999499
2·40	·9918025	2·90	·9981342	3·40	·9996631	3·90	·9999519
2·41	·9920237	2·91	·9981929	3·41	·9996752	3·91	·9999539
2·42	·9922397	2·92	·9982498	3·42	·9996869	3·92	·9999557
2·43	·9924506	2·93	·9983052	3·43	·9996982	3·93	·9999575
2·44	·9926564	2·94	·9983589	3·44	·9997091	3·94	·9999593
2·45	·9928572	2·95	·9984111	3·45	·9997197	3·95	·9999609
2·46	·9930531	2·96	·9984618	3·46	·9997299	3·96	·9999625
2·47	·9932443	2·97	·9985110	3·47	·9997398	3·97	·9999641
2·48	·9934309	2·98	·9985588	3·48	·9997493	3·98	·9999655
2·49	·9936128	2·99	·9986051	3·49	·9997585	3·99	·9999670
2·50	·9937903	3·00	·9986501	3·50	·9997674	4·00	·9999683

Percentage Points of the t Distribution

ν	$\alpha_1 = .10$ $\alpha_2 = .20$	.05 .10	.025 .050	.01 .02	.005 .010	.0025 .0050	.001 .002	.0005 .0010
1	3·078	6·314	12·706	31·821	63·657	127·32	318·31	636·62
2	1·886	2·920	4·303	6·965	9·925	14·089	22·327	31·598
3	1·638	2·353	3·182	4·541	5·841	7·453	10·214	12·924
4	1·533	2·132	2·776	3·747	4·604	5·598	7·173	8·610
5	1·476	2·015	2·571	3·365	4·032	4·773	5·893	6·869
6	1·440	1·943	2·447	3·143	3·707	4·317	5·208	5·959
7	1·415	1·895	2·365	2·998	3·499	4·029	4·785	5·408
8	1·397	1·860	2·306	2·896	3·355	3·833	4·501	5·041
9	1·383	1·833	2·262	2·821	3·250	3·690	4·297	4·781
10	1·372	1·812	2·228	2·764	3·169	3·581	4·144	4·587
11	1·363	1·796	2·201	2·718	3·106	3·497	4·025	4·437
12	1·356	1·782	2·179	2·681	3·055	3·428	3·930	4·318
13	1·350	1·771	2·160	2·650	3·012	3·372	3·852	4·221
14	1·345	1·761	2·145	2·624	2·977	3·326	3·787	4·140
15	1·341	1·753	2·131	2·602	2·947	3·286	3·733	4·073
16	1·337	1·746	2·120	2·583	2·921	3·252	3·686	4·015
17	1·333	1·740	2·110	2·567	2·898	3·222	3·646	3·965
18	1·330	1·734	2·101	2·552	2·878	3·197	3·610	3·922
19	1·328	1·729	2·093	2·539	2·861	3·174	3·579	3·883
20	1·325	1·725	2·086	2·528	2·845	3·153	3·552	3·850
21	1·323	1·721	2·080	2·518	2·831	3·135	3·527	3·819
22	1·321	1·717	2·074	2·508	2·819	3·119	3·505	3·792
23	1·319	1·714	2·069	2·500	2·807	3·104	3·485	3·767
24	1·318	1·711	2·064	2·492	2·797	3·091	3·467	3·745
25	1·316	1·708	2·060	2·485	2·787	3·078	3·450	3·725
26	1·315	1·706	2·056	2·479	2·779	3·067	3·435	3·707
27	1·314	1·703	2·052	2·473	2·771	3·057	3·421	3·690
28	1·313	1·701	2·048	2·467	2·763	3·047	3·408	3·674
29	1·311	1·699	2·045	2·462	2·756	3·038	3·396	3·659
30	1·310	1·697	2·042	2·457	2·750	3·030	3·385	3·646
40	1·303	1·684	2·021	2·423	2·704	2·971	3·307	3·551
60	1·296	1·671	2·000	2·390	2·660	2·915	3·232	3·460
120	1·289	1·658	1·980	2·358	2·617	2·860	3·160	3·373
∞	1·282	1·645	1·960	2·326	2·576	2·807	3·090	3·291

α_1 is the upper-tail value of the distribution with ν degrees of freedom, appropriate for use in a one-tailed test; use α_2 for a two-tailed test.

Percentage Points of the χ^2 Distribution

α ν	0·990	0·975	0·950	0·900	0·100	0·050	0·025	0·010
1	157088.10⁻⁹	982069.10⁻⁹	393214.10⁻⁸	0·0157908	2·70554	3·84146	5·02389	6·63490
2	0·0201007	0·0506356	0·102587	0·210721	4·60517	5·99146	7·37776	9·21034
3	0·114832	0·215795	0·351846	0·584374	6·25139	7·81473	9·34840	11·3449
4	0·297109	0·484419	0·710723	1·063623	7·77944	9·48773	11·1433	13·2767
5	0·554298	0·831212	1·145476	1·61031	9·23636	11·0705	12·8325	15·0863
6	0·872090	1·23734	1·63538	2·20413	10·6446	12·5916	14·4494	16·8119
7	1·239043	1·68987	2·16735	2·83311	12·0170	14·0671	16·0128	18·4753
8	1·64650	2·17973	2·73264	3·48954	13·3616	15·5073	17·5345	20·0902
9	2·08790	2·70039	3·32511	4·16816	14·6837	16·9190	19·0228	21·6660
10	2·55821	3·24697	3·94030	4·86518	15·9872	18·3070	20·4832	23·2093
11	3·05348	3·81575	4·57481	5·57778	17·2750	19·6751	21·9200	24·7250
12	3·57057	4·40379	5·22603	6·30380	18·5493	21·0261	23·3367	26·2170
13	4·10692	5·00875	5·89186	7·04150	19·8119	22·3620	24·7356	27·6882
14	4·66043	5·62873	6·57063	7·78953	21·0641	23·6848	26·1189	29·1412
15	5·22935	6·26214	7·26094	8·54676	22·3071	24·9958	27·4884	30·5779
16	5·81221	6·90766	7·96165	9·31224	23·5418	26·2962	28·8454	31·9999
17	6·40776	7·56419	8·67176	10·0852	24·7690	27·5871	30·1910	33·4087
18	7·01491	8·23075	9·39046	10·8649	25·9894	28·8693	31·5264	34·8053
19	7·63273	8·90652	10·1170	11·6509	27·2036	30·1435	32·8523	36·1909
20	8·26040	9·59078	10·8508	12·4426	28·4120	31·4104	34·1696	37·5662
21	8·89720	10·28293	11·5913	13·2396	29·6151	32·6706	35·4789	38·9322
22	9·54249	10·9823	12·3380	14·0415	30·8133	33·9244	36·7807	40·2894
23	10·19567	11·6886	13·0905	14·8480	32·0069	35·1725	38·0756	41·6384
24	10·8564	12·4012	13·8484	15·6587	33·1962	36·4150	39·3641	42·9798
25	11·5240	13·1197	14·6114	16·4734	34·3816	37·6525	40·6465	44·3141
26	12·1981	13·8439	15·3792	17·2919	35·5632	38·8851	41·9232	45·6417
27	12·8785	14·5734	16·1514	18·1139	36·7412	40·1133	43·1945	46·9629
28	13·5647	15·3079	16·9279	18·9392	37·9159	41·3371	44·4608	48·2782
29	14·2565	16·0471	17·7084	19·7677	39·0875	42·5570	45·7223	49·5879
30	14·9535	16·7908	18·4927	20·5992	40·2560	43·7730	46·9792	50·8922
40	22·1643	24·4330	26·5093	29·0505	51·8051	55·7585	59·3417	63·6907
50	29·7067	32·3574	34·7643	37·6886	63·1671	67·5048	71·4202	76·1539
60	37·4849	40·4817	43·1880	46·4589	74·3970	79·0819	83·2977	88·3794
70	45·4417	48·7576	51·7393	55·3289	85·5270	90·5312	95·0232	100·425
80	53·5401	57·1532	60·3915	64·2778	96·5782	101·879	106·629	112·329
90	61·7541	65·6466	69·1260	73·2911	107·565	113·145	118·136	124·116
100	70·0649	74·2219	77·9295	82·3581	118·498	124·342	129·561	135·807

APPENDIX TABLE 4

Percentage Points of the F Distribution $\alpha = .10$

v_2 \ v_1	1	2	3	4	5	6	7	8	9	10	12	15	20	24	30	40	60	120	∞
1	39·86	49·50	53·59	55·83	57·24	58·20	58·91	59·44	59·86	60·19	60·71	61·22	61·74	62·00	62·26	62·53	62·79	63·06	63·33
2	8·53	9·00	9·16	9·24	9·29	9·33	9·35	9·37	9·38	9·39	9·41	9·42	9·44	9·45	9·46	9·47	9·47	9·48	9·49
3	5·54	5·46	5·39	5·34	5·31	5·28	5·27	5·25	5·24	5·23	5·22	5·20	5·18	5·18	5·17	5·16	5·15	5·14	5·13
4	4·54	4·32	4·19	4·11	4·05	4·01	3·98	3·95	3·94	3·92	3·90	3·87	3·84	3·83	3·82	3·80	3·79	3·78	3·76
5	4·06	3·78	3·62	3·52	3·45	3·40	3·37	3·34	3·32	3·30	3·27	3·24	3·21	3·19	3·17	3·16	3·14	3·12	3·10
6	3·78	3·46	3·29	3·18	3·11	3·05	3·01	2·98	2·96	2·94	2·90	2·87	2·84	2·82	2·80	2·78	2·76	2·74	2·72
7	3·59	3·26	3·07	2·96	2·88	2·83	2·78	2·75	2·72	2·70	2·67	2·63	2·59	2·58	2·56	2·54	2·51	2·49	2·47
8	3·46	3·11	2·92	2·81	2·73	2·67	2·62	2·59	2·56	2·54	2·50	2·46	2·42	2·40	2·38	2·36	2·34	2·32	2·29
9	3·36	3·01	2·81	2·69	2·61	2·55	2·51	2·47	2·44	2·42	2·38	2·34	2·30	2·28	2·25	2·23	2·21	2·18	2·16
10	3·29	2·92	2·73	2·61	2·52	2·46	2·41	2·38	2·35	2·32	2·28	2·24	2·20	2·18	2·16	2·13	2·11	2·08	2·06
11	3·23	2·86	2·66	2·54	2·45	2·39	2·34	2·30	2·27	2·25	2·21	2·17	2·12	2·10	2·08	2·05	2·03	2·00	1·97
12	3·18	2·81	2·61	2·48	2·39	2·33	2·28	2·24	2·21	2·19	2·15	2·10	2·06	2·04	2·01	1·99	1·96	1·93	1·90
13	3·14	2·76	2·56	2·43	2·35	2·28	2·23	2·20	2·16	2·14	2·10	2·05	2·01	1·98	1·96	1·93	1·90	1·88	1·85
14	3·10	2·73	2·52	2·39	2·31	2·24	2·19	2·15	2·12	2·10	2·05	2·01	1·96	1·94	1·91	1·89	1·86	1·83	1·80
15	3·07	2·70	2·49	2·36	2·27	2·21	2·16	2·12	2·09	2·06	2·02	1·97	1·92	1·90	1·87	1·85	1·82	1·79	1·76
16	3·05	2·67	2·46	2·33	2·24	2·18	2·13	2·09	2·06	2·03	1·99	1·94	1·89	1·87	1·84	1·81	1·78	1·75	1·72
17	3·03	2·64	2·44	2·31	2·22	2·15	2·10	2·06	2·03	2·00	1·96	1·91	1·86	1·84	1·81	1·78	1·75	1·72	1·69
18	3·01	2·62	2·42	2·29	2·20	2·13	2·08	2·04	2·00	1·98	1·93	1·89	1·84	1·81	1·78	1·75	1·72	1·69	1·66
19	2·99	2·61	2·40	2·27	2·18	2·11	2·06	2·02	1·98	1·96	1·91	1·86	1·81	1·79	1·76	1·73	1·70	1·67	1·63
20	2·97	2·59	2·38	2·25	2·16	2·09	2·04	2·00	1·96	1·94	1·89	1·84	1·79	1·77	1·74	1·71	1·68	1·64	1·61
21	2·96	2·57	2·36	2·23	2·14	2·08	2·02	1·98	1·95	1·92	1·87	1·83	1·78	1·75	1·72	1·69	1·66	1·62	1·59
22	2·95	2·56	2·35	2·22	2·13	2·06	2·01	1·97	1·93	1·90	1·86	1·81	1·76	1·73	1·70	1·67	1·64	1·60	1·57
23	2·94	2·55	2·34	2·21	2·11	2·05	1·99	1·95	1·92	1·89	1·84	1·80	1·74	1·72	1·69	1·66	1·62	1·59	1·55
24	2·93	2·54	2·33	2·19	2·10	2·04	1·98	1·94	1·91	1·88	1·83	1·78	1·73	1·70	1·67	1·64	1·61	1·57	1·53
25	2·92	2·53	2·32	2·18	2·09	2·02	1·97	1·93	1·89	1·87	1·82	1·77	1·72	1·69	1·66	1·63	1·59	1·56	1·52
26	2·91	2·52	2·31	2·17	2·08	2·01	1·96	1·92	1·88	1·86	1·81	1·76	1·71	1·68	1·65	1·61	1·58	1·54	1·50
27	2·90	2·51	2·30	2·17	2·07	2·00	1·95	1·91	1·87	1·85	1·80	1·75	1·70	1·67	1·64	1·60	1·57	1·53	1·49
28	2·89	2·50	2·29	2·16	2·06	2·00	1·94	1·90	1·87	1·84	1·79	1·74	1·69	1·66	1·63	1·59	1·56	1·52	1·48
29	2·89	2·50	2·28	2·15	2·06	1·99	1·93	1·89	1·86	1·83	1·78	1·73	1·68	1·65	1·62	1·58	1·55	1·51	1·47
30	2·88	2·49	2·28	2·14	2·05	1·98	1·93	1·88	1·85	1·82	1·77	1·72	1·67	1·64	1·61	1·57	1·54	1·50	1·46
40	2·84	2·44	2·23	2·09	2·00	1·93	1·87	1·83	1·79	1·76	1·71	1·66	1·61	1·57	1·54	1·51	1·47	1·42	1·38
60	2·79	2·39	2·18	2·04	1·95	1·87	1·82	1·77	1·74	1·71	1·66	1·60	1·54	1·51	1·48	1·44	1·40	1·35	1·29
120	2·75	2·35	2·13	1·99	1·90	1·82	1·77	1·72	1·68	1·65	1·60	1·55	1·48	1·45	1·41	1·37	1·32	1·26	1·19
∞	2·71	2·30	2·08	1·94	1·85	1·77	1·72	1·67	1·63	1·60	1·55	1·49	1·42	1·38	1·34	1·30	1·24	1·17	1·00

v_1 is the numerator degrees of freedom and v_2 is the denominator degrees of freedom.

(continued)

Percentage Points of the F Distribution α = .05

ν_2 \ ν_1	1	2	3	4	5	6	7	8	9	10	12	15	20	24	30	40	60	120	∞
1	161.4	199.5	215.7	224.6	230.2	234.0	236.8	238.9	240.5	241.9	243.9	245.9	248.0	249.1	250.1	251.1	252.2	253.3	254.3
2	18.51	19.00	19.16	19.25	19.30	19.33	19.35	19.37	19.38	19.40	19.41	19.43	19.45	19.45	19.46	19.47	19.48	19.49	19.50
3	10.13	9.55	9.28	9.12	9.01	8.94	8.89	8.85	8.81	8.79	8.74	8.70	8.66	8.64	8.62	8.59	8.57	8.55	8.53
4	7.71	6.94	6.59	6.39	6.26	6.16	6.09	6.04	6.00	5.96	5.91	5.86	5.80	5.77	5.75	5.72	5.69	5.66	5.63
5	6.61	5.79	5.41	5.19	5.05	4.95	4.88	4.82	4.77	4.74	4.68	4.62	4.56	4.53	4.50	4.46	4.43	4.40	4.36
6	5.99	5.14	4.76	4.53	4.39	4.28	4.21	4.15	4.10	4.06	4.00	3.94	3.87	3.84	3.81	3.77	3.74	3.70	3.67
7	5.59	4.74	4.35	4.12	3.97	3.87	3.79	3.73	3.68	3.64	3.57	3.51	3.44	3.41	3.38	3.34	3.30	3.27	3.23
8	5.32	4.46	4.07	3.84	3.69	3.58	3.50	3.44	3.39	3.35	3.28	3.22	3.15	3.12	3.08	3.04	3.01	2.97	2.93
9	5.12	4.26	3.86	3.63	3.48	3.37	3.29	3.23	3.18	3.14	3.07	3.01	2.94	2.90	2.86	2.83	2.79	2.75	2.71
10	4.96	4.10	3.71	3.48	3.33	3.22	3.14	3.07	3.02	2.98	2.91	2.85	2.77	2.74	2.70	2.66	2.62	2.58	2.54
11	4.84	3.98	3.59	3.36	3.20	3.09	3.01	2.95	2.90	2.85	2.79	2.72	2.65	2.61	2.57	2.53	2.49	2.45	2.40
12	4.75	3.89	3.49	3.26	3.11	3.00	2.91	2.85	2.80	2.75	2.69	2.62	2.54	2.51	2.47	2.43	2.38	2.34	2.30
13	4.67	3.81	3.41	3.18	3.03	2.92	2.83	2.77	2.71	2.67	2.60	2.53	2.46	2.42	2.38	2.34	2.30	2.25	2.21
14	4.60	3.74	3.34	3.11	2.96	2.85	2.76	2.70	2.65	2.60	2.53	2.46	2.39	2.35	2.31	2.27	2.22	2.18	2.13
15	4.54	3.68	3.29	3.06	2.90	2.79	2.71	2.64	2.59	2.54	2.48	2.40	2.33	2.29	2.25	2.20	2.16	2.11	2.07
16	4.49	3.63	3.24	3.01	2.85	2.74	2.66	2.59	2.54	2.49	2.42	2.35	2.28	2.24	2.19	2.15	2.11	2.06	2.01
17	4.45	3.59	3.20	2.96	2.81	2.70	2.61	2.55	2.49	2.45	2.38	2.31	2.23	2.19	2.15	2.10	2.06	2.01	1.96
18	4.41	3.55	3.16	2.93	2.77	2.66	2.58	2.51	2.46	2.41	2.34	2.27	2.19	2.15	2.11	2.06	2.02	1.97	1.92
19	4.38	3.52	3.13	2.90	2.74	2.63	2.54	2.48	2.42	2.38	2.31	2.23	2.16	2.11	2.07	2.03	1.98	1.93	1.88
20	4.35	3.49	3.10	2.87	2.71	2.60	2.51	2.45	2.39	2.35	2.28	2.20	2.12	2.08	2.04	1.99	1.95	1.90	1.84
21	4.32	3.47	3.07	2.84	2.68	2.57	2.49	2.42	2.37	2.32	2.25	2.18	2.10	2.05	2.01	1.96	1.92	1.87	1.81
22	4.30	3.44	3.05	2.82	2.66	2.55	2.46	2.40	2.34	2.30	2.23	2.15	2.07	2.03	1.98	1.94	1.89	1.84	1.78
23	4.28	3.42	3.03	2.80	2.64	2.53	2.44	2.37	2.32	2.27	2.20	2.13	2.05	2.01	1.96	1.91	1.86	1.81	1.76
24	4.26	3.40	3.01	2.78	2.62	2.51	2.42	2.36	2.30	2.25	2.18	2.11	2.03	1.98	1.94	1.89	1.84	1.79	1.73
25	4.24	3.39	2.99	2.76	2.60	2.49	2.40	2.34	2.28	2.24	2.16	2.09	2.01	1.96	1.92	1.87	1.82	1.77	1.71
26	4.23	3.37	2.98	2.74	2.59	2.47	2.39	2.32	2.27	2.22	2.15	2.07	1.99	1.95	1.90	1.85	1.80	1.75	1.69
27	4.21	3.35	2.96	2.73	2.57	2.46	2.37	2.31	2.25	2.20	2.13	2.06	1.97	1.93	1.88	1.84	1.79	1.73	1.67
28	4.20	3.34	2.95	2.71	2.56	2.45	2.36	2.29	2.24	2.19	2.12	2.04	1.96	1.91	1.87	1.82	1.77	1.71	1.65
29	4.18	3.33	2.93	2.70	2.55	2.43	2.35	2.28	2.22	2.18	2.10	2.03	1.94	1.90	1.85	1.81	1.75	1.70	1.64
30	4.17	3.32	2.92	2.69	2.53	2.42	2.33	2.27	2.21	2.16	2.09	2.01	1.93	1.89	1.84	1.79	1.74	1.68	1.62
40	4.08	3.23	2.84	2.61	2.45	2.34	2.25	2.18	2.12	2.08	2.00	1.92	1.84	1.79	1.74	1.69	1.64	1.58	1.51
60	4.00	3.15	2.76	2.53	2.37	2.25	2.17	2.10	2.04	1.99	1.92	1.84	1.75	1.70	1.65	1.59	1.53	1.47	1.39
120	3.92	3.07	2.68	2.45	2.29	2.17	2.09	2.02	1.96	1.91	1.83	1.75	1.66	1.61	1.55	1.50	1.43	1.35	1.25
∞	3.84	3.00	2.60	2.37	2.21	2.10	2.01	1.94	1.88	1.83	1.75	1.67	1.57	1.52	1.46	1.39	1.32	1.22	1.00

(continued)

APPENDIX TABLE 4 (continued)

Percentage Points of the F Distribution α = .01

ν_2 \ ν_1	1	2	3	4	5	6	7	8	9	10	12	15	20	24	30	40	60	120	∞
1	4052	4999·5	5403	5625	5764	5859	5928	5981	6022	6056	6106	6157	6209	6235	6261	6287	6313	6339	6366
2	98·50	99·00	99·17	99·25	99·30	99·33	99·36	99·37	99·39	99·40	99·42	99·43	99·45	99·46	99·47	99·47	99·48	99·49	99·50
3	34·12	30·82	29·46	28·71	28·24	27·91	27·67	27·49	27·35	27·23	27·05	26·87	26·69	26·60	26·50	26·41	26·32	26·22	26·13
4	21·20	18·00	16·69	15·98	15·52	15·21	14·98	14·80	14·66	14·55	14·37	14·20	14·02	13·93	13·84	13·75	13·65	13·56	13·46
5	16·26	13·27	12·06	11·39	10·97	10·67	10·46	10·29	10·16	10·05	9·89	9·72	9·55	9·47	9·38	9·29	9·20	9·11	9·02
6	13·75	10·92	9·78	9·15	8·75	8·47	8·26	8·10	7·98	7·87	7·72	7·56	7·40	7·31	7·23	7·14	7·06	6·97	6·88
7	12·25	9·55	8·45	7·85	7·46	7·19	6·99	6·84	6·72	6·62	6·47	6·31	6·16	6·07	5·99	5·91	5·82	5·74	5·65
8	11·26	8·65	7·59	7·01	6·63	6·37	6·18	6·03	5·91	5·81	5·67	5·52	5·36	5·28	5·20	5·12	5·03	4·95	4·86
9	10·56	8·02	6·99	6·42	6·06	5·80	5·61	5·47	5·35	5·26	5·11	4·96	4·81	4·73	4·65	4·57	4·48	4·40	4·31
10	10·04	7·56	6·55	5·99	5·64	5·39	5·20	5·06	4·94	4·85	4·71	4·56	4·41	4·33	4·25	4·17	4·08	4·00	3·91
11	9·65	7·21	6·22	5·67	5·32	5·07	4·89	4·74	4·63	4·54	4·40	4·25	4·10	4·02	3·94	3·86	3·78	3·69	3·60
12	9·33	6·93	5·95	5·41	5·06	4·82	4·64	4·50	4·39	4·30	4·16	4·01	3·86	3·78	3·70	3·62	3·54	3·45	3·36
13	9·07	6·70	5·74	5·21	4·86	4·62	4·44	4·30	4·19	4·10	3·96	3·82	3·66	3·59	3·51	3·43	3·34	3·25	3·17
14	8·86	6·51	5·56	5·04	4·69	4·46	4·28	4·14	4·03	3·94	3·80	3·66	3·51	3·43	3·35	3·27	3·18	3·09	3·00
15	8·68	6·36	5·42	4·89	4·56	4·32	4·14	4·00	3·89	3·80	3·67	3·52	3·37	3·29	3·21	3·13	3·05	2·96	2·87
16	8·53	6·23	5·29	4·77	4·44	4·20	4·03	3·89	3·78	3·69	3·55	3·41	3·26	3·18	3·10	3·02	2·93	2·84	2·75
17	8·40	6·11	5·18	4·67	4·34	4·10	3·93	3·79	3·68	3·59	3·46	3·31	3·16	3·08	3·00	2·92	2·83	2·75	2·65
18	8·29	6·01	5·09	4·58	4·25	4·01	3·84	3·71	3·60	3·51	3·37	3·23	3·08	3·00	2·92	2·84	2·75	2·66	2·57
19	8·18	5·93	5·01	4·50	4·17	3·94	3·77	3·63	3·52	3·43	3·30	3·15	3·00	2·92	2·84	2·76	2·67	2·58	2·49
20	8·10	5·85	4·94	4·43	4·10	3·87	3·70	3·56	3·46	3·37	3·23	3·09	2·94	2·86	2·78	2·69	2·61	2·52	2·42
21	8·02	5·78	4·87	4·37	4·04	3·81	3·64	3·51	3·40	3·31	3·17	3·03	2·88	2·80	2·72	2·64	2·55	2·46	2·36
22	7·95	5·72	4·82	4·31	3·99	3·76	3·59	3·45	3·35	3·26	3·12	2·98	2·83	2·75	2·67	2·58	2·50	2·40	2·31
23	7·88	5·66	4·76	4·26	3·94	3·71	3·54	3·41	3·30	3·21	3·07	2·93	2·78	2·70	2·62	2·54	2·45	2·35	2·26
24	7·82	5·61	4·72	4·22	3·90	3·67	3·50	3·36	3·26	3·17	3·03	2·89	2·74	2·66	2·58	2·49	2·40	2·31	2·21
25	7·77	5·57	4·68	4·18	3·85	3·63	3·46	3·32	3·22	3·13	2·99	2·85	2·70	2·62	2·54	2·45	2·36	2·27	2·17
26	7·72	5·53	4·64	4·14	3·82	3·59	3·42	3·29	3·18	3·09	2·96	2·81	2·66	2·58	2·50	2·42	2·33	2·23	2·13
27	7·68	5·49	4·60	4·11	3·78	3·56	3·39	3·26	3·15	3·06	2·93	2·78	2·63	2·55	2·47	2·38	2·29	2·20	2·10
28	7·64	5·45	4·57	4·07	3·75	3·53	3·36	3·23	3·12	3·03	2·90	2·75	2·60	2·52	2·44	2·35	2·26	2·17	2·06
29	7·60	5·42	4·54	4·04	3·73	3·50	3·33	3·20	3·09	3·00	2·87	2·73	2·57	2·49	2·41	2·33	2·23	2·14	2·03
30	7·56	5·39	4·51	4·02	3·70	3·47	3·30	3·17	3·07	2·98	2·84	2·70	2·55	2·47	2·39	2·30	2·21	2·11	2·01
40	7·31	5·18	4·31	3·83	3·51	3·29	3·12	2·99	2·89	2·80	2·66	2·52	2·37	2·29	2·20	2·11	2·02	1·92	1·80
60	7·08	4·98	4·13	3·65	3·34	3·12	2·95	2·82	2·72	2·63	2·50	2·35	2·20	2·12	2·03	1·94	1·84	1·73	1·60
120	6·85	4·79	3·95	3·48	3·17	2·96	2·79	2·66	2·56	2·47	2·34	2·19	2·03	1·95	1·86	1·76	1·66	1·53	1·38
∞	6·63	4·61	3·78	3·32	3·02	2·80	2·64	2·51	2·41	2·32	2·18	2·04	1·88	1·79	1·70	1·59	1·47	1·32	1·00

Fisher's Z Transformed Value

r	Z	r	Z
·00	·0000	·50	·5493
1	·0100	1	·5627
2	·0200	2	·5763
3	·0300	3	·5901
4	·0400	4	·6042
·05	·0500	·55	·6184
6	·0601	6	·6328
7	·0701	7	·6475
8	·0802	8	·6625
9	·0902	9	·6777
·10	·1003	·60	·6931
1	·1104	1	·7089
2	·1206	2	·7250
3	·1307	3	·7414
4	·1409	4	·7582
·15	·1511	·65	·7753
6	·1614	6	·7928
7	·1717	7	·8107
8	·1820	8	·8291
9	·1923	9	·8480
·20	·2027	·70	·8673
1	·2132	1	·8872
2	·2237	2	·9076
3	·2342	3	·9287
4	·2448	4	·9505
·25	·2554	·75	0·973
6	·2661	6	0·996
7	·2769	7	1·020
8	·2877	8	1·045
9	·2986	9	1·071
·30	·3095	·80	1·099
1	·3205	1	1·127
2	·3316	2	1·157
3	·3428	3	1·188
4	·3541	4	1·221
·35	·3654	·85	1·256
6	·3769	6	1·293
7	·3884	7	1 333
8	·4001	8	1·376
9	·4118	9	1·422
·40	·4236	·90	1·472
1	·4356	1	1·528
2	·4477	2	1·589
3	·4599	3	1·658
4	·4722	4	1·738
·45	·4847	·95	1·832
6	·4973	6	1·946
7	·5101	7	2·092
8	·5230	8	2·298
9	·5361	9	2·647

APPENDIX TABLE 6
Orthogonal Polynomials

J	Trend	$j=1$	2	3	4	5	6	7	8	9	10	Σc_j^2
$J = 3$	linear	−1	0	1								2
	quadratic	1	−2	1								6
$J = 4$	linear	−3	−1	1	3							20
	quadratic	1	−1	−1	1							4
	cubic	−1	3	−3	1							20
$J = 5$	linear	−2	−1	0	1	2						10
	quadratic	2	−1	−2	−1	2						14
	cubic	−1	2	0	−2	1						10
	quartic	1	−4	6	−4	1						70
$J = 6$	linear	−5	−3	−1	1	3	5					70
	quadratic	5	−1	−4	−4	−1	5					84
	cubic	−5	7	4	−4	−7	5					180
	quartic	1	−3	2	2	−3	1					28
	quintic	−1	5	−10	10	−5	1					252
$J = 7$	linear	−3	−2	−1	0	1	2	3				28
	quadratic	5	0	−3	−4	−3	0	5				84
	cubic	−1	1	1	0	−1	−1	1				6
	quartic	3	−7	1	6	1	−7	3				154
	quintic	−1	4	−5	0	5	−4	1				84
$J = 8$	linear	−7	−5	−3	−1	1	3	5	7			168
	quadratic	7	1	−3	−5	−5	−3	1	7			168
	cubic	−7	5	7	3	−3	−7	−5	7			264
	quartic	7	−13	−3	9	9	−3	−13	7			616
	quintic	−7	23	−17	−15	15	17	−23	7			2184
$J = 9$	linear	−4	−3	−2	−1	0	1	2	3	4		60
	quadratic	28	7	−8	−17	−20	−17	−8	7	28		2772
	cubic	−14	7	13	9	0	−9	−13	−7	14		990
	quartic	14	−21	−11	9	18	9	−11	−21	14		2002
	quintic	−4	11	−4	−9	0	9	4	−11	4		468
$J = 10$	linear	−9	−7	−5	−3	−1	1	3	5	7	9	330
	quadratic	6	2	−1	−3	−4	−4	−3	−1	2	6	132
	cubic	−42	14	35	31	12	−12	−31	−35	−14	42	8580
	quartic	18	−22	−17	3	18	18	3	−17	−22	18	2860
	quintic	−6	14	−1	−11	−6	6	11	1	−14	6	780

Critical Values for Dunnett's Procedure
One-Tailed, $\alpha = .05$
(The columns represent J = number of treatment means [excluding the control])

d.f.	1	2	3	4	5	6	7	8	9
5	2.02	2.44	2.68	2.85	2.98	3.08	3.16	3.24	3.30
6	1.94	2.34	2.56	2.71	2.83	2.92	3.00	3.07	3.12
7	1.89	2.27	2.48	2.62	2.73	2.82	2.89	2.95	3.01
8	1.86	2.22	2.42	2.55	2.66	2.74	2.81	2.87	2.92
9	1.83	2.18	2.37	2.50	2.60	2.68	2.75	2.81	2.86
10	1.81	2.15	2.34	2.47	2.56	2.64	2.70	2.76	2.81
11	1.80	2.13	2.31	2.44	2.53	2.60	2.67	2.72	2.77
12	1.78	2.11	2.29	2.41	2.50	2.58	2.64	2.69	2.74
13	1.77	2.09	2.27	2.39	2.48	2.55	2.61	2.66	2.71
14	1.76	2.08	2.25	2.37	2.46	2.53	2.59	2.64	2.69
15	1.75	2.07	2.24	2.36	2.44	2.51	2.57	2.62	2.67
16	1.75	2.06	2.23	2.34	2.43	2.50	2.56	2.61	2.65
17	1.74	2.05	2.22	2.33	2.42	2.49	2.54	2.59	2.64
18	1.73	2.04	2.21	2.32	2.41	2.48	2.53	2.58	2.62
19	1.73	2.03	2.20	2.31	2.40	2.47	2.52	2.57	2.61
20	1.72	2.03	2.19	2.30	2.39	2.46	2.51	2.56	2.60
24	1.71	2.01	2.17	2.28	2.36	2.43	2.48	2.53	2.57
30	1.70	1.99	2.15	2.25	2.33	2.40	2.45	2.50	2.54
40	1.68	1.97	2.13	2.23	2.31	2.37	2.42	2.47	2.51
60	1.67	1.95	2.10	2.21	2.28	2.35	2.39	2.44	2.48
120	1.66	1.93	2.08	2.18	2.26	2.32	2.37	2.41	2.45
∞	1.64	1.92	2.06	2.16	2.23	2.29	2.34	2.38	2.42

(*continued*)

Critical Values for Dunnett's Procedure

One-Tailed, $\alpha = .01$

d.f.	1	2	3	4	5	6	7	8	9
5	3.37	3.90	4.21	4.43	4.60	4.73	4.85	4.94	5.03
6	3.14	3.61	3.88	4.07	4.21	4.33	4.43	4.51	4.59
7	3.00	3.42	3.66	3.83	3.96	4.07	4.15	4.23	4.30
8	2.90	3.29	3.51	3.67	3.79	3.88	3.96	4.03	4.09
9	2.82	3.19	3.40	3.55	3.66	3.75	3.82	3.89	3.94
10	2.76	3.11	3.31	3.45	3.56	3.64	3.71	3.78	3.83
11	2.72	3.06	3.25	3.38	3.48	3.56	3.63	3.69	3.74
12	2.68	3.01	3.19	3.32	3.42	3.50	3.56	3.62	3.67
13	2.65	2.97	3.15	3.27	3.37	3.44	3.51	3.56	3.61
14	2.62	2.94	3.11	3.23	3.32	3.40	3.46	3.51	3.56
15	2.60	2.91	3.08	3.20	3.29	3.36	3.42	3.47	3.52
16	2.58	2.88	3.05	3.17	3.26	3.33	3.39	3.44	3.48
17	2.57	2.86	3.03	3.14	3.23	3.30	3.36	3.41	3.45
18	2.55	2.84	3.01	3.12	3.21	3.27	3.33	3.38	3.42
19	2.54	2.83	2.99	3.10	3.18	3.25	3.31	3.36	3.40
20	2.53	2.81	2.97	3.08	3.17	3.23	3.29	3.34	3.38
24	2.49	2.77	2.92	3.03	3.11	3.17	3.22	3.27	3.31
30	2.46	2.72	2.87	2.97	3.05	3.11	3.16	3.21	3.24
40	2.42	2.68	2.82	2.92	2.99	3.05	3.10	3.14	3.18
60	2.39	2.64	2.78	2.87	2.94	3.00	3.04	3.08	3.12
120	2.36	2.60	2.73	2.82	2.89	2.94	2.99	3.03	3.06
∞	2.33	2.56	2.68	2.77	2.84	2.89	2.93	2.97	3.00

(*continued*)

Critical Values for Dunnett's Procedure

Two-Tailed, $\alpha = .05$

d.f.	1	2	3	4	5	6	7	8	9
5	2.57	3.03	3.29	3.48	3.62	3.73	3.82	3.90	3.97
6	2.45	2.86	3.10	3.26	3.39	3.49	3.57	3.64	3.71
7	2.36	2.75	2.97	3.12	3.24	3.33	3.41	3.47	3.53
8	2.31	2.67	2.88	3.02	3.13	3.22	3.29	3.35	3.41
9	2.26	2.61	2.81	2.95	3.05	3.14	3.20	3.26	3.32
10	2.23	2.57	2.76	2.89	2.99	3.07	3.14	3.19	3.24
11	2.20	2.53	2.72	2.84	2.94	3.02	3.08	3.14	3.19
12	2.18	2.50	2.68	2.81	2.90	2.98	3.04	3.09	3.14
13	2.16	2.48	2.65	2.78	2.87	2.94	3.00	3.06	3.10
14	2.14	2.46	2.63	2.75	2.84	2.91	2.97	3.02	3.07
15	2.13	2.44	2.61	2.73	2.82	2.89	2.95	3.00	3.04
16	2.12	2.42	2.59	2.71	2.80	2.87	2.92	2.97	3.02
17	2.11	2.41	2.58	2.69	2.78	2.85	2.90	2.95	3.00
18	2.10	2.40	2.56	2.68	2.76	2.83	2.89	2.94	2.98
19	2.09	2.39	2.55	2.66	2.75	2.81	2.87	2.92	2.96
20	2.09	2.38	2.54	2.65	2.73	2.80	2.86	2.90	2.95
24	2.06	2.35	2.51	2.61	2.70	2.76	2.81	2.86	2.90
30	2.04	2.32	2.47	2.58	2.66	2.72	2.77	2.82	2.86
40	2.02	2.29	2.44	2.54	2.62	2.68	2.73	2.77	2.81
60	2.00	2.27	2.41	2.51	2.58	2.64	2.69	2.73	2.77
120	1.98	2.24	2.38	2.47	2.55	2.60	2.65	2.69	2.73
∞	1.96	2.21	2.35	2.44	2.51	2.57	2.61	2.65	2.69

(continued)

Critical Values for Dunnett's Procedure
Two-Tailed, $\alpha = .01$

d.f.	1	2	3	4	5	6	7	8	9
5	4.03	4.63	4.98	5.22	5.41	5.56	5.69	5.80	5.89
6	3.71	4.21	4.51	4.71	4.87	5.00	5.10	5.20	5.28
7	3.50	3.95	4.21	4.39	4.53	4.64	4.74	4.82	4.89
8	3.36	3.77	4.00	4.17	4.29	4.40	4.48	4.56	4.62
9	3.25	3.63	3.85	4.01	4.12	4.22	4.30	4.37	4.43
10	3.17	3.53	3.74	3.88	3.99	4.08	4.16	4.22	4.28
11	3.11	3.45	3.65	3.79	3.89	3.98	4.05	4.11	4.16
12	3.05	3.39	3.58	3.71	3.81	3.89	3.96	4.02	4.07
13	3.01	3.33	3.52	3.65	3.74	3.82	3.89	3.94	3.99
14	2.98	3.29	3.47	3.59	3.69	3.76	3.83	3.88	3.93
15	2.95	3.25	3.43	3.55	3.64	3.71	3.78	3.83	3.88
16	2.92	3.22	3.39	3.51	3.60	3.67	3.73	3.78	3.83
17	2.90	3.19	3.36	3.47	3.56	3.63	3.69	3.74	3.79
18	2.88	3.17	3.33	3.44	3.53	3.60	3.66	3.71	3.75
19	2.86	3.15	3.31	3.42	3.50	3.57	3.63	3.68	3.72
20	2.85	3.13	3.29	3.40	3.48	3.55	3.60	3.65	3.69
24	2.80	3.07	3.22	3.32	3.40	3.47	3.52	3.57	3.61
30	2.75	3.01	3.15	3.25	3.33	3.39	3.44	3.49	3.52
40	2.70	2.95	3.09	3.19	3.26	3.32	3.37	3.41	3.44
60	2.66	2.90	3.03	3.12	3.19	3.25	3.29	3.33	3.37
120	2.62	2.85	2.97	3.06	3.12	3.18	3.22	3.26	3.29
∞	2.58	2.79	2.92	3.00	3.06	3.11	3.15	3.19	3.22

Critical Values for Dunn's (Bonferroni's) Procedure

		Number of contrasts										
ν	α	2	3	4	5	6	7	8	9	10	15	20
2	0.01	14.071	17.248	19.925	22.282	24.413	26.372	28.196	29.908	31.528	38.620	44.598
	0.05	6.164	7.582	8.774	9.823	10.769	11.639	12.449	13.208	13.927	17.072	19.721
	0.10	4.243	5.243	6.081	6.816	7.480	8.090	8.656	9.188	9.691	11.890	13.741
	0.20	2.828	3.531	4.116	4.628	5.089	5.512	5.904	6.272	6.620	8.138	9.414
3	0.01	7.447	8.565	9.453	10.201	10.853	11.436	11.966	12.453	12.904	14.796	16.300
	0.05	4.156	4.826	5.355	5.799	6.185	6.529	6.842	7.128	7.394	8.505	9.387
	0.10	3.149	3.690	4.115	4.471	4.780	5.055	5.304	5.532	5.744	6.627	7.326
	0.20	2.294	2.734	3.077	3.363	3.610	3.829	4.028	4.209	4.377	5.076	5.628
4	0.01	5.594	6.248	6.751	7.166	7.520	7.832	8.112	8.367	8.600	9.556	10.294
	0.05	3.481	3.941	4.290	4.577	4.822	5.036	5.228	5.402	5.562	6.214	6.714
	0.10	2.751	3.150	3.452	3.699	3.909	4.093	4.257	4.406	4.542	5.097	5.521
	0.20	2.084	2.434	2.697	2.911	3.092	3.250	3.391	3.518	3.635	4.107	4.468
5	0.01	4.771	5.243	5.599	5.888	6.133	6.346	6.535	6.706	6.862	7.491	7.968
	0.05	3.152	3.518	3.791	4.012	4.197	4.358	4.501	4.630	4.747	5.219	5.573
	0.10	2.549	2.882	3.129	3.327	3.493	3.638	3.765	3.880	3.985	4.403	4.718
	0.20	1.973	2.278	2.503	2.683	2.834	2.964	3.079	3.182	3.275	3.649	3.928
6	0.01	4.315	4.695	4.977	5.203	5.394	5.559	5.704	5.835	5.954	6.428	6.782
	0.05	2.959	3.274	3.505	3.690	3.845	3.978	4.095	4.200	4.296	4.675	4.956
	0.10	2.428	2.723	2.939	3.110	3.253	3.376	3.484	3.580	3.668	4.015	4.272
	0.20	1.904	2.184	2.387	2.547	2.681	2.795	2.895	2.985	3.066	3.385	3.620
7	0.01	4.027	4.353	4.591	4.782	4.941	5.078	5.198	5.306	5.404	5.791	6.077
	0.05	2.832	3.115	3.321	3.484	3.620	3.736	3.838	3.929	4.011	4.336	4.574
	0.10	2.347	2.618	2.814	2.969	3.097	3.206	3.302	3.388	3.465	3.768	3.990
	0.20	1.858	2.120	2.309	2.457	2.579	2.684	2.775	2.856	2.929	3.214	3.423
8	0.01	3.831	4.120	4.331	4.498	4.637	4.756	4.860	4.953	5.038	5.370	5.613
	0.05	2.743	3.005	3.193	3.342	3.464	3.569	3.661	3.743	3.816	4.105	4.316
	0.10	2.289	2.544	2.726	2.869	2.987	3.088	3.176	3.254	3.324	3.598	3.798
	0.20	1.824	2.075	2.254	2.393	2.508	2.605	2.690	2.765	2.832	3.095	3.286
9	0.01	3.688	3.952	4.143	4.294	4.419	4.526	4.619	4.703	4.778	5.072	5.287
	0.05	2.677	2.923	3.099	3.237	3.351	3.448	3.532	3.607	3.675	3.938	4.129
	0.10	2.246	2.488	2.661	2.796	2.907	3.001	3.083	3.155	3.221	3.474	3.658
	0.20	1.799	2.041	2.212	2.345	2.454	2.546	2.627	2.698	2.761	3.008	3.185
10	0.01	3.580	3.825	4.002	4.141	4.256	4.354	4.439	4.515	4.584	4.852	5.046
	0.05	2.626	2.860	3.027	3.157	3.264	3.355	3.434	3.505	3.568	3.813	3.989
	0.10	2.213	2.446	2.611	2.739	2.845	2.934	3.012	3.080	3.142	3.380	3.552
	0.20	1.779	2.014	2.180	2.308	2.413	2.501	2.578	2.646	2.706	2.941	3.108
11	0.01	3.495	3.726	3.892	4.022	4.129	4.221	4.300	4.371	4.434	4.682	4.860
	0.05	2.586	2.811	2.970	3.094	3.196	3.283	3.358	3.424	3.484	3.715	3.880
	0.10	2.186	2.412	2.571	2.695	2.796	2.881	2.955	3.021	3.079	3.306	3.468
	0.20	1.763	1.993	2.154	2.279	2.380	2.465	2.539	2.605	2.663	2.888	3.048
12	0.01	3.427	3.647	3.804	3.927	4.029	4.114	4.189	4.256	4.315	4.547	4.714
	0.05	2.553	2.770	2.924	3.044	3.141	3.224	3.296	3.359	3.416	3.636	3.793
	0.10	2.164	2.384	2.539	2.658	2.756	2.838	2.910	2.973	3.029	3.247	3.402
	0.20	1.750	1.975	2.133	2.254	2.353	2.436	2.508	2.571	2.628	2.845	2.999
13	0.01	3.371	3.582	3.733	3.850	3.946	4.028	4.099	4.162	4.218	4.438	4.595
	0.05	2.526	2.737	2.886	3.002	3.096	3.176	3.245	3.306	3.361	3.571	3.722
	0.10	2.146	2.361	2.512	2.628	2.723	2.803	2.872	2.933	2.988	3.198	3.347
	0.20	1.739	1.961	2.116	2.234	2.331	2.412	2.482	2.544	2.599	2.809	2.958
14	0.01	3.324	3.528	3.673	3.785	3.878	3.956	4.024	4.084	4.138	4.347	4.497
	0.05	2.503	2.709	2.854	2.967	3.058	3.135	3.202	3.261	3.314	3.518	3.662
	0.10	2.131	2.342	2.489	2.603	2.696	2.774	2.841	2.900	2.953	3.157	3.301
	0.20	1.730	1.949	2.101	2.217	2.312	2.392	2.460	2.520	2.574	2.779	2.924
15	0.01	3.285	3.482	3.622	3.731	3.820	3.895	3.961	4.019	4.071	4.271	4.414
	0.05	2.483	2.685	2.827	2.937	3.026	3.101	3.166	3.224	3.275	3.472	3.612
	0.10	2.118	2.325	2.470	2.582	2.672	2.748	2.814	2.872	2.924	3.122	3.262
	0.20	1.722	1.938	2.088	2.203	2.296	2.374	2.441	2.500	2.553	2.754	2.896

(*continued*)

Critical Values for Dunn's (Bonferroni's) Procedure

ν	α	\multicolumn{11}{c}{Number of contrasts}										
		2	3	4	5	6	7	8	9	10	15	20
16	0.01	3.251	3.443	3.579	3.684	3.771	3.844	3.907	3.963	4.013	4.206	4.344
	0.05	2.467	2.665	2.804	2.911	2.998	3.072	3.135	3.191	3.241	3.433	3.569
	0.10	2.106	2.311	2.453	2.563	2.652	2.726	2.791	2.848	2.898	3.092	3.228
	0.20	1.715	1.929	2.077	2.190	2.282	2.359	2.425	2.483	2.535	2.732	2.871
17	0.01	3.221	3.409	3.541	3.644	3.728	3.799	3.860	3.914	3.963	4.150	4.284
	0.05	2.452	2.647	2.783	2.889	2.974	3.046	3.108	3.163	3.212	3.399	3.532
	0.10	2.096	2.298	2.439	2.547	2.634	2.708	2.771	2.826	2.876	3.066	3.199
	0.20	1.709	1.921	2.068	2.179	2.270	2.346	2.411	2.468	2.519	2.713	2.849
18	0.01	3.195	3.379	3.508	3.609	3.691	3.760	3.820	3.872	3.920	4.102	4.231
	0.05	2.439	2.631	2.766	2.869	2.953	3.024	3.085	3.138	3.186	3.370	3.499
	0.10	2.088	2.287	2.426	2.532	2.619	2.691	2.753	2.806	2.857	3.043	3.174
	0.20	1.704	1.914	2.059	2.170	2.259	2.334	2.399	2.455	2.505	2.696	2.830
19	0.01	3.173	3.353	3.479	3.578	3.658	3.725	3.784	3.835	3.881	4.059	4.185
	0.05	2.427	2.617	2.750	2.852	2.934	3.004	3.064	3.116	3.163	3.343	3.470
	0.10	2.080	2.277	2.415	2.520	2.605	2.676	2.738	2.791	2.839	3.023	3.152
	0.20	1.699	1.908	2.052	2.161	2.250	2.324	2.388	2.443	2.493	2.682	2.813
20	0.01	3.152	3.329	3.454	3.550	3.629	3.695	3.752	3.802	3.848	4.021	4.144
	0.05	2.417	2.605	2.736	2.836	2.918	2.986	3.045	3.097	3.143	3.320	3.445
	0.10	2.073	2.269	2.405	2.508	2.593	2.663	2.724	2.777	2.824	3.005	3.132
	0.20	1.695	1.902	2.045	2.154	2.241	2.315	2.378	2.433	2.482	2.668	2.798
21	0.01	3.134	3.308	3.431	3.525	3.602	3.667	3.724	3.773	3.817	3.987	4.108
	0.05	2.408	2.594	2.723	2.822	2.903	2.970	3.028	3.080	3.125	3.300	3.422
	0.10	2.067	2.261	2.396	2.498	2.581	2.651	2.711	2.764	2.810	2.989	3.114
	0.20	1.691	1.897	2.039	2.147	2.234	2.306	2.369	2.424	2.472	2.656	2.785
22	0.01	3.118	3.289	3.410	3.503	3.579	3.643	3.698	3.747	3.790	3.957	4.075
	0.05	2.400	2.584	2.712	2.810	2.889	2.956	3.014	3.064	3.109	3.281	3.402
	0.10	2.061	2.254	2.387	2.489	2.572	2.641	2.700	2.752	2.798	2.974	3.098
	0.20	1.688	1.892	2.033	2.141	2.227	2.299	2.361	2.415	2.463	2.646	2.773
23	0.01	3.103	3.272	3.392	3.483	3.558	3.621	3.675	3.723	3.766	3.930	4.046
	0.05	2.392	2.574	2.701	2.798	2.877	2.943	3.000	3.050	3.094	3.264	3.383
	0.10	2.056	2.247	2.380	2.481	2.563	2.631	2.690	2.741	2.787	2.961	3.083
	0.20	1.685	1.888	2.028	2.135	2.221	2.292	2.354	2.407	2.455	2.636	2.762
24	0.01	3.089	3.257	3.375	3.465	3.539	3.601	3.654	3.702	3.744	3.905	4.019
	0.05	2.385	2.566	2.692	2.788	2.866	2.931	2.988	3.037	3.081	3.249	3.366
	0.10	2.051	2.241	2.373	2.473	2.554	2.622	2.680	2.731	2.777	2.949	3.070
	0.20	1.682	1.884	2.024	2.130	2.215	2.286	2.347	2.400	2.448	2.627	2.752
25	0.01	3.077	3.243	3.359	3.449	3.521	3.583	3.635	3.682	3.723	3.882	3.995
	0.05	2.379	2.558	2.683	2.779	2.856	2.921	2.976	3.025	3.069	3.235	3.351
	0.10	2.047	2.236	2.367	2.466	2.547	2.614	2.672	2.722	2.767	2.938	3.058
	0.20	1.679	1.881	2.020	2.125	2.210	2.280	2.341	2.394	2.441	2.619	2.743
26	0.01	3.066	3.230	3.345	3.433	3.505	3.566	3.618	3.664	3.705	3.862	3.972
	0.05	2.373	2.551	2.675	2.770	2.847	2.911	2.966	3.014	3.058	3.222	3.337
	0.10	2.043	2.231	2.361	2.460	2.540	2.607	2.664	2.714	2.759	2.928	3.047
	0.20	1.677	1.878	2.016	2.121	2.205	2.275	2.335	2.388	2.435	2.612	2.735
27	0.01	3.056	3.218	3.332	3.419	3.491	3.550	3.602	3.647	3.688	3.843	3.952
	0.05	2.368	2.545	2.668	2.762	2.838	2.902	2.956	3.004	3.047	3.210	3.324
	0.10	2.039	2.227	2.356	2.454	2.534	2.600	2.657	2.707	2.751	2.919	3.036
	0.20	1.675	1.875	2.012	2.117	2.201	2.270	2.330	2.383	2.429	2.605	2.727
28	0.01	3.046	3.207	3.320	3.407	3.477	3.536	3.587	3.632	3.672	3.825	3.933
	0.05	2.363	2.539	2.661	2.755	2.830	2.893	2.948	2.995	3.038	3.199	3.312
	0.10	2.036	2.222	2.351	2.449	2.528	2.594	2.650	2.700	2.744	2.911	3.027
	0.20	1.672	1.872	2.009	2.113	2.196	2.266	2.326	2.378	2.424	2.599	2.720
29	0.01	3.037	3.197	3.309	3.395	3.464	3.523	3.574	3.618	3.658	3.809	3.916
	0.05	2.358	2.534	2.655	2.748	2.823	2.886	2.940	2.987	3.029	3.189	3.301
	0.10	2.033	2.218	2.346	2.444	2.522	2.588	2.644	2.693	2.737	2.903	3.018
	0.20	1.671	1.869	2.006	2.110	2.193	2.262	2.321	2.373	2.419	2.593	2.713

(*continued*)

Critical Values for Dunn's (Bonferroni's) Procedure

ν	α	Number of contrasts										
		2	3	4	5	6	7	8	9	10	15	20
30	0.01	3.029	3.188	3.298	3.384	3.453	3.511	3.561	3.605	3.644	3.794	3.900
	0.05	2.354	2.528	2.649	2.742	2.816	2.878	2.932	2.979	3.021	3.180	3.291
	0.10	2.030	2.215	2.342	2.439	2.517	2.582	2.638	2.687	2.731	2.895	3.010
	0.20	1.669	1.867	2.003	2.106	2.189	2.258	2.317	2.369	2.414	2.587	2.707
40	0.01	2.970	3.121	3.225	3.305	3.370	3.425	3.472	3.513	3.549	3.689	3.787
	0.05	2.323	2.492	2.608	2.696	2.768	2.827	2.878	2.923	2.963	3.113	3.218
	0.10	2.009	2.189	2.312	2.406	2.481	2.544	2.597	2.644	2.686	2.843	2.952
	0.20	1.656	1.850	1.983	2.083	2.164	2.231	2.288	2.338	2.382	2.548	2.663
60	0.01	2.914	3.056	3.155	3.230	3.291	3.342	3.386	3.425	3.459	3.589	3.679
	0.05	2.294	2.456	2.568	2.653	2.721	2.777	2.826	2.869	2.906	3.049	3.148
	0.10	1.989	2.163	2.283	2.373	2.446	2.506	2.558	2.603	2.643	2.793	2.897
	0.20	1.643	1.834	1.963	2.061	2.139	2.204	2.259	2.308	2.350	2.511	2.621
120	0.01	2.859	2.994	3.087	3.158	3.215	3.263	3.304	3.340	3.372	3.493	3.577
	0.05	2.265	2.422	2.529	2.610	2.675	2.729	2.776	2.816	2.852	2.987	3.081
	0.10	1.968	2.138	2.254	2.342	2.411	2.469	2.519	2.562	2.600	2.744	2.843
	0.20	1.631	1.817	1.944	2.039	2.115	2.178	2.231	2.278	2.319	2.474	2.580
∞	0.01	2.806	2.934	3.022	3.089	3.143	3.188	3.226	3.260	3.289	3.402	3.480
	0.05	2.237	2.388	2.491	2.569	2.631	2.683	2.727	2.766	2.800	2.928	3.016
	0.10	1.949	2.114	2.226	2.311	2.378	2.434	2.482	2.523	2.560	2.697	2.791
	0.20	1.618	1.801	1.925	2.018	2.091	2.152	2.204	2.249	2.289	2.438	2.540

APPENDIX TABLE 9
Critical Values for the Studentized Range Statistic
$\alpha = .10$

v \ J or r	2	3	4	5	6	7	8	9	10
1	8.929	13.44	16.36	18.49	20.15	21.51	22.64	23.62	24.48
2	4.130	5.733	6.773	7.538	8.139	8.633	9.049	9.409	9.725
3	3.328	4.467	5.199	5.738	6.162	6.511	6.806	7.062	7.287
4	3.015	3.976	4.586	5.035	5.388	5.679	5.926	6.139	6.327
5	2.850	3.717	4.264	4.664	4.979	5.238	5.458	5.648	5.816
6	2.748	3.559	4.065	4.435	4.726	4.966	5.168	5.344	5.499
7	2.680	3.451	3.931	4.280	4.555	4.780	4.972	5.137	5.283
8	2.630	3.374	3.834	4.169	4.431	4.646	4.829	4.987	5.126
9	2.592	3.316	3.761	4.084	4.337	4.545	4.721	4.873	5.007
10	2.563	3.270	3.704	4.018	4.264	4.465	4.636	4.783	4.913
11	2.540	3.234	3.658	3.965	4.205	4.401	4.568	4.711	4.838
12	2.521	3.204	3.621	3.922	4.156	4.349	4.511	4.652	4.776
13	2.505	3.179	3.589	3.885	4.116	4.305	4.464	4.602	4.724
14	2.491	3.158	3.563	3.854	4.081	4.267	4.424	4.560	4.680
15	2.479	3.140	3.540	3.828	4.052	4.235	4.390	4.524	4.641
16	2.469	3.124	3.520	3.804	4.026	4.207	4.360	4.492	4.608
17	2.460	3.110	3.503	3.784	4.004	4.183	4.334	4.464	4.579
18	2.452	3.098	3.488	3.767	3.984	4.161	4.311	4.440	4.554
19	2.445	3.087	3.474	3.751	3.966	4.142	4.290	4.418	4.531
20	2.439	3.078	3.462	3.736	3.950	4.124	4.271	4.398	4.510
24	2.420	3.047	3.423	3.692	3.900	4.070	4.213	4.336	4.445
30	2.400	3.017	3.386	3.648	3.851	4.016	4.155	4.275	4.381
40	2.381	2.988	3.349	3.605	3.803	3.963	4.099	4.215	4.317
60	2.363	2.959	3.312	3.562	3.755	3.911	4.042	4.155	4.254
120	2.344	2.930	3.276	3.520	3.707	3.859	3.987	4.096	4.191
∞	2.326	2.902	3.240	3.478	3.661	3.808	3.931	4.037	4.129

v \ J or r	11	12	13	14	15	16	17	18	19
1	25.24	25.92	26.54	27.10	27.62	28.10	28.54	28.96	29.35
2	10.01	10.26	10.49	10.70	10.89	11.07	11.24	11.39	11.54
3	7.487	7.667	7.832	7.982	8.120	8.249	8.368	8.479	8.584
4	6.495	6.645	6.783	6.909	7.025	7.133	7.233	7.327	7.414
5	5.966	6.101	6.223	6.336	6.440	6.536	6.626	6.710	6.789
6	5.637	5.762	5.875	5.979	6.075	6.164	6.247	6.325	6.398
7	5.413	5.530	5.637	5.735	5.826	5.910	5.988	6.061	6.130
8	5.250	5.362	5.464	5.558	5.644	5.724	5.799	5.869	5.935
9	5.127	5.234	5.333	5.423	5.506	5.583	5.655	5.723	5.786
10	5.029	5.134	5.229	5.317	5.397	5.472	5.542	5.607	5.668
11	4.951	5.053	5.146	5.231	5.309	5.382	5.450	5.514	5.573
12	4.886	4.986	5.077	5.160	5.236	5.308	5.374	5.436	5.495
13	4.832	4.930	5.019	5.100	5.176	5.245	5.311	5.372	5.429
14	4.786	4.882	4.970	5.050	5.124	5.192	5.256	5.316	5.373
15	4.746	4.841	4.927	5.006	5.079	5.147	5.209	5.269	5.324
16	4.712	4.805	4.890	4.968	5.040	5.107	5.169	5.227	5.282
17	4.682	4.774	4.858	4.935	5.005	5.071	5.133	5.190	5.244
18	4.655	4.746	4.829	4.905	4.975	5.040	5.101	5.158	5.211
19	4.631	4.721	4.803	4.879	4.948	5.012	5.073	5.129	5.182
20	4.609	4.699	4.730	4.855	4.924	4.987	5.047	5.103	5.155
24	4.541	4.628	4.708	4.780	4.847	4.909	4.966	5.021	5.071
30	4.474	4.559	4.635	4.706	4.770	4.830	4.886	4.939	4.988
40	4.408	4.490	4.564	4.632	4.695	4.752	4.807	4.857	4.905
60	4.342	4.421	4.493	4.558	4.619	4.675	4.727	4.775	4.821
120	4.276	4.353	4.422	4.485	4.543	4.597	4.647	4.694	4.738
∞	4.211	4.285	4.351	4.412	4.468	4.519	4.568	4.612	4.654

J for Tukey, r for Newman-Keuls

(continued)

Estimates rather than real
Columns = # of groups
Rows = # of df

v \ J or r	2	3	4	5	6	7	8	9	10
1	17.97	26.98	32.82	37.08	40.41	43.12	45.40	47.36	49.07
2	6.085	8.331	9.798	10.88	11.74	12.44	13.03	13.54	13.99
3	4.501	5.910	6.825	7.502	8.037	8.478	8.853	9.177	9.462
4	3.927	5.040	5.757	6.287	6.707	7.053	7.347	7.602	7.826
5	3.635	4.602	5.218	5.673	6.033	6.330	6.582	6.802	6.995
6	3.461	4.339	4.896	5.305	5.628	5.895	6.122	6.319	6.493
7	3.344	4.165	4.681	5.060	5.359	5.606	5.815	5.998	6.158
8	3.261	4.041	4.529	4.886	5.167	5.399	5.597	5.767	5.918
9	3.199	3.949	4.415	4.756	5.024	5.244	5.432	5.595	5.739
10	3.151	3.877	4.327	4.654	4.912	5.124	5.305	5.461	5.599
11	3.113	3.820	4.256	4.574	4.823	5.028	5.202	5.353	5.487
12	3.082	3.773	4.199	4.508	4.751	4.950	5.119	5.265	5.395
13	3.055	3.735	4.151	4.453	4.690	4.885	5.049	5.192	5.318
14	3.033	3.702	4.111	4.407	4.639	4.829	4.990	5.131	5.254
15	3.014	3.674	4.076	4.367	4.595	4.782	4.940	5.077	5.198
16	2.998	3.649	4.046	4.333	4.557	4.741	4.897	5.031	5.150
17	2.984	3.628	4.020	4.303	4.524	4.705	4.858	4.991	5.108
18	2.971	3.609	3.997	4.277	4.495	4.673	4.824	4.956	5.071
19	2.960	3.593	3.977	4.253	4.469	4.645	4.794	4.924	5.038
20	2.950	3.578	3.958	4.232	4.445	4.620	4.768	4.896	5.008
24	2.919	3.532	3.901	4.166	4.373	4.541	4.684	4.807	4.915
30	2.888	3.486	3.845	4.102	4.302	4.464	4.602	4.720	4.824
40	2.858	3.442	3.791	4.039	4.232	4.389	4.521	4.635	4.735
60	2.829	3.399	3.737	3.977	4.163	4.314	4.441	4.550	4.646
120	2.800	3.356	3.685	3.917	4.096	4.241	4.363	4.468	4.560
∞	2.772	3.314	3.633	3.858	4.030	4.170	4.286	4.387	4.474

v \ J or r	11	12	13	14	15	16	17	18	19
1	50.59	51.96	53.20	54.33	55.36	56.32	57.22	58.04	58.83
2	14.39	14.75	15.08	15.38	15.65	15.91	16.14	16.37	16.57
3	9.717	9.946	10.15	10.35	10.53	10.69	10.84	10.98	11.11
4	8.027	8.208	8.373	8.525	8.664	8.794	8.914	9.028	9.134
5	7.168	7.324	7.466	7.596	7.717	7.828	7.932	8.030	8.122
6	6.649	6.789	6.917	7.034	7.143	7.244	7.338	7.426	7.508
7	6.302	6.431	6.550	6.658	6.759	6.852	6.939	7.020	7.097
8	6.054	6.175	6.287	6.389	6.483	6.571	6.653	6.729	6.802
9	5.867	5.983	6.089	6.186	6.276	6.359	6.437	6.510	6.579
10	5.722	5.833	5.935	6.028	6.114	6.194	6.269	6.339	6.405
11	5.605	5.713	5.811	5.901	5.984	6.062	6.134	6.202	6.265
12	5.511	5.615	5.710	5.798	5.878	5.953	6.023	6.089	6.151
13	5.431	5.533	5.625	5.711	5.789	5.862	5.931	5.995	6.055
14	5.364	5.463	5.554	5.637	5.714	5.786	5.852	5.915	5.974
15	5.306	5.404	5.493	5.574	5.649	5.720	5.785	5.846	5.904
16	5.256	5.352	5.439	5.520	5.593	5.662	5.727	5.786	5.843
17	5.212	5.307	5.392	5.471	5.544	5.612	5.675	5.734	5.790
18	5.174	5.267	5.352	5.429	5.501	5.568	5.630	5.688	5.743
19	5.140	5.231	5.315	5.391	5.462	5.528	5.589	5.647	5.701
20	5.108	5.199	5.282	5.357	5.427	5.493	5.553	5.610	5.663
24	5.012	5.099	5.179	5.251	5.319	5.381	5.439	5.494	5.545
30	4.917	5.001	5.077	5.147	5.211	5.271	5.327	5.379	5.429
40	4.824	4.904	4.977	5.044	5.106	5.163	5.216	5.266	5.313
60	4.732	4.808	4.878	4.942	5.001	5.056	5.107	5.154	5.199
120	4.641	4.714	4.781	4.842	4.898	4.950	4.998	5.044	5.086
∞	4.552	4.622	4.685	4.743	4.796	4.845	4.891	4.934	4.974

(continued)

303

Critical Values for the Studentized Range Statistic

$\alpha = .10$

v \ J or r	2	3	4	5	6	7	8	9	10
1	90.03	135.0	164.3	185.6	202.2	215.8	227.2	237.0	245.6
2	14.04	19.02	22.29	24.72	26.63	28.20	29.53	30.68	31.69
3	8.261	10.62	12.17	13.33	14.24	15.00	15.64	16.20	16.69
4	6.512	8.120	9.173	9.958	10.58	11.10	11.55	11.93	12.27
5	5.702	6.976	7.804	8.421	8.913	9.321	9.669	9.972	10.24
6	5.243	6.331	7.033	7.556	7.973	8.318	8.613	8.869	9.097
7	4.949	5.919	6.543	7.005	7.373	7.679	7.939	8.166	8.368
8	4.746	5.635	6.204	6.625	6.960	7.237	7.474	7.681	7.863
9	4.596	5.428	5.957	6.348	6.658	6.915	7.134	7.325	7.495
10	4.482	5.270	5.769	6.136	6.428	6.669	6.875	7.055	7.213
11	4.392	5.146	5.621	5.970	6.247	6.476	6.672	6.842	6.992
12	4.320	5.046	5.502	5.836	6.101	6.321	6.507	6.670	6.814
13	4.260	4.964	5.404	5.727	5.981	6.192	6.372	6.528	6.667
14	4.210	4.895	5.322	5.634	5.881	6.085	6.258	6.409	6.543
15	4.168	4.836	5.252	5.556	5.796	5.994	6.162	6.309	6.439
16	4.131	4.786	5.192	5.489	5.722	5.915	6.079	6.222	6.349
17	4.099	4.742	5.140	5.430	5.659	5.847	6.007	6.147	6.270
18	4.071	4.703	5.094	5.379	5.603	5.788	5.944	6.081	6.201
19	4.046	4.670	5.054	5.334	5.554	5.735	5.889	6.022	6.141
20	4.024	4.639	5.018	5.294	5.510	5.688	5.839	5.970	6.087
24	3.956	4.546	4.907	5.168	5.374	5.542	5.685	5.809	5.919
30	3.889	4.455	4.799	5.048	5.242	5.401	5.536	5.653	5.756
40	3.825	4.367	4.696	4.931	5.114	5.265	5.392	5.502	5.599
60	3.762	4.282	4.595	4.818	4.991	5.133	5.253	5.356	5.447
120	3.702	4.200	4.497	4.709	4.872	5.005	5.118	5.214	5.299
∞	3.643	4.120	4.403	4.603	4.757	4.882	4.987	5.078	5.157

v \ J or r	11	12	13	14	15	16	17	18	19
1	253.2	260.0	266.2	271.8	277.0	281.8	286.3	290.4	294.3
2	32.59	33.40	34.13	34.81	35.43	36.00	36.53	37.03	37.50
3	17.13	17.53	17.89	18.22	18.52	18.81	19.07	19.32	19.55
4	12.57	12.84	13.09	13.32	13.53	13.73	13.91	14.08	14.24
5	10.48	10.70	10.89	11.08	11.24	11.40	11.55	11.68	11.81
6	9.301	9.485	9.653	9.808	9.951	10.08	10.21	10.32	10.43
7	8.548	8.711	8.860	8.997	9.124	9.242	9.353	9.456	9.554
8	8.027	8.176	8.312	8.436	8.552	8.659	8.760	8.854	8.943
9	7.647	7.784	7.910	8.025	8.132	8.232	8.325	8.412	8.495
10	7.356	7.485	7.603	7.712	7.812	7.906	7.993	8.076	8.153
11	7.128	7.250	7.362	7.465	7.560	7.649	7.732	7.809	7.883
12	6.943	7.060	7.167	7.265	7.356	7.441	7.520	7.594	7.665
13	6.791	6.903	7.006	7.101	7.188	7.269	7.345	7.417	7.485
14	6.664	6.772	6.871	6.962	7.047	7.126	7.199	7.268	7.333
15	6.555	6.660	6.757	6.845	6.927	7.003	7.074	7.142	7.204
16	6.462	6.564	6.658	6.744	6.823	6.898	6.967	7.032	7.093
17	6.381	6.480	6.572	6.656	6.734	6.806	6.873	6.937	6.997
18	6.310	6.407	6.497	6.579	6.655	6.725	6.792	6.854	6.912
19	6.247	6.342	6.430	6.510	6.585	6.654	6.719	6.780	6.837
20	6.191	6.285	6.371	6.450	6.523	6.591	6.654	6.714	6.771
24	6.017	6.106	6.186	6.261	6.330	6.394	6.453	6.510	6.563
30	5.849	5.932	6.008	6.078	6.143	6.203	6.259	6.311	6.361
40	5.686	5.764	5.835	5.900	5.961	6.017	6.069	6.119	6.165
60	5.528	5.601	5.667	5.728	5.785	5.837	5.886	5.931	5.974
120	5.375	5.443	5.505	5.562	5.614	5.662	5.708	5.750	5.790
∞	5.227	5.290	5.348	5.400	5.448	5.493	5.535	5.574	5.611

Critical Values for Duncan's New Multiple Range Test

$$\alpha = .05$$

ν \ r	2	3	4	5	6	7	8	9	10	12	14	16	18	20
1	18.0	18.0	18.0	18.0	18.0	18.0	18.0	18.0	18.0	18.0	18.0	18.0	18.0	18.0
2	6.09	6.09	6.09	6.09	6.09	6.09	6.09	6.09	6.09	6.09	6.09	6.09	6.09	6.09
3	4.50	4.50	4.50	4.50	4.50	4.50	4.50	4.50	4.50	4.50	4.50	4.50	4.50	4.50
4	3.93	4.01	4.02	4.02	4.02	4.02	4.02	4.02	4.02	4.02	4.02	4.02	4.02	4.02
5	3.64	3.74	3.79	3.83	3.83	3.83	3.83	3.83	3.83	3.83	3.83	3.83	3.83	3.83
6	3.46	3.58	3.64	3.68	3.68	3.68	3.68	3.68	3.68	3.68	3.68	3.68	3.68	3.68
7	3.35	3.47	3.54	3.58	3.60	3.61	3.61	3.61	3.61	3.61	3.61	3.61	3.61	3.61
8	3.26	3.39	3.47	3.52	3.55	3.56	3.56	3.56	3.56	3.56	3.56	3.56	3.56	3.56
9	3.20	3.34	3.41	3.47	3.50	3.52	3.52	3.52	3.52	3.52	3.52	3.52	3.52	3.52
10	3.15	3.30	3.37	3.43	3.46	3.47	3.47	3.47	3.47	3.47	3.47	3.47	3.47	3.48
11	3.11	3.27	3.35	3.39	3.43	3.44	3.45	3.46	3.46	3.46	3.46	3.46	3.47	3.48
12	3.08	3.23	3.33	3.36	3.40	3.42	3.44	3.44	3.46	3.46	3.46	3.46	3.47	3.48
13	3.06	3.21	3.30	3.35	3.38	3.41	3.42	3.44	3.45	3.45	3.46	3.46	3.47	3.47
14	3.03	3.18	3.27	3.33	3.37	3.39	3.41	3.42	3.44	3.45	3.46	3.46	3.47	3.47
15	3.01	3.16	3.25	3.31	3.36	3.38	3.40	3.42	3.43	3.44	3.45	3.46	3.47	3.47
16	3.00	3.15	3.23	3.30	3.34	3.37	3.39	3.41	3.43	3.44	3.45	3.46	3.47	3.47
17	2.98	3.13	3.22	3.28	3.33	3.36	3.38	3.40	3.42	3.44	3.45	3.46	3.47	3.47
18	2.97	3.12	3.21	3.27	3.32	3.35	3.37	3.39	3.41	3.43	3.45	3.46	3.47	3.47
19	2.96	3.11	3.19	3.26	3.31	3.35	3.37	3.39	3.41	3.43	3.44	3.46	3.47	3.47
20	2.95	3.10	3.18	3.25	3.30	3.34	3.36	3.38	3.40	3.43	3.44	3.46	3.46	3.47
22	2.93	3.08	3.17	3.24	3.29	3.32	3.35	3.37	3.39	3.42	3.44	3.45	3.46	3.47
24	2.92	3.07	3.15	3.22	3.28	3.31	3.34	3.37	3.38	3.41	3.44	3.45	3.46	3.47
26	2.91	3.06	3.14	3.21	3.27	3.30	3.34	3.36	3.38	3.41	3.43	3.45	3.46	3.47
28	2.90	3.04	3.13	3.20	3.26	3.30	3.33	3.35	3.37	3.40	3.43	3.45	3.46	3.47
30	2.89	3.04	3.12	3.20	3.25	3.29	3.32	3.35	3.37	3.40	3.43	3.44	3.46	3.47
40	2.86	3.01	3.10	3.17	3.22	3.27	3.30	3.33	3.35	3.39	3.42	3.44	3.46	3.47
60	2.83	2.98	3.08	3.14	3.20	3.24	3.28	3.31	3.33	3.37	3.40	3.43	3.45	3.47
100	2.80	2.95	3.05	3.12	3.18	3.22	3.26	3.29	3.32	3.36	3.40	3.42	3.45	3.47
∞	2.77	2.92	3.02	3.09	3.15	3.19	3.23	3.26	3.29	3.34	3.38	3.41	3.44	3.47

(continued)

Critical Values for Duncan's New Multiple Range Test

$$\alpha = .01$$

v \ r	2	3	4	5	6	7	8	9	10	12	14	16	18	20
1	90.0	90.0	90.0	90.0	90.0	90.0	90.0	90.0	90.0	90.0	90.0	90.0	90.0	90.0
2	14.0	14.0	14.0	14.0	14.0	14.0	14.0	14.0	14.0	14.0	14.0	14.0	14.0	14.0
3	8.26	8.5	8.6	8.7	8.8	8.9	8.9	9.0	9.0	9.0	9.1	9.2	9.3	9.3
4	6.51	6.8	6.9	7.0	7.1	7.1	7.2	7.2	7.3	7.3	7.4	7.4	7.5	7.5
5	5.70	5.96	6.11	6.18	6.26	6.33	6.40	6.44	6.5	6.6	6.6	6.7	6.7	6.8
6	5.24	5.51	5.65	5.73	5.81	5.88	5.95	6.00	6.0	6.1	6.2	6.2	6.3	6.3
7	4.95	5.22	5.37	5.45	5.53	5.61	5.69	5.73	5.8	5.8	5.9	5.9	6.0	6.0
8	4.74	5.00	5.14	5.23	5.32	5.40	5.47	5.51	5.5	5.6	5.7	5.7	5.8	5.8
9	4.60	4.86	4.99	5.08	5.17	5.25	5.32	5.36	5.4	5.5	5.5	5.6	5.7	5.7
10	4.48	4.73	4.88	4.96	5.06	5.13	5.20	5.24	5.28	5.36	5.42	5.48	5.54	5.55
11	4.39	4.63	4.77	4.86	4.94	5.01	5.06	5.12	5.15	5.24	5.28	5.34	5.38	5.39
12	4.32	4.55	4.68	4.76	4.84	4.92	4.96	5.02	5.07	5.13	5.17	5.22	5.24	5.26
13	4.26	4.48	4.62	4.69	4.74	4.84	4.88	4.94	4.98	5.04	5.08	5.13	5.14	5.15
14	4.21	4.42	4.55	4.63	4.70	4.78	4.83	4.87	4.91	4.96	5.00	5.04	5.06	5.07
15	4.17	4.37	4.50	4.58	4.64	4.72	4.77	4.81	4.84	4.90	4.94	4.97	4.99	5.00
16	4.13	4.34	4.45	4.54	4.60	4.67	4.72	4.76	4.79	4.84	4.88	4.91	4.93	4.94
17	4.10	4.30	4.41	4.50	4.56	4.63	4.68	4.72	4.75	4.80	4.83	4.86	4.88	4.89
18	4.07	4.27	4.38	4.46	4.53	4.59	4.64	4.68	4.71	4.76	4.79	4.82	4.84	4.85
19	4.05	4.24	4.35	4.43	4.50	4.56	4.61	4.64	4.67	4.72	4.76	4.79	4.81	4.82
20	4.02	4.22	4.33	4.40	4.47	4.53	4.58	4.61	4.65	4.69	4.73	4.76	4.78	4.79
22	3.99	4.17	4.28	4.36	4.42	4.48	4.53	4.57	4.60	4.65	4.68	4.71	4.74	4.75
24	3.96	4.14	4.24	4.33	4.39	4.44	4.49	4.53	4.57	4.62	4.64	4.67	4.70	4.72
26	3.93	4.11	4.21	4.30	4.36	4.41	4.46	4.50	4.53	4.58	4.62	4.65	4.67	4.69
28	3.91	4.08	4.18	4.28	4.34	4.39	4.43	4.47	4.51	4.56	4.60	4.62	4.65	4.67
30	3.89	4.06	4.16	4.22	4.32	4.36	4.41	4.45	4.48	4.54	4.58	4.61	4.63	4.65
40	3.82	3.99	4.10	4.17	4.24	4.30	4.34	4.37	4.41	4.46	4.51	4.54	4.57	4.59
60	3.76	3.92	4.03	4.12	4.17	4.23	4.27	4.31	4.34	4.39	4.44	4.47	4.50	4.53
100	3.71	3.86	3.98	4.06	4.11	4.17	4.21	4.25	4.29	4.35	4.38	4.42	4.45	4.48
∞	3.64	3.80	3.90	3.98	4.04	4.09	4.14	4.17	4.20	4.26	4.31	4.34	4.38	4.41

Critical Values for the Bryant–Paulson Procedure

$\alpha = .05$

ν	$J = 2$	$J = 3$	$J = 4$	$J = 5$	$J = 6$	$J = 7$	$J = 8$	$J = 10$	$J = 12$	$J = 16$	$J = 20$
					$X = 1$						
2	7·96	11·00	12·99	14·46	15·61	16·56	17·36	18·65	19·68	21·23	22·40
3	5·42	7·18	8·32	9·17	9·84	10·39	10·86	11·62	12·22	13·14	13·83
4	4·51	5·84	6·69	7·32	7·82	8·23	8·58	9·15	9·61	10·30	10·82
5	4·06	5·17	5·88	6·40	6·82	7·16	7·45	7·93	8·30	8·88	9·32
6	3·79	4·78	5·40	5·86	6·23	6·53	6·78	7·20	7·53	8·04	8·43
7	3·62	4·52	5·09	5·51	5·84	6·11	6·34	6·72	7·03	7·49	7·84
8	3·49	4·34	4·87	5·26	5·57	5·82	6·03	6·39	6·67	7·10	7·43
10	3·32	4·10	4·58	4·93	5·21	5·43	5·63	5·94	6·19	6·58	6·87
12	3·22	3·95	4·40	4·73	4·98	5·19	5·37	5·67	5·90	6·26	6·53
14	3·15	3·85	4·28	4·59	4·83	5·03	5·20	5·48	5·70	6·03	6·29
16	3·10	3·77	4·19	4·49	4·72	4·91	5·07	5·34	5·55	5·87	6·12
18	3·06	3·72	4·12	4·41	4·63	4·82	4·98	5·23	5·44	5·75	5·98
20	3·03	3·67	4·07	4·35	4·57	4·75	4·90	5·15	5·35	5·65	5·88
24	2·98	3·61	3·99	4·26	4·47	4·65	4·79	5·03	5·22	5·51	5·73
30	2·94	3·55	3·91	4·18	4·38	4·54	4·69	4·91	5·09	5·37	5·58
40	2·89	3·49	3·84	4·09	4·29	4·45	4·58	4·80	4·97	5·23	5·43
60	2·85	3·43	3·77	4·01	4·20	4·35	4·48	4·69	4·85	5·10	5·29
120	2·81	3·37	3·70	3·93	4·11	4·26	4·38	4·58	4·73	4·97	5·15
					$X = 2$						
2	9·50	13·18	15·59	17·36	18·75	19·89	20·86	22·42	23·66	25·54	26·94
3	6·21	8·27	9·60	10·59	11·37	12·01	12·56	13·44	14·15	15·22	16·02
4	5·04	6·54	7·51	8·23	8·80	9·26	9·66	10·31	10·83	11·61	12·21
5	4·45	5·68	6·48	7·06	7·52	7·90	8·23	8·76	9·18	9·83	10·31
6	4·10	5·18	5·87	6·37	6·77	7·10	7·38	7·84	8·21	8·77	9·20
7	3·87	4·85	5·47	5·92	6·28	6·58	6·83	7·24	7·57	8·08	8·46
8	3·70	4·61	5·19	5·61	5·94	6·21	6·44	6·82	7·12	7·59	7·94
10	3·49	4·31	4·82	5·19	5·49	5·73	5·93	6·27	6·54	6·95	7·26
12	3·35	4·12	4·59	4·93	5·20	5·43	5·62	5·92	6·17	6·55	6·83
14	3·26	3·99	4·44	4·76	5·01	5·22	5·40	5·69	5·92	6·27	6·54
16	3·19	3·90	4·32	4·63	4·88	5·07	5·24	5·52	5·74	6·07	6·33
18	3·14	3·82	4·24	4·54	4·77	4·96	5·13	5·39	5·60	5·92	6·17
20	3·10	3·77	4·17	4·46	4·69	4·88	5·03	5·29	5·49	5·81	6·04
24	3·04	3·69	4·08	4·35	4·57	4·75	4·90	5·14	5·34	5·63	5·86
30	2·99	3·61	3·98	4·25	4·46	4·62	4·77	5·00	5·18	5·46	5·68
40	2·93	3·53	3·89	4·15	4·34	4·50	4·64	4·86	5·04	5·30	5·50
60	2·88	3·46	3·80	4·05	4·24	4·39	4·52	4·73	4·89	5·14	5·33
120	2·82	3·38	3·72	3·95	4·13	4·28	4·40	4·60	4·75	4·99	5·17

X is the number of covariates

(*continued*)

Critical Values for the Bryant–Paulson Procedure

α = .05

v	J = 2	J = 3	J = 4	J = 5	J = 6	J = 7	J = 8	J = 10	J = 12	J = 16	J = 20
					X = 3						
2	10·83	15·06	17·82	19·85	21·45	22·76	23·86	25·66	27·08	29·23	30·83
3	6·92	9·23	10·73	11·84	12·72	13·44	14·06	15·05	15·84	17·05	17·95
4	5·51	7·18	8·25	9·05	9·67	10·19	10·63	11·35	11·92	12·79	13·45
5	4·81	6·16	7·02	7·66	8·17	8·58	8·94	9·52	9·98	10·69	11·22
6	4·38	5·55	6·30	6·84	7·28	7·64	7·94	8·44	8·83	9·44	9·90
7	4·11	5·16	5·82	6·31	6·70	7·01	7·29	7·73	8·08	8·63	9·03
8	3·91	4·88	5·49	5·93	6·29	6·58	6·83	7·23	7·55	8·05	8·42
10	3·65	4·51	5·05	5·44	5·75	6·01	6·22	6·58	6·86	7·29	7·62
12	3·48	4·28	4·78	5·14	5·42	5·65	5·85	6·17	6·43	6·82	7·12
14	3·37	4·13	4·59	4·93	5·19	5·41	5·59	5·89	6·13	6·50	6·78
16	3·29	4·01	4·46	4·78	5·03	5·23	5·41	5·69	5·92	6·27	6·53
18	3·23	3·93	4·35	4·66	4·90	5·10	5·27	5·54	5·76	6·09	6·34
20	3·18	3·86	4·28	4·57	4·81	5·00	5·16	5·42	5·63	5·96	6·20
24	3·11	3·76	4·16	4·44	4·67	4·85	5·00	5·25	5·45	5·75	5·98
30	3·04	3·67	4·05	4·32	4·53	4·70	4·85	5·08	5·27	5·56	5·78
40	2·97	3·57	3·94	4·20	4·40	4·56	4·70	4·92	5·10	5·37	5·57
60	2·90	3·49	3·83	4·08	4·27	4·43	4·56	4·77	4·93	5·19	5·38
120	2·84	3·40	3·73	3·97	4·15	4·30	4·42	4·62	4·77	5·01	5·19

α = .01

v	J = 2	J = 3	J = 4	J = 5	J = 6	J = 7	J = 8	J = 10	J = 12	J = 16	J = 20
					X = 1						
2	19·09	26·02	30·57	33·93	36·58	38·76	40·60	43·59	45·95	49·55	52·24
3	10·28	13·32	15·32	16·80	17·98	18·95	19·77	21·12	22·19	23·82	25·05
4	7·68	9·64	10·93	11·89	12·65	13·28	13·82	14·70	15·40	16·48	17·29
5	6·49	7·99	8·97	9·70	10·28	10·76	11·17	11·84	12·38	13·20	13·83
6	5·83	7·08	7·88	8·48	8·96	9·36	9·70	10·25	10·70	11·38	11·90
7	5·41	6·50	7·20	7·72	8·14	8·48	8·77	9·26	9·64	10·24	10·69
8	5·12	6·11	6·74	7·20	7·58	7·88	8·15	8·58	8·92	9·46	9·87
10	4·76	5·61	6·15	6·55	6·86	7·13	7·35	7·72	8·01	8·47	8·82
12	4·54	5·31	5·79	6·15	6·43	6·67	6·87	7·20	7·46	7·87	8·18
14	4·39	5·11	5·56	5·89	6·15	6·36	6·55	6·85	7·09	7·47	7·75
16	4·28	4·96	5·39	5·70	5·95	6·15	6·32	6·60	6·83	7·18	7·45
18	4·20	4·86	5·26	5·56	5·79	5·99	6·15	6·42	6·63	6·96	7·22
20	4·14	4·77	5·17	5·45	5·68	5·86	6·02	6·27	6·48	6·80	7·04
24	4·05	4·65	5·02	5·29	5·50	5·68	5·83	6·07	6·26	6·56	6·78
30	3·96	4·54	4·89	5·14	5·34	5·50	5·64	5·87	6·05	6·32	6·53
40	3·88	4·43	4·76	5·00	5·19	5·34	5·47	5·68	5·85	6·10	6·30
60	3·79	4·32	4·64	4·86	5·04	5·18	5·30	5·50	5·65	5·89	6·07
120	3·72	4·22	4·52	4·73	4·89	5·03	5·14	5·32	5·47	5·69	5·85

(*continued*)

Critical Values for the Bryant–Paulson Procedure

$\alpha = .01$

Critical Values for the Bryant–Paulson Procedure, $\alpha = .01$

ν	$J = 2$	$J = 3$	$J = 4$	$J = 5$	$J = 6$	$J = 7$	$J = 8$	$J = 10$	$J = 12$	$J = 16$	$J = 20$
					$X = 2$						
2	23·11	31·55	37·09	41·19	44·41	47·06	49·31	52·94	55·82	60·20	63·47
3	11·97	15·56	17·91	19·66	21·05	22·19	23·16	24·75	26·01	27·93	29·38
4	8·69	10·95	12·43	13·54	14·41	15·14	15·76	16·77	17·58	18·81	19·74
5	7·20	8·89	9·99	10·81	11·47	12·01	12·47	13·23	13·84	14·77	15·47
6	6·36	7·75	8·64	9·31	9·85	10·29	10·66	11·28	11·77	12·54	13·11
7	5·84	7·03	7·80	8·37	8·83	9·21	9·53	10·06	10·49	11·14	11·64
8	5·48	6·54	7·23	7·74	8·14	8·48	8·76	9·23	9·61	10·19	10·63
10	5·02	5·93	6·51	6·93	7·27	7·55	7·79	8·19	8·50	8·99	9·36
12	4·74	5·56	6·07	6·45	6·75	7·00	7·21	7·56	7·84	8·27	8·60
14	4·56	5·31	5·78	6·13	6·40	6·63	6·82	7·14	7·40	7·79	8·09
16	4·42	5·14	5·58	5·90	6·16	6·37	6·55	6·85	7·08	7·45	7·73
18	4·32	5·00	5·43	5·73	5·98	6·18	6·35	6·63	6·85	7·19	7·46
20	4·25	4·90	5·31	5·60	5·84	6·03	6·19	6·46	6·67	7·00	7·25
24	4·14	4·76	5·14	5·42	5·63	5·81	5·96	6·21	6·41	6·71	6·95
30	4·03	4·62	4·98	5·24	5·44	5·61	5·75	5·98	6·16	6·44	6·66
40	3·93	4·48	4·82	5·07	5·26	5·41	5·54	5·76	5·93	6·19	6·38
60	3·83	4·36	4·68	4·90	5·08	5·22	5·35	5·54	5·70	5·94	6·12
120	3·73	4·24	4·54	4·75	4·91	5·05	5·16	5·35	5·49	5·71	5·88
					$X = 3$						
2	26·54	36·26	42·64	47·36	51·07	54·13	56·71	60·90	64·21	69·25	73·01
3	13·45	17·51	20·17	22·15	23·72	25·01	26·11	27·90	29·32	31·50	33·13
4	9·59	12·11	13·77	15·00	15·98	16·79	17·47	18·60	19·50	20·87	21·91
5	7·83	9·70	10·92	11·82	12·54	13·14	13·65	14·48	15·15	16·17	16·95
6	6·85	8·36	9·34	10·07	10·65	11·13	11·54	12·22	12·75	13·59	14·21
7	6·23	7·52	8·36	8·98	9·47	9·88	10·23	10·80	11·26	11·97	12·51
8	5·81	6·95	7·69	8·23	8·67	9·03	9·33	9·84	10·24	10·87	11·34
10	5·27	6·23	6·84	7·30	7·66	7·96	8·21	8·63	8·96	9·48	9·88
12	4·94	5·80	6·34	6·74	7·05	7·31	7·54	7·90	8·20	8·65	9·00
14	4·72	5·51	6·00	6·36	6·65	6·89	7·09	7·42	7·69	8·10	8·41
16	4·56	5·30	5·76	6·10	6·37	6·59	6·77	7·08	7·33	7·71	8·00
18	4·44	5·15	5·59	5·90	6·16	6·36	6·54	6·83	7·06	7·42	7·69
20	4·35	5·03	5·45	5·75	5·99	6·19	6·36	6·63	6·85	7·19	7·45
24	4·22	4·86	5·25	5·54	5·76	5·94	6·10	6·35	6·55	6·87	7·11
30	4·10	4·70	5·06	5·33	5·54	5·71	5·85	6·08	6·27	6·56	6·78
40	3·98	4·54	4·88	5·13	5·32	5·48	5·61	5·83	6·00	6·27	6·47
60	3·86	4·39	4·72	4·95	5·12	5·27	5·39	5·59	5·75	6·00	6·18
120	3·75	4·25	4·55	4·77	4·94	5·07	5·18	5·37	5·51	5·74	5·90

ANSWERS
TO SELECTED CHAPTER PROBLEMS

Chapter 1

Odd-Numbered Answers to Conceptual Problems

1. c.
3. a.
5. d.
7. a.
9. b.
11. d.
13. True.
15. False.
17. Yes.

Odd-Numbered Answers to Computational Problems

1. a, $b = .8571$, $a = 1.9716$, b, $Y' = 7.1142$.
3. a, $b = -.6658$, $a = 9.8616$; b, $Y' = 3.8694$.

Chapter 2

Odd-Numbered Answers to Conceptual Problems

1. a.
3. False.
5. False.
7. No.

Odd-Numbered Answers to Computational Problems

1. Intercept $= 28.0952$, $b_1 = .0381$, $b_2 = .8333$, $SS_{res} = 21.4294$, $SS_{reg} = 1128.5706$, $F = 105.3292$ (reject at .01), $s_{res}^2 = 5.3574$, $s(b_1) = .0058$, $s(b_2) = .1545$, $t_1 = 6.5343$ (reject at .01), $t_2 = 5.3923$ (reject at .01), F increment in $X_1 = 42.6604$ (reject at .01), F increment in $X_2 = 29.1627$ (reject at .01).
3. $r_{12.3} = .0934$.
5. $df_{reg} = 4$, $df_{res} = 40$, $df_{tot} = 44$, $SS_{reg} = 80$, $SS_{tot} = 480$, $MS_{res} = 10$, $F = 2$, critical value $= 2.61$, fail to reject H_0.
7. $r_{13.2} = .5305$, $r_{1(3.2)} = .5187$.

Chapter 3

Odd-Numbered Answers to Conceptual Problems

1. a.
3. c.
5. e.
7. b.
9. d.
11. True.
13. True.
15. False.
17. No.

Odd-Numbered Answers to Computational Problems

1. $df_{betw} = 3$, $df_{with} = 60$, $df_{tot} = 63$, $SS_{with} = 9.00$, $MS_{betw} = 3.25$, $MS_{with} = 0.15$, $F = 21.6666$, critical value $= 2.76$ (reject H_0).
3. $SS_{betw} = 150$, $SS_{tot} = 1{,}110$, $df_{betw} = 3$, $df_{with} = 96$, $df_{tot} = 99$, $MS_{betw} = 50$, $MS_{with} = 10$, critical value approximately 2.7 (reject H_0).

Chapter 4

Odd-Numbered Answers to Conceptual Problems

1. No.
3. d.
5. d.
7. b.
9. c.
11. True.
13. False.

Odd-Numbered Answers to Computational Problems

1. Contrast $= -5$; standard error $= 1.0$; $t = -5$; critical value $= 5.10$; fail to reject.

3. Standard error $= .3719$; $q_1 = (8 - 4.8)/.3719 = 8.6045$; $q_2 = (8 - 6)/.3719 = 5.3778$; $q_3 = (6 - 4.8)/.3719 = 3.2267$

   For Tukey, critical value 3.674; first two contrasts are significant. For NK, critical value of first contrast 3.674; first contrast is significant. For NK, critical value of second and third contrasts 3.014; second and third contrasts are significant.

5. a, $\mu_1 - \mu_2, \mu_3 - \mu_4, (\mu_1 + \mu_2)/2 - (\mu_3 + \mu_4)/2$; b, No, as c_j not equal to 0; c, H_0: $\mu_1 - [(\mu_2 + \mu_3 + \mu_4)/3]$.

Chapter 5

Odd-Numbered Answers to Conceptual Problems

1. c.
3. a.
5. c.
7. e.
9. b.
11. b.
13. d.
15. False.
17. No.

Odd-Numbered Answers to Computational Problems

1. $SS_{with} = 225, df_A = 1, df_B = 2, df_{AB} = 2, df_{with} = 150, df_{tot} = 155, MS_A = 6.15, MS_B = 5.30, MS_{AB} = 4.55, MS_{with} = 1.50, F_A = 4.10, F_B = 3.5333, F_{AB} = 3.0333$, critical value for A approximately 3.91, reject H_0 for A, critical value for B and AB approximately 3.06, reject H_0 for B and fail to reject H_0 for AB.

3. $SS_A = 14700$, $SS_B = 18367.125$, $SS_{AB} = 1386.375$, $SS_{with} = 42418.5$, $SS_{tot} = 76872$, $df_A = 1$, $df_B = 2$, $df_{AB} = 2$, $df_{with} = 42$, $df_{tot} = 47$, $MS_A = 14{,}700$, $MS_B = 9{,}183.5625$, $MS_{AB} = 693.1875$, $MS_{with} = 1{,}009.9648$, $F_A = 14.555$, $F_B = 9.093$, $F_{AB} = .6863$, critical value for A approximately 7.31, reject H_0 for A, critical value for B and AB approximately 5.18, reject H_0 for B but not for AB.

Means: factor A, level 1 = 62, level 2 = 97; factor B, level 1 = 54.688, level 2 = 81.313, level 3 = 102.5; with Scheffé, only levels 1 and 3 are different.

Chapter 6

Odd-Numbered Answers to Conceptual Problems

1. b.
3. b.
5. c.
7. c.
9. b.
11. c.
13. no.

Answers to Computational Problems

1. The adjusted groups means are all equal to 150; this resulted because the adjustment moved the mean for group 1 up to 150 and the mean for group 3 down to 150.

2. ANOVA results: $SS_{betw} = 4763.275$, $SS_{with} = 9636.7$, $df_{betw} = 3$, $df_{with} = 36$, $MS_{betw} = 1587.758$, $MS_{with} = 267.686$, $F = 5.931$, critical value approximately 2.88 (reject H_0). Means in order: 32.5, 60.4, 53.1, 39.9. ANCOVA results: $SS_{betw} = 5402.046$, $SS_{with} = 3880.115$, $df_{betw} = 3$, $df_{with} = 35$, $MS_{betw} = 1800.682$, $MS_{with} = 110.8604$, $F = 16.24$, critical value approximately 2.88 (reject H_0), $SS_{cov} = 5117.815$, $F_{cov} = 46.164$, critical value approximately 4.12 (reject H_0). Means in order: 30.7617, 61.2544, 53.1295, 40.7544.

Chapter 7

Odd-Numbered Answers to Conceptual Problems

1. b.
3. c.
5. False.
7. No.

Answers to Computational Problems

1. $SS_{with} = 1.9$, $df_A = 2$, $df_B = 1$, $df_{AB} = 2$, $df_{with} = 18$, $df_{tot} = 23$, $MS_A = 1.82$, $MS_B = .57$, $MS_{AB} = 1.035$, $MS_{with} = .1056$, $F_A = 1.7585$, $F_B = 5.3977$, $F_{AB} = 9.8011$, critical value for AB =

6.01 (reject H_0 for AB), critical value for B = 8.29 (fail to reject H_0 for B), critical value for A = 99 (fail to reject H_0 for A).

2. $SS_{sub} = 12.4687$, $SS_{rater} = 187.3438$, $SS_{SR} = 25.4063$, $MS_{sub} = 1.7812$, $MS_{rater} = 62.4479$, $MS_{SR} = 1.2098$, $F = 51.6184$, critical value = 3.07 (reject H_0). $q_{1-4} = 15.7577$, $q_{2-4} = 13.8281$, $q_{3-4} = 6.7533$, $q_{1-3} = 9.0044$, $q_{2-3} = 7.0749$, $q_{1-2} = 1.9295$. Tukey: critical value approximately 3.95, reject all but q_{1-2}. Newman–Keuls: critical value for $r = 4$ approximately 3.95, critical value for $r = 3$ approximately 3.57, critical value for $r = 2$ approximately 2.95, reject all but q_{1-2}.

Chapter 8

Odd-Numbered Answers to Conceptual Problems

1. d.
3. d.
5. a.
7. False.
9. No.

Answers to Computational Problems

1. a, yes; b, at age 4 type 1 is most effective, at age 6 type 2 is most effective, and at age 8 type 2 is most effective.
2. $SS_{tot} = 560$, $df_A = 2$, $df_B = 1$, $df_{AB} = 2$, $df_{with} = 24$, $df_{tot} = 29$, $MS_A = 100$, $MS_B = 100$, $MS_{AB} = 10$, $MS_{with} = 10$, $F_A = 10$, $F_B = 10$, $F_{AB} = 1$, critical value for B = 4.26 (reject H_0 for B), critical value for A and AB = 3.40 (reject H_0 for A and fail to reject H_0 for AB).

INDEX

A